Disconnecting the Dots

the Dots

How CIA and FBI officials helped enable
9/11 and evaded government investigations

Kevin Fenton

DISCONNECTING THE DOTS: HOW CIA AND FBI OFFICIALS HELPED ENABLE 9/11 AND EVADED GOVERNMENT INVESTIGATIONS

Published by:
TrineDay LLC
PO Box 577
Walterville, OR 97489
1-800-556-2012
www.TrineDay.com
publisher@TrineDay.net

Library of Congress Control Number: 2010941379

Fenton, Kevin — Author
Disconnecting the Dots—1st ed.
p. cm.
Print (ISBN-13) 978-0-9841858-5-6 (ISBN-10) 0-9841858-5-2
Epub (ISBN-13) 978-1-936296-19-4 (ISBN-10) 1-936296-19-5
Mobi (ISBN-13) 978-1-936296-20-0 (ISBN-10) 1-936296-20-9
1. September 11 Terrorist Attacks, 2001. 2. Intelligence service -- United States. 3. Governmental investigations -- United States. 4. National security -- United States. I. Fenton, Kevin. II. Title

FIRST EDITION
10 9 8 7 6 5 4 3 2 1

Printed in the USA
Distribution to the Trade by:
Independent Publishers Group (IPG)
814 North Franklin Street
Chicago, Illinois 60610
312.337.0747
www.ipgbook.com

Publisher's Foreword

All of this was brought upon us in a single day – and night fell on a different world, a world where freedom itself is under attack.... They hate our freedoms – our freedom of religion, our freedom of speech, our freedom to vote and assemble and disagree with each other.... Either you are with us, or you are with the terrorists.

— George W. Bush, September 20, 2001
Address to a Joint Session of Congress

I have already said that I am not involved in the 11 September attacks in the United States. As a Muslim, I try my best to avoid telling a lie. I had no knowledge of these attacks, nor do I consider the killing of innocent women, children and other humans as an appreciable act. Islam strictly forbids causing harm to innocent women, children and other people. Such a practice is forbidden even in the course of a battle.

— Osama bin Laden, September 28, 2001
Ummat (Pakistani newspaper)

(a)(1) The Director of the Federal Bureau of Investigation or a designee of the Director (whose rank shall be no lower than Assistant Special Agent in Charge) may make an application for an order requiring the production of any tangible things (including books, records, papers, documents, and other items) for an investigation to protect against international terrorism or clandestine intelligence activities, provided that such investigation of a United States person is not conducted solely upon the basis of activities protected by the first amendment to the Constitution.

...

(d) No person shall disclose to any other person (other than those persons necessary to produce the tangible things under this section) that the Federal Bureau of Investigation has sought or obtained tangible things under this section.

— Uniting and Strengthening America by Providing Appropriate Tools Required to Intercept and Obstruct Terrorism Act (USA PATRIOT ACT)
Signed into law on October 26, 2001

This president is trying to bring to himself all the power to become an emperor – to create Empire America. If you go along like sheep, that is what will happen.

— Jim McDermott (D – WA), October 7, 2002
Seattle Times

On 9 11, four planes for two hours were able to drive around, fly around even one hour in the direction going toward the west and then turn around and comeback. The military air force was not able to interdict them. It's [un]imaginable!

— Andreas Von Buelow, February 8, 2004
Former assistant German defense minister, and member of the German Bundestag
Alex Jones Radio Show

For those who might question the reasoning and importance for re-examining the [9/11] Commission's report, the events that led up to and the day of September 11th, one only has to recall the enormous ramifications that the attacks of September 11th have had on our country.... [Only] an honest re-evaluation of how the 9/11 attacks could have happened will allow us to reverse the adverse consequences of overreaching laws and the existing loopholes in our security systems in order to allow us to be safer in the future.

— Lorie Van Auken, Jully 22, 2005
9-11 widow and founding member of the 9-11 Family Steering Committee
Congressional Briefing

What we do know is that government officials decided not to inform a lawfully constituted body, created by Congress and the president, to investigate one the greatest tragedies to confront this country. We call that obstruction.

— Thomas H. Kean & Lee H. Hamilton, January 2, 2008
Chair & Vice-Chair of The 9-11 Commission
New York Times

The evidence that Al-Qaeda is actually an arm of the U.S. government is voluminous.... This whole thing was not engineered from a cave in Afghanistan ...

— Daniel Hamburg, Feb 22, 2008
former U.S. Congressman
Alex Jones Radio Show

So who cares that the 9/11 Commission chose to believe that Dick Cheney did not enter the White House bunker until 'shortly before 10:00', twenty minutes after the strike on the Pentagon? Surely the Vice President would not fib, so the Commission threw out the testimony of several eyewitnesses, including Norman Mineta, the Transportation Secretary. Mineta must have been making it all up when he testified that he joined Cheney in the bunker at about 9:20 and heard Cheney reaffirm an apparent stand-down order just before the Pentagon was struck.

— Ray McGovern, March 2008
former CIA Analyst and Presidential Briefer
Amazon.com Book Review

... two of the terrorists who crashed Flight 77 into the Pentagon on 9/11 [Nawaf al Hazmi and Khalid al Mihdhar] managed to escape FBI detection the previous month [August 2001] because an agent on the West Coast was denied help from the criminal-investigative side of his own agency.

— Karl Rove, March 2010
Courage and Consequence

Tonight, I can report to the American people and to the world that the United States has conducted an operation that killed Osama bin Laden ...

— Barack Obama, May 1, 2011
Address to the the Nation

Onwards to the utmost of futures
Peace,
Kris Millegan
Publisher
TrineDay
May 7, 2011

Contents

Prologue — *Every place that something could have gone wrong in this over a year and a half, it went wrong* 1

PART 1:
SANA'A, YEMEN

1. *The [NSA] refused to exploit the conduit and threatened legal action against the Agency officer who advised of its existence* 7

2. *One of the most important pieces of information the FBI would ever discover* 13

3. *[Redacted]* 22

4. *A secret coded indicator placed there by the Saudi government, warning of possible terrorist affiliation* 28

PART 2:
KUALA LUMPUR, MALAYSIA

5. *This is not a matter for the FBI* 37

6. *She stated that she had no recollection* 50

7. *He did not know why James briefed him about the Almihdhar information* 55

8. *Something apparently was dropped somewhere and we don't know where that was* 59

9. *There was pressure on people not to disclose what really happened* 62

10. *Amongst the finest we have* 67

11. *It appears Barbara Grewe conducted the interviews with "John" and "Jane"* 71

12. *Who chaired that meeting? Khalid Shaikh Mohammed chaired that meeting* 82

13. *There is no evidence of any tracking efforts* 97

14. *Captain Queeg* 106

15. *I know nobody read that cable* 116

16. *AA 77–3 indiv have been followed since Millennium* + Cole ... 127

17. *The FBI could have potentially linked them through financial records to the other Flight 77 hijackers* 131

PART 3:
SAN DIEGO

18. *Two al-Qaeda guys living in California–are you kidding me?* 139

19. *[The CIA's Counterterrorist Center] sent one officer to NSA for a brief period of time in 2000, but failed to send others, citing resource constraints* 146

20. *[As a result, NSA regularly provided information about these targets to the FBI ...]* 149

21. *Neither the contents of the calls nor the physics of the intercepts allowed us to determine that one end of the calls was in the United States* 154

22. *For the commission's staff, Fort Meade might as well have been Kabul* 156

23. *SOCOM lawyers would not permit the sharing of the U.S. person information regarding terrorists located domestically due to "fear of potential blowback"* 168

PART 4:
ADEN, YEMEN

24. *Further connections had been made between Almihdhar and al-Qaeda* 177

25. *As far as the Cole bombing, a U.S. investigator said the phone was used by the bombers to "put everything together"* 180

26. *One has also been identified as playing key roles in both the East African Embassy attacks and the USS* Cole *attack* 186

27. *This is a high threshold to cross* 190

28. *Hampered the pursuit of justice in the death of seventeen American sailors* 193

29. *The "Khallad" mentioned by al-Quso could actually be Khalid Almihdhar or one of his associates* 201

30. *In addition, the cable identified the third traveler as Salah Saeed Mohammed Bin Yousaf* 210

31. *The number that he called in Yemen to reach Ahmed al-Hada was 9671200578* 214

PART 5:
WASHINGTON AND NEW YORK

32. *He was focused on Malaysia* 225

33. *"John" asked her to do the research in her free time* 230

34. *Someone saw something that wasn't there* 243

35. *Shouting match* 248

36. *What's the story with the Almihdhar information, when is it going to get passed ... when is it going to get passed* 256

37. *The bad guys were in Yemen on this conversation* 259

38. *How bad things look in Malaysia* 265

39. *Major-league killer* 270

40. *Khalid Midhar should be very high interest anyway* 274

41. *They're coming here* 283

42. *The Minneapolis Airplane IV crowd* 289

43. *I had no idea that the Bureau wasn't aware of what its own people were doing* 300

44. *Donna was unable to recall how she first discovered the information on the Khallad identification* 307

45. *If this guy is in the country, it's not because he's going to fucking Disneyland* 310

46. *Someday someone will die* 323

47. *He ran into the bathroom and retched* 337

48. *Searches of readily available databases could have unearthed the driver's licenses, the car registration, and the telephone listing* 341

49. *Find and kill ... Khalid Shaikh Mohammed* 356

50. *We didn't know they were here until it was too late* 365

Epilogue — *They were lucky over and over again* 370

Appendix A — *... And over again* 383

Appendix B — *Alhazmi and Almihdhar were Saudi agents* 387

Documents 393

Bibliography 404

Index 407

Acknowledgements 419

Joint Inquiry into Intelligence Community Activities before and after the Terrorist Attacks of September 11, 2001

Senate Select Committee on Intelligence – 107th Congress

Carl Levin (D-MI)

Evan Bayh (D-IN)

James Inhofe (R-OK)

Richard Lugar (R-IN)

Dianne Feinstein (D-CA)

Bob Graham Chairman (D-FL)

Orrin Hatch (R-UT)

Pat Roberts (R-KS)

John Edwards (D-NC)

Ron Wyden (D-OR)

Fred Thompson (R-TN)

Barbara Mikulski (D-MD)

Jon Kyl (R-AZ)

John D. Rockefeller (D-WV)

Richard Shelby Vice Chairman (R-AL)

Richard Durbin (D-IL)

Mike DeWine (R-OH)

House Permanent Select Committee on Intelligence – 107th Congress

Nancy Pelosi Ranking Dem. (D-CA)

Richard Burr (R-NC)

Peter Hoekstra (R-MI)

Michael Castle (R-DE)

Saxby Chambliss (R-GA)

Sherwood Boehlert (R-NY)

Terry Everett (R-AL)

Tim Roemer (D-IN)

Bud Cramer (D-AL)

Jane Harman (D-CA)

Sanford Bishop (D-GA)

Collin Peterson (D-MN)

Ray LaHood (R-IL)

Jim Gibbons (R-NV)

Porter Goss Chairman (R-FL)

Gary Condit (D-CA)

Doug Bereuter (R-NE)

Duke Cunningham (R-CA)

Silvestre Reyes (D-TX)

Leonard Boswell (D-IA)

The two Intelligence Committees of Congress (pictured previous page) possessed the requisite security clearances and already knew much relevant information. Among those no longer in Congress are Gary Condit, defeated after evident involvement with a murdered intern, Randall "Duke" Cunningham, who resigned after pleading guilty to bribery charges, and Porter Goss, who became CIA Director. Its report and many other sources refer to the panel as the "Joint Inquiry." My label, "9/11 Congressional Inquiry," is intended to emphasize the responsibility of Congress, which also established the 9/11 Commission. "Joint Inquiry" will appear in some quoted material.

Executive Director Philip Zelikow was the *éminence grise* of the 9/11 Commission. With a law degree from the University of Houston and a Ph.D. from Tufts, Zelikow served in both the Reagan and George H.W. Bush administrations and was on George W. Bush's transition team in 2000-01. He has held professorships at Harvard and the University of Virginia, specializing in recent presidencies, and has co-authored books with both Condoleezza Rice and Ernest May.

The 9/11 Commission

The National Commission on Terrorist Attacks upon the United States, established by law in November 2002, eight months before the 9/11 Congressional Inquiry would publish its report, included five Democrats and five Republicans, all former politicians and public officials. Standing, from left: Richard Ben-Veniste (D), once counsel in the Watergate Special Prosecutor's Office; John F. Lehman (R), Secretary of the Navy under President Reagan; Timothy J. Roemer, who also served on the 9/11 Congressional Inquiry, ex-Representative from Indiana; James R. Thompson (R), ex-Governor of Illinois; Bob Kerrey (D), ex-Senator from Nebraska; and Slade Gorton (R), ex-Senator from Washington. Seated, from left: Fred F. Fielding (R), former White House counsel to Presidents Reagan and George W. Bush; Lee H. Hamilton, Vice Chairman (D), ex-Representative from Indiana; Thomas H. Keane, Chairman (R), ex-Governor of New Jersey; and Jamie S. Gorelick (D), Deputy Attorney General in the Clinton administration. Kerrey was a replacement for former Senator Max Cleland (D-GA), who resigned in December 2003 with complaints that the White House was managing the supposedly independent Commission. Given the Commission's purview, *The 9/11 Commission Report* of July 2004 was thoroughly inadequate; p. xv: "Our mandate was sweeping. The law directed us to investigate 'facts and circumstances relating to the terrorist attacks of September 11, 2001,' including those relating to intelligence agencies, law enforcement agencies ..."

Prologue

Every place that something could have gone wrong in this over a year and a half, it went wrong

W e may think we understand why 9/11 happened, and, indeed, after several official investigations, numerous books and countless press articles, many intelligence failures before 9/11 are well known. Among them are the failure to watchlist two of the hijackers, Khalid Almihdhar and Nawaf Alhazmi; the failure to exploit intercepts of their telephone calls; the failure to follow them to the US; the failure to search the belongings of one of their apparent associates, Zacarias Moussaoui, who was arrested three weeks before 9/11; the failure to find Almihdhar just before the attacks. These were not simple failures, but *ongoing* failures

What is less well known is that most, or perhaps all, of these particular failures were the fault of one small coterie of intelligence officials grouped around Alec Station, the CIA's bin Laden unit. They will be known here as the "Alec Station group," though they included FBI agents as well.

It is important to highlight the significance of these events. It has become a commonplace that 9/11 changed the world. Primarily, it led to the "global war on terror," the invasions of Afghanistan and Iraq, which together have cost many tens, if not hundreds, of thousands of lives. It also had a major impact in the West itself, through the climate of fear it engendered and the security measures that followed. Nine days after the attacks, President George Bush stood before Congress and famously asked, "Why do they hate us? ... They hate our freedoms."[1] He then wasted no time in beginning to dismantle those freedoms. Other western societies eagerly followed the US. We also had the abuses of Abu Ghraib and Guan-

---

1. President George W. Bush, Address to a Joint Session of Congress, September 20, 2001, http://www.greatdreams.com/bush_speech_92001.htm.

tanamo, significant increases in military spending, and mundane burdens such as longer lines at airports.

All this was avoidable. The 9/11 hijackers were not larger-than-life super-terrorists; neither were they "clean skins" with no hint of previous association with al-Qaeda. When we examine their tradecraft, we can see that they were simply not very good covert operators and kept getting things wrong. Among their many blunders: making calls to a number monitored by the National Security Agency and traveling on marked passports.

The rewritten, redacted executive summary of the CIA inspector general's report into that agency's pre-9/11 failings, the only version available, claimed there was no one "silver bullet" that would have prevented the attacks.[2] You could argue that this was strictly true: there was not *one* silver bullet, but a whole magazine of them. The perspective of a deputy chief of Alec Station, Tom Wilshire, was stated in testimony to the 9/11 Congressional Inquiry:

> Every place that something could have gone wrong in this over a year and a half, it went wrong. All the processes that had been put in place, all the safeguards, everything else, they failed at every possible opportunity. Nothing went right.[3]

The official government reports, by the 9/11 Congressional Inquiry, the 9/11 Commission, the Justice Department inspector general and the CIA inspector general,[4] as well as accounts in the mainstream media, give the impression that this string of failures was caused by bad luck, interagency rivalry and systemic error. Put simply, the US intelligence community had the relevant dots, but failed to connect them.

However, there are good reasons to disbelieve that explanation. In addition to the improbably large number of failures, we must consider that the failures concerned a small group of people—

---

2. OIG Report on CIA Accountability With Respect to the 9/11 Attacks, June 2005, p. vii, http://www.fas.org/irp/cia/product/oig-911.pdf.

3. US Congress, Report of the Joint Inquiry into the Terrorist Attacks of September 11, 2001 by the House Permanent Select Committee on Intelligence and the Senate Select Committee on Intelligence, July 24, 2003 [hereinafter: 9/11 Congressional Inquiry report], p. 151, http://news.findlaw.com/hdocs/docs/911rpt/.

4. As noted, only a redacted version of the executive summary of a rewritten report by the CIA's inspector general is publicly available. It is unclear whether the NSA inspector general's office ever wrote a report on that agency's pre-9/11 behavior.

Almihdhar, Alhazmi and a few associates—and were perpetrated by another small group of people—centered on, but apparently not headed by, Tom Wilshire himself.

This book will show that, properly understood, 9/11 was less a failure by some intelligence community officials to connect the dots, than a success by other officials in disconnecting them. Had they not prevented their colleagues from learning certain pieces of information, these colleagues would probably have thwarted the 9/11 attacks, for example by placing Almihdhar and Alhazmi under surveillance, or even arresting them for their part in a prior terrorist attack, the bombing of the USS *Cole* in Yemen.

Furthermore, once honest investigators began to learn information pointing to Almihdhar, Alhazmi and their associates, over the summer of 2001, the Alec Station group worked diligently to prevent any but the most restricted dissemination of the information. Then, after 9/11, they actively participated in a whitewash of their actions, though the official bodies that have issued reports on the events must share that blame.[5]

Nonetheless, these reports allow an accurate reconstruction of many key events through a record of interactions among key players. These include e-mails providing clear insights into how the operation was carried out.

In the popular imagination of what a "spy" does, some see James Bond, flirting in casinos at Monte Carlo. At the other extreme is a grittier scene, where the spy is badly paid and meets with even worse characters in dimly lit basements. Neither of these myths captures the reality we are to deal with. People sat at their computers and wrote reports—apparently intended to be found by investigators—that said, for example, they had done things they had not actually done. Enabling 9/11 was a job done at the office, with memos.

Another important note should be added here. The first, official draft of history, that the US intelligence community failed to connect the dots, is simply wrong. Here is the second draft of history, based on sources currently available. There are other historical re-

5. The concept of individuals disconnecting the dots in the run-up to 9/11 was previously employed by Peter Lance in his book *Triple Cross* (New York: Regan, 2006). As far as I know, I am the first to apply it to the subsequent investigations, where some investigators appear to have begun to work out what had really happened, but then fudged their conclusions and omitted key facts from the various reports.

cords that are not yet available. Indeed, it is likely that most of the relevant material is still classified. If and when that material becomes available, we will be able to revise our understanding of what happened, arriving at an even more accurate picture.

One thing that will become apparent is that the previous investigations into 9/11, by the 9/11 Congressional Inquiry, the 9/11 Commission, the Department of Justice inspector general and the CIA inspector general, were inadequate. Their various failings will be underlined as we proceed.

Although the initial Congressional Inquiry made an attempt to properly investigate within its limited mandate, both the Justice Department inspector general's report and *The 9/11 Commission Report* omit information that should not have been omitted, and to such an extent that their good faith must be questioned. These two reports are, in short, whitewashes. The CIA inspector general's report was rewritten at the insistence of the Agency's management, in part because it criticized too strongly the officials with whose performance this book finds fault, and only a redacted executive summary of the rewritten version has been made available. All this is grossly inadequate, and, if the American people and the international community are ever to understand 9/11, a new, truly independent inquiry must take place.

Finally, I would like to highlight the fact that this book contains almost no original reporting. With a few very minor exceptions, I did not speak to any officials or sources, either on or off the record. Nearly everything you read here has been in the public record, mostly for several years, and comes from those very government reports, from publicly available court documents, and from the mainstream media. All the information here could have been put together by others, including media and government agencies with resources dwarfing those of a solitary author. Why they have not done so is another important question deserving of an answer.

Part 1: Sana'a, Yemen

AMERICAN AIRLINES • FLIGHT 77 SUSPECTS • (PENTAGON)

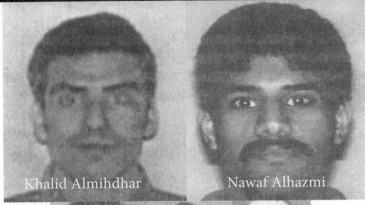

Khalid Almihdhar   Nawaf Alhazmi

Majed Moqed   Salem Alhazmi   Hani Hanjour

AMERICAN AIRLINES • FLIGHT 11 SUSPECTS • (WORLD TRADE CENTER)

Mohamed Atta   Abdulaziz Alomari   Wail Alshehri   Waleed Alshehri   Satam M.A. al Suqami

UNITED AIRLINES • FLIGHT 175 SUSPECTS • (WORLD TRADE CENTER)

Marwan Alshehhi   Hamza Alghamdi   Fayez Ahmed Banihammad   Mohand Alshehri   Ahmed Alghamdi

UNITED AIRLINES • FLIGHT 93 SUSPECTS • (PENNSYLVANIA)

Saeed Alghamdi   Ahmed Ibrahim A. Alhaznawi   Ahmed Alnami   Ziad Samir Jarrah

The [NSA] refused to exploit the conduit and threatened legal action against the Agency officer who advised of its existence

A history of 9/11 could start in many places, with Osama bin Laden's declaration of jihad against the US in February 1998, with Operation Bojinka, a forerunner of the September 11 plot devised in the mid-1990s, or even earlier, with the start of US funding for the Afghan mujaheddin a few months before the Soviet invasion of Afghanistan.

We start with a minor engagement north of Kabul, Afghanistan's capital, in 1996 or 1997, because this is where Ahmed al-Hada's rise to become a top US counterterrorist surveillance target began. To appreciate the position of his son-in-law, Flight 77 hijacker Khalid Almihdhar, in the al-Qaeda hierarchy, to understand what the Alec Station group did—and possibly why they did it—we need to know about al-Hada, because al-Hada's activities form one background against which the events of 9/11 occurred.

Although the relationship between al-Qaeda and the Taliban was not always as close as it has been portrayed, Arab camp commanders close to al-Qaeda did allow their trainees to go and fight in Afghanistan. When the Taliban was pushed back to the edge of Kabul by a Northern Alliance offensive beginning in October 1996, a group of Arab fighters went to strengthen the Taliban's lines. They suffered a major defeat, incurring at least ten fatalities, and the remainder fled to the nearby mountains. This group of six fighters included al-Hada and two others who would later become well known: Mohamed al-Owhali and an operative now known to the world as Azzam.

According to the FBI, in the mountains al-Owhali and his comrades "engaged in severe fighting with his enemies and were able to defend their position and repel the attack." This engagement later became known as the "C" formation battle. The Bureau wrote,

> [Al-Owhali's] actions while fighting in the "c" formation battle and while in the mountains earned him significant prominence and honor within his group and in the bin Laden camps. He stated that he had earned such a reputation and loyalty during these struggles that he was allowed to carry his rifle in the camps even around bin Laden.[1]

Al-Owhali and Azzam would use the status they gained in Afghanistan to win a place on the team that in 1998 bombed the US embassy in Nairobi, Kenya, and al-Hada would help them. In fact, al-Hada would be a key link between the bombers in Africa and Osama bin Laden in Afghanistan, even though he soon fell under surveillance by the NSA.

James Bamford, a widely acknowledged expert on the NSA, described how this began:

> A devoted follower of bin Laden, al-Hada offered to turn his house [in Sana'a, Yemen,] into a secret operations center for his friend in Afghanistan. While the rugged Afghan landscape provided bin Laden with security, it was too isolated and remote to manage the day-to-day logistics for his growing worldwide terrorist organization. His sole tool of communication was a gray, battery-powered $7,500 Compact-M satellite phone ...
>
> Bin Laden needed to set up a separate operations center somewhere outside Afghanistan, somewhere with access to regular telephone service and close to major air links. He took al-Hada up on his offer, and the house in Yemen quickly became the epicenter of bin Laden's war against America, a logistics base to coordinate his attacks, a switchboard to pass on orders, and a safe house where his field commanders could meet to discuss and carry out operations.[2]

---

1. FBI form 302 (Form for Reporting Information That May Become Testimony), dated September 9, 1998, summarizing interviews of Mohammad al-Owhali, http://www.vaed.uscourts.gov/notablecases/moussaoui/exhibits/defense/767.pdf.
2. James Bamford, *The Shadow Factory: The Ultra-Secret NSA from 9/11 to the Eavesdropping on America* (New York: Doubleday, 2008) [hereinafter: Bamford 2008], p. 8. In the quoted passage Bamford refers to al-Hada simply as "Hada," not using the "al-" prefix. However, I have altered the name to "al-Hada" in the quoted passage in order to ensure the continuity of names. Likewise, all

Bin Laden used his last satellite phone from November 1996 until September 1998, when he stopped making calls on it, possibly due to the US missile strikes following the East African embassy bombings. The calls were intercepted by the NSA and tens of thousands of pages of transcripts were produced.[3] According to some reports, the top destination for calls from bin Laden's satellite phone was Britain,[4] bin Laden's center of operations in Europe, where the government often turned a blind eye to, or even encouraged, Islamist militancy. The US had monitored other phones bin Laden used before November 1996. When FBI agents from New York's Joint Terrorism Task Force were allowed to review the files on bin Laden at the CIA's Counterterrorist Center (CTC) in October 1995, they found forty files of material, mostly the result of electronic eavesdropping.[5]

In January 1996, the CIA established its first "virtual" station—assigned an issue, rather than a locale—as the second Clinton administration was venturing boldly into uncharted waters at the "end of history." The station was organized as part of the CTC, and originally assigned to investigate "terrorist financial links," although it soon became the Agency's Osama bin Laden unit. The original chief was Michael Scheuer, an Agency old hand whose zeal in the effort against al-Qaeda earned him enemies as well as friends among his intelligence agency colleagues. He had a son named Alec, and this provided the station with its code name. While various Alec Station personnel and associates are singled out for criticism in this book, Michael Scheuer is not among them.

Yemen was the second most popular destination for calls from bin Laden's phone, although reports conflict over how many times he called it. Exactly how many of these calls went to al-Hada's com-

---

Arabic names are rendered in uniform fashion throughout this book, so bin Laden is always bin Laden and never Binladin, Almihdhar is always Almihdhar, never al-Mihdhar or simply Mihdhar, and so on.

3. There are various stories about how the NSA came to intercept bin Laden's phone calls, and there is also a story that the NSA could track the phone even when it was switched off. The full truth of the matter is not known at the time of writing.

4. Nick Fielding and Dipesh Gadhery, "Al-Qaeda's Satellite Phone Records Revealed," *Sunday Times* (London), March 24, 2002; Mark Hosenball and Daniel Klaidman, "Calling al-Qaeda: Questions about Iran," *Newsweek*, February 17, 2002.

5. John Miller and Michael Stone with Chris Mitchell, *The Cell: Inside the 9/11 Plot and Why the FBI and CIA Failed to Stop It* (New York: Hyperion, 2002), pp. 148–49.

munications hub in Sana'a (the "Yemen hub") is also unknown, although *Los Angeles Times* journalist Terry McDermott, who wrote a book about the September 11 attacks, said that it was "dozens," and Bamford wrote that it was over two hundred.[6]

The NSA began monitoring the hub in 1996,[7] probably spurred by bin Laden's first calls to it. As we will see, the phone number was crucial for 9/11, not only because some of the hijackers called it, but because Khalid Almihdhar lived at the hub with his family. Upon learning of the hub, the NSA promptly kept this secret and told none of the other agencies in the intelligence community about it.

Alec Station learned what the NSA was doing by chance in late 1996. Station chief Scheuer later wrote,

> From a CIA officer detailed to another Intelligence Community (IC) agency [the NSA] and serving overseas, the bin Laden unit learned of the availability of a communications conduit used by bin Laden and al-Qaeda [the Yemen hub]. The [NSA] refused to exploit the conduit and threatened legal action against the Agency officer who advised of its existence. This officer bravely continued to supply the information; and I asked senior Agency officers to intervene with the [NSA]. There ensued a desultory interagency discussion without resolution.[8]

The NSA did not want the CIA to have the raw intelligence, but agreed to provide summaries of the information. These summaries, which usually came late, were largely useless, and Scheuer knew it. The reason was that al-Qaeda operatives used a simple code system, substituting words like "tourism" and "playing football" for "jihad," and "wedding" for "bombing" or "attack." Scheuer commented,

> Over time, if you read enough of these conversations, you first get clued into the fact that maybe "bottle of milk" doesn't mean bottle of milk, and if you follow it long enough, you develop a

6. Terry McDermott, "The Plot," *Los Angeles Times*, September 1, 2002, http://articles.latimes.com/2002/sep/01/nation/na-plot-1; PBS, *NOVA*, "The Spy Factory," February 3, 2009, http://www.pbs.org/wgbh/nova/transcripts/3602_spyfactory.html. Bamford 2008 states that all 221 calls to Yemen went to al-Hada's house. Some other accounts, such as one given at the trial of the embassy bombers, state that bin Laden first called the Yemen hub after the embassy bombings. As he made over 200 calls to Yemen before September 1998, I find this highly unlikely.
7. Bamford 2008, p. 16.
8. Michael Scheuer, "How *Not* to Catch a Terrorist," *Atlantic*, December 2004, http://www.theatlantic.com/doc/200412/anonymous.

sense of what they're really talking about. But it's not possible to do unless you have the verbatim transcript.[9]

Therefore, Alec Station and "several other senior CIA officers" requested transcripts rather than summaries.[10] This happened repeatedly over a period of about two years. James Bamford described the situation:

> Before 9/11 Scheuer knew how important the house was, he knew NSA was eavesdropping on the house. He went to NSA, went to the head of operations for NSA, and ... Barbara McNamara, and asked for transcripts of the conversations coming into and going out of the house. And the best the NSA would do would be to give them brief summaries every ... once a week or something like that, you know, just a report, not the actual transcripts or anything. And so he got very frustrated, he went back there and they still refused.[11]

He continued:

> Eventually the CIA built their own intercept facility in the Indian Ocean area, I think it was on Madagascar, where they were intercepting the same signals. The whole thing was directed at that house, trying to get the signals going in and out of that house, the telephone calls. But because the technology was not as good as NSA's they were only picking up half of the conversations, apparently it was downlink, they weren't able to get the uplink, you need a satellite.
>
> And so the CIA, Mike Scheuer, went back to NSA and said look, you know, we're able to get, you know, half the conversations here, but we still need the other half, and NSA still wouldn't give them the other half. I mean this is absurd, but this is what was going on.

Throughout this book we will encounter officials who fail to recall events they really should remember, and here is the first. 9/11 Commission staffers Lorry Fenner and Gordon Lederman asked Barbara McNamara about the failure to give Scheuer what he wanted. The memo based upon her interview says,

> She does not recall being personally [asked] to provide about transcripts or raw data.... But sharing of raw data is not done

9. "The Spy Factory," see note 6.
10. Michael Scheuer, see note 8.
11. "Scott Horton Interviews James Bamford," *Antiwar.com*, October 22, 2008, http://antiwar.com/radio/2008/10/22/james-bamford-2/.

routinely by NSA unless they get a specific request for a specific item. She said that she does not remember people asking for raw data, but if they wanted it NSA would have provided it.[12]

To their credit, Fenner and Lederman picked up on this. The memo says,

> In response to a specific question, she responded that she has no memory of [Deputy CIA Director General John] Gordon having come to NSA to complain about [the CIA's Counterterrorist Center] not having received transcripts/raw data.

We obviously cannot prove that the meeting did not simply slip McNamara's mind during the interview. Nevertheless, the failure to provide what Scheuer wanted made the NSA look very bad, especially in hindsight, and pretending not to recall it may well have seemed a useful tactic.

While the NSA and CIA were arguing, al-Qaeda's plot to bomb US embassies in East Africa was moving forward, and the Yemen hub was being used as a key support facility. Not only was the NSA not exploiting the intelligence the Yemen hub was generating to thwart the plot, it was preventing Alec Station from doing so as well.

On August 7, 1998, truck bombs severely damaged the US embassies in Nairobi, Kenya, and Dar es Salaam, Tanzania, killing over 200, including twelve Americans.

12. 9/11 Commission, "Memo of 9/11 Commission Interview of Former NSA Deputy Director Barbara McNamara," December 15, 2003, http://www.scribd.com/doc/23252626/Memo-of-9-11-Commission-Interview-of-Former-NSA-Deputy-Director-Barbara-McNamara.

—2—

One of the most important pieces of information the FBI would ever discover

In April or May of 1998, Mohamed al-Owhali, who had by then been chosen as one of the suicide bombers for the upcoming embassy attacks, was instructed by al-Qaeda to travel to Yemen and was given a false Iraqi passport to do so. He stayed with al-Hada in Sana'a for several weeks, and a call was placed to his parents in Saudi Arabia.[1]

As al-Owhali thought it was too dangerous for him to go to Saudi Arabia, his father came down to the Yemen hub, and al-Hada agreed to relay messages between the two of them so that al-Owhali could communicate with his family. In addition, a false Yemeni passport was obtained for al-Owhali by an al-Qaeda leader named Abd al-Rahim al-Nashiri.

Al-Hada then instructed al-Owhali to return to Pakistan, where he made a martyrdom video with another al-Qaeda leader known as Khallad bin Attash.[2] He then traveled to Kenya in early August to carry out his suicide mission. When he got there, one of his main tasks was to get his mind ready for the suicide bombing. This entailed several calls to his old friend al-Hada, the last of which ended just as al-Owhali was about to get in the bomb-laden truck and drive to the embassy to blow it up.

These calls were listed in detail at the embassy bombings trial in early 2001. Al-Owhali called the Yemen hub once on August 5, twice on August 6, and again in the morning of August 7, just be-

---

1. This and the description of al-Owhali's actions in subsequent paragraphs are based on an FBI 302 (Form for Reporting Information That May Become Testimony), dated September 9, 1998, of interviews of Mohammad al-Owhali, http://www.vaed.uscourts.gov/notablecases/moussaoui/exhibits/defense/767.pdf.
2. *Khallad* bin Attash is an alias, but sources disagree on whether his true given name is Walid or Tawfiq. As he was tracked simply as "Khallad" before his surname was discovered, and as this name remains the name by which he is most commonly identified, "Khallad bin Attash" is the name used in this book.

fore the bombing, when he spoke to al-Hada for 20 minutes, 43 seconds.[3] The NSA, which had been monitoring the hub for two years by this point, must have intercepted these calls.

We need to ask what the NSA was doing in all of this. It was already aware of al-Hada's phone, and the volume of traffic between it and bin Laden in Afghanistan indicated its importance. How could the NSA possibly have missed al-Owhali, given that several calls must have mentioned him and his travel arrangements?

The calls al-Owhali made to al-Hada's phone in the days shortly before the bombing were a flashing red arrow pointing to the safe house in Nairobi where the bomb had been built. Yet there is no record of the NSA doing anything about this, and no record of any subsequent investigation of the NSA's inaction.[4]

This was the first time the NSA failed to act on information from the Yemen hub to prevent a terrorist attack against US interests. It would not be the last. The exact same failure—inaction on actionable intelligence from the Yemen hub—happened before the USS *Cole* bombing in 2000 and before 9/11. According to public information, there was no investigation of this intelligence failure before the embassy bombings. The review after the *Cole* bombing was extremely cursory at best, and the investigation of the NSA after 9/11 was practically non-existent. Asked if the NSA's inspector general had written a report about the failure before the embassy bombings, James Bamford responded that he had never heard of any such report and that the NSA's inspector general mostly wrote reports about "employee complaints and not about failed policies."[5]

There are some simple questions that need to be asked here. How many calls between the Yemen hub, bin Laden and the bombers in Africa did the NSA intercept, and why did it not do anything about them? There must have been recordings, transcripts of these calls, a whole section at the NSA devoted to monitoring the Yemen

3. *United States v. Usama bin Laden et al.*, trial transcript of day 14, March 7, 2001, http://cryptome.org/usa-v-ubl-14.htm; *United States v. Usama bin Laden et al.*, trial transcript of day 23, March 27, 2001, http://cryptome.org/usa-v-ubl-23.htm.
4. There are other questions about how the embassy bombings could have happened, as the bombers included several informers for western intelligence and were under surveillance by numerous agencies. However, this is beyond the scope of this book.
5. PBS, *NOVA*, "Ask the Expert," February 9, 2009, http://www.pbs.org/wgbh/nova/spyfactory/ask.html.

hub. What did these people do, who are they, and how did they keep screwing up?

Due to the way the bombing was carried out, al-Owhali survived. However, as he was supposed to have been killed in the attack, there was no extraction plan to get him out of the country. Unfamiliar with the city, he was unable to find the safe house he had stayed at, and returned to the area of the hotel where he had checked in when he first arrived in Kenya.

From the hotel he made a series of calls to al-Hada, telling him to inform bin Attash that he had not died in the attack and that he needed money and documents so that he could flee Kenya. Al-Hada was then called three times by Osama bin Laden or a person using his phone. One call was on August 10 and lasted for 2.7 minutes, and two more were made the next day, both lasting less than a minute.[6]

These calls, which pointed to al-Owhali's location in Kenya, must have been noticed by the NSA—there had, after all, just been a major terrorist attack with 200-plus fatalities, and bin Laden was certainly a significant suspect even at this early stage in the bombings inquiry. Bin Laden called his operations center—the operations center which had previously had heavy contacts with operatives in one of the cities that was attacked—and repeatedly spoke to an operative there. How much more suspicious could it be? Nevertheless, the NSA sat on this information. In fact, there is no mention of the NSA being of any help at all during the investigation.

Despite this, the FBI was able to locate al-Owhali. There are contradictory stories about exactly how he was arrested, but it appears he was finally detained based on a tip from a local who thought him suspicious. However, the Bureau was also trying to trace him based on phone information.[7]

---

6. *United States v. Usama bin Laden et al.*, trial transcript of day 23, March 27, 2001, http://cryptome.info/usa-v-ubl-23.htm. The embassy bombings trial will be discussed in more detail in subsequent chapters. Allegedly based on billing records, a witness for the government, a paralegal specialist at the US attorney's office in New York named Margot Hitpas, claimed that there were no other calls between bin Laden's satellite phone and al-Hada except these three. Given the circumstances of the case and that much heavier traffic was credibly reported by both McDermott and Bamford, Hitpas' claim appears to be incorrect.

7. Lawrence Wright, *The Looming Tower: Al-Qaeda's Road to 9/11* (London: Allen Lane, 2006) [hereinafter: Wright 2006], pp. 275-79.

The contradictory stories are interesting in their own right. The initial stories claimed that al-Owhali was arrested based on a tip from a taxi driver who took him to a hotel where he stayed after the bombing; these accounts made no mention of his calls to the Yemen hub.[8] Later accounts, written after the trial in early 2001, mention the hub.[9]

The amount of misinformation, and possibly disinformation, about the embassy bombings is startling. In a 2005 book, former CIA officer Gary Berntsen, who led the Agency team that investigated the bombing in Kenya, even claimed that Hezbollah was initially suspected, and that responsibility could not be pinned on al-Qaeda until August 15, eight days after the attacks. He lists the breaks occurring on this day as the arrest of al-Owhali, which actually happened three days earlier, and the fact of one of his colleagues noticing a newspaper article about the arrest of another of the bombers, Mohammed Saddiq Odeh, in Pakistan.[10]

Generally, Odeh is said to have been arrested because he became agitated during a routine airport check hours before the bombing and gave himself away.[11] However, according to UPI, he was stopped based on an alert from the CIA,[12] which had been monitoring al-Qaeda operatives in East Africa for years. Whatever the true story of Odeh's arrest, it is unlikely it remained unknown to the CIA until August 15. Any disinformation regarding the embassy bombings may have been designed to obscure the Yemen hub's role in the plot.

A close observer of counterterrorism efforts can see that there are sometimes parallel accounts of the capture or questioning of al-Qaeda operatives. For example, compare the Odeh incident to

---

8. See, for example, Simon Reeve, *The New Jackals: Ramzi Yousef, Osama bin Laden and the Future of Terrorism* (London: André Deutsch Press, 1999), p. 201; also Karl Vick, "Assault on a U.S. Embassy: A Plot Both Wide and Deep," *Washington Post*, November 23, 1998, http://www.washingtonpost.com/wp-dyn/content/article/2007/08/10/AR2007081001730.html.

9. Wright 2006, pp. 275-79; also Jason Burke, "Dead Man Walking," *Observer* (UK), August 5, 2001, http://www.guardian.co.uk/theobserver/2001/aug/05/life1.lifemagazine8.

10. Gary Berntsen and Ralph Pezzullo, *Jawbreaker: The Attack on Bin Laden and Al-Qaeda: A Personal Account by the CIA's Key Field Commander* (New York: Three Rivers Press, 2005), pp. 24-26.

11. See, for example, John Miller and Michael Stone with Chris Mitchell, *The Cell: Inside the 9/11 Plot and Why the FBI and CIA Failed to Stop It* (New York: Hyperion, 2002), p. 212; also Peter Bergen, *Holy War Inc.: Inside the Secret World of Osama bin Laden* (London: Phoenix, 2004), p. 116.

12. "Analysis: Anatomy of a Bombing Cell," UPI, January 2, 2001, http://www.highbeam.com/doc/1P1-38896418.html.

the stopping of alleged 9/11 hijacker pilot Ziad Jarrah in Dubai in January 2001, also said to be due to a mistake made by Jarrah[13] and to his being tracked by the CIA.[14] The arrest of Djamel Beghal in the same place in 2001 is also attributed both to his name being on a watch list[15] and to his losing his cool during routine questioning.[16]

When interviewed by the FBI, al-Owhali admitted to calling al-Hada's number. Ironically, the agent who got him to admit this was John Anticev, one of the agents whose surveillance of the 1993 World Trade Center bombers had ended a few months before they murdered six people in New York.[17]

The secret of al-Hada's phone was now no longer confined to the NSA and CIA. Author Lawrence Wright highlighted the importance of the information: "This Yemeni telephone number would prove to be one of the most important pieces of information the FBI would ever discover, allowing investigators to map the links of the al-Qaeda network all across the globe." The FBI made a link chart based on intercepts of calls made to and from the Yemen hub. The chart, posted on the wall of the "bullpen" at the FBI's New York office, showed all the operatives around the world who talked to the hub.[18] Information gleaned based on the intercepts was reportedly used to thwart many attacks, including ones against the US embassy in Paris and the US consulate in Istanbul.[19]

Wright's comment about this being "one of the most important pieces of information" is, if anything, an understatement. Al-Qaeda was no longer a secret organization: the FBI and other US agencies

---

13. He allegedly had a passport overlay that marked him as an extremist and was carrying radical books and tapes; see 9/11 Commission, *The 9/11 Commission Report: Final Report of the National Commission on Terrorist Attacks upon the United States* (New York: W. W. Norton, 2004) [hereinafter: *9/11 CR*], p. 496 n97.

14. Terry McDermott, *Perfect Soldiers: The 9/11 Hijackers, Who They Were, Why They Did It* (London: Pontico's, 2005), pp. 294-95.

15. Steven Erlanger and Chris Hedges, "Terror Cells Slip Through Europe's Grasp," *New York Times*, December 28, 2001, http://www.pulitzer.org/archives/6580.

16. See, for example, Sean O'Neill and Daniel McGrory, *The Suicide Factory: Abu Hamza and the Finsbury Park Mosque* (London: Harper Perennial, 2006), pp. 93-94.

17. See Wright 2006, p. 277; also Peter Lance, *1,000 Years for Revenge: International Terrorism and the FBI* (New York: HarperCollins, 2003), pp. 86-88. The translator at the interviews of al-Owhali, according to the FBI 302, was Mike Feghali. Feghali was also later involved in the case of Sibel Edmonds, an FBI translator who accused people at the Bureau of wrongdoing following 9/11.

18. Wright 2006, pp. 277-78, 343.

19. David E. Kaplan and Kevin Whitelaw, "Pieces of the 9/11 Puzzle," *US News and World Report*, March 7, 2004, http://www.usnews.com/usnews/news/articles/040315/15nine11.htm.

knew where al-Qaeda agents were all over the world, and had a good idea of what they were doing.

There are two versions of the CIA's role in monitoring the hub after this. One was set out by Michael Scheuer:

> After the bombing of two U.S.-based embassies in East Africa, the senior CIA managers asked what the bin Laden unit needed most to enhance the attack against al-Qaeda. I again raised our dire need for verbatim reports derived from electronic collection. These senior managers ordered this to be arranged. After receiving less than a dozen such transcripts the process stopped. Despite repeated requests, I failed to get the flow of data restored.[20]

Scheuer further noted,

> Also, tragically, no member of the bin Laden unit was asked to testify before the State Department's accountability boards for the 1998 embassy bombings. This exclusion ensured that the systemic problems embedded in the Intelligence Community— which had become overwhelmingly clear before the 1998 al-Qaeda attacks—were not raised before the only pre-9/11 panel that might have been able to initiate remedial action.

The alternative account is that the CIA was more involved in monitoring the phone. According to English journalist Barry Wigmore, "Helped by the National Security Agency, the CIA staked out the house and waited." In addition to the NSA intercepting al-Hada's calls, he said, the CIA placed bugs in the house and even monitored it with spy satellites, which "photographed every visitor."[21] Lawrence Wright claimed that the CIA "had jurisdiction over conversations on the al-Hada phone."[22]

---

20. Michael Scheuer, "How *Not* to Catch a Terrorist," *Atlantic*, December 2004, http://www.the-atlantic.com/doc/200412/anonymous.

21. Barry Wigmore, "9/11: The 7 Missed Clues," *Sunday Mirror* (London), June 9, 2002, http://find-articles.com/p/articles/mi_qn4161/is_/ai_n12841550. No confirmation could be found from US sources for the bugs inside the house and the spy satellites, although both would certainly make sense given the hub's importance to counterterrorism efforts. The *Sunday Mirror* is not regarded as a publication of the first rank in terms of journalistic quality, although Wigmore is a reporter who does write on national security issues and many of the other facts contained in the article are correct. Presumably, Wigmore's article was based on British sources, indicating that British intelligence, probably GCHQ, was involved in monitoring the hub. As we will see, the hub definitely was being monitored by one of the NSA's foreign partners.

22. Lawrence Wright, "The Agent: Did the C.I.A. stop an F.B.I. Detective from Preventing 9/11?" *New Yorker*, July 10 and 17, 2006, http://www.lawrencewright.com/WrightSoufan.pdf.

While there is a tension between these two versions, that tension may be more apparent than real. Scheuer was fired from his position a few months after the embassy bombings and then lost contact with events at Alec Station, so he may not have known what happened after he left. As we will see, shortly after Scheuer left, the CIA did obtain access to the transcripts from the NSA, but voluntarily surrendered it a short time later.

The CIA's involvement on the ground in Yemen is a key fact. The NSA claims that it voluntarily cut itself off from a portion of the intelligence produced by monitoring the hub—it decided not to trace calls between the hub and the US, which would have led it straight to 9/11 hijackers Khalid Almihdhar and Nawaf Alhazmi. However, given the CIA's involvement in the surveillance of al-Hada's house, the CIA could have obtained, and probably did obtain, information about the calls that the NSA failed to collect. For example, a list of the destinations of calls could easily be obtained from the phone company in Yemen.

One point that needs to be stressed here is that a conscious decision must have been made to allow al-Hada and his associates to continue to operate. Along with the various other conspirators who were tried in the US, there was enough information to bring charges against al-Hada for the bombings. Indeed, because of Mohamed al-Owhali's calls to al-Hada, the connection to al-Hada was a major plank in the case against al-Qaeda and its leader, Osama bin Laden. The CIA's rendition program was already running, and al-Hada could have been snatched in Yemen or while on the move.

The decision to allow al-Hada to continue to operate reportedly did generate some good intelligence. However, given the quality and quantity of the intelligence, it is hard to understand how the attack on the USS *Cole* and 9/11 were able to succeed.

It is also remarkable that al-Qaeda allowed this to happen, allowed the US to map its global network. Bin Laden stopped using his satellite phone in September 1998 and appears to have done so because he thought the US was aware of it. If that was the reason he ceased using the phone, then it certainly would have been prudent to no longer use the same communications hub, or any number he had called with the compromised satellite phone.

In addition, according to the *New York Daily News*, "US officials said [Samir] al-Hada was questioned after the 1998 bombings of the U.S. embassies in Kenya and Tanzania."[23] Samir al-Hada was Ahmed's son and helped him run the operations center. This interview would have been another clue telling al-Qaeda that the Yemen hub was being monitored. Yet, as we will see, not only did al-Qaeda continue to use it for mundane affairs, they also used the number to coordinate their next two major attacks, the bombing of the USS *Cole* and 9/11. And the US quite obviously failed to prevent these attacks.[24]

Two key questions here: why did al-Qaeda continue to use a phone it should have known was compromised, and why did the US not take full advantage of the intelligence this generated? The answer to the first may be that al-Qaeda was simply a poor-quality organization whose members had received some training, but not enough to make them experienced covert operatives on a par with the world's major intelligence services. Several examples of poor tradecraft by al-Qaeda operatives, including those engaged in the 9/11 plot, will be highlighted below. The second question—why did the US not take advantage of the intelligence—is harder to answer.

The connection between the embassy bombings and Khalid Almihdhar, who lived at the Yemen hub with his wife Hoda al-Hada (Ahmed's daughter and Samir's sister) is murky. He knew some of the players involved in the bombings, such as Azzam, al-Hada, bin Attash, al-Nashiri and alleged 9/11 mastermind Khalid Shaikh Mohammed, although in the case of the last two it is unclear whether he first met them before or after the embassy attacks.

In the leading international justification for invading Afghanistan after 9/11, British Prime Minister Tony Blair stated that one of the nineteen hijackers "has also been identified as playing key roles in both the East African Embassy attacks and the USS *Cole* attack."[25] US officials later told the *New York Times* that Blair was talking

---

23. Leo Standora, "9/11 Terrorist's in-law Kills Self Fleeing Police," *New York Daily News*, February 14, 2002.
24. One possible explanation for this is that al-Qaeda used this channel for information it wanted the US to know. However, information about the *Cole* bombing and 9/11 was passed over the phone. Assuming there was no secret deal between anyone in al-Qaeda and the US, it is unlikely al-Qaeda would want any such information revealed.
25. Tony Blair, "Statement to Parliament (US terror attacks)," October 4, 2001, http://www.number10.gov.uk/Page1606.

about Almihdhar, and that Almihdhar was definitely involved in the *Cole* attack, but only "possibly" in the embassy bombings.[26]

It is possible that Blair, whose reputation for truthfulness was shredded by the WMD-in-Iraq affair, was making this up, or at least letting his imagination get the better of him. However, there is some evidence directly linking Almihdhar to the embassy bombings. A Yemeni police official told Agence France-Presse that Almihdhar had "made a number of overseas calls to Ahmed al-Hada ... who was then in Sana'a, before, during and after the attacks in Nairobi and Dar es Salaam." AFP added that it was the FBI who told the Yemeni authorities that "Almihdhar made calls to the house of Samir al-Hada in Sana'a between August 5 and 16, 1998."[27]

The *Yemen Times* had a slightly different take on the calls, reporting that sources told it that Samir al-Hada's "contact with Almihdhar during the attacks on the US embassies in Nairobi and Dar es Salaam in 1998 was monitored."[28] There is nothing to say that the calls concerned the embassy bombings in any way, as Almihdhar may have been discussing family matters with his relatives, or even other terror attacks. However, this certainly could have been the start of a case linking Almihdhar to the bombings.

---

26. Jeff Gerth and Don Van Natta Jr., "US Traces Path of Hijacker Tied to Other Attacks," *New York Times*, October 6, 2001.
27. Hammoud Mounasser, "Yemeni killed in blast was involved in Cole, US embassies attacks: police," Agence France-Presse , February 15, 2002.
28. "Al-Hada linked to Cole, US embassies' bombing," *Yemen Times*, February 18, 2002, http://www.yementimes.com/02/iss08/front.htm.

— 3 —

[Redacted]

The NSA continued to monitor Khalid Almihdhar's calls in 1999, giving rise to one of the most cryptic passages in the 9/11 Congressional Inquiry report. It concerned an intercept of calls to and from the al-Hada home, referred to in the report as a "suspected terrorist facility." On page 11, the Inquiry report included the following:

> [In early 1999, the National Security Agency (NSA) analyzed communications involving a suspected terrorist facility in the Middle East that had previously been linked to al-Qaeda activities directed against US interests. Information obtained [...] included, among other things, the full name of future hijacker Nawaf Alhazmi. Beyond the fact that the communications involved a suspected terrorist facility in the Middle East, the communications did not, in NSA's view at the time, feature any other terrorist-related information. The information was not published because the individuals mentioned in the communications were unknown to NSA, and, according to NSA, the information did not meet NSA's reporting thresholds. NSA has explained that these thresholds are flexible, sometimes changing daily, and consist of several factors, including: the priority of the intelligence requirement; the apparent intelligence value of the information; the level of customer interest in the topic; the current situation; and the volume of intercepts to be analyzed and reported].

Later, on page 155, the Congressional Inquiry went over the same episode again:

> [In early 1999, NSA analyzed communications involving a suspected terrorist facility in the Middle East, some of which were associated with Nawaf Alhazmi and Khalid [...], who NSA now believes to have been Khalid Almihdhar. [... ... ...
> ... ...
> ... ...

… … … … … … … … … … … … … … … ….]. These communications were the first indication NSA had of a link between Almihdhar and Alhazmi. They were not disseminated in NSA SIGINT
reporting because the persons were unknown and the subject
matter did not meet NSA reporting thresholds. Those thresholds
vary, depending on the judgment of the NSA analyst who is re-
viewing the intercept and the subject, location, and content of the
intercept].

[In early 1999, another organization obtained the same or similar communications and published the information in a report
it gave to NSA. NSA's practice was to review such reports and
disseminate those responsive to U.S. intelligence requirements.
For an undetermined reason, NSA did not disseminate the […]
report. It was not until early 2002 during the Joint [Congres-
sional] Inquiry that NSA realized that it had the […] report in
its databases and subsequently disseminated it to CIA and other
customers].

Let's try and tease some meaning out of these passages, although
the reader's normal inclination would be to give up, thinking all
sense had been redacted out of them, and perhaps confused by the
forest of brackets. First, we need to understand that information in
the Congressional Inquiry report was redacted in two ways. One
was the traditional way, where the information was deleted and replaced with square brackets and a line of dots between them. The
other way was more subtle. Some passages with sensitive information were reworded to take the sensitive information out, replacing
it with generalities, and these paragraphs were marked with square
brackets at the start and end. This happened to all three paragraphs
quoted above.

First, let us examine the reasons for non-dissemination from
the NSA itself. We are told that the reasons are (1) the individuals
mentioned in the communications were unknown to NSA, and, (2)
according to NSA, the information did not meet NSA's reporting
thresholds, which are variable.

But why was the information disseminated by the other intelligence agency to the NSA, and why did the NSA then disseminate it
in 2002? And what is the function of the sentence beginning "NSA
has explained that these thresholds are flexible"?

Reading between the lines, it appears that what the Congressional Inquiry is trying to tell us is that the information should have been disseminated, but was not—this is what "NSA has explained that these thresholds are flexible" means when translated from redacted-speak into English. In addition, the members of the Congressional Inquiry are saying they could not find out why the NSA did not do this because the NSA *would not tell them*.

The fact that the report from the foreign intelligence agency was disseminated in 2002 indicates that the information was of importance, and that it was not just merely biographical information about the two men. So what were they talking about, and what was the foreign intelligence agency?

The NSA has four main foreign partners, with which it makes up a group known as the "Five Eyes." The other agencies are the NSA equivalents in the world's other main Anglo-Saxon countries: Britain, Canada, Australia and New Zealand. Of these, the NSA's British counterpart, the Government Communications Headquarters (GCHQ), is the largest and most important. If a short list were drawn up of the likely candidates for the foreign intelligence agency that provided the report about the Yemen hub, the name at the top of the list would be GCHQ. If GCHQ were involved in the surveillance of the Yemen hub, this might also account for how British journalist Barry Wigmore was able to obtain information about the operation not available to his counterparts across the Atlantic.[1]

Later, in the summer, the NSA intercepted more calls involving Almihdhar at the hub. The identity of the person he spoke to and the content of the intercepts are so sensitive that a whole passage regarding these communications is redacted in the Congressional Inquiry's

---

1. See Chapter 2 note 21 and related text. Former British intelligence officer John Hughes-Wilson, in his book *Military Intelligence Blunders and Cover-ups* (London: Constable & Robinson, 2004), writes (pp. 384, 386), "Early in 1999 NSA intercepted the name of one Nawaf Alhazmi as a likely al-Qaeda hijacker. The information was filed but apparently not passed on." He repeated the claim later in the book: "Alhazmi was also well known to the NSA at Fort Meade, Maryland. Their signals intelligence operators had intercepted a message in 1999 proving that Alhazmi was an al-Qaeda terrorist and that he was plotting to hijack American airliners. They had, however, apparently not told the CIA or FBI." I am unsure of Hughes-Wilson's claims, relegating them to this note. A *Sunday Times* report stated that British intelligence warned the US of an al-Qaeda plot using civilian aircraft in unconventional ways. This may be a reference to the foreign intelligence warning discussed in the Congressional Inquiry report; see Nicholas Rufford, "MI6 warned US of Al-Qaeda attacks," *Sunday Times* (London), June 9, 2002, http://www.propagandamatrix.com/mi6_warned_us_of_al_qaeda_attacks.htm.

report. After the redacted passage, the Inquiry comments, "At about the same time, the name [of al-Qaeda leader] Khallad [bin Attash] came to the attention of the NSA for the first time," so the calls may have involved bin Attash in some way. Generally, when the NSA failed to disseminate information to other intelligence agencies, the report specifies there was no dissemination, but there is no such comment for these calls, meaning the information was probably disseminated.[2]

The NSA analyzed more communications involving the Yemen hub later in the summer, and Almihdhar's first name was mentioned, but the NSA reportedly still did not know his last name. Presumably, he was one of the parties to the calls, but the NSA did not disseminate any information about them.

It is worth noting that these intercepts were entirely ignored in the 9/11 Commission's final report, which makes no mention of them.[3] Nevertheless, all the Commissioners knew of these calls, as they read the unredacted, classified version of the Congressional Inquiry report. One of them, Tim Roemer, even served as a member of the House Intelligence Committee, one of the bodies responsible for drafting the Inquiry's report.[4] In fact, the Commissioners were mandated by statute to "first review the information compiled by, and the findings, conclusions, and recommendations of, the Joint [Congressional] Inquiry."[5]

Regardless of what was said in the NSA's intercepts of Almihdhar's and Alhazmi's communications in the first eleven months of 1999, the mere fact of the intercepts should have merited a mention and discussion in the main body of the report, yet it was omitted. As we will see, this was because the 9/11 Commission had little apparent interest in the NSA and what it knew of the hijackers.

Here, we need to point out a gap in the official accounts. As we saw above, Almihdhar is reported to have called the Yemen hub from another country at the time of the embassy bombings, and he

2. 9/11 Congressional Inquiry report, pp. 155-56.
3. For the Congressional Inquiry's heavily redacted sections on these intercepts, see pp. 155-57 of its report. The first NSA intercept of communications involving Almihdhar mentioned in *The 9/11 Commission Report* (p. 181) is from late 1999.
4. The 9/11 Commission also hired some of the Congressional Inquiry's staff, Miles Kara, Michael Jacobson and Dana Lesemann, although Lesemann was fired by the Commission's Executive Director Philip Zelikow before the report was completed.
5. Thomas H. Kean and Lee H. Hamilton, *Without Precedent: The Inside Story of the 9/11 Commission* (New York: Alfred A. Knopf, 2006), pp. 65-69.

then stayed at the hub for some time. According to Wigmore, such people were photographed coming and going, and there were bugs inside the house. We are told that the NSA did not know Almih-dhar's last name, but there is deafening silence on what the CIA's Yemen station knew about the hub itself.

The CIA learned of the hub in 1996, so by the beginning of December 1999 they would have had over three years to learn Almih-dhar's last name. While it can be difficult to penetrate militant Islamist groups and discover their leaders' plans, finding out people's names is not so hard. Paying a local journalist to obtain biographical information, which can be as simple as going to the local registry office, is relatively easy.

We also need to take into account the closeness of Islamist militants in Yemen to the government. There are a string of examples showing that the Yemeni government turned a blind eye to what radicals were doing on numerous occasions. One of the most notorious examples of this is the fact that some of the operatives initially convicted in Yemen of blowing up the USS *Cole* are now free.[6] What links did Yemen's security apparatus have to al-Hada? And what did the CIA know of this?

It is also interesting to note that the CIA itself was linked to Yemeni militants. Veteran CIA contractor Billy Waugh, famous as one of the agents who found Carlos the Jackal in Sudan, wrote in his autobiography (emphases added),

> These loosely organized groups—led but not dominated by al-Qaeda—espouse terror and destruction as a tool for moving Islam to the top of the religious powers. I have spoken to some of these terrorists, and they consider terror attacks against the general public their only outlet to hurt and destroy the infidels who have wrongfully ousted them from their homes so many years in the past. *I worked right there with these al-Qaeda operatives* and heard these arguments first hand many times, especially *during an assignment in Yemen*.[7]

---

6. Craig Whitlock, "Probe of USS Cole Bombing Unravels," *Washington Post*, May 4, 2008, http://www.washingtonpost.com/wp-dyn/content/article/2008/05/03/AR2008050302047_pf.html.
7. Billy Waugh and Tim Keown, *Hunting the Jackal: A Special Forces and CIA Soldier's Fifty Years on the Frontlines of the War Against Terrorism* (New York: Avon Books, 2004), p. 303. It is unclear when this happened, although Waugh worked for the CIA between 1989 and 2001.

Obviously, we need to know whether Waugh was the only CIA operative in Yemen who met militants. Which militants did he meet? Did they include Ahmed al-Hada or his associates? And, by the way, what was a CIA contractor doing working "right there" with "al-Qaeda operatives"? Weren't they supposed to be enemies?

Finally, we need to highlight the fact that there were relatively few core al-Qaeda operatives at this time. This is shown by the way operatives were re-used from one operation to another. For example, Khallad bin Attash made a martyrdom video with one of the embassy bombers, is alleged to be one of the masterminds of the *Cole* attack, and passed on messages to the 9/11 hijackers. There were lots of radical Islamists in Asia, but very few of them lived at al-Qaeda's main operations center. This makes the alleged lack of information on Almihdhar at this time all the more bizarre. If we knew what the CIA and NSA really knew about al-Hada, Almihdhar and the hub at this time, we might be a lot closer to solving the puzzle of 9/11.

— 4 —

A secret coded indicator placed there by the Saudi government, warning of possible terrorist affiliation

T he NSA and CIA were not the only agencies interested in Khalid Almihdhar and Nawaf Alhazmi. Saudi Arabia's General Intelligence Directorate (GID) was too.

The nature of the men's relationship with the Saudi authorities is complicated and in dispute. In some accounts, the Saudis simply monitored them; in others they were witting Saudi agents; a third option is that the Saudis attempted to recruit them when they were in the US, but failed; a fourth is that they were not Saudi agents, but the CIA convinced itself they were. All this speculation is based, among other things, on a mountain of evidence about their contacts with Saudi agents, known and presumed. Not all of it need interest us, as this book is primarily about the handling of the hijackers by US intelligence officials. However, the Saudi issue must be mentioned.

After 9/11, three top Saudi officials claimed that Saudi intelligence had been aware of the two men, and that they had been watchlisted in Saudi Arabia. A fourth official said that the Saudis had tracked some of the hijackers, presumably including Almihdhar and Alhazmi, through watchlisting them.

Prince Turki, head of the GID until August 2001, said that by late 1999 Almihdhar and Alhazmi "were on our watch list from previous activities of al-Qaeda, in both the embassy bombings and attempts to smuggle arms into the kingdom in 1997."[1] This was confirmed by Saeed Badeeb, the GID's chief analyst under Turki, and Nawaf Obaid, a security consultant to the Saudi government.[2]

Prince Bandar, a former Saudi ambassador to the US who was known as "Bandar Bush" due to his closeness to the president's family,

1. Mark Follman, "Did the Saudis Know about 9/11?" *Salon* , October 18, 2003, http://dir.salon.com/story/news/feature/2003/10/18/saudis/.
2. Wright 2006, pp. 310-11, 448.

28

said in 2007 that Saudi Arabia had tracked the hijackers. According to his comments, the Saudis had been "actively following" most of the 9/11 hijackers "with precision." Bandar added, "If US security authorities had engaged their Saudi counterparts in a serious and credible manner, in my opinion, we would have avoided what happened."[3] One of the methods of this tracking will be discussed below.

Prince Turki, Badeeb and Obaid also said that they had informed the CIA of the link between al-Qaeda on the one hand and Almihdhar and Alhazmi on the other. Obaid specified that the CIA official told was the Agency's station chief in Saudi Arabia. However, the CIA denied this. Turki initially stood by his claim, but retracted it after becoming ambassador to the US a few years later, a retraction we may take with a healthy dose of salt. According to the Saudis, this notification occurred around the fall of 1999.[4]

However, a cryptic passage in the 9/11 Congressional Inquiry report hints at a closer relationship between Alhazmi and Saudi intelligence. It says that Alhazmi "returned to Saudi Arabia in early 1999, where, [… … … … … … … … … …], he disclosed information about the East Africa embassy bombings."[5] The method in which he disclosed it is unknown, but one possibility is that it was in a discussion with an agent of Saudi intelligence. Another is that he called a line monitored by the NSA—this could even be the content of the early 1999 intercept discussed in the previous chapter. Whatever the method was, the Congressional Inquiry learned of it. The way in which Alhazmi learned the information is also unknown, although it could simply have been from Almihdhar, with whom he was traveling at the time.

* * *

One Saudi tracking method was revealed in 2008 by James Bamford. This was by means of a "secret coded indicator placed there [in suspects' passports] by the Saudi government, warning of possible terrorist affiliation."[6] This appears to have been the use of the

---

3. "Ex-Saudi ambassador: Kingdom could have helped U.S. prevent 9/11," CNN, November 2, 2007, http://www.cnn.com/2007/WORLD/meast/11/01/saudiarabia.terrorism/index.html.
4. Wright 2006, pp. 310-11, 448. John Brennan, later a senior counterterrorism official in the Obama administration, was station chief in Riyadh in the late 1990s. However, he may well have vacated the position by the time of this notification.
5. 9/11 Congressional Inquiry report, p. 131.
6. Bamford 2008, p. 58.

words "Holy Capital," a reference to Mecca's status in Islam, as the place of issue for passports issued in Mecca.[7] The indicator had been in use for some time, and had even been placed on the Saudi passports of three of the men who bombed the World Trade Center in 1993. Which three is not known, although Ahmad Ajaj, an associate of lead bomber Ramzi Yousef, did have a Saudi passport.[8]

Three of the hijackers definitely had this indicator of extremism in their passports. One was Nawaf Alhazmi, who obtained a new passport on March 21, 1999, used it to obtain a US visa on April 3, and then left Saudi Arabia.

Another was Khalid Almihdhar. He received a passport with the indicator on April 6, 1999, used it to obtain a US visa the next day, and then left Saudi Arabia.[9] Almihdhar re-entered Saudi Arabia in late 2000 and stayed for two or three months, leaving in February 2001.[10] He re-entered Saudi Arabia again on May 26,[11] and obtained a new passport, which was again tagged by the authorities, six days later.[12] He obtained a US visa on June 13, and then left for the US on July 4, 2001.[13]

The third was Salem Alhazmi, who obtained a passport with the indicator on April 4, 1999, and got a US visa with it the same day,

7. A 9/11 Commission document refers to the passports of Almihdhar and Salem Alhazmi as "'Holy Capital' passports"; see "Suggested Travel Document Illustrations for the Commission Report" (undated), http://www.scribd.com/doc/16729054/T5-B6-Graphics-for-Final-Report-Fdr-Memo-and-Email-Re-Graphics-w-Chp-5-Pgs-191. An FBI document found in the 9/11 Commission's files stated of each of these two passports, "This passport was issued at 'Holy Capital'"; see FBI PENTTBOM document 265A-NY-280350, http://www.scribd.com/doc/16842138/T5-B50-Hijacker-Primary-Docs-AA-77-1-of-2-Fdr-Al-Mihdhar-Tab-FBI-PENTTBOM-Memo-Re-CD-Found-81502-Redacted-and-Unredacdted-Versions-340. A draft of the 9/11 Commission's staff report on the terrorists' travel (see note 8) states that the passport Almihdhar used in 1999 "was issued in 'Makkah' and contains the words 'Holy Capital'"; see "The September 11 Attacks and the U.S. Borders," June 21, 2004, p. 7, http://www.scribd.com/doc/17518806/T5-B38-Team-5-Presentations-Fdr-Draft-Monograph-on-Terrorist-Travel-Appendix-Not-Scanned-052. An FBI notice issued on July 2, 2003 stated, "Numerous Al Qaeda terrorists have also carried Saudi passports issued in the Holy Capital, another term for the city of Mecca"; see David Johnston, "Citing Low Level Threat, Officials Plan No Special Terror Alert for Holiday Weekend," New York Times, July 2, 2003, http://www.nytimes.com/2003/07/03/us/threats-responses-intelligence-citing-low-threat-level-officials-plan-no-special.html?pagewanted=1.
8. 9/11 Commission, "9/11 and Terrorist Travel: Staff Report of the National Commission on Terrorist Attacks Upon the United States," August 21, 2004 [hereinafter: Terrorist Travel report], pp. 46-47, 61. The final draft of this staff report does not contain any references to "Holy Capital."
9. Terrorist Travel report, p. 9.
10. 9/11 CR, p. 237.
11. Bamford 2008, p. 64.
12. 9/11 CR, p. 496; Terrorist Travel report, pp. 24, 27.
13. Terrorist Travel report, pp. 24, 27, 33, 49.

then left Saudi Arabia.[14] Salem allegedly returned to Saudi Arabia and took a flight from there to Beirut, Lebanon, in November 2000.[15] He must have soon returned to Saudi Arabia, because he left again on January 1, 2001, this time to go to Yemen.[16] He arrived back in Saudi Arabia on June 13, 2001,[17] obtained a new marked passport three days later, obtained a second US visa four days after that,[18] and then left Saudi Arabia again.

Other hijackers may also have been tracked using the indicator. The 9/11 Commission speculated, "It is likely that many of the hijackers' passports contained indicators of extremism," and thought Ahmed Alnami and Ahmed Alhaznawi were particularly likely candidates.[19]

Apparently, US immigration and consular officials were not trained to recognize these indicators before 9/11. Before the World Trade Center bombing, the CIA had produced a Red Book instructing immigration officials on how to recognize terrorists by looking at their passports. However, the last edition was published in 1992, and radical Islamists linked to the WTC bombing and the fighting in Bosnia were found to have obtained a copy in 1995.[20]

The CIA did not disseminate the information about the indicator *after* 9/11 either. It learned of the indicator no later than February 14, 2003, but a year later immigration inspectors had still not been warned.[21]

* * *

The hijackers' US visas are interesting in their own right. An investigation by the *National Review* found that the visa applications were of extremely poor quality, and information missing from them

14. Federal Bureau of Investigation, "Working Draft Chronology of Events for Hijackers," p. 40, http://www.historycommons.org/sourcedocuments/2001/pdfs/fbi911timeline1-105.pdf; Terrorist Travel report, p. 33.
15. *9/11 CR*, p. 240.
16. Federal Bureau of Investigation, see note 14, p. 116.
17. *United States v. Zacarias Moussaoui*, "Stipulation [Regarding flights hijacked on September 11, 2001; September 11, 2001 deaths; al Qaeda; chronology of hijackers' activities; Zacarias Moussaoui; and the Computer Assisted Passenger Pre-screening System (CAPPS)]," Part A, p. 35, http://www.vaed.uscourts.gov/notablecases/moussaoui/exhibits/prosecution/ST00001.html
18. *9/11 CR*, pp. 563-64; Terrorist Travel report, pp. 9, 25-26, 33.
19. *9/11 CR*, pp. 563-4; Terrorist Travel report, p. 7.
20. Terrorist Travel report, pp. 45-46, 61, 63, 69, 102.
21. Ibid., pp. 25, 27, 41.

meant that they should have been rejected.[22] However, with one exception, all the visa applications were granted. Most of the hijackers' visas—fifteen out of a total of twenty-three—were issued at the US consulate in Jeddah, Saudi Arabia, and most of these, eleven or twelve, were issued by the same consular official, Shayna Steinger.[23]

The most controversial of the visa applications Steinger granted was that of Hani Hanjour, whom she originally rejected. Steinger first testified about the visas in August 2002 before the House Committee on Government Reform. She claimed that she had issued Hanjour's visa under the Visa Express program and that the initial denial was about calling him in for an interview: "I remember that I had refused him for interview, because he had applied for a tourist visa and he said that his reason for going to the United States was to study."[24]

This account is untrue—the visa was not granted under the Visa Express program, which was not introduced until the following spring. In addition, Hanjour appears to have been at the consulate when the denial was issued. Steinger later gave a different account of her actions to the 9/11 Commission, which referred to her using the aliases "Consular Official No. 3," "Consular Official No. 11," and "Tom" in its Terrorist Travel report.[25] Steinger went on to serve in various positions around the Middle East and in Washington. In 2008, she was elevated to a seat on the board of the American Foreign Service Association, an organization representing around 15,000 US government officials working abroad.[26]

22. Joel Mowbray, "Visas that Should Have Been Denied," *National Review*, October 9, 2002, http://www.nationalreview.com/mowbray/mowbray100902.asp.

23. The Commission's Terrorist Travel report makes an error with its numbers, claiming that the hijackers only received twenty-two visas, but it omits Salem Alhazmi's visa issued in April 1999, also in Jeddah. The Commission's claim that Steinger issued only eleven of the visas also appears to be incorrect. Analysis of the Commission's supporting documentation indicates she actually issued twelve visas to the hijackers: Ahmed Alghamdi (September 3, 2000), Saeed Alghamdi (September 4, 2000), Hani Hanjour (September 25, 2000), Waleed and Wail Alshehri (October 24, 2000), Ahmed Alnami (October 28, 2000), Ahmed Alhaznawi (November 12, 2000), Ahmed Alnami again (April 23, 2001), Saeed Alghamdi (June 12, 2001), Abdulaziz Alomari (June 18, 2001), Khalid Almihdhar (June 13, 2001), and Salem Alhazmi (June 20, 2001); 9/11 Commission, "Chronology of Saudi Visa Applications," December 30, 2002, http://www.scribd.com/doc/16842336/T5-B51-Hijacker-Primary.

24. Terrorist Travel report, p. 37.

25. Terrorist Travel report, pp. 37-38, 125-26, 148.

26. "Notes from the Boards," *AFSA News*, January 2008, http://www.afsa.org/fsj/jan08/afsa_news.pdf.

In this context it is interesting to note that during the Soviet-Afghan War, it was the US Consulate in Jeddah that served as one terminus of an underground railroad sending radical Islamist fighters to the US. These visas were issued by CIA officers working undercover at the consulate as consular officials.[27]

The 9/11 Commission even noted "eerie parallels" with the case of the "Blind Sheikh," Sheikh Omar Abdul-Rahman, who had repeatedly entered the US despite being the spiritual head of al-Gama'a al-Islamiyya, an Egyptian terrorist organization. When in the US, the Blind Sheikh was linked to the 1993 World Trade Center bombers and was eventually convicted for his part in the "Day of Terror" plot. The Commission examined the case in detail in its Terrorist Travel report, purporting to debunk the claims that the CIA had been involved in the issuance of his visas.[28]

Pulitzer Prize-winning journalist and author Tim Wiener had a different take on the matter:

> His visa had been issued in the capital of Sudan by a member of the Central Intelligence Agency in Khartoum, said Joe O'Neill, the chargé d affaires at the American embassy. The Agency knew that he was traveling in the area looking for a visa and never told us. It must have been a mistake, O'Neill thought. That name should have showed up like a shot. In fact, CIA officers had reviewed seven applications by Abdul-Rahman to enter the United States and said yes six times. I can't tell you what a terrible thing it is that that had happened, O'Neill said. It was atrocious.[29]

It is also worth noting that in the spring of 1989 al-Gama'a al-Islamiyya was engaged in secret, back-channel talks with the US.[30] These talks may have started before this period and continued after it.

The authority the Commission relied on for its purported debunking was a set of talking points for the CIA director that said the Agency's inspector general had found the CIA did not issue the Sheikh with the visas for "CIA operational purposes." The claim

27. Joseph Trento, *Prelude to Terror* (New York: Carroll & Graf, 2005), pp. 344-46.
28. Terrorist Travel report, pp. 49-52, 62.
29. Tim Weiner, *Legacy of Ashes: The History of the CIA* (London: Penguin, 2007), p. 512.
30. Memo from US Embassy in Cairo, "Summary of Conversations with a Member of 'The Islamic Group,' aka 'Al-Jihad,'" April 25, 1989, http://intelfiles.egoplex.com/1989-04-25-gamaat.pdf; Memo from US Embassy in Cairo, "Conversations with a Member of 'The Islamic Group,'" May 3, 1989, http://intelfiles.egoplex.com/1989-05-03-gamaat.pdf. These documents were obtained by terrorism analyst J.M. Berger of Intelwire.

was that the visas were issued to the Sheikh as a favor for services rendered in the Soviet-Afghan War and/or so he could continue with his own activities, not in support of a specific CIA operation. As it happened, one of the Sheikh's main activities in the US was to raise funds for the jihad in Bosnia, conducted against the Bosnian Serbs, a Russian proxy.

Part 2:

Kuala Lumpur, Malaysia

https://www.cia.gov/news-information/press-releases-statements/press-release-archive-2005/pr10052005.html

CENTRAL INTELLIGENCE AGENCY
THE WORK OF A NATION. THE CENTER OF INTELLIGENCE.

Search

Press Releases & Statements

CIA Home > News & Information > Press Releases &
Statements > Press Release Archive 2005 > Statement
on CIA Office of the Inspector General Report

Statement on CIA Office of the Inspector General Report

CIA Director Porter J. Goss Statement on CIA Office of the Inspector General Report, "CIA Accountability with Respect to the 9/11 Attacks"

October 5, 2005

Sidebar navigation:

CIA Home
About CIA
Careers
Offices of CIA
▾News & Information
  ▸Press Releases & Statements
    ▸Press Release Archive 2005
      ▸Statement on CIA Office of the Inspector General Report
  Speeches & Testimony
  CIA & The War on Terrorism
  Featured Story Archive
  What's New on CIA.gov
  Your News
Library
Kids' Page
Contact CIA

Mission
The Central Intelligence Agency (CIA) is an independent US Government agency responsible for providing national security intelligence to senior US policymakers.

To learn more, visit CIA Vision, Mission & Values.

Press Release Archive:

2008
2007
2006
2005
2004
2003
2002
2001
2000
1999
1998

... Just as with the other IC agencies that conducted similar 9/11 OIG reviews, in no way does this report suggest that any one person or group of people could have prevented 9/11. Of the officers named in this report, about half have retired from the Agency, and those who are still with us are amongst the finest we have.

After great consideration of this report and its conclusions, I will not convene an accountability board to judge the performances of any individual CIA officers. I have talked to each of the named current employees and am familiar with their abilities and dedication to our mission. I remember well the time period prior to 9/11, and it was a time of great challenge for the intelligence community. CIA resources were inadequate, and hiring had been at a historic low. During this time period, certain individuals were asked to "step-up." These officers were "stars" who had excelled in their areas, so the CIA leadership singled them out to take on some tough assignments. Unfortunately, time and resources were not on their side, despite their best efforts to meet unprecedented challenges....

Part of Director Porter Goss' statement regarding his refusal to convene any accountability boards to review the performances of CIA officials prior to 9/11, which had been recommended by the CIA inspector general.

5

This is not a matter for the FBI

A key al-Qaeda gathering, a summit meeting of sorts, at which 9/11 was planned, took place in Kuala Lumpur, Malaysia, in early January 2000. The CIA and a local Malaysian intelligence service monitored it. Nawaf Alhazmi and Khalid Almihdhar along with other al-Qaeda leaders attended. The meeting was discussed by the investigations and the media. All the accounts, however, omitted crucial facts, and thus wrongly minimized the importance of this gathering.

In December 1999, during a major alert due to a perceived set of forthcoming al-Qaeda attacks to mark the Millennium, the NSA had intercepted a call involving the Yemen hub. It was between Khallad bin Attash and Almihdhar, and indicated that a number of operatives, referred to by the NSA as "Khalid," "Nawaf," and "Salem," would be traveling to Malaysia for a summit with other al-Qaeda operatives. The Khalid was Almihdhar, although the NSA reportedly did not know his full name at this point. Nawaf and Salem were the Alhazmi brothers.

The NSA already associated Nawaf Alhazmi with the Yemen hub's phone thanks to the intercepts earlier in the year, and if they had searched their database, they would have found his name. They also figured that Salem was Nawaf's brother, so, if they had found Nawaf's last name, they would have found Salem's too. The NSA did not search its database, but it did send a report of the intercept to both the CIA and the FBI.[1]

The CIA officer responsible for the Yemen hub, referred to only as "Michelle" in the Justice Department inspector general's report, presumably read this cable when it came in.[2] It is unclear who else

1. *9/11 CR*, pp. 181; Wright 2006, pp. 310-11; 9/11 Congressional Inquiry report, pp. 143-44.
2. She was identified as the officer responsible for the Yemen hub by Mark Rossini, an FBI agent detailed to Alec Station; PBS, *NOVA*, "The Spy Factory," February 3, 2009, http://www.pbs.org/wgbh/nova/transcripts/3602_spyfactory.html. She is referred to as "Michael" in *The 9/11 Commission Report*, although it refers to her as a woman. In *The Dark Side*, author Jane Mayer calls the

read the report at this time, although Tom Wilshire, a deputy chief of Alec Station, did access cables about the surveillance on January 5,[3] and it is reasonable to assume he knew about the NSA report when it came in. He later told the Congressional Inquiry, "this intelligence [the NSA surveillance] provided a kind of a tuning fork that buzzed when two individuals [Alhazmi and Almihdhar] reportedly planning a trip to Kuala Lumpur were linked indirectly to a support element [the Yemen hub] that we suspected had played a role with the Africa bombers."[4]

Michelle, who later helped Wilshire prevent information from reaching the FBI, is said to be the one who identified these links, although they would have been obvious at the time.[5] In any case, the CIA realized that the summit was so important that information about it was briefed to CIA and FBI leaders, National Security Adviser Sandy Berger and other top officials at the start of 2000.[6]

The CIA's Counterterrorist Center was concerned about these reports. An anonymous desk officer speculated that "something more nefarious is afoot,"[7] and a senior intelligence official told James Bamford in 2003,

We knew that some guys that looked as though they were al-Qaeda-associated were traveling to KL [Kuala Lumpur]. We didn't know what they were going to do there. We were trying to find that. And we were concerned that there might be an attack, because it wasn't just Almihdhar and Alhazmi, it was also eleven young guys—which was a term that was used for operatives traveling. We didn't have the names of the others, and on Alhazmi we only had his first name, "Nawaf." So the concern was: What are they doing? Is this a prelude to an attack in KL—what's happening here?[8]

officer "Mike," and mistakenly states that she was male.
3. US Department of Justice, Office of the Inspector General, A Review of the FBI's Handling of Intelligence Information Related to the September 11 Attacks, November 2004 (released June 16, 2006) [hereinafter: Justice Department IG report], p. 240.
4. US Congress, The House Permanent Select Committee On Intelligence and the Senate Select Committee On Intelligence, The Intelligence Community's Knowledge of the September 11 Hijackers Prior to September 11, 2001: Hearing before the Joint Inquiry of the Senate Select Committee on Intelligence and the House Permanent Select Committee on Intelligence, September 20, 2002.
5. Justice Department IG report, p. 239.
6. 9/11 CR, pp. 181-82.
7. Ibid., p. 181.
8. James Bamford, A Pretext for War: 9/11, Iraq, and the Abuse of America's Intelligence Agen-

* * *

A note of caution should be sounded here, as the desk officer who wrote about "something nefarious" may have been Michelle or Tom Wilshire, and, in any case, the "something nefarious" quote does not directly indicate that the CIA thought there was going to be an attack in Malaysia itself. Likewise, the senior intelligence official who told Bamford the CIA thought there might be an attack in Malaysia may have been Wilshire, or one of his associates.

There is no public record of the CIA warning Malaysia of the possibility of an attack during the summit in January 2000, or even in May and July 2001, when Wilshire would say he thought there was going to be an al-Qaeda attack there. On the other hand, if such a warning was sent, then there is no specific reason it should have been made public, as intelligence agencies are particularly unwilling to disclose information about contacts with foreign services.

As described below, when Alec Station withheld information about the 9/11 hijackers from the FBI, "Michelle" justified this by saying that the next al-Qaeda attack was going to be in Southeast Asia. Tom Wilshire, a central figure in the withholding of information, repeatedly generated documentation stating his concern that al-Qaeda might attack in Southeast Asia, specifically Malaysia. In hindsight, this was obviously wrong, as neither the USS *Cole* bombing nor 9/11 was in Malaysia, or anywhere else in Southeast Asia.

It could be argued that the CIA officers made a genuine mistake in assuming this. They simply saw al-Qaeda operatives linked to the Yemen hub traveling to Malaysia and meeting with local militants there, then put two and two together.

It could also be argued that some or all of these officers simply made this claim up to get colleagues to go along with them when they suggested doing things that should not have been done, and to lay a false trail—build an excuse in advance—in the event of a later investigation. The evidence supporting both positions will be highlighted where it occurs in the narrative. Here, you should simply bear in mind that when a CIA officer expresses concern over a possible al-Qaeda attack in Southeast Asia, both the statement and the officer should be treated with caution.

---

cies (New York: Anchor Books, 2005) [hereinafter: Bamford 2005], p. 222.

Al-Qaeda did not carry out attacks in all countries in which it operated. Some countries were regarded simply as bases of operations where the organization raised funds and recruited. Probably the best-known such country was Britain, where the security services welcomed with open arms a raft of Islamist radicals keen on supporting the jihad against the Russian-backed Serbs in Bosnia and the Russians themselves in Chechnya. As a result of the hospitality they received from the British, al-Qaeda sympathizers in Britain promised the local security services not to carry out attacks there.

Al-Qaeda regarded Malaysia in a similar way. Faiz abu Baker Bafana, a leading operative for the al-Qaeda affiliate Jemaah Islamiyya, said in 2002 during a deposition for the Zacarias Moussaoui trial,

> [Moussaoui] was saying about this, the jihad—I mean, he was talking about jihad, and I was saying that jihad would be, you know, in Indonesia, and Malaysia will be the economic base. They donate money to—for jihad.
>
> And [Moussaoui] say that it more important that America be the, more important that we bring down rather than other areas, and you want to do business in Malaysia for this purpose, to finance the jihad, that the government or the U.S. or the Malaysian government knows what you-all are doing, and we should just either rob a bank or do kidnapping for—to get money rather than doing business in Malaysia, which I feel like it's not appropriate, because if we do that, then we are putting ourself in trouble in Malaysia as we are being—as we are looking for a safe place in Malaysia to do business.[9]

So it should be borne in mind that when the Alec Station officers said they were worried about an attack in Malaysia, they were claiming they were unaware al-Qaeda regarded the country as an economic base, not a target for attacks.

In addition, Malaysia was well-known as a destination with lax visa rules for Muslim visitors, a practice that carried on after 9/11.[10] According to the 9/11 Commission, Khallad bin Attash told the CIA under interrogation that "Malaysia was an ideal destination because its government did not require citizens of Saudi Arabia or other Gulf

9. *United States v. Zacarias Moussaoui*, March 8, 2006, morning session, http://cryptome.org/usa-v-zm-030806-01.htm.
10. Simon Montlak, "Tired of post-9/11 hassles, Arab tourists head east." *Christian Science Monitor*, August 18, 2004, http://www.csmonitor.com/2004/0818/p07s02-wome.html, Alexandra A. Seno, "Invasion Of The Ninjas," *Newsweek*, July 22, 2002, http://www.newsweek.com/id/100949

states to have a visa."[11] (Please note: this information may be considered unreliable because of the "enhanced interrogation methods" used on detainees. However, public information indicates known radicals did travel to Malaysia on numerous occasions.)

The fact that visas were not required made it an ideal meeting point for Islamist terrorists. As we will see, it appears Khalid Almihdhar returned here twice, in October 2000 and May or June of 2001, to discuss with Bafana an attack that was to take place in Singapore. It is certainly possible that people whose business it was to track terrorists before 9/11 would have known this, and known that operatives going to Malaysia did not necessarily signify an attack in Malaysia.

In this context it is appropriate to recall the 1996 Bojinka plot, in which alleged 9/11 mastermind Khalid Shaikh Mohammed and his associate Ramzi Yousef planned to blow up eleven airliners in Southeast Asia, mostly on their way to the US. The countries from which the airlines would leave were South Korea, the Philippines, Singapore, Hong Kong, Taiwan, and Japan; Thailand was used as a transit point, and the bombers planned to hide out in Pakistan after the attacks.[12] Part of the Bojinka plot's financial architecture, the front company Konsonjaya, was based in Malaysia, and this had been known to investigators since 1996.[13]

It is also worth noting how completely penetrated Jemaah Islamiyya was at this point. Many of its leaders lived in a single Malaysian village, Sungai Manggis. In fact, there were so many of them there that the security services dubbed the village "Terror HQ." One of the top militants, Fauzi Hasbi, was actually an Indonesian government mole. He lived across the street from a leading militant known as "Hambali," who met Almihdhar and Alhazmi in Kuala Lumpur.[14] Another Indonesian mole who penetrated the or-

11. *9/11 CR*, p. 158.
12. Simon Reeve, *The New Jackals: Ramzi Yousef, Osama bin Laden and the Future of Terrorism* (London: André Deutsch Press, 1999), pp. 90-91. Most accounts say that the Bojinka plot involved twelve, not eleven airliners. However, in this book Reeve actually details which flights were to be blown up, so his account was used here.
13. Peter Lance, *1,000 Years for Revenge: International Terrorism and the FBI*, (New York: Harper-Collins, 2003), 303-04.
14. Simon Elegant, "Asia's Own Osama," *Time*, April 1, 2001, http://www.time.com/time/asia/features/malay_terror/hambali.html; Terry McDermott, "The Plot," *Los Angeles Times*, September 1, 2002, http://articles.latimes.com/2002/sep/01/nation/na-plot; Widjajanto and Rommy Fibri, "Sermons in Sungai Manggis," *Tempo*, October 29, 2002, http://www.worldpress.org/Asia/830.cfm, "Inside Indo-

ganization was known only as Dadang.[15] If there was a major plot by al-Qaeda in Southeast Asia, the locals certainly had informants in high places who could have learned of it, and this information could have been passed to the CIA.

* * *

After receiving notification from the NSA, the CIA decided to track Khalid Almihdhar and Nawaf Alhazmi on their way to Kuala Lumpur, from Yemen and Pakistan respectively. When Almihdhar changed planes in Dubai, a copy of his passport was made. There are two versions of this story. In one, Almihdhar's passport was photocopied at the airport while he was changing planes. In the other, the CIA broke into his hotel room as he overnighted in Dubai and copied his passport there.[16]

Whichever version is true, the CIA found a US visa in the passport. The visa was due to expire in April, and a check on immigration records showed that Almihdhar had not yet used it. Therefore, the CIA figured, Almihdhar intended to come to the US in the following couple of months.[17]

The CIA also learned information about Alhazmi's flight, but he is reported to have changed his reservation twice, meaning that the CIA missed him at the airport in Pakistan on the way to Malaysia.[18]

Veteran FBI agent Jack Cloonan highlighted the great importance of the information about the Malaysia summit to US intelligence:

> How often do you get into someone's suitcase and find multiple-entry visas? And how often do you know there's going to be an organizational meeting of al-Qaeda, anyplace in the world? The chances are slim to none! This is as good as it gets. It's a home run in the ninth inning of the World Series. This is the kind of case

nesia's War on Terror," *SBS Dateline*, October 12, 2005, http://www.adelaideinstitute.org/Australia/indonesia.htm; Maria Ressa, *Seeds of Terror* (New York: Free Press, 2003).

15. Ken Conboy, *INTEL: Inside Indonesia's Intelligence Service*, (London: Equinox, 2003), pp. 212-13.

16. For example, Bamford (see note 9) says Almihdhar's passport was copied at the airport (p. 223), but Wright's *Looming Tower* says it was copied in his hotel room (p. 311). According to an FBI chronology of the attacks (p. 51), Almihdhar stayed at a hotel called the Nihar: http://www.historycommons.org/sourcedocuments/2001/pdfs/fbi911timeline1-105.pdf.

17. Wright 2006, p. 311.

18. 9/11 Commission Staff Statement No. 2, "Three 9/11 Hijackers: Identification, Watchlisting, and Tracking," http://www.9-11Commission.gov/staff_statements/staff_statement_2.pdf.

you hope your whole life for. That's why you do all this work, you have thousands of cases, you've got agents spending their lives doing all kinds of stuff, responding to every crank call that comes in, and here you are. This is what you would dream about. This is what you trained for. What you planned for, what you hope for. You want to be lucky. And that was being lucky.[19]

The visa information was reported in a cable to Alec Station, where it was accessed by Doug Miller, an FBI agent on detail to the station. Miller knew the FBI had already received some information about the Malaysia summit, but, prior to the discovery of Almihdhar's US visa, there was nothing of particular importance for the Bureau, a domestic agency. Realizing the significance of the new information, Miller drafted an official cable for the FBI, warning them of Almihdhar's US visa and of a link between him and the 1998 African embassy bombings.[20]

Learning of the draft cable to the Bureau, Tom Wilshire instructed "Michelle" to tell Miller to hold off on it, and she attached a note saying, "pls hold off on [the cable] for now per [Tom Wilshire]."[21] Miller was also told, "This is not a matter for the FBI."[22] But, confused as to why he would have to hold off on the cable, he complained to another FBI detailee to Alec Station, Mark Rossini.

"Doug came to me and said, 'What the fuck?'" Rossini later told James Bamford. Rossini took the matter up with Michelle. "So the next day I went to her and said, 'What's with Doug's cable? You've got to tell the bureau about this.' She put her hand on her hip and said, 'Look, the next attack is going to happen in Southeast Asia—it's not the FBI's jurisdiction. When we want the FBI to know about it, we'll let them know. The next bin Laden attack's going to happen in Southeast Asia.'"[23] The implication here was that the CIA was aware

19. Jane Mayer, *The Dark Side* (New York: Doubleday, 2008), p. 18.
20. Wright 2006, 311-12; Justice Department IG report, pp. 239-42.
21. Justice Department IG report, p. 240.
22. Wright 2006, p. 311.
23. Bamford 2008, p. 19-20. Bamford identifies this officer as a woman, and it would be logical for Rossini to take the matter up with "Michelle," the officer who prevented Miller from sending the cable. Therefore, it is highly likely that Bamford's officer is in fact the officer named Michelle in the Justice Department IG report. The Justice Department IG calls Michelle a "desk officer" (p. 239), as does *The 9/11 Commission Report* (p. 502). Bamford identifies the woman as a deputy unit chief, but this seems unlikely, as the unit is reported to have had two deputy chiefs at this time, Wilshire and the FBI detailee known as "Eric" in the Justice Department IG report. There were other

of this alleged attack in Southeast Asia, planned to thwart it and any interference by the FBI could disrupt such a sensitive operation.

Miller followed up with Wilshire a few days later, asking if the draft cable should be remade in some way before it could be sent, but received no reply and dropped the matter.[24] Although he was an FBI agent, he was stationed at the CIA and the information had come to him through CIA channels. It was unthinkable for him or Rossini to pass on the information without explicit permission. Had he done so, he would have been fired.[25]

To his credit, Rossini later regretted his actions,[26] telling PBS' *NOVA* in January 2009, "I can't come up with a rational reason why I didn't break the rules, pick up the phone, and tell that the hijackers, or really bad guys, are in the U.S. And I don't know if I'll ever be able to come to terms with that. I don't know. I really don't know."[27]

management positions in addition to unit chief and deputy unit chief at this time, so the female officer may have filled one of these positions, such as head of operations, or she may simply have been a desk officer to whom Wilshire tended to delegate important tasks.

24. Wright 2006, 311-12.

25. Jeff Stein, "FBI Prevents Agents from Telling 'Truth' About 9/11 on PBS," *Congressional Quarterly*, October 1, 2008, http://blogs.cqpolitics.com/spytalk/2008/10/fbi-prevents-agents-from-telli.html.

26. Rossini resigned from the FBI after apparently searching the Bureau's computers to obtain information for his girlfriend. The searches were made in the first half of 2007, and Rossini resigned in November 2008, by which time the case had gotten into the media. I considered the possibility that when Rossini, who stated he could not recall Miller's blocked cable in 2004, changed his story for accounts published in 2008, he did it for reasons other than getting the real truth out. He seems to have been unpopular with some of the CIA officers at Alec Station and was close to FBI manager John O'Neill, who was at daggers drawn with Scheuer and then Richard Blee, Scheuer's replacement and Wilshire's superior. However, Rossini does not fit the mold of a bitter ex-employee. He pleaded guilty at his trial and did not allege a witch hunt against him. In addition, the change to his story actually cast the FBI, the organization that had just forced him out, in a good light. The damp criticism of him and Miller voiced by the Justice Department inspector general had no impact on his career, as he subsequently became a briefer at a key CIA meeting with Director Tenet and then a press spokesman for the FBI's New York office. The documentary record clearly shows that Miller read the incoming cables and drafted one to the FBI that was never sent. It also shows that Rossini read Miller's draft cable and four of the incoming cables it was based on. Given the amount of material they read, their claims of bad memory to the Justice Department IG are incredible. In addition, an article in *Congressional Quarterly* (see note 26) says that Rossini and Miller first changed their story for an internal FBI investigation into its 9/11 failings, which presumably occurred some time before 2007. Lawrence Wright's 2006 account that Miller was told "this is not a matter for the FBI" is sourced to Rossini, meaning that he changed at least this part of his story before he even made the searches for which he was forced out. The documentary record also clearly establishes that Michelle and Wilshire were the officers who blocked the cable. It was Michelle who attached the note to the draft cable referencing Wilshire, and it was Wilshire to whom Miller appealed a week later.

27. PBS, *NOVA*, "The Spy Factory," February 3, 2009, http://www.pbs.org/wgbh/nova/tran-

This is one of the key events on the road to 9/11. Had the notification been passed to the FBI and the two men's names placed on the US watch list, domestic authorities would have been all over them as soon as they entered the US in mid-January 2000. As we will see, the hijackers' tradecraft was poor and surveillance of Alhazmi and Almihdhar would have led investigators to the other hijackers. In addition, the two men later moved in with an FBI counterterrorism informant, Abdussattar Shaikh, which certainly could have been exploited by the Bureau.[28]

In addition to failing to notify the Bureau, the CIA also failed to add Almihdhar's name to the main US watch list. This omission is especially odd because in the middle of the previous month the Counterterrorist Center had sent all CIA stations and bases a circular entitled "Terrorism Guidance" stressing the importance of watchlisting:

> It is important to flag terrorist personality information in DO [Directorate of Operations] intelligence reporting for [the State Department watch list program] so that potential terrorists may be watchlisted. Information for inclusion in [the State Department watch list program] must raise a reasonable suspicion that the individual is a possible terrorist.... Information for [the State Department watch list] program should be based on the following priorities:
>
> – known or suspected terrorists who pose or may pose a present threat to U.S. interests in the United States or abroad ...[29]

* * *

The important question here: why did Wilshire and "Michelle" block notification to the FBI of Almihdhar's US visa?

---

scripts/3602_spyfactory.html.

28. They moved in with the FBI informant in May 2000. After Almihdhar went back to the Middle East in June, Alhazmi stayed there alone. Shaikh allegedly mentioned the two men in passing to his handler, Steve Butler, later claiming that they didn't break the law, so why would he say much about them to the FBI. Nonetheless, Shaikh's interview memo in the 9/11 Commission's files shows he knew Alhazmi was working illegally; "9/11 Commission MFR for FBI Informer Abdussattar Shaikh," April 23, 2004, http://www.scribd.com/doc/15877639/911-Commission-MFR-for-FBI-Informer-Abdussattar-Shaikh. Butler refused to be interviewed by the Department of Justice inspector general, but he *was* interviewed by the Congressional Inquiry. Although broke from his divorce, Shaikh managed to hire an expensive lawyer who prevented the Congressional Inquiry from getting his testimony, and joint chairman Senator Bob Graham speculated that the FBI had paid for this lawyer; Bob Graham with Jeff Nussbaum, *Intelligence Matters: The CIA, the FBI, Saudi Arabia, and the Failure of America's War on Terror* (New York: Random House, 2004), pp. 160-66.
29. 9/11 Congressional Inquiry report, Appendix: "CTC Watchlisting Guidance, December 1999."

One interpretation of Michelle's claim that the next al-Qaeda attack would be in Southeast Asia is that it was an expression of a genuinely held (but incorrect, as it turned out) belief. If so, it would have to be based on intelligence reporting, but what intelligence reporting? There are no public reports of any such reporting at the CIA, so there is reason to withhold judgment on whether Michelle genuinely believed what she told Rossini was true.

In late 1999 and early 2000, al-Qaeda was working on a number of plots: a ship-bombing operation in Yemen, a hotel bombing in Jordan and an attack on Los Angeles airport (which were collectively known as the "Millennium Plot"[30]), as well as 9/11. According to alleged 9/11 mastermind Khalid Shaikh Mohammed, at this stage the 9/11 plot was divided into two sections. One was to be in the US, the other in Southeast Asia. KSM divulged this information about the later-canceled Southeast Asia portion of 9/11 under CIA questioning using "enhanced techniques," rendering it unreliable, but it was confirmed by another detainee, Khallad bin Attash. Bin Attash was also tortured, but two detainees saying the same thing lends more credibility than just one.

There is some limited evidence to back this up: bin Attash claimed that he took specific casing flights in Southeast Asia, from Kuala Lumpur to Bangkok and then to Hong Kong and back, to gain information about flight procedures for that portion of the attacks. These flights either have been or can be confirmed using the manifests, and such confirmation would enhance the credibility of the statements about the Southeast Asian part of the plot.

Further, KSM said the reason for the Southeast Asian section was that bin Attash, originally slated to go to the US to participate in 9/11, failed to obtain a US visa, and this was a way to use him and similar operatives who would have trouble getting visas because they were Yemenis. Bin Attash's denied visa application was located after 9/11, making this statement at least plausible.[31]

So if Wilshire and Michelle genuinely were aware of an al-Qaeda plot in Southeast Asia at this time, it was probably the 9/11 plot, which, in addition to the subsequently aborted Southeast Asian leg, also had the US section that was implemented. Could Wilshire and

---

30. *9/11 CR*, pp. 176-80 for an account of the Millennium Plot.
31. Ibid., pp. 155-59.

Michelle have known of one section without knowing of the other? It is hard to see how.

However, for various reasons that will be explained, it is more likely that this was just an excuse invented by Wilshire, Michelle or one of their associates, because Doug Miller and Mark Rossini needed to be told something to win their cooperation despite their reservations.

In any case, even if Wilshire and Michelle were aware of an al-Qaeda plot in Southeast Asia, how could they be certain that there was not also another one focused on the US, and that Almihdhar was not involved in this?

Given al-Qaeda's long record of opposition to the US and its foreign policy, how could the information that one of its top operatives intended to come to the US be construed in such a way that the CIA genuinely thought there was no chance of him participating in an operation inside the US, but that he must be part of some Southeast Asian plot? This is especially questionable because another al-Qaeda operative had been arrested on the US-Canadian border just over two weeks earlier with a car full of explosives and a map of Los Angeles.

If Wilshire and Michelle had thought there was to be an attack in Southeast Asia, then news of Almihdhar's US visa would certainly have given them pause for thought. Al-Qaeda is a terrorist organization headquartered in South Asia—Afghanistan and Pakistan—with supporters in the Middle East, in particular Saudi Arabia and Yemen, and elsewhere in Asia. If it were planning to attack in Southeast Asia, it would not have to send an operative involved in the planning to the US, where Almihdhar and Alhazmi lived in places like San Diego; Falls Church, Virginia; and Paterson, New Jersey. These locations have no strategic value for a terrorist organization planning to hijack an airliner out of Singapore, due to the geographical and cultural distance. A terrorist organization planning to hijack airliners or bomb something in Southeast Asia should really base its operations there. It is hard to understand how this fact could have been lost on Wilshire and Michelle.

Another reason an al-Qaeda operative planning an operation in Southeast Asia would not come to the US is that it is difficult to operate in the US, but relatively easy in Southeast Asia. After all, there was a support network comprising hundreds, if not thousands of

Southeast Asians who had been trained and had fought in Afghanistan. There were even training camps full of radical Muslim fighters in Southeast Asia, partly funded by Osama bin Laden. In the US, on the other hand, there were relatively few al-Qaeda members, especially after the arrests of operatives such as Ali Mohammed and Wadih El-Hage following the embassy bombings. Entering the US made pulling off an operation elsewhere much harder. It is hard to find a reason for Khalid Almihdhar entering the US other than his desire to carry out an attack in the US.

Even if Tom Wilshire and his associates did genuinely believe that Almihdhar wanted to come to the US to facilitate an attack on the other side of the world, it would still make sense to follow him and determine his contacts in the US. The people he met inside America—US residents or citizens—would be of enormous interest to the intelligence community because they were meeting with a man plotting a terrorist attack in Southeast Asia. It would make sense to monitor Almihdhar in the US, to foil the planned attack in Southeast Asia, and then to roll up his contacts.

A caveat should be added here: it is argued above that, based on the evidence they had, Wilshire and Michelle could not reasonably have dismissed the possibility of Almihdhar's intent to participate in a terrorist attack inside the US. However, Wilshire, Michelle's boss, may have told her he had additional inside information supporting this unlikely theory in order to induce her to stop Miller and Rossini from sending the information to the FBI.

Whatever the motivation behind concealing the information from the FBI, it is highly likely that this pre-dated January 5, 2000, when Miller wrote the draft cable and it was blocked by Wilshire and Michelle. Miller began writing the cable at 9:30 a.m., Michelle accessed it at 10:30 a.m., and attached the note to it telling Miller not to send it at 4:00 p.m., an interval of six and a half hours from drafting to the instruction not to send it.[32] Presumably, the cable was blocked to cover a CIA operation that was already in progress, but the purpose of that alleged operation is not yet known with certainty. It is highly improbable that the information came in and then a deputy unit chief simply decided to block its passage to the FBI on a whim.

---

32. Justice Department IG report, p. 240.

As will we see, more people than Miller, Rossini, Michelle and Wilshire were involved in withholding information about Almihdhar from the FBI and others. One of them was Wilshire's boss Richard Blee.[33] It is therefore likely that the instruction to withhold the information originated not with Wilshire, but with Blee or someone above him, either in the CIA's formal or informal hierarchy.

Blocking Doug Miller's cable was crucial, and it is the first known occasion on which the CIA withheld information from the FBI about Almihdhar and the Malaysia summit. It was not to be the last. It was also an occasion about which two of the participants, Miller and Rossini, have apparently confessed to wrongdoing and implicated two of their associates, Tom Wilshire and "Michelle." What they have said about the two must necessarily color our view of their subsequent actions, as well as those of the other officers and agents who assisted Wilshire.

---

33. Regarding my identification of Richard Blee: Blee's name is generally redacted in documents about 9/11. He is usually referred to as simply "Rich," his alias in Steve Coll's *Ghost Wars*, James Bamford's *A Pretext for War* and Gary Berntsen's *Jawbreaker*, although he is "Richard" in *The 9/11 Commission Report*. His last initial was revealed by former CIA Director George Tenet in *At the Center of the Storm*, and a column about him by *Harper's* magazine journalist Ken Silverstein ("Meet the CIA's New Baghdad Station Chief," January 27, 2007, http://www.harpers.org/archive/2007/01/meet-the-cias-new-2007-01-28) stated that his father was a famous CIA officer. After the 9/11 Commission's files were opened by the National Archives in 2009, my associate, Erik Larson, scanned 8,000 of them and uploaded them to the document archive site Scribd. Although Blee's name is mostly redacted in the Commission's files, it was left in one of them: undated notes by staffers Dan Byman and Mike Hurley. The notes read, "No one anticipated (well a few like Clarke, Black, Blee) what these people would do, or their single-minded determination, or that it would adapt to events and change to be more lethal" ("Miscellaneous 9/11 Commission Staff Notes about Drafting the Final Report," http://www.scribd.com/doc/16095055/Miscellaneous-911-Commission-Staff-Notes-about-Drafting-the-Final-Report). Blee's father would be David Blee, a key figure in counterintelligence and anti-Soviet operations during the Cold War. David Blee's *New York Times* obituary confirms he had a son named Richard; James Risen, "David H. Blee, 83, C.I.A. Spy Who Revised Defector Policy," *New York Times*, August 17, 2000, http://www.nytimes.com/2000/08/17/us/david-h-blee-83-cia-spy-who-revised-defector-policy.html?pagewanted=1.

6

She stated that she had no recollection

Acouple of hours after blocking Doug Miller's cable, "Michelle" sent several CIA stations a different cable summarizing the information that had been collected on Khalid Almihdhar and three other individuals who were also possibly traveling to Malaysia. The cable began,

> After following the various reports, some much more credible than others, regarding a possible [bin Laden]-associated threat against U.S. interests in East Asia, we wish to note that there indeed appears to be a disturbing trend of [bin Laden] associates traveling to Malaysia, perhaps not for benign reasons.[1]

It also said, "We need to continue the effort to identify these travelers and their activities to determine if there is any true threat posed."[2]

The cable summarized CIA information about several individuals planning to travel to Malaysia, and in the paragraph about Almihdhar, Michelle wrote that his travel documents, including a multiple entry US visa, had been copied and passed "to the FBI for further investigation."

The Justice Department's inspector general investigated this cable:

> When we interviewed Michelle, she stated that she had no recollection of who told her that Almihdhar's travel documents had been passed to the FBI or how they had been passed. She said she would not have been the person responsible for passing the documents. According to Michelle, the language in the cable stating "[the documents] had been passed" suggested to her that someone else told her

---

1. Justice Department IG report, pp. 242-43. This is also the source for the following paragraphs. Note the discrepancy between what she told Rossini, that the next al-Qaeda attack would be in Southeast Asia, and what she wrote in a cable she sent the day before, when there was only "a possible [bin Laden]-associated threat against U.S. interests in East Asia."
2. Wright 2006, p. 311.

that they had already been passed, but she did not know who it was. The CIA Deputy Chief of the bin Laden Unit [Wilshire] also said he had no recollection of this cable, and he did not know whether the information had been passed to the FBI.

Neither we nor the CIA OIG [CIA's Office of Inspector General] was able to locate any other witness who said they remembered anything about Almihdhar's travel documents being passed to the FBI, or any other documents that corroborated the statement that the documents were in fact passed to the FBI.

Michelle must have known that the claim that Almihdhar's visa information had been passed to the FBI was false at the time she wrote this cable, as she was one of the officers who had just blocked passage. As we saw in the last chapter, she also discussed the blocking of Miller's cable with Mark Rossini the next day, which would certainly have reminded her of the fact that she had blocked it. Yet, she took no action to pass information about Almihdhar's visa to the FBI.

Her claim to have "no recollection" of the events is not credible, although such claims are constantly repeated throughout the Justice Department inspector general's report by all the participants in the events. As we will see, both Doug Miller and Rossini also told the Justice Department inspector general they had no recollection of the events, but later recalled them and apparently said that they had been pressured to lie to the inspector general.

In addition, at that time it was standard practice at Alec Station to make sure that information like this had been received. The CIA inspector general commented that it "found no indication that anyone in [the Counterterrorist Center] checked to ensure FBI receipt of the information, which, a few [Alec] Station officers said, should have been routine practice."[3]

What was the purpose of the "misstatement" in Michelle's cable that said information about Almihdhar's visa had been passed to the FBI?

The cable would have had two benefits for the Alec Station group. The first would be to prevent other officers from trying to share the information with the FBI—if the FBI already knew it, why tell them again? The other would be that officers who concealed the

3. OIG Report on CIA Accountability With Respect to the 9/11 Attacks, June 2005, p. xv, http://www.fas.org/irp/cia/product/oig-911.pdf.

information from the FBI could later claim they believed they had done nothing of the kind.

After 9/11, when it became apparent that Alec Station had failed to do what it should have done—immediately passed the information to the FBI—this cable assumed great significance. The CIA could point to Michelle's cable as evidence that they thought they had done what they were supposed to do—even though they had not. This claim was made, for example, by George Tenet, CIA director in the run-up to 9/11, in his 2007 book (emphasis added):

> Once this e-mail came to the CIA [saying that Almihdhar had a US visa], it was opened by CIA officers and three FBI officers detailed to the Counterterroris[t] Center. A senior CIA officer on the scene recently said to me, "Once Almihdhar's picture and visa information were received, everyone agreed that the information should immediately be sent to the FBI. Instructions were given to do so. There was a contemporaneous e-mail in CIA staff traffic [Michelle's cable], which CIA and FBI employees had access to, indicating that the data had in fact been sent to the FBI. *Everyone believed it had been done.*

After describing Miller's blocked cable, Tenet added,

> No excuses. However, overworked men and women who, by their actions, were saving lives around the world all believed the information had been shared with the FBI.[4]

The identity of the senior CIA officer quoted by Tenet is not known, but his or her version of events is far from the truth. Nobody involved in the cable's blocking believed the information had been sent to the FBI, not Miller, not Rossini, not "Michelle," not Wilshire.

In the light of this we can surmise that even at this point Tom Wilshire and his associates, or at least one of them, knew that the whole operation would or could end in an attack, that there would be an investigation, and that it was necessary to create a contemporary document containing a lie so that they could be protected from the investigation. As we will see, this was not the last time that such documents were created by Alec Station officers involved in concealing information from the FBI.

4. George Tenet, *At the Center of the Storm: My Years at the CIA* (London: Harper Press, 2007) [hereinafter: Tenet 2007], pp. 195-96. Throughout the book, and elsewhere, Tenet mistakenly refers to the CTC as the "Counterterror*ism*" Center.

Michelle's claim that Almihdhar's visa information had been passed to the FBI had an added benefit when the investigations started. In addition to the witness interviews and document searches by the Justice Department and CIA inspectors general mentioned above, the 9/11 Congressional Inquiry also spent some time examining the issue of whether the information about Almihdhar's visa was passed to the FBI (although, as set out below, the Congressional Inquiry never found Miller's cable). Staff director Eleanor Hill said the Congressional Inquiry's research included "interviews of the author of the message [Michelle], who cannot remember the information being passed; interviews of other CIA and FBI individuals who also have no recollection of it being passed; and contemporaneous e-mails, both within the CIA and the FBI, that indicate while briefings of other issues were provided to the FBI regarding those individuals, that there was no mention of the visa or the information about the possible travel to the U.S."[5]

So the investigators were sent chasing a red herring, on which they expended valuable resources.

Tenet's relationship to the concealing of the information from the FBI is unclear. Did he authorize it, or was it done behind his back? Whichever the case, he certainly busted a gut to cover up for the actors after 9/11, commenting to the Congressional Inquiry,

> I have interviewed this officer [Michelle]. She's a terrific officer. She believes she never would have written this cable [saying the information about Almihdhar's visa had been passed to the FBI] unless she believes this had happened.[6]

It seems either Michelle lied to Tenet or Tenet lied to the Congressional Inquiry, possibly both. Tenet certainly did lie to the Congressional Inquiry on a related matter, as we will later see.

Another "misstatement" before the Congressional Inquiry may have been a lie of Michelle's. By James Bamford's account, an "FBI official" stated that a CIA officer from the Directorate of Intelligence lied to the Inquiry about the sharing of information concerning Almihdhar, claiming she physically brought information about

---

5. "Testimony from the Joint Intelligence Committee," *New York Times*, October 17, 2002, http://www.nytimes.com/2002/10/17/politics/18ITEXT.html?ei=5070&en=9ddb1047607578ac&ex=12 27848400&pagewanted=print&position=top.
6. Ibid.

Almihdhar to FBI headquarters in Washington. However, the FBI then checked the visitors' logs and found that she was never in the building during the period in question: "Then she said she gave it to somebody else, she said, 'I may have faxed it down—I don't remember.'"[7] It is unclear who the female CIA officer might be, and this incident is entirely omitted from all the official reports. However, "Michelle" is the only female CIA officer known to have been involved in the withholding of the information about Almihdhar and Alhazmi, making her a likely candidate.[8]

7. Bamford 2005, pp. 224-25.
8. Another interpretation is that the FBI official is confused and is really referring to Margaret Gillespie, an FBI agent detailed to Alec Station for several years at this point. She is reported to have come to FBI headquarters for a meeting with Wilshire on August 22, 2001.

He did not know why James briefed him about the Almihdhar information

A t the same time as "Michelle" and Tom Wilshire were busy blocking Doug Miller's cable and generating a false message saying Almihdhar's visa information had been passed to the FBI, a parallel set of events was unfolding at the Bureau.

A CIA officer known only as "James" accessed two of the cables from the field that reported on Almihdhar's US visa a few hours after they were drafted. He also accessed Miller's draft cable to the FBI, although he told the CIA inspector general he had no recollection of this. He declined to be interviewed by the Justice Department inspector general.[1]

At this point James had been detailed to the FBI, where he was attached to its Strategic Information Operations Center (SIOC) during the Millennium threat period. During the night of January 5, 2000, James briefed an FBI supervisory special agent in the Bureau's bin Laden unit, known only as "Bob," on what the CIA knew of the Malaysia meetings. Although he knew Almihdhar had a US visa and must have known that this information was of great interest to the FBI, he failed to mention it in the briefing. The Justice Department inspector general observed,

> James wrote an e-mail to several CIA employees in which he stated that he was detailing "exactly what [he] briefed [the FBI] on" in the event the FBI later complained that they were not provided with all of the information about Almihdhar. This e-mail did not discuss Almihdhar's passport or U.S. visa.

Bob did not recall the briefing, although he did locate a "scant contemporaneous note" saying that it had occurred. The Justice Department inspector general continued (emphasis added):

---

1. Justice Department IG report, pp. 239, 241, 245-47, 250-51.

Bob told the OIG that he does not believe that he had been told in this conversation about Almihdhar's U.S. visa. Bob stated to us that the presence of a U.S. visa in Almihdhar's passport would have been extremely important and would have triggered a more significant response than his minimal notes.

Bob also told the OIG that he did not know why James chose to brief him about Almihdhar. Bob said that he was not a designated point of contact for the CIA while the SIOC was activated, although he also said that he did not know whether there was a designated point of contact in the SIOC. Bob said that he knew James because James had previously been detailed from the CTC [Counterterrorist Center] to FBI Headquarters and had worked in ITOS [the International Terrorism Operations Section] with Bob.

The next morning, the CIA reported more information about Almihdhar and what he was doing in Kuala Lumpur. After reading this cable, James went out and briefed another FBI officer, known only as "Ted." The Justice Department inspector general noted,

In the same e-mail in which he had detailed what he told Bob, James provided specifics of what he told Ted. The e-mail also stated that the CIA would "continue to run this down and keep the FBI in the loop." The e-mail did not contain any reference to Almihdhar's passport or U.S. visa.

Ted then prepared an update for FBI leaders, who were being briefed on al-Qaeda's Malaysia summit. The update did not contain any reference to Almihdhar's passport or visa. The Justice Department inspector general continued (emphasis added):

Although he said he did not recall these events, Ted asserted he did not believe that he had received Almihdhar's passport or U.S. visa information because if he had he would have unquestionably recognized their significance and documented such information in the update for the executive briefing.

Ted told the OIG that he did not know why James briefed him about the Almihdhar information. Like Bob, Ted stated he was not a designated point of contact for the CIA while the SIOC was activated. Ted also knew James because of James' previous detail to ITOS in FBI Headquarters when Ted served as an SSA [supervisory special agent] in the RFU [Radical Fundamentalist Unit].

Based on James' documentation, we know that the briefings contained practically all the relevant details about Almihdhar, except the things the FBI really needed to know—that Almihdhar had a US visa and that he was probably coming to the US. So why did James give these briefings to Bob and Ted?

In this context we should note that after the second cable came in on January 6, 2000, another CIA detailee to the FBI asked James for information about Almihdhar, because an FBI contact had requested an update. James then fired off a series of e-mails basically telling the other CIA officer that he had already briefed the FBI, so there was no need for the other CIA officer to do so.

The explanation that offers itself here is that James gave the briefings precisely so he could later say that he had briefed the FBI. This prevented other CIA officers from wanting to brief the FBI about something they thought it already knew, and was also handy when the investigators came calling after 9/11. His e-mail to the other CIA officer even makes the point about a later investigation explicitly, as the Justice Department inspector general pointed out in its conclusion:

> Moreover, James wrote a detailed e-mail to document the contents of his conversations with Bob and Ted. Since the stated purpose of James' e-mail was to prevent the FBI from later claiming he had failed to brief them on some important details, he had every incentive to include all relevant details in that e-mail. At the time he wrote this e-mail, he had read three of the CIA cables indicating that Almihdhar had a U.S. visa, as well as the draft CIR [Miller's cable]. Yet, James' e-mail contained no mention of Almihdhar's passport or visa.

James knew Almihdhar had a US visa and, as a CIA officer detailed to the FBI, must have known this was extremely important information to the Bureau. Yet he failed to mention it in two briefings as well as a series of e-mails about Almihdhar to a CIA counterpart. Given the close parallels with the actions of Wilshire and Michelle, it is reasonable to assume that James was acting in concert with them, and was part of a plot to keep from the FBI the information that Almihdhar had a US visa and presumably intended to enter the US.

Having said this, the position of "James" in this operation is uncertain. Miller and Rossini are at the bottom, "Michelle" is in the middle and Wilshire near the top. James' relationship to them and what he knew cannot be definitely determined. Even if the purpose of the operation was to enable an al-Qaeda attack in the US, there is no reason to suppose that James would have known this at the time, or even ever. It is entirely possible that James acted the way he did simply because he was told that the CIA did not want the FBI trying to muscle in on a delicate CIA operation that was already ongoing.[2]

---

2. Other actions apparently in support of the operation to withhold information from the FBI were later taken by anonymous CIA officers, for example by a CIA officer in Islamabad around January 2001 and by one or more CIA officers in Yemen from the autumn of 2000. It is possible that James is one of these officers, as he could have been reassigned from the FBI to Islamabad or Yemen in the intervening time. However, this is far from certain, and there is no indication of it. Therefore, the two briefings and the e-mails on January 5-6, 2000 are the only known involvement of "James" in the operation to withhold information about Almihdhar from the FBI.

8

Something apparently was dropped somewhere and we don't know where that was

We now turn to the treatment of Doug Miller's unsent cable by the various post-9/11 inquiries: by the 9/11 Congressional Inquiry, the Justice Department inspector general, the CIA inspector general and the 9/11 Commission.

The first of these inquiries to start investigating and issue its report was the 9/11 Congressional Inquiry. This investigation was much narrower than that of the 9/11 Commission, and it focused exclusively on the intelligence failures that preceded the attacks. Despite this, it never found Doug Miller's cable. In fact, Miller's cable was not discovered by investigators until February 2004, fourteen months after the Congressional Inquiry ended.[1] Although the Inquiry devoted considerable energy to the non-passage of Almihdhar's visa information to the FBI, it reached few conclusions:

> Thus, at the time of the Malaysia meeting, the CIA had passport information regarding Almihdhar, including his U.S. visa. A CIA officer, who was working as a CTC Supervisor [Wilshire], testified before the Joint Inquiry that a CTC cable in early 2000 noted that Almihdhar's passport information had been "passed to the FBI," but the CIA was unable to "confirm either passage or receipt of the information" and, thus, could not identify "the exact details … that were passed." The Joint Inquiry found no record of the visa information at FBI Headquarters.[2]

Clearly, the Congressional Inquiry did not get to the bottom of the matter. However, what is most remarkable is what occurred when the Congressional Inquiry had Tom Wilshire testify publicly, albeit from behind a screen and anonymously in order to hide his

---

1. Justice Department IG report, p. 227.
2. 9/11 Congressional Inquiry report, p. 145.

identity.[3] Naturally, the issue of the non-passage of Almihdhar's visa information came up several times, but the Inquiry never resolved it fully. In his prepared statement, Wilshire glossed over the incident, saying,

> While the [Malaysia] meeting was in progress, the CIA officers detailed to the FBI, CTC [the CIA's Counterterrorist Center] kept the FBI advised of developments via verbal briefings ... We prefer to document significant transfers of information, both to assure ourselves that it was passed and also to create a detailed record for our own operations officers and analysts who at a later date draw on such data to do a variety of tasks. In this case, CTC did not formally document to the FBI the conversations between the CIA referrants and the FBI supervisors they briefed. CTC did note in a cable to the field that Almihdhar's passport information had been passed to the FBI, but to date, we have been unable to confirm either passage or receipt of the information, so we cannot say what the exact details were that were passed.

It is striking that he did not point out that it was he who had blocked the passage of Miller's cable.

Senator Carl Levin, one of the members most knowledgeable about the inquiry's work, commented during the same hearing,

> And the CIA, we know, monitored the al-Qaeda members there, including the two people at issue [Alhazmi and Almihdhar]. They knew that these two people had, at least in one case, already had a visa to go to the United States. That information was not put into the watch list. It was not shared with the FBI. It knew that Almihdhar had a multiple-entry visa, as a matter of fact, and knew of his ties to al-Qaeda. Two failures there – not placed on the watch list, not shared with the FBI.

Levin appeared not to realize that the reason the information had not been passed to the FBI was because the man sitting right in front of him had blocked the relevant cable.

3. US Congress, The House Permanent Select Committee On Intelligence and the Senate Select Committee On Intelligence, The Intelligence Community's Knowledge of the September 11 Hijackers Prior to September 11, 2001: Hearing before the Joint Inquiry of the Senate Select Committee on Intelligence and the House Permanent Select Committee on Intelligence, September 20, 2002. The panel on which Wilshire testified also included FBI agent Steve Bongardt and FBI manager Michael Rolince, whose roles in pre-9/11 events will be described in detail below.

Under questioning from Representative Richard Burr, Wilshire again fudged the issue: "We had the basic visa information on Almihdhar and that wasn't passed." Burr then asked, "To the best of your knowledge was the FBI ever notified?" Wilshire replied,

> The best of my knowledge the intent was to notify the FBI and I believe the people involved in the operation thought the FBI had been notified. Something apparently was dropped somewhere and we don't know where that was.

There was certainly intent to notify the FBI, in particular on the part of Doug Miller, but the statement "I believe the people involved in the operation thought the FBI had been notified" beggars belief. The way the sentence is constructed implies that Wilshire was not involved in the operation, but the very opposite is true. He was not just one of the people involved in the operation, he was one of the managers running it. The statement that "something apparently was dropped somewhere and we don't know where that was" is equally incredible. What was dropped was that he himself blocked the cable.

Wilshire then discussed the two hijackers' connection to the 1998 African embassy bombings and claimed "that's why that information was documented as having been passed to the FBI, and then I can't explain why it was not, but the intent was to pass it." Again, *he* blocked the cable. Are we supposed to accept as fact that he found his own actions to have been unexplainable?

The key question that should have been asked of Wilshire about the failure to inform the FBI of Almihdhar's US visa: "Why did you block the cable?" It was not asked, it was not answered. Although some aspects of the Congressional Inquiry's work can be praised, it failed very badly here.

Other elements of Wilshire's testimony to the 9/11 Congressional Inquiry will be discussed as the narrative proceeds.

There was pressure on people not to disclose what really happened

The Congressional Inquiry was succeeded by three more investigations into 9/11: by the Justice Department inspector general, the CIA inspector general and the 9/11 Commission. The first named was also the first to finalize its report, in early July 2004.[1]

Doug Miller's draft cable was discovered by the Justice Department inspector general in a roundabout fashion. As we have seen, the cable was not found by the Congressional Inquiry and did not arrive at the Justice Department with any documents sent by the Inquiry. The inspector general also interviewed several of the participants in late 2002, including Tom Wilshire, "Michelle" and Margaret Gillespie, another of Wilshire's associates who read the cables about Almihdhar's visa,[2] but there is no record of any of them mentioning the cable. In May 2003, the CIA inspector general sent his Justice Department counterpart several more documents relevant to both their inquiries, but Miller's cable was again strangely absent. In February 2004, a Justice Department inspector general employee was scanning a list of cables accessed by FBI detailees to the CIA and noticed Miller's draft, which the CIA inspector general then obtained and provided. The draft cable's discovery meant that several interviewees had to be re-interviewed so they could be asked about it.[3]

1. The report issued in July 2004 was classified and has never been made public. An unclassified version of the report, omitting classified information, was drafted later that year, but publication was delayed because of the Moussaoui trial and only a heavily redacted unclassified version was published in 2005. An unredacted unclassified version was published after the end of the Moussaoui trial in 2006.
2. Wilshire was interviewed by the Justice Department IG on November 1, 2002; see *9/11 CR*, p. 537. "Michelle" was interviewed on October 31, 2002; see *9/11 CR*, p. 502. Gillespie was interviewed on October 29, 2002; see 9/11 CR, p. 538.
3. Justice Department IG report, p. 227.

Although the Justice Department inspector general spent over two dozen pages of its report on the cable, it concluded, "We were unable to determine why this [the passage of the information about Almihdhar's US visa to the FBI] did not occur."[4] Despite this, the overall impression is that the inspector general thought that it was just some bureaucratic snafu, as the report goes on to discuss the usual suspect of "systemic problems." The possibility of intentional wrongdoing in relation to the blocking of Miller's cable is not even articulated in the report.

Despite this, the report is full of passages like this one:

> As discussed above, Dwight [Doug Miller] told the OIG [office of inspector general] that he did not even recall writing the [cable about Almihdhar's US visa] or even being aware of the Malaysia meetings or of the fact that Almihdhar had a U.S. visa. Eric [another FBI detailee to Alec Station, and its other deputy chief] told the OIG that his CIA counterpart – the CIA Bin Laden Unit Deputy Chief [Wilshire] – mentioned the Malaysia meetings and that surveillance photos had been taken, but Eric did not recall ever hearing anything about Almihdhar having a U.S. visa. Mary [Margaret Gillespie] told the OIG that she did not recall even being contemporaneously aware of the Malaysia meetings.[5]

After fording through the endless lists of key actors who cannot remember a single thing about the most important actions they took in their lives, the reader cannot help but wonder whether it is possible to believe they could have all lost their memories so completely. Nor can one help but wonder whether the Justice Department inspector general believed in such comprehensive memory loss. Might these people have been hiding something?

A hint that Mark Rossini's memory was not quite as bad as he claimed came with the publication of *The Looming Tower* by Lawrence Wright in 2006. As we know, Wright described the blocking of the cable: "Miller was told, 'This is not a matter for the FBI.'" Wright sourced this quote to an interview with Rossini.[6]

Commenting that Miller's alias in the Justice Department inspector general's report was "Dwight," Wright presumably had read the report and knew that Rossini was telling him something

---

4. Ibid., p. 255.
5. Ibid., p. 254; Gillespie was interviewed on October 29, 2002, *9/11 CR*, p. 538.
6. Wright 2006, pp. 311, 423.

he had failed to recall for the Justice Department inspector general. Wright did not trouble himself, however, to point this out to his readers, either in the book or in a 2006 article for the *New Yorker* entitled "The Agent: Did the C.I.A. stop an F.B.I. detective from preventing 9/11?"[7]

The *Congressional Quarterly* in October 2008 reported what had likely happened in a Justice Department inspector general interview of Miller and Rossini:

> Under pressure from the CIA, they [Miller and Rossini] kept the full truth from the Justice Department's Inspector General, which looked into the FBI's handling of pre-9/11 intelligence in 2004.
>
> "There was pressure on people not to disclose what really happened," said sources close to the IG investigation.
>
> Rossini, in particular, is said to have felt threatened that the CIA would have him prosecuted for violating the Intelligence Identities Protection Act if he told the IG investigators what really happened inside the CTC [Counterterrorist Center].
>
> CIA officials were in the room when he and Miller, as well as a sympathetic CIA officer, were questioned.
>
> The IG investigators showed them copies of CTC intelligence reports and e-mails.
>
> But the FBI agents suddenly couldn't remember details about who said what, or who reported what, to whom, about the presence of two al-Qaeda agents in the U.S. prior to the 9/11 attacks.[8]

This is an amazing tale: the Justice Department inspector general was suspicious of Miller and Rossini—who wouldn't be?—but decided to question them together. If an investigator had suspicions of people he was investigating, would it not be wise to question them separately? Questioning suspects separately is a basic tenet of investigatory work, something of which the United States Department of Justice should be very aware. Yet this basic tenet was violated.

What's more, we are told that the investigators not only questioned them together, but also in the presence of representatives from the CIA, an organization they suspected had, together with

7. Lawrence Wright, "The Agent: Did the C.I.A. stop an F.B.I. Detective from Preventing 9/11?" *New Yorker*, July 10 and 17, 2006, http://www.lawrencewright.com/WrightSoufan.pdf.

8. Jeff Stein, "FBI Prevents Agents from Telling 'Truth' About 9/11 on PBS," *Congressional Quarterly*, October 1, 2008, http://blogs.cqpolitics.com/spytalk/2008/10/fbi-prevents-agents-from-telli.html. This passage apparently refers to the interview of Miller and Rossini in February 2004, after Miller's draft cable had been found.

Miller and Rossini, withheld information from the FBI and might want to pressure the two men to keep their mouths shut. How could the circumstances have been less conducive to getting Miller and Rossini to reveal what they knew?

One might legitimately wonder whether the Justice Department inspector general genuinely wanted to find the truth. As we will see, this was by no means the investigation's sole failing. In this author's opinion, the whole report reads like the Justice Department inspector general's office started to connect some of the dots and figure out what had really happened, but did not like where this was taking it, and rapidly began to disconnect them again.

In addition to the various communications between the investigations by the Justice Department inspector general and the 9/11 Commission, there is a direct staff link: one of the investigators working for the inspector general, Barbara Grewe, subsequently moved to the 9/11 Commission,[9] where she handled the same issues.[10] In several cases the Commission made the same mistakes that the Justice Department's report had, such as accepting the simultaneous amnesias of Doug Miller and Mark Rossini.

However, there's more. From the same *Congressional Quarterly* article:

> But [Rossini] and Miller did come clean during an internal FBI investigation, which remains under wraps.
>
> Sources with direct knowledge of the FBI's internal probe say that the agents provided the bureau with unadulterated versions of their CTC experiences, including orders they were given by the center's then-Deputy Director, Tom Wilshire, to withhold intelligence about the movement of al-Qaeda operatives into the country from the FBI.

This clearly implies that the FBI, which is part of the Justice Department, learned that the Justice Department inspector general's report was based on a raft of falsehoods, and then decided to keep this secret while the entire US intelligence community was re-organized and the US made war in Afghanistan and Iraq.

---

9. "An Inside View of the 9/11 Commission," *Michigan Law* (University of Michigan Law School), March 7, 2005, http://www.law.umich.edu/newsandinfo/Pages/march2005.aspx.
10. Philip Zelikow, "Shenon-Zelikow Correspondence about the 9/11 Commission (2007)," http://www.fas.org/irp/news/2008/02/zelikow.pdf. Grewe was transferred within the Commission in late 2003, giving her more involvement in CIA-FBI issues.

Only seven years had to pass before the *Congressional Quarterly*, based on research for a book by James Bamford, decided to write about this episode. Given that Rossini and Miller apparently "misspoke" to the Justice Department's inspector general and that their statements definitively shaped a key section of its report, the entire report should be treated with extreme caution at all points, and some sections must be discarded entirely.

10

Amongst the finest we have

The full CIA inspector general's report is still not public. An executive summary was pried from the CIA in August 2007, thanks to a campaign by relatives of the attacks' victims and Congressional legislation. The summary has the following to say about the blocking of Doug Miller's cable (emphases added):

> Agency officers also failed to pass the travel information about the two terrorists [Almihdhar and Alhazmi] to the FBI in the pre-scribed channels. The Team found that an FBI officer assigned to CTC [Miller] on 5 January 2000 drafted a message about the terrorists' travel that was to be sent from CIA to the FBI in the proper channels. *Apparently because it was in the wrong format or needed editing, the message was never sent.* On the same date, another CTC officer ["Michelle"] sent a cable to several Agency addressees reporting that the information and Almihdhar's travel documents had been passed to the FBI. *The officer* who drafted this cable *does not recall how this information was passed.* The Team has not been able to confirm that the information was passed, or that it was not passed. Whatever the case, the Team found no indication that anyone in CTC checked to ensure FBI receipt of the information, which, a few [Alec] Station officers said, should have been routine practice.[1]

Two dubious claims immediately leap out in this passage. First, the non-sending of Miller's cable is attributed to its apparently be-ing "in the wrong format or need[ing] editing." It is a virtual cer-tainty that the cable was blocked because Wilshire and/or Michelle did not want the FBI to know the information about Almihdhar's visa, as this would make the Bureau interested in Almihdhar.

Second, Michelle is said not to recall "how this information was passed." As Michelle was one of the officers who blocked the cable,

---

1. OIG Report on CIA Accountability With Respect to the 9/11 Attacks, June 2005 , pp. xiv-xv, http://www.fas.org/irp/cia/product/oig-911.pdf.

she knew the claim she made that the FBI had been informed was false, and there are no reasons to believe her claims of memory loss.

* * *

What should be borne in mind here is that the executive summary that was published was the executive summary of a re-written report. The original report did not find favor with CIA Director Porter Goss, and he recommended that it be re-written. The problem was that the original report actually held the officials who had performed badly accountable for their failures. Goss wanted the accountability taken out of the report, and that is what he got.[2] The re-written version did not directly hold any of the CIA officers accountable for poor performance; it merely recommended that accountability boards be convened to determine whether they should be punished.

The revised report recommended that accountability boards be convened to assess the performance of the following CIA officers and managers:

- Director of Central Intelligence George Tenet (July 1997-July 2004), for failing to personally resolve differences between the CIA and NSA that impeded counterterrorism efforts.

- CIA Executive Director David Carey (July 1997-March 2001), CIA Executive Director A.B. "Buzzy" Krongard (March 2001-2004, resigned shortly after Goss became DCI in September), CIA Deputy Director for Operations Jack Downing (1997-1999), and CIA Deputy Director for Operations James Pavitt (1999-July 2004, resigned one day after Tenet) for failing to properly manage CIA counterterrorism funds.

- CIA Counterterrorist Center Chief Jeff O'Connell (1997-1999) for failing to properly manage CIA counterterrorism funds, for staffing Alec Station with officers lacking experience, expertise and training, for failing to ensure units under him coordinated coverage of Khalid Shaikh Mohammed, for poor leadership of the CIA's watchlisting program, for poor management of a program under which officers were loaned between the CIA and other agencies, and for failing to send officers to the NSA to review its material.

2. Douglas Jehl, "C.I.A. Chief Seeks Change in Inspector's 9/11 Report," *New York Times* November 2, 2004, http://www.nytimes.com/2004/11/02/politics/02intel.html.

- CIA Counterterrorist Center Chief Cofer Black (Summer 1999-December 2002, moved to counterterrorism position at State Department, then served as vice-chairman of notorious private security contractor Blackwater USA from 2004-2008) for failing to properly manage CIA counterterrorism funds, for staffing Alec Station with officers lacking experience, expertise and training, for failing to ensure units under him coordinated coverage of KSM, for poor leadership of the CIA's watchlisting program, possibly for failing to ensure the FBI was informed Alhazmi had entered the US, possibly for failing to do anything about Alhazmi and Almihdhar in 2001, for poor management of a program where officers were loaned between the CIA and other agencies, and for failing to send officers to the NSA to review its material.

- Chief of Alec Station Richard Blee. Some sections of the executive summary appear to refer to Blee, but are redacted. It seems to criticize him for failing to properly oversee operations related to KSM, failing to ensure the FBI was informed Alhazmi had entered the US, and failing to do anything about Alhazmi and Almihdhar in 2001.

- Deputy Chief of Alec Station Tom Wilshire. Some sections of the executive summary appear to refer to Wilshire, but are redacted. It seems to criticize him for failing to ensure the FBI was informed Alhazmi had entered the US, and for failing to do anything about Alhazmi and Almihdhar in 2001.

- Unnamed officer, possibly head of the CIA's renditions branch, for failing to properly oversee operations related to KSM.

- Unnamed officer, for failing to ensure the FBI was informed Alhazmi had entered the US, and for failing to do anything about Alhazmi and Almihdhar in 2001.

- Unnamed officer(s), for failure to produce any coverage of KSM from 1997 to 2001; the type of coverage that should have been provided is redacted in the publicly released executive summary.

The re-written report with its recommendations for accountability boards was presented to Director Goss in June 2005. A few months later, Goss turned around and told the inspector general that he was not going to convene any after all. This meant that *none* of the CIA officers who performed badly in the run-up to 9/11 were punished in any way by the Agency. Goss minced no words: "Of the officers named in this report, about half have retired from the Agency, and those who are still with us are amongst the finest we have."[3]

Richard Blee was still with the Agency at this time, and it appears Tom Wilshire was as well. They were among the officers the CIA director thought were "amongst the finest we have." As we will see, Blee not only appears to be a key player in frustrating the passage to the FBI of information that could have prevented 9/11. He was also at the heart of some very controversial events afterwards.

---

3. Central Intelligence Agency, "CIA Director Porter J. Goss Statement on CIA Office of the Inspector General Report, 'CIA Accountability with respect to the 9/11 Attacks,'" October 5, 2005, https://www.cia.gov/news-information/press-releases-statements/press-release-archive-2005/pr10052005.html. See page 36 herein for more of Goss' statement.

11

It appears Barbara Grewe conducted the interviews with "John" and "Jane"

D espite what we have already seen in other reports, the treatment of this incident by the 9/11 Commission is remarkable. In its narrative, the Commission spent one page and eight lines of its over-500 page final report discussing the NSA intercept of the call to Khalid Almihdhar in December 1999 and the CIA's tracking and alleged loss of Almihdhar, Alhazmi and others during al-Qaeda's Malaysia summit. In the middle of this we find this innocuous paragraph:[1]

> Though Nawaf's trail was temporarily lost, the CIA soon identified "Khalid" as Khalid Almihdhar.[44] He was located leaving Yemen and tracked until he arrived in Kuala Lumpur on January 5, 2000.[45] Other Arabs, unidentified at the time, were watched as they gathered with him in the Malaysian capital.[46]

The Commission's description of the blocking of Doug Miller's cable is relegated to a small-type endnote, number 44 in the above passage. Given the text of the paragraph in which the endnote number is included, the reader would not even expect to find key information about Miller's cable in the endnote, being much more likely to expect the sourcing for the information in the sentence. The relevant section of the endnote reads,

> [Almihdhar's] Saudi passport—which contained a visa for travel to the United States—was photocopied and forwarded to CIA headquarters. This information was not shared with FBI headquarters until August 2001. An FBI agent [Miller] detailed to the bin Laden Unit at CIA attempted to share this information with colleagues at FBI headquarters. A CIA desk officer ["Michelle"] instructed him not to send the cable with

---

1. *9/11 CR*, pp. 181-82.

this information. Several hours later, this same desk officer drafted a cable distributed solely within CIA alleging that the visa documents had been shared with the FBI. She admitted she did not personally share the information and cannot identify who told her they had been shared. We are unable to locate anyone who claimed to have shared the information. Contemporaneous documents contradict the claim that they were shared.[2]

Although it mentioned Tom Wilshire by his alias "John" numerous times in its report, the Commission entirely omitted his role in this particular event, giving readers the false impression that "Michelle" acted on her own initiative when asking Miller not to send the cable. As we will see, this is not the only time the Commission omitted Wilshire's role in key events. For example, it also failed to mention him in its discussion of the Zacarias Moussaoui case.

It is unclear which staffer actually wrote the endnote. An internal 9/11 Commission document found at the National Archives specifies the lead drafter for each section of the report.[3] It gives the lead drafter for section 6.1, which contains the reference to endnote 44, as Sarah Linden. Commission staffers approached about the endnote in 2009 could not say definitively who wrote it. I was unable to reach Linden. Whoever wrote the endnote, the Commission's files make it clear that it was based on research headed by Barbara Grewe.

Grewe was the key 9/11 Commission staffer responsible for investigating the matters this book looks into. As mentioned above, she first worked on the Justice Department inspector general's investigation of the FBI's performance before 9/11, where she was a special investigative counsel.[4] According to her résumé found in the 9/11 Commission's files, while working on the Justice Department probe she:

> Directed examination of prior intelligence community's knowledge of two of the Pentagon hijackers.

2. Ibid., p. 502 n44.
3. 9/11 Commission, "Table of Contents for Cite Checkers," undated, http://www.scribd.com/doc/15907138/SD-B1-Cite-Team-Table-of-Contents-for-Cite-Checkers-3-Lists-of-Standard-Endnote-Examples-Quick-Style-Guide.
4. 9/11 Commission, "Commission Staff (in alphabetical order)," undated, http://www.9-11Commission.gov/about/bios_staff.htm; "Barbara A. Grewe," *Center for American Progress*, April 16, 2008, http://www.americanprogressaction.org/events/2008/inf/GreweBarbara.html.

Examined intelligence sharing between the FBI and CIA, investigated management of new counterterrorism priorities and reviewed intelligence storage and retrieval systems.

Drafted sections of final report relating to the two hijackers [Almihdhar and Alhazmi].[5]

Grewe left the Justice Department's probe while it was still in progress and went over to the Commission. According to an article written when she gave a talk at the University of Michigan, "A former colleague of Grewe, who worked in the US Department of Justice Office of Inspector General, recommended her to the Commission as it began its work in spring 2003."[6]

Grewe was initially assigned as the leader of the Commission's Team 6, which was responsible for investigating law enforcement and intelligence efforts inside the United States. One of first tasks for each team on the 9/11 Commission was to draft a workplan, setting out key questions for the investigation, suggested readings, documents it intended to request and witnesses it intended to interview. Team 6's workplan is unique because it also contains what it calls a "premise statement," which sets out the basis for its work.[7]

There are several problems with the premise statement, which has a tendency to heap the blame on the FBI and give the CIA and NSA a free pass. For example, it says, "The U.S. Intelligence Community generally, and the FBI more specifically, were aware prior to attacks that three of these individuals had ties to al-Qaeda." The FBI was actually only aware that *two* of the hijackers, Almihdhar and Alhazmi, had ties to al-Qaeda, and it only learned that they had entered the US in the summer of 2001.

Further, when the FBI's investigation of the two men began, as we will see, *the senior official involved was none other than Tom Wilshire,* who had by then moved to the Bureau. It was Wilshire, not "the FBI more specifically," who had detailed knowledge of the two men's links to al-Qaeda. The premise statement also introduces the concept of "systemic failure," a fine idea if an investigator wants to not hold any specific person accountable:

5. Resume of Barbara A. Grewe (undated), http://www.scribd.com/doc/15740882/Resume-of-911-Commission-Staffer-Barbara-Grewe. The two hijackers are Almihdhar and Alhazmi.
6. Jared Wadley, "9/11 Commission counsel to speak March 24," University Record Online, March 14, 2005, http://www.ur.umich.edu/0405/Mar14_05/18.shtml.
7. 9/11 Commission, "Team 6 Workplan," undated, http://www.scribd.com/doc/13279679/Workplan-for-911-Commissions-Team-6.

Based on previous reviews, it is now clear that the FBI did not respond aggressively and appropriately to all of the available intelligence, and failed in many respects to "connect the dots" prior to the attacks. Less closely studied is the extent to which the FBI's inability to detect the hijackers' activities and associations while in the United States represented a systemic intelligence failure.

The Bureau certainly did not respond "aggressively and appropriately" to the intelligence, but this failure can be laid firmly at the door of Wilshire and his associates. And the reason the dots could not be connected appears to be that the Alec Station group was disconnecting them.

The statement also sets up a false dichotomy: either the hijackers' ability to avoid detection by the FBI while in the United States was an indication of excellent operational tradecraft by the hijackers, or it represented a failure on the part of the FBI. Clearly there are other possibilities, such as a failure by Alec Station to pass along the relevant information, but if these are excluded at the outset, it is so much easier to reach a preordained conclusion.

Barbara Grewe also played a role in the controversy over the use of "minders" by government departments to accompany witnesses in private interviews by the Commission. This practice met with initial resistance by the Commission. At a press conference on July 7, 2003 Commission Chairman Tom Kean said, "I think the Commission feels unanimously that it's some intimidation to have somebody sitting behind you all the time who you either work for or works for your agency. You might get less testimony than you would."[8]

However, just over two months later Kean had performed an about-face:

Talking to staff, what they have told me is that as they've done these interviews, that the interviewees are encouragingly frank; that they by and large have not seemed to be intimidated in any way in their answers. In fact, it's the opposite in some cases. So, that's very, very encouraging.[9]

8. Philip Shenon, "9/11 Commission Says U.S. Agencies Slow Its Inquiry," *New York Times*, July 8, 2003, http://www.nytimes.com/2003/07/08/politics/08CND-TERR.html.
9. 9/11 Commission, "9/11 Commission Releases Interim Report, Transcript of Press Briefing with Thomas H. Kean, Chair, Lee Hamilton, Vice Chair," September 23, 2003, http://www.9-11Commission.gov/archive/2003-09-23_press_briefing.pdf.

One of the reasons for this change of heart can be found in minutes of a 9/11 Commission meeting in mid-September 2003:

> In response to a question on minders, Team Leader Grewe notes they were not obstructionist, and did not get in the way of candor.[10]

The assessment of Grewe and Kean was disputed by other Commission staff. A mere nine days after Kean had said interviewees were being "encouragingly frank," three staffers, including Team 2 leader Kevin Scheid, sent an internal memo featuring three main complaints about the minders.

Perhaps the worst problem was that the minders "answered questions directed at witnesses." According to the memo, this was inappropriate because the Commission needed to understand not how the intelligence community was supposed to function, but "how the intelligence community functions in actuality." However, "When we have asked witnesses about certain roles and responsibilities within the intelligence community, minders have preempted witnesses' responses by referencing formal polices and procedures. As a result, witnesses have not responded to our questions," meaning they did not tell the Commission how the intelligence community actually worked and what they thought their jobs to actually be.

Minders also acted as "monitors, reporting to their respective agencies on Commission staffs lines of inquiry and witnesses' verbatim responses." The three staffers thought this "conveys to witnesses that their superiors will review their statements and may engage in retribution." They believed that "the net effect of minders' conduct, whether intentionally or not, is to intimidate witnesses and to interfere with witnesses providing full and candid responses." Another problem with the verbatim note-taking was that it meant agencies could alert future witnesses to the Commission's lines of inquiry, which "permits agencies to prepare future witnesses either explicitly or implicitly."

Finally, the minders positioned "themselves physically and have conducted themselves in a manner that we believe intimidates witnesses from giving full and candid responses to our questions. Minders generally have sat next to witnesses at the table and across

10. 9/11 Commission, "Minutes of the September 9-10, 2003 Meeting," http://www.scribd.com/doc/15838253/FO-B2-Commission-Meeting-92303-Fdr-Table-of-Contents-and-Tab-1-Entire-Contents-Minutes-of-91003-Meeting-643.

from Commission staff, conveying to witnesses that minders are participants in interviews and are of equal status to witnesses."

The memo made it clear that the problems were not occurring only with witnesses talking to Team 2, but also in "other teams' interviews." A hand-written note on a draft of the memo says, "not one agency or minder—also where we've sat in on other teams' interviews."[11]

It is hard to imagine how the situation described by the memo could be worse, although one might hypothesize that these staffers were encountering problems Barbara Grewe was not. Whatever the case, this offers us some insight into what sort of investigator Grewe was—one who did not much object to minders. Recall that it was minders—"CIA officials ... in the room"—that provided one of the reasons advanced for the poor memories of Mark Rossini and Doug Miller when they were interviewed about Miller's blocked cable. We do not know that Grewe was present at that interview, although the chances of this are extremely high.

In the late fall of 2003, Grewe left Team 6 and moved to another team called Special Projects.[12] Whereas before she was only responsible for investigating the FBI, this move gave her specific responsibility for FBI-CIA interaction, a main topic of this book. The Commission's executive director Philip Zelikow said that the move "brought Barbara into the CIA part of the work and gave her a lead role in developing our draft on some of the specific FBI-CIA operational problems before 9/11 and on the 'summer of threat.'"[13] Grewe also worked on the Moussaoui case and, at Special Projects, on the NSA's surveillance of the Yemen hub.

I investigated whether Barbara Grewe had angled for this move in order to gain power over this area of the report. However, a source close to the 9/11 Commission, who does not want to be named because of the sensitivity of the issue, said the transfer had more to do with a personality clash with other staffers. A set of internal Commission e-mails provides some support for this. Shortly

11. 9/11 Commission memo from Kevin Scheid, Col. Lorry Fenner, and Gordon Lederman, "Executive Branch Minders' Intimidation of Witnesses," October 2, 2003, http://www.scribd.com/doc/13279605/911-Commission-Memo-Executive-Branch-Minders-Intimidation-of-Witnesses.
12. 9/11 Commission, "Minutes of the November 6-7, 2003 Meeting," November 7, 2003, http://www.scribd.com/doc/15877535/Minutes-of-911-Commission-Meeting-on-November-67-2003.
13. Philip Zelikow, "Shenon-Zelikow Correspondence about the 9/II Commission (2007)," p. 52, http://www.fas.org/irp/news/2008/02/zelikow.pdf.

before the move, another Commission team leader, Dieter Snell, wrote to Grewe,

> Hi Barbara. Hope your Miami trip went well. I wanted to give you a heads up on our current planning for DSM [Designated Sensitive Material] interviews at WFO [the FBI's Washington Field Office] next week … Once again Mike's participation in as many interviews as possible will be important for us to maximize our effectiveness … Please let me know if this is OK with you. Thanks.

Mike is Commission staffer Mike Jacobson, who was officially on Team 6, but also helped out another team regarding the links between the Saudi government and the hijackers. Grewe's reply on October 4 was altogether different in tone:

> I do not believe this request is reasonable for the following reasons. First, you cried wolf over LA and essentially demanded that Mike be made available in contravention of our previous agreement as to the time he would devote to DSM matters. This was extremely detrimental to Team 6's previously planned work. I do not believe it is fair that just because you decide to schedule things at a particular time that Mike should be expected to drop all Team 6 work. In my view you already cashed your get out of jail free card.

This dispute evidently had been going on for some time. Here is a particularly choice passage from a September 19 e-mail from Grewe:

> I do not appreciate the gratuitous denigration of my team's work as "cookie cutter" interviews. They are far from that. And if anyone thinks the work my team is doing is something a trained monkey can do, then I am willing to turn the trouble over to someone else and let them try it for a spell.[14]

Whatever the initial reason for the move, Barbara Grewe certainly was even more heavily involved in the CIA-FBI issue thereafter. Of the documents produced by the 9/11 Commission, she was the lead drafter for Chapter 8 of the final report, "The System Was Blinking Read," which dealt with several of the intelligence failures in the summer of 2001 that are discussed below.[15] She also made a significant contribution to the Commission's Staff Statement No.

14. The e-mails can be found at http://www.scribd.com/doc/15644649/DM-B4-Jacobson-Fdr-2-Emails-Re-Time-Conflicts-and-Priorities-Re-Work-of-Staff-Member-Mike-Jacobson-331.
15. 9/11 Commission, see note 3; Philip Zelikow, see note 13, p. 52.

10, "Threats and Responses in 2001," part of which she read out at a Commission hearing.[16] Finally, she wrote a monograph entitled "Legal Barriers to Information Sharing," discussing the "wall" between intelligence and criminal investigations. The wall's great significance in our narrative will become apparent as we proceed.

Barbara Grewe was also present at the Commission's interviews of two of the key actors this book focuses on: Tom Wilshire and an associate of his at the FBI, Dina Corsi. Although records of these interviews have not yet been declassified, Kirsten Wilhelm of the National Archives was able to provide some information about them. "It appears Barbara Grewe conducted the interviews with 'John' [Wilshire] and 'Jane' [Corsi]," said Wilhelm.[17] Grewe was also present at the interviews of Richard Blee;[18] Ali Soufan,[19] the FBI agent who ran the *Cole* bombing investigation, two of whose three interviews she led; and Steve Bongardt, one of his assistants.[20]

Not all the interviews the Commission relied on for its report were conducted by the Commission itself; output from interviews by other agencies was also used. The 9/11 Commission cites interviews of the following witnesses by the Justice Department inspector general in its endnotes: FBI attorneys Marion "Spike" Bowman and Sherry Sabol, "Michelle," Wilshire, FBI bin Laden agent Jennifer Maitner, FBI Islamabad agent "Michael D," a CIA officer known only as "Chris," Dina Corsi, CIA officer Clark Shannon, FBI *Cole* investigator Russell Fincher, Steve Bongardt, Margaret Gillespie, FBI bin Laden unit acting chief Rodney Middleton and FBI agent Robert Fuller, as well as numerous FBI personnel involved in the Zacarias Moussaoui case. Barbara Grewe may have conducted these interviews, and certainly drew on them when drafting her sections of the Commission's and Justice Department inspector general's reports.

16. National Commission on Terrorist Attacks upon the United States, Tenth Public Hearing, April 13, 2004, http://govinfo.library.unt.edu/911/archive/hearing10/9-11Commission_Hearing_2004-04-13.htm.
17. E-mail to the author from Kirsten Wilhelm of the National Archives, January 26, 2009.
18. E-mail to the author from Kirsten Wilhelm of the National Archives, February 9, 2009. The others present at this interview were Philip Zelikow, Alexis Albion, Kevin Scheid and Doug MacEachin.
19. E-mail to the author from Kirsten Wilhelm of the National Archives, February 3, 2009.
20. She was accompanied at this interview by another Commission staffer, Quinn John Tamm, Jr.; see 9/11 Commission, "Memorandum for the Record: Interview of Steven Bongardt," November 13, 2003, http://www.scribd.com/doc/23252061/9-11-Commission-Memo-on-Interview-of-FBI-Agent-Steve-Bongardt.

There is understandably some overlap between the lists of 9/11 Commission and Justice Department inspector general interviewees. However, it appears the Commission did not interview Mark Rossini or "Michelle,"[21] nor others this book will discuss later.

After most Commission interviews, one of the Commission staffers who had conducted them drafted a document called a "memorandum for the record," or MFR. Many of these MFRs were released in January 2009 by the National Archives. However, the MFRs for the interviews of Tom Wilshire and Dina Corsi were not among them, neither were they among the set of MFRs that were still classified or still to be reviewed. As far as the archives could tell, no MFR had been drafted for these two interviews. In fact, although the archives could locate some notes—which are still classified—of the interview of Wilshire, it could find no written record of what Corsi had said in her interview.[22]

The lack of an MFR for Tom Wilshire is astounding. He was involved in almost everything that went wrong before 9/11 and, as such, this was about the most important interview the Commission conducted. It should have received high-level attention and even been attended by some of the Commissioners, but, in the event, the relevant staffer could not even be bothered to write a memo about it.

The Commission and the Justice Department inspector general made many of the same mistakes. For example, they both omitted Wilshire's role in the Moussaoui case as well as significant facts about the *Cole* investigation.[23] There can be little doubt that Barbara Grewe was the staffer behind the Commission's conclusions criticized in this book. Some time after the Commission's activities ended, Grewe was hired by the MITRE Corporation, a contractor for the CIA, NSA and a whole alphabet soup of similar agencies.[24]

All this should be borne in mind when assessing the Commission's conclusions about Tom Wilshire and Alec Station: the lead

21. The *Congressional Quarterly* article by Jeff Stein (see Chapter 5 note 26) also stated that Miller was not interviewed by the 9/11 Commission. He was actually interviewed on December 16, 2003 (*9/11 CR*, p. 504 n83). However, as investigators did not discover his draft cable until the next year, he could not have been asked about it.
22. E-mail to the author from Kirsten Wilhelm of the National Archives, January 26, 2009.
23. The Commission's report and the unclassified Justice Department IG report also omitted a key e-mail sent by Wilshire on August 23, 2001, although this e-mail was probably mentioned in the classified version of the Justice Department IG report.
24. "Free Event Features 9/11 Commission Members," Bellvue University, August 9, 2007.

investigator worked on another investigation that made the same mistakes, she failed to draft the appropriate records that would have fully informed others on the Commission's staff about two key interviews, she wrote a lot of the passages in the final report that failed to point out Alec Station's errors, and she was subsequently hired by a CIA contractor. At the very least, being hired by a contractor for an agency you have just taken it easy on in a high profile report represents the appearance of impropriety.

* * *

Given the uncertainty over who wrote the endnote, it is appropriate to look at how endnotes got added to *The 9/11 Commission Report*. Some of the details were revealed in Philip Shenon's excellent 2008 book, *The Commission: The Uncensored History of the 9/11 Investigation*. Based on interviews with the 9/11 Commission's staff, Shenon recounts two vignettes concerning how some of the report's hundreds of endnotes came to be written.

In the first, the Commission's vice chairman, Lee Hamilton, asked a staffer, Alexis Albion, to prepare a comparison of how former President Bill Clinton and President George W. Bush talked about terrorism in their public speeches before 9/11. Albion found that, whereas Clinton talked about the threat of non-state terrorists often and on important occasions, Bush hardly ever mentioned this, and when he did he mostly talked about missile defense. However, the Commission's executive director, Philip Zelikow, a close associate of Bush's National Security Adviser Condoleezza Rice, became enraged by the comparison and demanded it be removed from the final report. As Zelikow was Albion's superior, the comparison was deleted, although, according to Shenon:

> Albion later got a small dose of revenge. She figured, correctly, that in the chaos of the final days of writing and editing the report, Zelikow would not pay too much attention to the drafting of footnotes. So she wrote footnotes that summarized the comparisons between Bush and Clinton and snuck them in.[25]

In the second vignette, two of the Commission's investigators discovered material linking Khalid Almihdhar and Nawaf Alhazmi

25. Philip Shenon, *The Commission: The Uncensored History of the 9/11 Investigation* (New York: Twelve, 2008), pp. 396-98. The two endnotes to which Shenon refers are numbers 2 and 164 of Chapter 6.

to Saudi Arabia's intelligence agency, the GID. However, their team leader, Dieter Snell, insisted that this material be deleted from the report, as he was not one-hundred-percent certain of their links to Saudi intelligence. Zelikow backed the team leader and had much of the material deleted from the report's main text, but allowed it to remain in the form of notes.[26]

Finally, another factor may have been at work here. In his 2008 book, former Alec Station chief Michael Scheuer made the following claim:

> In early 2004, the 9/11 Commissioners indicated that they were intending to name [a young] CIA officer as the only individual to be publicly identified for a pre-9/11 failure. A group of senior CIA officers ... let it be known that if that officer was named, information about the pre-9/11 negligence of several very senior US officials would find its way into the media. The Commissioners dropped the issue.[27]

It is unclear which CIA officer Scheuer is referring to, although the number of relatively junior CIA officers the 9/11 Commission might have named due to a pre-attack failure is relatively small. If one were to compile a short list of such officers who should be named as having failed in some way, then Tom Wilshire would certainly be the first name on that list by some margin, although "Michelle" would also be a candidate.

One possible explanation could go like this: the 9/11 Commission had the blocking of Miller's cable in the main text of the report, naming Wilshire and/or Michelle. The CIA officers complained and made their threat. The Commission moved the information to an endnote, deleting Wilshire's role in the event entirely. Alternatively, the Commission just deleted it after being threatened, and a staffer put it back in as an endnote. However, it should be stressed that this is speculation, and the real course of events is not known.

26. Ibid., pp. 398-99.
27. Michael Scheuer, *Marching Toward Hell: America and Islam after Iraq* (New York: Free Press, 2008), p. 273. I am told Scheuer was approached by a journalist about this matter, but declined to reveal more details.

81

Who chaired that meeting? Khalid Shaikh Mohammed chaired that meeting

The US learned of Khalid Almihdhar's visa when he was on his way to a January 2000 al-Qaeda summit in Malaysia. The CIA has made a number of claims about the summit and why it failed to exploit the information it could, should, and probably did gather about it. However, when the Agency's claims are subjected to scrutiny, they do not hold up. The main issue examined here is the identities of the al-Qaeda operatives who attended the summit, although there are some additional problems, such as what was done with the surveillance video and photos from the summit that showed these operatives.

There is some dispute over who was there. It is known and accepted that Almihdhar, Nawaf Alhazmi, and Khallad bin Attash attended, as did one of bin Attash's associates known as Abu Bara al Taizi.[1] The apartment used for the summit was owned by a Malaysian operative named Yazid Sufaat,[2] and Almihdhar was monitored meeting with an Iraqi named Ahmad Hikmat Shakir at the airport.[3]

A full list of the meeting's attendees, as least according to the CIA, has never been published. The CIA claims that it did not then know who the people at the meeting were—it either did not know their names at all, or knew their names but did not recognize their importance—and that it did not regard the meeting as "important."[4]

---

1. *9/11 CR*, p. 158.
2. Ibid., p. 159.
3. Ibid., p. 502.
4. The CIA's claim that it did not think the meeting was important at the time was made to 9/11 Congressional Inquiry investigators; see US Congress, The House Permanent Select Committee On Intelligence and the Senate Select Committee On Intelligence, The Intelligence Community's Knowledge of the September 11 Hijackers Prior to September 11, 2001: Hearing before the Joint Inquiry of the Senate Select Committee on Intelligence and the House Permanent Select Committee on Intelligence, September 20, 2002.

This might depend on one's definition of "important"—officers from eight CIA stations and six friendly foreign intelligence services were all asked to help track Almihdhar on his way to the summit,[5] indicating some priority was allocated to it, despite the many leads in play at the time due to the Millennium alert. In addition, as pointed out earlier, National Security Adviser Sandy Berger was briefed. Presumably, Alec Station did not bother the national security adviser with every trifle.

According to Cofer Black, head of the CIA's Counterterrorist Center, "We were not able to learn what the men did during that meeting, but we were able to identify other participants."[6] Although they were able to identify other participants, they allegedly did not begin to appreciate the meeting's significance until almost a year later. CIA Director George Tenet told the 9/11 Congressional Inquiry,

> The Malaysian meeting took on greater significance in December 2000 when the investigation of the October 2000 USS *Cole* bombing linked some of Khalid Almihdhar's Malaysia connections with *Cole* bombing suspects.[7]

However, the attendees listed by the press and elsewhere are of such significance that their mere presence at the summit would clearly make it important. If these people really did attend—and there is good evidence of this—then the claim that the CIA thought the meeting unimportant would be untenable.

Al-Qaeda did not regularly hold summits outside Afghanistan. In fact, this is the only such summit known, before or after 9/11. This was a unique opportunity for the CIA. Recall the quote from FBI veteran Jack Cloonan about this being "as good as it gets," "a home run in the ninth inning of the World Series," and "the kind of case you hope your whole life for."[8]

The summit's other reported attendees included:

- Khalid Shaikh Mohammed, the alleged mastermind of 9/11 and a well-known radical Islamist at that point. The CIA had

---

5. Oliver Schröm and Dirk Laabs, "The Deadly Mistakes of the US Intelligence Agency (Part 1)," *Stern*, August 13, 2003.
6. Statement of Cofer Black: Joint Investigation into September 11, September 26, 2002, http://www.fas.org/irp/congress/2002_hr/092602black.html.
7. 9/11 Congressional Inquiry report, p. 149.
8. Jane Mayer, *The Dark Side* (New York: Doubleday, 2008), p. 18.

been actively looking to rendition KSM to the US since 1997 for his part in the Bojinka plot to blow up US airliners over the Pacific or dive them into buildings.[9]

- Abd al-Rahim al-Nashiri, an al-Qaeda leader in the Arabian peninsula and a key player in the attempted bombing of the USS *The Sullivans* and the attack on the USS *Cole*. According to a *Los Angeles Times* article published less than a month after 9/11, Yemeni authorities said that al-Nashiri had attended the Malaysia summit.[10] Al-Nashiri's attendance was confirmed by Rohan Gunaratna and Senator Bob Graham, chairman of the 9/11 Congressional Inquiry.[11]

- "Hambali," operational head of the al-Qaeda affiliate Jemaah Islamiyya. Hambali was also an associate of KSM and had been involved in the Bojinka plot. The 9/11 Commission commented, "Hambali arranged lodging for them [the al-Qaeda operatives including Almihdhar, Alhazmi and bin Attash] and helped them purchase airline tickets for their onward travel." According to the US Treasury Department and CNN, he was actually videotaped at the meeting with Almihdhar and Alhazmi.[12] A photo of Hambali had been obtained

9. For a timeline of KSM's activities, see http://www.historycommons.org/timeline. jsp?timeline=complete_911_timeline&other_al-qaeda_operatives=khalidShaikMohammed. For the 9/11 Commission's summary about KSM see *9/11 CR*, pp. 145-50. Please note much of the information contained in this section of the Commission's report was obtained using torture and is therefore unreliable. For the CIA's Renditions Branch looking for KSM since 1997, see *9/11 CR*, p. 276.

10. Jeffrey Gettleman, "Under U.S. pressure, strategic nation formerly cozy with Iraq's Hussein has booted out 'Afghan Arabs,'" *Los Angeles Times* , October 10, 2001. The article refers to al-Nashiri as "Al Safani." This is a known alias for al-Nashiri; see Office of the Director of National Intelligence, Detainee Biographies, September 7, 2006, http://www.dni.gov/announcements/content/DetaineeBiographies.pdf.

11. Rohan Gunaratna, *Inside al-Qaeda: Global Network of Terror* (New York: Berkley Trade, 2003), p. 188; Bob Graham with Jeff Nussbaum, *Intelligence Matters: The CIA, the FBI, Saudi Arabia, and the Failure of America's War on Terror* (New York: Random House, 2004), p. 59. Graham refers to al-Nashiri as "Muhammad Omar al-Harazi," but this is another alias for al-Nashiri; see "Family connection between attacks on USS Cole and U.S. embassy," CNN, December 11, 2000, http://archives. cnn.com/2000/US/12/11/cole.family.connection/index.html. Al-Nashiri's presence at the summit completely invalidates the Congressional Inquiry's conclusions about the meeting. Presumably, Graham remained unaware of "al-Harazi's" real identity.

12. Maria Ressa, "'95 Philippine plot had echoes of September 11," CNN, March 14, 2002, http:// archives.cnn.com/2002/WORLD/asiapcf/southeast/03/14/philippines.yousef.plot/; Maria Ressa, "The quest for SE Asia's Islamic 'super' state," CNN, August 29, 2002, http://edition.cnn.com/2002/ WORLD/asiapcf/southeast/07/30/seasia.state/; US Department of the Treasury, "Statement by the Treasury Department Regarding Today's Designation of Two Leaders of Jemaah Islamiyah," January 24, 2003, http://www.nefafoundation.org/miscellaneous/WestCoast/Treasury_JI.pdf; *9/11 CR*, p. 150-52.

when the Bojinka plot was broken up,[13] so Hambali's links to the summit certainly should have indicated its importance.

Now let's look more closely at the evidence regarding these three critical attendees. Numerous press accounts have put KSM at the summit, as has counterterrorism expert Rohan Gunaratna, who told the 9/11 Commission in public testimony,

> Khalid Shaikh Mohammed ... the mastermind of 9/11 ... organized that whole operation. The first planning meeting of 9/11 was held from the 5th to the 8th of January in Kuala Lumpur. Who chaired that meeting? Khalid Shaikh Mohammed chaired that meeting.[14]

Gunaratna also told the Commission that he had unique access to classified information from the CIA's interrogations of KSM and that he knew this from that source. *Newsweek* set out what this would mean:

> If true, Gunaratna's claims about Mohammed's presence would make the intelligence failure of the CIA even greater. It would mean the agency literally watched as the 9-11 scheme was hatched—and had photographs of the attack's mastermind, Khalid Shaikh Mohammed, doing the plotting.[15]

The 9/11 Commission completely ignored this in its final report, which contains *no listing of the summit's attendees*. The Commission must have known KSM was said to attend, because Gunaratna, a witness it selected, told them so publicly. However, the final report is a blank on this, although it curiously does mention that KSM met with Alhazmi, bin Attash and others until just before the summit started.[16]

Gunaratna said KSM was in Kuala Lumpur in response to questioning from Commissioner Tim Roemer. Roemer's response was to say, "Let me pursue that line of questioning in a minute," and then

---

13. "May 23, 1999: FBI Connects Hambali to Bojinka Front Company," *History Commons*, March 21, 2007, http://www.historycommons.org/context.jsp?item=a052399hambalikonsonjaya&scale=0 #a052399hambalikonsonjaya, citing Brendan Pereira, "Preacher Was Close to WTC Bombers," *New Straits Times*, February 2, 2002.

14. National Commission on Terrorist Attacks upon the United States, Public Hearing, July 9, 2003, http://govinfo.library.unt.edu/911/archive/hearing3/9-11Commission_Hearing_2003-07-09.htm.

15. Michael Isikoff and Mark Hosenball, "Did the CIA Watch a Key 9-11 Plotter Plan the Strikes," *Newsweek*, July 9, 2003.

16. *9/11 CR*, pp. 156-58.

start talking about terrorism finance and public diplomacy with the other witnesses on the panel. None of the other Commissioners returned to the topic of KSM's attendance at the Malaysia summit.

Reports the Commission got about what certain detainees said came from the CIA, which held and interrogated them. If the CIA did not want the Commissioners to know something the detainees said, it could simply decide not to tell them. If KSM had been in Kuala Lumpur and the CIA had missed him—or actively decided not to capture him for whatever reason—and KSM admitted being at the summit during his interrogations, the CIA could simply omit to pass reports of those statements on to the Commission.

The Commission never subpoenaed the CIA, it merely issued the Agency document requests, which were not backed by any legal imperative. The Commission realized the interrogation reports were of little value and repeatedly asked to interview the detainees in person. However, the CIA kept refusing, and the Commission eventually gave up. The Commission's chairman and vice-chairman, Tom Kean and Lee Hamilton, later blamed this failure on a lack of help from the victims' families and the media.[17] And the CIA certainly did ignore some of the document requests: for hundreds of hours of videotape of the detainees' behavior in interrogations and in their cells.[18]

We should not forget that at the time of the Malaysia summit KSM had been indicted for his role in Bojinka, and the CIA was actively seeking to rendition him to the US for trial.[19] The CIA also knew he had been involved in the 1993 World Trade Center bombing and had flown to Nairobi, Kenya, before the attack on the US embassy there.[20] Malaysia had previously consented to the rendition to the US of one of KSM's associates.[21] This raises the important question of why KSM was not seized at the time.

17. Philip Shenon, *The Commission: The Uncensored History of the 9/11 Investigation* (New York: Twelve, 2008), pp. 181-83; Thomas H. Kean and Lee H. Hamilton, *Without Precedent: The Inside Story of the 9/11 Commission* (New York: Alfred A. Knopf, 2006), pp. 119-23.
18. Thomas Kean and Lee Hamilton, "Stonewalled by the CIA," *New York Times*, January 2, 2008, http://www.nytimes.com/2008/01/02/opinion/02kean.html.
19. *9/11 CR*, pp. 276-77.
20. 9/11 Congressional Inquiry, pp. 310-13.
21. Wali Khan Amin Shah, one of KSM's co-plotters in Bojinka, was renditioned to the US from Malaysia in December 1995 to face trial; see James C. McKinley Jr., "F.B.I. Arrests Man in Far East, Charged in Plot to Bomb Planes," *New York Times*, December 13, 1995, http://query.nytimes.com/gst/fullpage.html?res=9C03EED81639F930A25751C1A963958260.

Furthermore, by 2000 the CIA was aware that Abd al-Rahim al-Nashiri was a very important figure in al-Qaeda. In *At the Center of the Storm*, George Tenet described a meeting he had with the Saudis about al-Nashiri in 1998. The Saudis had uncovered a plot headed by al-Nashiri, whom Tenet calls "head of al-Qaeda operations in the Arabian peninsula," to smuggle antitank missiles into Saudi Arabia before a scheduled visit to the country by Vice President Al Gore. However, the Saudis had failed to report all the details of the operation to the CIA. Tenet considered obtaining the information so important that he made "a quick trip to Saudi Arabia" and obtained an audience: not with the head of Saudi intelligence, but with Prince Naif, the interior minister and a very powerful figure in the country. Naif did not want to provide the information, so Tenet placed his hand on Naif's knee, "something you are never supposed to do with royalty," and threatened, in the event of a successful al-Qaeda attack against US interests, to tell the *Washington Post* that it was Saudi Arabia's fault because it had withheld information. Tenet got what he wanted within a week.[22]

The US intelligence community had a photo of al-Nashiri, so he could have been positively identified at the Kuala Lumpur meeting. At this time the US also knew he had facilitated the 1998 African embassy bombings. One of the bombers, Mohamed al-Owhali, identified al-Nashiri as a person he knew under the name "Bilal" when questioned by the FBI soon after the attacks.[23] It is not known where the FBI obtained the photo in which al-Owhali identified al-Nashiri, but one possibility is that it was a product of Tenet's trip to Saudi Arabia.

Given that al-Nashiri is reported to have attended by three credible sources, was known to be important at the time of the meeting, and the US had a photo of him, it is hard to understand how the CIA could possibly have thought the Malaysia summit to be unimportant.

The presence of Hambali is another serious blow to the CIA's claim they did not appreciate the meeting's import at the time. The US had a photograph of Hambali, his connection to Bojinka and

---

22. Tenet 2007, pp. 105-06.
23. *9/11 CR,* pp. 152-53; Federal Bureau of Investigation, "302 of Interviews of Mohammed al-Owhali," September 9, 1998, http://www.vaed.uscourts.gov/notablecases/moussaoui/exhibits/defense/767.pdf.

KSM was already known,[24] and he was on tape standing next to Almihdhar, who the CIA knew had a US visa.[25]

Recall that Hambali lived across the road from a government informer, Fauzi Hasbi, in the village of Sungai Manggis. One of the other residents at this "Terror HQ" was Abu Bakar Bashir, a leading radical cleric exiled from his home in Indonesia, and allegedly the spiritual head of Jemaah Islamiyya. A fourth resident was Abdullah Sungkar, another notorious extremist.[26] Hambali lived there openly, throwing annual feasts for hundreds of people.[27] In the spring of 2001, the Malaysians developed more information about Hambali showing him to be a top terrorist, and this information, together with a photo of him, found its way into the local press by August 2001.[28] In the same month as the summit, January 2000, Hambali chaired a meeting of regional militant leaders near Kuala Lumpur—attended by an informer—and they set up a radical umbrella organization to better coordinate their activities.[29]

However, the US failed to warn the Malaysians about Hambali. Although it knew of Hambali's role in Bojinka,[30] partly through finding his photo on Ramzi Yousef's captured computer, it did not share this with the Malaysians. As a result, the Malaysians did not arrest either Hambali or Yazid Sufaat, the summit's host, although they identified both of them.[31] Neither did the Malaysian authorities learn more about the summit. The US also failed to follow up on Hambali, despite their knowledge of him. Four of the other Bojinka conspirators were in jail in the US, and one of them had even been arrested in Malaysia and renditioned to face trial in New York.

---

24. *9/11 CR*, p. 489.

25. This summit was not Hambali's only connection to 9/11. In early September 2001 he was in Karachi with KSM and was aware of the attack date; see Stewart Bell, "Canadian Admits to Role in Hunt for 'White Meat': Confessions to the FBI," *National Post*, January 18, 2003).

26. Widjajanto and Rommy Fibri, "Sermons in Sungai Manggis," *Tempo*, October 29, 2002, http://www.worldpress.org/Asia/830.cfm; Maria Ressa, *Seeds of Terror* (New York: Free Press, 2003).

27. Simon Elegant, "Asia's Own Osama," *Time*, April 1, 2001, http://www.time.com/time/asia/features/malay_terror/hambali.html.

28. "Gun-Running and Bank Heist," *Malay Mail* (Kuala Lumpur), August 16, 2003; Tony Emmanuel, "Gun-running Racket," *New Straits Times*, August 18, 2001; Abdul Razak Ahmad, "Militant member tells of his experience and beliefs," *New Straits Times*, September 9, 2001.

29. "Inside Indonesia's War on Terror," *SBS Dateline*, October 12, 2005, http://www.adelaideinstitute.org/Australia/indonesia.htm; Ken Conboy, *INTEL: Inside Indonesia's Intelligence Service* (London: Equinox Publishing, 2003), pp. 212-13.

30. *9/11 CR*, p. 489 n14

31. "May 23, 1999: FBI Connects Hambali to Bojinka Front Company," see note 13.

Given that the Malaysians identified Hambali and then passed on their intelligence, it would be extremely hard for the CIA to claim that they did not realize he was there.

* * *

Also present at the summit was Ramzi bin al-Shibh, a close associate of three of the alleged 9/11 pilots (Mohamed Atta, Marwan Alshehhi and Ziad Jarrah) who lived in Germany with them. Bin al-Shibh was a key link in the 9/11 plot and relayed messages between al-Qaeda leaders in Asia and the plotters in the US, sometimes meeting them in person.[32]

The summit may have included some other people, such as Fahad al-Quso, one of the *Cole* bombers; Nawaf Alhazmi's brother Salem; "20th hijacker" Mohamed al-Khatani; and other unnamed Egyptian Islamic Jihad operatives. Claims of their attendance, however, cannot be verified.

So the meeting, planned during the period of high alert over the Millennium and held just after it, was attended by lots of high-ranking al-Qaeda leaders. How clear could it be that something really important was happening? Yet the CIA maintains that it did not appreciate the summit's significance.

While the summit is sometimes said to be a planning meeting for the attack on the *Cole* and/or for 9/11, one of its functions was very likely as a meet-up of plotters in another attack, on the USS *The Sullivans*. That attack was attempted on January 3, 2000 as a part of the wave of bombings known as the Millennium Plot, but it had failed. It employed the same means as the later attack on the *Cole*: a small boat was loaded with explosives in Aden harbor with the intention of it approaching a US warship, *The Sullivans*, as the boat's crew detonated the explosives. The attack failed because the bombers put too much explosive in their boat, and it sank. Given that many of the people at the meeting, in particular bin Attash and al-Nashiri, but also KSM, Almihdhar, bin al-Shibh, al-Quso and Al-

---

32. Oliver Schröm, "Deadly Mistakes," *Die Zeit*, October 2, 2002, http://www.antiwar.com/article.php?articleid=2305; Peter Finn, "Yemeni Fugitive Was Critical to Unfolding of Sept. 11 Plot," Washington Post, July 14, 2002, http://www.washingtonpost.com/ac2/wp-dyn?pagename=article&node=&contentId=A1503-2002Jul13&notFound=true; Maria Ressa, "Uncovering Southeast Asia's Jihad Network," CNN, February 26, 2004, http://edition.cnn.com/2002/WORLD/asiapcf/southeast/10/29/asia.jihad.1/.

hazmi, were later involved in or linked to the *Cole* operation, it is likely they were all involved in *The Sullivans* failure.

The treatment of this summit by the various official reports is very strange. While the presence of al-Nashiri is not widely known, KSM is widely reported to have attended, and Hambali's attendance is confirmed. Hambali was one of the key players in Bojinka, a plot that could have killed over 4,000 people had all the airliners been destroyed. The idea that his presence did not make the summit important, but the discovery of bin Attash, Osama bin Laden's "run boy" did,[33] is bizarre. Yet the 9/11 Commission passes over this problem without missing a beat; the Justice Department inspector general's report does not mention Hambali once in its 379 pages; the 9/11 Congressional Inquiry likewise ignores him and lets George Tenet's assertion that bin Attash was "the most important figure" at the meeting pass without challenge.[34]

* * *

Besides the issue of who attended, there are other problems with the accounts of the Kuala Lumpur meeting.

Primarily, reports say that the summit was not bugged and what the attendees said there was not recorded. According to author Jane Mayer, an attempt by the Malaysians to plant hidden microphones failed,[35] although such a failure is not reported by other sources. One problem with the alleged failure to plant microphones is the length of the summit, which went on for four days. If an attempt failed on the first day, why not simply try again? Also recall "Michelle's" excuse when she told Mark Rossini not to send the cable notifying the FBI of Almihdhar's visa: the next al-Qaeda attack was to be in Southeast Asia. Given that the CIA reportedly thought these people were traveling for "nefarious" purposes, listening to what they were saying should have been an extremely high priority, especially during a high-threat period.

We are left to wonder whether the claims of non-bugging are false, and the meeting really was bugged, perhaps by the CIA acting independently of the Malaysians. Another possible explanation

---

33. *9/11 CR* (p. 192) recounts that a joint FBI/CIA source handled out of Islamabad called bin Attash a "run boy" for bin Laden.

34. 9/11 Congressional Inquiry report, p. 144.

35. Jane Mayer, *The Dark Side* (New York: Doubleday, 2008), p. 14.

could be that one of the attendees was an informer, minimizing any need for recording the meeting.

There is also the issue of the Echelon signals-intelligence collection and analysis network. While the NSA vacuums up communications from around the globe, the agency can obviously not focus its attention on all of them, and much information collected is not scrutinized by humans. However, the NSA has the ability to focus its collection and analytic capacity on specific places. For example, before Ramzi bin al-Shibh and some members of KSM's family were captured in Karachi in September 2002, the NSA had increased its coverage of the city,[36] which reportedly led to the arrests. The Malaysians and the CIA could even see the attendees using a specific pay phone in front of the Kuala Lumpur apartment. What was the NSA doing with all of this?

Not much, according to statements by officials. The CIA later claimed that it knew one of the attendees was called Nawaf and that one of the three attendees who then flew to Thailand on January 8, 2000 had the last name Alhazmi. However, the Agency reportedly did not put these two names together, and did not ask the NSA what it knew. The NSA had the relevant information in its database. According to the 9/11 Commission, if asked, "NSA's analysts would promptly have discovered who Nawaf was, that his full name might be Nawaf Alhazmi, and that he was an old friend of Khalid [Almihdhar]."[37] According to James Bamford, this failure is "inexplicable."[38] And it is all the worse because the NSA knew Nawaf and Salem were brothers, so this would have given them Salem's last name as well.[39]

Further, when the NSA received a report from the CIA about Almihdhar on January 10, 2000, it did nothing with it. The report mentioned his travel to Kuala Lumpur, the name of a person who helped him there, and that his primary purpose for visiting Malaysia was to meet with other people.[40] The NSA had a lot of information about Almihdhar it had not yet disseminated, but the receipt of the CIA report did not cause it to do anything with that information.

---

36. Ron Suskind, *The One Percent Doctrine: Deep Inside America's Pursuit of its Enemies Since 9/11* (New York: Simon & Schuster, 2006), p.140.
37. *9/11 CR*, pp. 353-54.
38. Bamford 2005, p. 227.
39. 9/11 Congressional Inquiry report, p. 145.
40. Ibid., p. 156.

At the summit, the attendees were videotaped by security services on the first day. Hambali was videotaped with Alhazmi and Almihdhar, the Iraqi Shakir was videotaped, and bin al-Shibh is also said to have been videotaped.[41] However, the next three days were not videotaped. The summit was so important that the national security adviser was briefed on it during a very busy period, but not important enough to videotape every day? The video of the first day arrived at the CIA some time in February, but the Agency did not show much interest in it.[42]

Only photographs were taken on the next three days. A lot of photos were taken, and the German newspaper *Die Zeit* commented, "As the terrorists left the [condominium where the summit was held], the Malaysian police clicked away with their cameras. There was enough material for a whole photo series."[43] Information about the surveillance and the photos were passed to the CIA at once.[44]

To date, none of the photos have been made public, and information about them is scanty. However, it is known that the photos include:

- Three high-quality surveillance photos later shown to the FBI. One is shot from a low angle and shows Almihdhar and Alhazmi standing by a tree. The two others in this set appear to show Almihdhar and Alhazmi individually, and would also later be shown to Yemeni authorities (together with the first photo with the tree) and an FBI asset in Pakistan.[45]

- More photos of Almihdhar "meeting with other al-Qaeda operatives." He is also "photographed in various locations meeting with several different people." The photos of Almihdhar include ones taken at his hotel, which was discovered by the Malaysians, and more coming and going from the condominium where the meeting was held.[46]

41. Rohan Gunaratna, see note 11, p. 261; Stephen Braun, Bob Drogin, Mark Fineman, Lisa Getter, Greg Krikorian and Robert J. Lopez, "Haunted by Years of Missed Warnings," *Los Angeles Times*, October 14, 2001, http://articles.latimes.com/2001/oct/14/news/mn-57084. Hambali was videotaped with Almihdhar and Alhazmi; see US Treasury Department, "Statement by the Treasury Department Regarding Today's Designation of Two Leaders of Jemaah Islamiyah," January 24, 2003, http://www.nefafoundation.org/miscellaneous/WestCoast/Treasury_JI.pdf. Bin al-Shibh is also said to be shown on the video; see Ewan Thomas, "Gunning for Bin Laden," *Newsweek*, November 26, 2001, http://www.newsweek.com/id/76477.
42. Stephen Braun, et al., see note 41.
43. Oliver Schröm, see note 32.
44. Stephen Braun, et al., see note 41.
45. Wright 2006, p. 341.
46. Justice Department IG report, pp. 234, 243; Daniel Klaidman, Michael Isikoff and Mark Hosenball, "In-

- A picture of bin Attash, apparently standing by Alhazmi and Almihdhar.[47]

- Photos of USS *Cole* bomber Fahad al-Quso, or a person who looks like him, standing next to Almihdhar.[48]

- A picture of Ramzi bin al-Shibh next to Khallad bin Attash.[49]

- Photos including "Hambali," who was immediately recognized by Malaysian intelligence.

- Photos including Yazid Sufaat, the summit's host, who was also recognized by Malaysian intelligence.[50]

- Additional photos containing a new person, about which the CIA was informed on January 8. This person has never been identified.[51]

We know very little about what the CIA did with these photos. They showed a number of top al-Qaeda figures and were of huge importance, but, as far as we know, only three of them were circulated before 9/11. Where are the rest? And what, if anything, was done with them?

Some of the attendees, including Almihdhar, used an Internet café, spending many hours in front of the computers. Not only were the Malaysians monitoring them at the time, but they searched the computers' hard drives after they left.[52] This was a potential intelligence bonanza, and could have led to the e-mail accounts of senior al-Qaeda figures, as well as the chat rooms and websites they used. How often do the security services get to a computer that has just been used by an al-Qaeda leader? However, there is no public information about what the intelligence services gleaned from all of this.

vestigators Link Last Week's Attacks, Embassy Bombings in Africa, and USS Cole," *Newsweek*, September 20, 2001, http://www.newsweek.com/id/75817; Edward Helmore and Ed Vulliamy, "Saudi Hijacker 'Was Key Link to Bin Laden,'" *Observer* (UK), October 7, 2001, http://www.guardian.co.uk/world/2001/oct/07/terrorism.afghanistan3.

47. Justice Department IG report, p. 285; Wright 2006, p. 342.

48. Daniel Klaidman, Michael Isikoff and Mark Hosenball, see note 46.

49. Bob Drogin and Josh Meyer, "Yemen Files Aid Terror Inquiry," *Los Angeles Times*, October 17, 2001, http://www.latimes.com/news/nationworld/nation/la-101701probe,1,5057995.story; Oliver Schröm, see note 32.

50. Brendan Periera, "Unmasking Radical Preachers," *New Straits Times*, October 2, 2002.

51. Justice Department IG report, p. 247.

52. Oliver Schröm, see note 32; "January 7, 2000 or Shortly After: Malaysian Authorities Search Computers Used by Malaysia Summit Attendees," *History Commons*, April 12, 2008, http://www.historycommons.org/context.jsp?item=a010700harddrive&scale=0#a010700harddrive, citing Zachary Abuza, "Kuala Lumpur a Vital Hub for al-Qa'ida Strike Plans: Al-Qa'ida's South-East Asian Network," *Australian*, December 24, 2002.

If the same café was used more than once, then it would certainly be possible to install monitoring equipment in such a way that keystrokes and passwords were recorded.

On January 6 two of the summit's attendees, Nawaf Alhazmi and Khallad bin Attash, took side trips. One traveled to Singapore and the other to Thailand. The 9/11 Commission staff statement that revealed this does not make it clear which was which, but as associates of bin Attash had just arrived in Thailand, it is likely he went there and Alhazmi went to Singapore. Allegedly, the US was unable to obtain the travelers' details, but the CIA's Kuala Lumpur station speculated that one of the men might be what the Commission called "the still mysterious Nawaf." According to the Commission, the US tried to learn more about the trips "after the fact," but does not seem to have come up with much. Both men returned to Kuala Lumpur within twenty-four hours, but, reportedly, this was not registered by the authorities.[53]

These side trips represented an opportunity to learn more about the travelers, but this opportunity was seemingly not taken, even though obtaining the manifests for the flights they took and learning the names they were traveling under would have been a simple matter, and was actually done for the flight on which they left Kuala Lumpur two days later. Again, skepticism must be expressed about the claimed lack of exploitation of these trips—the summit was important enough to brief the national security adviser, but they couldn't get a flight manifest?

During the summit, according to a 2010 article in the *New York Observer*, the CIA came to believe that Ahmad Hikmat Shakir, the otherwise apparently unremarkable Iraqi, was gay, and that this could be used as leverage to recruit him, given the conservative Islamist circles he moved in. The Agency may have surmised that Shakir was not a high-level terrorist, but could be of value to them because he did know such people and might be able to provide access to them. Therefore, at some point during or shortly after the summit, the CIA reportedly broke into his apartment and also made a recruitment pitch, but their offer was rebuffed.[54] If true, this

53. 9/11 Commission Staff Statement No. 2, "Three Hijackers: Identification, Watchlisting and Tracking," p. 4, http://www.9-11Commission.gov/staff_statements/staff_statement_2.pdf.

54. Aram Roston, "The Gay Terrorist," *New York Observer*, March 16, 2010, http://www.observer.com/2010/politics/gay-terrorist?page=0. According to Roston, it was the failed recruitment that led the CIA to withhold information about Alhazmi and Almihdhar from the FBI until August 2001.

story shows that the CIA paid much more attention to the Malaysia summit at the time than it later claimed, a denial of interest left unchallenged in the Congressional Inquiry report, *The 9/11 Commission Report* and the Justice Department inspector general's report.

After the summit ended, the Malaysians continued to monitor the apartment, but the CIA lost interest and the surveillance stopped. Had the surveillance continued, the Malaysians would have noticed Zacarias Moussaoui there later that year. The Malaysians said they were surprised by the CIA's lack of interest after the summit. "We couldn't fathom it, really," said Rais Yatim, Malaysia's Legal Affairs minister. "There was no show of concern."[55]

* * *

What are we to make of this? It could not look more like the CIA was hiding something, but what? It must have been important even at this time, as it involved letting a lot of al-Qaeda's leaders continue to operate instead of detaining them. As we have seen, Miller's cable about Almihdhar was blocked on January 5, 2000, so whatever was up, it must have been known by then. The thrust of this book is that by the late summer of 2001 at least one of the people involved in the efforts to conceal this information from the FBI had decided to allow 9/11 to happen. However, precisely when this decision was taken is unclear, and it may well have been later than January 2000.

One suggestion made after 9/11 was that the CIA kept Almihdhar's presence in the US secret from the FBI to spite John O'Neill, an FBI terrorism investigator who had irked Alec Station. However, the extremely important nature of what was being withheld argues against this. The CIA might keep some details from the FBI because of personal animus, but the significance of this specific information makes that highly unlikely here.

This is highly unlikely for several reasons. For example, Doug Miller's cable was blocked almost immediately, before the Agency had time to think about recruiting Shakir. Further, as we will see, after the *Cole* bombing in October 2000, the CIA continued to protect Alhazmi, Almihdhar and bin Attash, and it is improbable that one failed recruitment would have induced it to continue the protection in such grave circumstances. And, of course, even if the Agency did attempt to recruit Shakir, this is no reason not to monitor Alhazmi and Almihdhar in the US, which should have been the FBI's responsibility. The reader will be provided additional reasons to doubt Roston's thesis as this narrative proceeds.

55. Michael Isikoff and Daniel Klaidman, "The Hijackers We Let Escape," *Newsweek*, June 10, 2002, http://holtz.org/Library/ToFile/The%20Hijackers%20We%20Let%20Escape.htm.

The Pentagon, September 11, 2001

There is no evidence of any tracking efforts

The official story of how the two hijackers eluded CIA-led surveillance in Malaysia also needs to be examined. On January 8, they flew from Kuala Lumpur to Bangkok, Thailand, together with Khallad bin Attash. The CIA allegedly lost them in Bangkok because it was unable to get a surveillance team to the airport in time to meet their flight.[1]

However, bin Attash had been monitored in Kuala Lumpur making calls from a pay phone in front of the apartment where the summit was being held, and one or more of these calls was to the Washington Hotel in Bangkok, where the three men stayed along with two others, Fahad al-Quso and Ibrahim al-Thawar, who would go on to be involved in the *Cole* bombing. There were also calls to al-Quso's house in Yemen, either from the pay phone, the Bangkok hotel, or both.

According to author Lawrence Wright, "Although the CIA later denied that it knew anything about the phone, the number was recorded in the Malaysians' surveillance log, which was given to the agency."[2] And CIA Counterterrorist Center Chief Cofer Black later commented on the calls in general: "They're acting kind of spooky. They're not using the phone in the apartment. They're going around, walking in circles, just like junior spies. Going up to phone booths, making a lot of calls. It's like, 'Who are these dudes?'"[3] The CIA therefore could have used the information gleaned from monitoring bin Attash to find where he was staying in Bangkok, but instead of explaining why it failed to do this, it simply provided a false excuse.

The briefings being given to CIA leaders were by Richard Blee, Tom Wilshire's boss and chief of Alec Station. The station received

1. *9/11 CR*, p. 181; bin Attash traveled under an alias he had previously used to apply for a US visa.
2. Lawrence Wright, "The Agent: Did the C.I.A. stop an F.B.I. Detective from Preventing 9/11?" *New Yorker*, July 10 and 17, 2006, http://www.lawrencewright.com/WrightSoufan.pdf.
3. Steve Coll, *Ghost Wars: The Secret History of the CIA, Afghanistan, and bin Laden, from the Soviet Invasion to September 10, 2001* (London: Penguin, 2004), pp. 487-88.

notification that Almihdhar and two others had left Kuala Lumpur on January 8[4] and had urged Bangkok station to find them the next day.[5] Despite this, in a briefing to his superiors on January 12, 2000, Blee claimed that the surveillance was ongoing and completely omitted any mention of the three men's departure to Thailand. Based on an interview of Blee, the 9/11 Commission said he "kept providing updates, unaware at first even that the Arabs had left Kuala Lumpur, let alone that their trail had been lost in Bangkok."[6]

The Commission commented,

> On January 12, the head of the CIA's al-Qaeda unit [Blee] told his bosses that surveillance in Kuala Lumpur was continuing. He may not have known that in fact Almihdhar and his companions had dispersed and the tracking was falling apart. U.S. officials in Bangkok regretfully reported the bad news on January 13. The names they had were put on a watchlist in Bangkok, so that Thai authorities might notice if the men left the country. On January 14, the head of the CIA's al-Qaeda unit again updated his bosses, telling them that officials were continuing to track the suspicious individuals who had now dispersed to various countries.
>
> Unfortunately, there is no evidence of any tracking efforts actually being undertaken by anyone after the Arabs disappeared into Bangkok. No other effort was made to create other opportunities to spot these Arab travelers in case the screen in Bangkok failed. Just from the evidence in Almihdhar's passport, one of the logical possible destinations and interdiction points would have been the United States. Yet no one alerted the INS or the FBI to look for these individuals. They arrived, unnoticed, in Los Angeles on January 15.[7]

This makes no sense. Alec Station was informed of the departure of the three men to Bangkok on January 8 and sent a cable to the CIA station in Bangkok instructing it to find them the next day. Yet Richard Blee, the station chief, told his superiors the surveillance in Malaysia was still ongoing four days after they had left. It is hard to imagine that he could have been so ignorant of the true situation. It is also unclear why the 9/11 Commission's investigators would take such a startling claim at face value.

4. Justice Department IG report, p. 247.
5. Ibid., Bamford 2005, p. 227.
6. *9/11 CR*, pp. 181, 502.
7. Ibid., p. 354.

The next day, January 13, Bangkok station told Alec Station that it could not locate the men, and the day after that, Blee claimed to his superiors that the tracking was continuing. Yet the Commission claimed there was "no evidence" that any tracking occurred in Bangkok, the only place they could have been tracked. They were staying at a hotel the CIA could have easily identified.

What's more, Blee failed to have a formal report drawn up about surveillance of the Malaysia summit. As James Bamford observed,

> Despite the importance of the operation, [Blee] had never bothered to write up and distribute an intelligence report on it—what is known as a TD, or Telegraphic Dissemination. "A TD would have gone to a lot of people," admitted [a] senior intelligence officer, "but we didn't do that." ...
> It was a serious blunder.[8]

Around January 15—the day Almihdhar and Alhazmi arrived in Los Angeles—Alec Station apparently ceased all efforts related to the operation. There were also missed opportunities to watchlist the two, as well as missed opportunities to ask other agencies, such as the NSA, for information about them.[9]

It seems that Richard Blee was hiding information from his superiors. Had he told them on January 12 or 14 that the men had slipped surveillance, he would have been ordered to find them. He appears not to have wanted to do this, at least officially.

However, there is also the possibility that he appeared to mislead his superiors because they themselves had indicated they did not want to know about this—that they did not want any paper trail that indicated they knew something that they might later prefer not to have known.

* * *

The discussion of Richard Blee and his role in the events leading to 9/11 will be complicated, but at the outset we need to understand four things about the CIA.

First, when the CIA began to be investigated in the 1970s for its involvement in a number of unsavory Cold War activities, in particular by the Senate's "Church Committee" (the Select Com-

---

8. Bamford 2005, p. 227.
9. Ibid., pp. 224-30.

mittee to Study Governmental Operations with Respect to Intelligence Activities, chaired by Senator Frank Church of Idaho), its response was to set up a parallel network. This network employed foreign intelligence agencies, and was most famously grouped around the Safari Club: private businessmen sympathetic to the CIA, loyal alumni and their trusted associates. Former CIA Associate Director Robert Crowley explained the purpose of this when he said that by "taking operations and putting them in the hands of private businessmen and other countries, Congressional accountability could be avoided."[10]

One of the most famous members of this parallel network was Edwin Wilson, an officer who left the CIA in 1971. Starting in the mid-'70s he established a series of front companies that were exploited by the Agency for numerous operations. The best-known project was his work on Libya, during which one of his contractors took photographs of military facilities hit in the 1986 bombing ordered by President Reagan. This contractor was Billy Waugh, who later worked "right there with these al-Qaeda operatives." Wilson was convicted of illegally shipping arms to the Libyans, but, after serving 27 years in jail, he finally managed to prove that he had dozens of contacts with the CIA and that the illegal things he did were at their request.[11]

Another well-known member of the parallel network was Miles Copeland, a leading official in the CIA's early years who left the Agency and went private, but never severed his ties to the world of intelligence. He defended the Agency from the Church Committee and was a player in the Iran-Contra affair, meeting with Israeli and Iranian representatives to facilitate missile transactions. A book by one of Copeland's associates, Larry Kolb, claims that Copeland later recruited Kolb, who used his cover as an international businessman to perform a number of services for the Agency.[12]

For a time, one of the senior figures in this parallel network was William Casey, CIA director from 1981 to 1987. Despite his formal

10. For the quote from Crowley, see Joseph Trento, *Prelude to Terror* (New York: Carroll & Graf, 2005), p. 98.
11. Wilson's story is described in Trento's *Prelude to Terror*. For Waugh taking photographs in Libya, see Billy Waugh and Tim Keown, *Hunting the Jackal: A Special Forces and CIA Soldier's Fifty Years on the Frontlines of the War Against Terrorism* (New York: Avon Books, 2004), pp. 153-54.
12. Larry Kolb, *Overworld* (London: Corgi, 2005).

position as head of the Agency and the large number of operatives under his official control, Casey repeatedly ran informal operations. In one instance, he sent two representatives to North Korea to cut a deal with its leaders on their nuclear program. The mission was a success, but by the time the two reported, Casey was so ill and so wrapped up in Iran-Contra that no attention was paid to it.[13] Another Casey success was Saudi support totaling millions of dollars for the Contra rebels. Nicaragua is hardly of pressing geopolitical concern for the Saudis, but they provided the money at the request of US officials sympathetic to the Contras.[14]

While the anti-Soviet jihad in Afghanistan is closely associated with official CIA operations, the parallel network was also busy there. For example, some of the money for the mujaheddin was apparently funneled through the transportation company EATSCO, which was linked to Wilson and another key player in the parallel network of that era, Ted Shackley.[15] In addition, the Saudis agreed to match US funding for the anti-Soviet mujaheddin, and the CIA administered and disbursed these funds, but they were not subject to the usual regulations on how the CIA spent its money.[16] Huge amounts of cash were skimmed off the top and deposited in the CIA-backed Bank of Credit and Commerce International, then made their way to accounts linked to A.Q. Khan, father of Pakistan's atomic bomb.[17]

According to author Ahmed Rashid, in 1986 Casey also approved the use of non-Afghan Islamist fighters in the Afghan War.[18] The CIA has repeatedly admitted thinking about giving money to these groups at that time, but claims it decided against this. Any CIA money for them would have been channeled through Pakistan's ISI security agency, which handled the vast majority of US and Saudi funds and weapons for the war. It is certainly possible that Casey

13. Joseph Trento, see note 9, pp. 288-89.
14. George Crile, *Charlie Wilson's War: The Extraordinary Story of How the Wildest Man in Congress and a Rogue CIA Agent Changed the History of Our Times* (New York: Grove Press, 2003), p. 341.
15. Joseph Trento, see note 9; the EATSCO affair is described in particular in the last third of the book.
16. George Crile, see note 13, p. 413.
17. Adrian Levy and Catherine Scott-Clark, *Deception: Pakistan, the United States and the Global Nuclear Weapons Conspiracy* (London: Atlantic Books, 2006), p. 125.
18. Ahmid Rashid, *Taliban* (London: Pan Books, 2001), p. 129. In addition to Arabs, these groups included Moros from the Philippines, Uighurs from Chinese Turkestan and Uzbeks from Soviet Central Asia. (Uzbeks also comprise a segment of the Afghan population.)

gave the ISI the green light to support these Islamists without telling any of his subordinates in Langley.

If the CIA had wanted to monitor the hijackers in the US, but had not wanted a paper trail inside the Agency about this surveillance—which would have been illegal—this parallel network could have been utilized to implement the surveillance off the books.

It is also possible that, instead of using a parallel network managed by US citizens, the intelligence service of a friendly country was used to monitor the hijackers. There is a wealth of information that shows Almihdhar and Alhazmi associated with several people thought to be agents of the Saudi government, particularly Omar al-Bayoumi, but also Osama Basnan and Fahad al-Thumairy. It is perfectly possible that the CIA asked the Saudis to monitor the two men in the US, which would have neatly sidestepped the prohibition against domestic CIA operations. However, as pointed out above, the relationship between the two men and the Saudi government remains murky.

There are also reports that Israeli agents were in the US at the same time as the hijackers, and it has been suggested that they may have been tracking the terrorists.[19] Mossad allegedly passed a warning to the US on August 23, 2001, and this warning may have named four of the hijackers, Alhazmi, Almihdhar, Mohamed Atta and Marwan Alshehhi.[20] Perhaps coincidentally, these are the same four hijackers reportedly identified by the Army's Able Danger data-mining project.

The second point about the CIA: it is a highly compartmentalized organization. What this means is that information is tightly held and only disclosed on a need-to-know basis. Officers based in one room do not necessarily know what the officers in the next room are doing.

Based on interviews with Gust Avrakotos, one of the CIA managers who had led US support for the anti-Soviet mujaheddin, author George Crile explained how this worked:

> [Avrakotos] knew that the CIA forcibly places blinders on all of its employees. As the thousands of operatives and analysts and administrators cross one another in the halls, Avrakotos knew

---

19. Christopher Ketcham, "The Israeli "art student" mystery," *Salon*, May 7, 2002, http://dir.salon.com/story/news/feature/2002/05/07/students/index.html.
20. Matthias Gebauer, "Mossad Agents Were On Atta's Tail," *Der Spiegel*, October 1, 2002, http://www.unansweredquestions.org/timeline/2002/derspiegel100102.html.

that precious few would have any idea what anyone else was doing. Even people in the same division or on the same floor understood that it was dangerous to look too curious, and so Avrakotos, the master of deception, walked through the white halls of Langley with the knowledge that no one would be trying to figure out what he was up to. In fact, they would be doing just the opposite. And for the chance encounter with old colleagues he knew exactly what kind of shrug to give, what kind of half lie to offer, what kind of air to affect. The whole exercise was remarkably simple—the idea being to make it seem as if he was engaged in something that others either should know about, if they were in the know, or shouldn't ask if they weren't.[21]

Third: power in the CIA is vested in its officers in a way different from a normal Western corporation. Usually, power in a corporation is hierarchical, with a chief executive officer or director general at the top, senior executives below him, and middle management below them. Although the CIA does officially have such a structure with a director at the top, senior managers supporting him, and then division and station chiefs, this structure is mitigated by other factors.

Due to the nature of their business and the shared danger, CIA officers often build up extraordinarily close personal bonds and relationships of trust, which can give a nominal subordinate influence with a nominal superior and also last even after an officer leaves the Agency.

Corporations do not regularly rotate their managers. The CIA, however, does, with many postings lasting three years, to give the officers a variety of experiences and to stop them getting too close to people or entities the Agency does not want them to get too close to.

In addition, some postings that may be technically at the same level are actually not. For example, all station chiefs are station chiefs, but the stations in Berlin during the Cold War, Saigon during the Vietnam War and Baghdad now are large and important in a way that Ouagadougou station, in the capital of Burkina Faso, never will be.

Finally, a number of officers are children of former officers. These children grow up plugged into their parent's network, which is of great help to them. For example, it makes background checks much

---

21. George Crile, see note 13, p. 93.

easier, as the CIA will already know a lot about a former division chief's son who accompanied his father on numerous postings and already knows several of the CIA's current and former leaders.

Richard Blee's father David was one of the officers of which the Agency is most proud. A former Office of Strategic Services agent in World War II, David made his name by spiriting Stalin's daughter to the West while he was station chief in New Delhi, India.[22] Later posted to headquarters, he ran the Soviet Division at the height of the Cold War and completely reformed the Agency's defector policy, which allowed it to build a large network of spies in Eastern Europe. He went on to head counterintelligence and, when the Agency celebrated its fiftieth birthday in 1997, was one of the fifty former officers honored by Director Tenet. He died in August 2000.[23]

* * *

What does all this mean?

Upon seeing that CIA officers did something wrong—withheld information from the FBI about Khalid Almihdhar and Nawaf Alhazmi for over a year and a half—it is natural to think that this must be something on which the CIA's leadership had agreed, an official operation that George Tenet and Counterterrorist Center chief Cofer Black approved. However, although Tenet's and Black's performances were not perfect before the attacks, and while they certainly did make false statements after 9/11 in an apparent attempt to cover up what happened, there is no evidence of their doing anything intentionally wrong before the attacks.

Withholding the information about Almihdhar and Alhazmi from the FBI only makes sense if the CIA was monitoring the two men in the US itself, either officially or off the books. Although he was not a senior manager at the CIA, Richard Blee's connections gave him access to the parallel network of loyal alumni and sym-

22. Richard accompanied his father on this posting; a yearbook of the American International School in Delhi for 1966-1967 contains a picture of a young Blee reading to his teacher, p. 26, http://www.aisaes.org/1966_namaste.pdf.
23. James Risen, "David H. Blee, 83, C.I.A. Spy Who Revised Defector Policy," *New York Times*, August 17, 2000, http://www.nytimes.com/2000/08/17/us/david-h-blee-83-cia-spy-who-revised-defector-policy.html?pagewanted=1; Harold Jackson; "David Blee: CIA chief who rescued the agency from paranoia," *Guardian* (UK), August 22, 2000, http://www.guardian.co.uk/news/2000/aug/22/guardianobituaries.haroldjackson.

pathizers who would have been needed to carry out off-the-books surveillance in the US. The compartmentalization would have stopped other officers at the Agency from treading on his toes.

Blee is the most senior officer whose poor performance—the incorrect briefings on January 12 and 14 and other actions described below—looks to have been intentional. Although Tom Wilshire, his deputy, appears much more heavily involved in any wrongdoing, Wilshire seems too junior to have acted on his own initiative; he was one of two deputy chiefs at a station with about two dozen officers.

We do not know exactly what happened, but if Blee had wanted to monitor the hijackers through a parallel network in the US while keeping this secret from the FBI and his superiors, he could have done so. Because of the diffuse nature of power at the CIA, he did not need approval from Black or Tenet; he could do it on his own.

Having said this, it should be stressed that this is just a possibility. Maybe Blee did discuss what was happening with others, either in the CIA's formal hierarchy or in the milieu of influential loyal alumni. We simply don't know.

— 14 —

Captain Queeg

Here we must pause to examine two more points in relation to Richard Blee.

The first is about his temperament and that of Alec Station, the unit he headed. This is how author Steve Coll described the station in 1999, when Blee took over:

> The bin Laden unit's analysts were so intense about their work that they made some of their CIA colleagues uncomfortable. The unit had about twenty-five professionals in the summer of 1999. They called themselves "the Manson Family" because they had acquired a reputation for crazed alarmism about the rising al-Qaeda threat. "Jonestown," said one person involved, asked to sum up the unit's atmosphere. "I outlawed Kool-Aid." Some of their colleagues thought they had lost their perspective. "It was a cult," recalled a second American official. "There was frustration: Why didn't everybody else share their views on things?"[1]

The Manson Family, headed by Charles Manson, of course went on an infamous killing spree in California in 1969. Jonestown was a settlement in Guyana where hundreds of members of Jim Jones' Peoples Temple died in a mass murder/suicide (complete with poisoned Kool-Aid) in 1978 after an inspection by a US congressman, who was also killed. These are not good comparisons, especially for a unit of the United States government's Central Intelligence Agency.

Blee fit right in with the station he inherited. Coll describes him as "sometimes emotional and combative,"[2] adding,

---

1. Steve Coll, *Ghost Wars: The Secret History of the CIA, Afghanistan, and bin Laden, from the Soviet Invasion to September 10, 2001* (London: Penguin, 2004), p. 456. The comment about outlawing Kool-Aid is intriguing, as is the reference to the summer of 1999, when Blee arrived at Alec Station. Presumably, the anonymous source here is Blee. There are various passages concerning Blee throughout the book that indicate he was one of Coll's sources.
2. Ibid.

Tall and intense, Rich was seen by some of his colleagues as typical of the unyielding zealots the unit had seemed to produce one after another since about 1997. The bin Laden team talked about the al-Qaeda threat in apocalyptic terms. And if you weren't with them, you were against them.[3]

Long after 9/11, *Newsweek* also reported on how Blee was perceived in a subsequent assignment:

[Blee] was a stickler for starting meetings on time (his own watch was always seven minutes fast) ... One slightly bitter spook, speaking anonymously to *Newsweek* to protect his identity, likened the station chief to Captain Queeg in *The Caine Mutiny*.[4]

The Caine Mutiny is a novel by Herman Wouk in which the fictional Captain Queeg is relieved of command of a WWII destroyer by his subordinates after they come to the conclusion that he is mad and will get the ship sunk during a storm.

Similar criticisms were echoed elsewhere, for example James Bamford said Blee had a "myopic obsession with bin Laden,"[5] and *Harper's* journalist Ken Silverstein reported that he had "frequently been divisive and ineffective in previous positions" and was a "terrible manager."[6]

Blee is the highest official we can tentatively identify as being part of any plot to withhold information about Almihdhar and Alhazmi. If he was doing this on the instructions of someone else, his temperament may have made him easier to manipulate, or simply more willing to go along. If he was acting alone, then this information about his temperament can inform our opinion about his motivations.

* * *

Another issue involves what happened to Blee after 9/11. One of his long-cherished plans as chief of Alec Station and then the Sunni Extremist Group[7] was to form stronger ties with Afghanistan's

3. Ibid., p. 540.
4. Evan Thomas, "The Ongoing Hunt for Osama bin Laden," *Newsweek*, August 28, 2007.
5. Bamford 2005, pp. 218-19.
6. Ken Silverstein, "Meet the CIA's New Baghdad Station Chief," *Harper's*, January 28, 2007, http://www.harpers.org/archive/2007/01/meet-the-cias-new-2007-01-28.
7. The CIA's Counterterrorist Center was re-organized in the first half of 2000. When "Eric," the FBI agent who had served as one of Alec Station's two deputy chiefs, was replaced by Charles Frahm

Northern Alliance, and Central Asian powers such as Uzbekistan, to attack Osama bin Laden in Afghanistan. Before 9/11, Blee had met repeatedly with Northern Alliance leaders and argued within the CIA that it should give the alliance more resources. However, other elements of the CIA had been lukewarm about this and had stopped any significant increases in support.[8] After 9/11 Blee got his way, and US forces joined up with the Northern Alliance and occupied Afghanistan.

In addition, Blee was appointed chief of the CIA's new station in Kabul. This was a substantial promotion from his position at the Counterterrorist Center, and was also right in the thick of the action after 9/11. Before the attacks, he had headed a couple of dozen analysts at CIA headquarters; now he had massive resources to help run a war for control of a country of twenty-five million inhabitants.

The officer Richard Blee replaced as the CIA's leader in Afghanistan was Gary Berntsen. In a book about his time at the CIA, Berntsen quotes himself as telling Blee, "You pushed for the job, now it's yours."[9] This indicates that it was Blee who had angled for the promotion, although, according to the *Newsweek* article quoted above, he had then only read one book about the country.

What is startling about Blee's replacement of Berntsen is its timing—right in the middle of the battle of Tora Bora. Berntsen commented, "I couldn't believe they were doing this in the middle of the most important battle of the war."[10]

Bin Laden was holed up in Tora Bora and surrounded by Afghan forces allied with the US, plus a handful of US troops. Berntsen,

in July 2000, Frahm became the deputy chief of this larger unit; see Justice Department IG report, pp. 229, 232, 320. This larger unit appears to be the Sunni Extremist Group, an entity mentioned in a report by the CIA's inspector general and George Tenet's *At the Center of the Storm* (p. 251); see OIG Report on CIA Accountability With Respect to the 9/11 Attacks, June 2005, p. xii, http://www.fas.org/irp/cia/product/oig-911.pdf. A CIA log entry made on 9/11 gave the technical Agency designation for Frahm as "DC/SEG/Law Enforcement"; see CIA, "Response to DCI Document Request Number 52, Item 2," undated, http://www.scribd.com/doc/14274557/CIA-Log-Entries-from-911-and-Related-Documents. The designation means Deputy Chief of the Sunni Extremist Group for Law Enforcement. The 9/11 Commission refers to Blee as "head of the section that included the bin Laden unit" and "a group chief with authority over the bin Laden unit"; see *9/11 CR*, pp. 142, 204.
8. Steve Coll, see note 1, pp. 459, 469-70, 539-40, 560.
9. Gary Berntsen and Ralph Pezzullo, *Jawbreaker: The Attack on Bin Laden and Al-Qaeda: A Personal Account by the CIA's Key Field Commander* (New York: Three Rivers Press, 2005), p. 305.
10. Ibid., p. 297.

recognizing that the situation was perilous and that some of the Afghans might not be reliable, requested boots on the ground:

> I also informed General Dell Dailey [of the Joint Special Operations Command (JSOC)] I'd sent a message to Langley requesting the introduction of ground forces into Tora Bora. He said, "Gary, you've done great down there. Now we'll finish it off."
>
> "With what?" I asked, venting my frustration. "Forty JSOC and a dozen SF [Special Forces] troops? You think that somehow they're going to block escape routes across hundreds of miles of caves and mountain passes? It's not enough."
>
> It didn't take a great military strategist to figure out that bin Laden was looking for a way out and would ultimately succeed in escaping. It was a twenty-four hour climb through the White Mountains from Tora Bora to Pakistan. Yet, General Dailey and CENTCOM continued to ignore my request for eight hundred U.S. ground troops.[11]

We know the rest. Berntsen was replaced soon after, the boots on the ground did not arrive, and bin Laden escaped to live on for another ten years. We know Berntsen's position on ground forces—he wanted them and he had good reason to want them. However, we do not know Blee's position. Did he ask for ground forces or not? Almost a decade after the event, we still don't know what he recommended.[12]

---

11. Ibid., p. 299.
12. According to media reports, Cofer Black was angry that bin Laden had got away and blamed it on a lack of US ground troops. When Black gave a story about this to the *Washington Post*, Secretary of Defense Donald Rumsfeld had him fired from the CIA, after which he took refuge in the State Department. See Barton Gellman and Thomas E. Ricks, "U. S. Concludes Bin Laden Escaped at Tora Bora," *Washington Post*, April 17, 2002, http://www.washingtonpost.com/ac2/wp-dyn/A62618-2002Apr16?language=printer; also Richard Sale, "Embarrassed Rumsfeld Fired CIA Official," UPI, July 28, 2004, http://www.neilrogers.com/news/articles/2004073012.html. Black issued a denial of sorts, although the wording makes it unclear what he was specifically denying; see Kevin McMurray, "Cofer Black, Out of the Shadows," *Men's Journal*, October 17, 2008, http://www.mensjournal.com/cofer-black. The Special Operations Command published a history of its operations during the invasion of Afghanistan that focuses on the battle of Tora Bora. Although there are several references to the CIA, this history does not mention Blee; "Operation ENDURING FREEDOM Afghanistan," *United States Special Operations Command History*, 6th Edition (2007). Neither is Blee mentioned in an examination of Tora Bora by the Senate Committee on Foreign Relations, although it does mention Berntsen; also mentioned are Berntsen's predecessor in Afghanistan, Gary Schroen; the CTC deputy director responsible for Afghan operations, Henry Crumpton; and an anonymous CIA officer, apparently the on-the-ground Agency leader at the battle; see US Senate Committee on Foreign Relations, Tora Bora Revisited: How We Failed to Get Bin Laden and Why It Matters Today, November 30, 2009, http://foreign.senate.gov/imo/media/doc/Tora_Bora_Report.pdf.

Speculation about what would have happened if bin Laden were caught is of limited value, but it is reasonable to presume this would have brought some form of closure after 9/11. Certainly, he would not have been available to periodically re-emerge and remind us of the threat.

* * *

While in Afghanistan, Blee was also involved in the CIA's rendition program. The program had been formalized by the Clinton administration in the mid-1990s, largely on the initiative of Blee's predecessor at Alec Station, Michael Scheuer. It seems the program's leadership passed to Blee after he replaced Scheuer in June 1999, but it was a relatively small program before 9/11.

Rendition was massively expanded after the attacks, and new elements were added. When a detainee was renditioned to a third country, such as Egypt or Syria, the US used the intelligence produced by interrogation, whereas before it had generally ignored this data, thinking it unreliable. In addition, the US also renditioned detainees to its own black sites, where "enhanced" techniques such as waterboarding were used.

Blee was station chief in a country, Afghanistan, from and to which many of the detainees were being renditioned and where they were being held. He is also known to be personally involved in the rendition of the first high-profile detainee, the militant training camp commander Ibn Shaikh al-Libi.

Al-Libi was captured in Afghanistan in December 2001 and initially interrogated by FBI agent Russell Fincher and a New York police detective. Fincher called a more experienced agent in New York, Jack Cloonan, to ask for guidance. Cloonan later gave an interview about what happened to the *American Prospect*.

> Says Cloonan: "I told them, 'When you get access, don't say anything at first. Sit; say hello after awhile; offer him tea, dates, figs. Point out where Mecca is; ask him if he wants to pray. And sit. And when he starts to look a little inquisitive, tell him who you are, and that he has rights and privileges, and that you're going to give him his rights. Just like any other interview.' So they do all this. And they start building rapport. And he starts talking about [shoe-bomber Richard] Reid and [Zacarias] Moussaoui. They're

getting good stuff, and everyone's getting the raw 302s [interview summaries] – the agency, the military, the director. But for some reason, the CIA chief of station in Kabul [Blee] is taking issue with our approach."

… A series of conference calls ensued among military, CIA, and FBI officials; in the end, over both the military and [FBI Director Robert] Mueller's objections, the CIA's prerogative carried the day—which meant al-Libi would be rendered to Cairo for interrogation by Egypt's intelligence service …

What Cloonan's agents told him happened next blew his mind. "My guys told me that a Toyota Tundra with a box in the back pulls up to the building," he recalls. "CIA officers come in, start shackling al-Libi up. Right before they duct tape his mouth, he tells our guys, 'I know this isn't your fault.' And as he's standing there, chained and gagged, this CIA guy gets up in his face and tells al-Libi he's going to fuck his mother. And then off he apparently goes to Cairo, in a box."[13]

This dispute was about more than one training camp manager being brutally tortured in Egypt.[14] Author and journalist James Risen concluded that the dispute between the CIA and FBI was finally resolved by President Bush himself, and he explained the significance of this:

By choosing the CIA over the FBI, Bush was rejecting the law enforcement approach to fighting terrorism that had been favored during the Clinton era. Bush had decided that al-Qaeda was a national security threat, not a law enforcement problem, and he did not want al-Qaeda operatives brought back to face trial in the United States, where they would come under the strict rules of the American legal system.[15]

This decision on what to do with al-Libi, apparently provoked by Blee's complaint about the FBI's handling of him, was a key milestone in the development of US detainee policy after 9/11. There had been some theoretical work done before this, some memos drafted, but al-Libi's was the first test case, and its resolution paved

13. Jason Vest, "Pray and Tell," *American Prospect*, June 19, 2005, http://www.prospect.org/cs/articles?articleId=9876.
14. Before being sent to Egypt, al-Libi was held on the USS *Bataan*, a craft that was also housing some other detainees; see "Top al Qaeda leader held aboard U.S. warship," CNN, January 8, 2002, http://edition.cnn.com/2002/WORLD/asiapcf/central/01/08/ret.afghan.prisoners/index.html.
15. James Risen, *State of War: The Secret History of the CIA and the Bush Administration* (New York: Free Press, 2006), p. 28.

the way for all that followed—the black sites, the enhanced techniques, the waterboarding, the "mild non-injurious physical contact," the ghost planes, the deleted videotapes.

Russell Fincher, the FBI agent from whom al-Libi was taken, was previously on the *Cole* investigation and had attended a June 11, 2001 meeting between the *Cole* investigators and three of Tom Wilshire's associates, to be described in detail below. At that meeting, the three associates refused to provide Fincher and another agent, Steve Bongardt, with relevant information about Khalid Almihdhar, with one of them citing the spurious justification of the "wall," a set of procedures that regulated the sharing of information between FBI intelligence agents and criminal investigators and prosecutors.

Wilshire's associates therefore had a track record of withholding information from FBI investigators in general, and Fincher in particular. By taking al-Libi away from Fincher as 2002 dawned, Blee also caused him and his colleagues to miss out on additional information. Is this just a coincidence?

After 9/11, the narrative that emerged was that the various government agencies had failed to connect the dots that would have stopped the plot, and that information-sharing issues were partially responsible for this. Therefore, the various agencies of the US government began to share information more freely. "The wall had come down," as Wright put it.[16]

But the CIA promptly re-built the wall. The first known use of harsh interrogation tactics by the CIA itself after 9/11 was on militant training camp facilitator Abu Zubaida, who was captured in Pakistan in late March 2002. Initially, he was interviewed by Ali Soufan, who had headed the *Cole* bombing probe and from whom, as described below, the CIA had withheld information about Almihdhar and Alhazmi. Although Soufan was initially successful in gaining information from Abu Zubaida, the CIA moved in, having been designated the lead agency for detainees in the Blee-inspired turf war over al-Libi. When the Agency started using its harsh techniques on Abu Zubaida, Soufan complained, but then, recognizing he was fighting a losing battle, left the interrogation in disgust. This pattern was repeated in the first months of the "War on Ter-

---

16. Lawrence Wright, "The Agent: Did the C.I.A. stop an F.B.I. Detective from Preventing 9/11?" *New Yorker*, July 10 and 17, 2006, http://www.lawrencewright.com/WrightSoufan.pdf.

ror," with FBI agents not wanting anything to do with the enhanced techniques.

In an op-ed piece for the *New York Times* in April 2009, Soufan wrote,

> One of the worst consequences of the use of these harsh techniques was that it reintroduced the so-called Chinese wall between the C.I.A. and F.B.I., similar to the communications obstacles that prevented us from working together to stop the 9/11 attacks. Because the bureau would not employ these problematic techniques, our agents who knew the most about the terrorists could have no part in the investigation. An F.B.I. colleague of mine who knew more about Khalid Shaikh Mohammed than anyone in the government was not allowed to speak to him.[17]

Here is what seems to be the established narrative behind the use of torture techniques by the Bush administration: the administration, in particular Vice President Dick Cheney, panicked after 9/11, perhaps fearing a second attack, and it would stop at nothing to prevent it.

The harsh techniques had arrived in the US through studies of procedures used by Communist intelligence services during the Cold War, including a military program called Survival, Evasion, Resistance and Escape (SERE), a part of which prepared US servicemen for the experience of torture by those intelligence services. One of the primary purposes of such interrogations was to generate false confessions: to make US prisoners make statements detrimental to the United States, which could then be exploited for propaganda purposes.

The established narrative holds that even though the reverse-engineered SERE techniques were originally designed to elicit false confessions, the administration somehow convinced itself that they would produce accurate intelligence. This despite the fact that the administration and Congress were replete with current and former officers who had been through the SERE program and knew exactly what it was about.

---

17. Ali Soufan, "My Tortured Decision," *New York Times*, April 22, 2009, http://www.nytimes.com/2009/04/23/opinion/23soufan.html?_r=1. The FBI agent who refused to participate in the questioning of KSM is presumably Frank Pellegrino.

We can posit a second narrative next to the established one: somebody in the administration knew that SERE was designed to produce false information *and supported it primarily for this reason*. The false information that was to be produced was to link al-Qaeda to Iraq, providing a justification for the invasion of that country, an invasion the Bush administration began planning in its very first days.[18] As we now know, al-Libi was tortured in Egypt, as a result of which he did falsely confess to cooperation between Iraq and al-Qaeda. This false confession then formed a key part of Secretary of State Colin Powell's embarrassing presentation to the UN before the invasion of Iraq.[19]

We can also posit a third narrative: after 9/11 CIA officials still wanted to shield information from the FBI because they wanted to keep the Bureau away from information from detainees which they feared would expose the protection the CIA had provided to the 9/11 hijackers. When assessing this theory, we should bear in mind that a close associate of Tom Wilshire and of "Michelle" at Alec Station before 9/11, known only as "Frances" and mentioned repeatedly by Jane Mayer in her 2008 book *The Dark Side*, became closely involved in torture after 9/11.

These three explanations are not mutually exclusive. Just because people—probably the vast majority of those involved in torture—genuinely believed it would produce good information does not mean others could not have had different motives. Although much is known about some aspects of the torture programs, their origins are shrouded in mystery. The disclosure of further documents from the crucial seven months before Abu Zubaida's capture, and more research, could help us answer the question of how this regime came to be implemented.

18. According to former Treasury Secretary Paul O'Neill, the very first National Security Council meeting of the Bush administration, on January 31, 2001, focused on what to do about Iraq and the possibility of invading it; see Ron Suskind, *The Price of Loyalty* (London: Simon & Schuster, 2004), pp. 70-75.
19. Michael Isikoff, "Iraq and al-Qaeda," *Newsweek*, July 5, 2004, http://www.newsweek.com/id/54310.

15

I know nobody read that cable

After the CIA allegedly lost Khalid Almihdhar, Nawaf Al-hazmi, and Khallad bin Attash in Bangkok, it asked the Thais to watchlist the three men, meaning that Almihdhar and Alhazmi's departure from Thailand on January 15, 2000 should have been noted and passed to the local CIA station. From there it would have gone to headquarters. Since the two men were flying to the US, they could have been picked up on arrival, or any time later. As they ended up lodging with an FBI counterterrorism informant in San Diego, it could have been a straightforward matter for the Bureau to get close to them.[1]

For some reason that has not yet been determined, their departure from Thailand was not reported promptly by the CIA station

---

1. Though the role of the informant, Abdussattar Shaikh, is beyond the scope of this book, his tale, as it is known (see also Chapter 5, note 28), is a passport to the murky world of intelligence and counter-intelligence operations. The Congressional Inquiry report (p. 51) called his association with the hijackers "the US intelligence community's best chance to unravel the Sept. 11 plot" before the disaster. When his position as the housemate/landlord of terrorists was revealed, the *San Diego Union-Tribune* of September 16, 2001 identified him as a "prominent Muslim leader," a "retired San Diego State University English professor," and essentially proclaimed him an innocent benefactor. Yet, according to investigator Daniel Hopsicker, "a visit to the various locations around San Diego where he was said to have worked reveals that Abdussattar Shaikh never taught at San Diego State, has never been a Professor of English, and possesses a phony PhD from a bogus diploma mill run by people with U.S. military and intelligence connections"; http://www.madcowprod.com/Shaikh.html. Born in 1935, Shaikh left his homeland as it was being partitioned into Hindu India and Muslim Pakistan after World War II. Apparently arriving in California around 1970, he rose to a position of prominence in the small but growing Muslim community in the San Diego area. During his many-months residence with Alhazmi, neighbors reported, he received short, late-night visits by cars with darkened windows and also may have been visited by hijackers Mohamed Atta and/or Hani Hanjour; http://www.historycommons.org/entity.jsp?entity=abdussattar_shaikh. For his service to the Islamic community, in October of 2009 Shaikh was honored in suburban Lemon Grove, where he had given Alhazmi and Almihdhar accommodations in his five-bedroom home: "We honor you, Dr. Shaikh, for the love and devotion you have shown to your adopted country. You have touched countless lives." The local press that covered the event made no mention of Shaikh's connection to 9/11, though it did note that he was "trained as a chaplain in the Red Cross"; "Abdussattar Shaikh, Co-founder of San Diego's Islamic Center, Honored for 50 Years of Service Promoting Religious Tolerance," *East County Magazine*, October 8, 2009, http://www.eastcountymagazine.org/node/2020.

in Bangkok. After a few weeks went by, a CIA officer in Malaysia noticed this lack of reporting and queried Bangkok about what had happened.[2] According to the 9/11 Commission:

> Presumably the departure information was obtained back in January, on the days that these individuals made their departures. Because the names were watchlisted by the Thai authorities we cannot yet explain the delay in reporting the news.[3]

The CIA station in Bangkok sat on this request for two weeks. Then it told the CIA station in Kuala Lumpur that there was a delay in responding due to difficulties in obtaining the requested information.[4] However, it appears the station already had this information and, even if it did not, it could have simply asked the Thais, who had watchlisted the men at the CIA's request.

There was a further problem when Bangkok station finally did send a cable reporting the departure information for the two men, on March 5. The cable omitted Almihdhar's name, only saying that Alhazmi had traveled to the US with a companion, even though the cable was drafted in response to a query from Kuala Lumpur about Almihdhar's whereabouts.

Most media accounts are wrong about this, claiming that the cable only reported Alhazmi's departure, not that of a companion as well. However, the executive summary of the re-written CIA inspector general's report is very clear on this point:

> Separately, in March 2000, two CIA field locations [Bangkok and Kuala Lumpur] sent to a number of addressees cables reporting that Alhazmi and another al-Qaeda associate had traveled to the United States. They were clearly identified in the cables as "UBL [Osama bin Laden] associates."[5]

Given that this cable was generated in response to a question about Almihdhar's whereabouts, and that Almihdhar was a known associate of Alhazmi and had flown with him from Kuala Lumpur to Bangkok, it would not be too difficult to deduce that Almihdhar

2. This happened on February 11, 2000. See *9/11 CR*, pp. 181 n52, 502; also Justice Department IG report, p. 247.
3. *9/11 CR*, p. 502 n53.
4. Justice Department IG report, pp. 247-48.
5. OIG Report on CIA Accountability With Respect to the 9/11 Attacks, June 2005, p. xv, http://www.fas.org/irp/cia/product/oig-911.pdf.

was this associate. Any check of the flight manifest or with immigration would have revealed the associate's identity. In any case, Bangkok station must have had Almihdhar's name, and it is hard to view the omission as anything but intentional. It was the name of an al-Qaeda terrorist who had just entered the US and, as such, incredibly important.

Almihdhar apparently later claimed that both he and Alhazmi thought they were followed on this flight. According to Khalid Shaikh Mohammed's "substitution for testimony" at Zacarias Moussaoui's trial: in the late summer of 2000, "Almihdhar also gave a report to Sheikh Mohammed, telling him of their problems with enrolling in language schools and that they believed they were surveilled from Thailand to the US. Sheikh Mohammed began having doubts about whether the two would be able to fulfill their mission in the US."[6] This information was obtained by the CIA using the "enhanced" techniques, and its reliability is therefore questionable. However, it was not self-serving for KSM, and it does not look like something the CIA actively wanted to hear, so it may be accurate.

The hijackers were allegedly followed on two other occasions. According to one of their associates, Ramzi bin al-Shibh, the hijackers told him that Ziad Jarrah and Marwan Alshehhi were followed by "security officers" on cross-country casing flights inside the US. This statement was made while bin al-Shibh was still at liberty.[7]

Comparison of the hijackers' flight bookings and their actual flights shows that on several occasions they booked an extra flight with a similar itinerary, but then took only one, apparently hoping to avoid surveillance. On at least one occasion, Alhazmi's flight from Karachi to Kuala Lumpur on January 5, 2000, the ruse worked. The double bookings clearly indicate that the hijackers were concerned about surveillance of their travels.

Between January 15 and March 5, 2000, the CIA's Bangkok station racked up a total of six errors: it failed to locate Alhazmi, Almihdhar and bin Attash in Thailand, although the CIA had information that bin Attash had called a hotel in Bangkok, a logical place to

6. *United States v. Zacarias Moussaoui*, "Substitution for the Testimony of Khalid Shaikh Mohammed," July 31, 2006, http://www.vaed.uscourts.gov/notablecases/moussaoui/exhibits/defense/941.pdf.
7. Yosri Fouda and Nick Fielding, *Masterminds of Terror: The Truth Behind the Most Devastating Terrorist Attack the World Has Ever Seen* (Edinburgh: Mainstream, 2003), p. 135.

start looking for them; it claimed to be searching for the three men unsuccessfully, but the 9/11 Commission found "no evidence of any tracking efforts actually being undertaken by anyone"; it failed to report their departure when they left and to respond promptly to the query from Kuala Lumpur station asking about Almihdhar's whereabouts; it then claimed that it was having trouble obtaining the departure information, although it either already had it or could obtain it easily; and when it finally reported the departure of the two men, it failed to name Almihdhar in its cable.

Some of these errors, such as the failure to pick up surveillance at the airport, may seem genuine errors of the sort made by all complex organizations. However, Bangkok station's behavior when being queried about the cable is highly suspicious. Why claim it did not have the departure information and would have difficulty obtaining it, when it probably already had it or could get it easily? And why omit Almihdhar's name from the March 5 cable?

Contrast this with Kuala Lumpur station. It can certainly be criticized for not bugging the summit, or rather not having the Malaysians do it. Despite this, the list of its failures is shorter, and there is no occasion where credulity must necessarily be stretched beyond the breaking point to believe an explanation.

In addition, on more than one occasion Kuala Lumpur station took actions to assist tracking of the hijackers that were above and beyond what was required of it. The first occurred when it prodded Bangkok station for the departure information about Almihdhar mentioned above. This cable caused serious problems for Bangkok station, which was forced to make the improbable claim it did not have the information and would have trouble getting it, and then to report on Alhazmi's travel to the US.

A second is noted in a cable sent in response to Bangkok's March 5 cable reporting the travel by Alhazmi and an associate to the US. This cable, dated the next day, commented that Bangkok's cable had been read "with interest."[8] The station that sent this cable is not named, although Kuala Lumpur is a likely candidate, as it was this station that requested the departure information from Bangkok. This cable was widely cited during the post-9/11 investigations and proved embarrassing to the Agency.

---

8. Justice Department IG report, p. 248.

The third occasion was a visit to Kuala Lumpur by FBI agent Frank Pellegrino looking for Khalid Shaikh Mohammed some time after the summit. Fellow Bureau agent Jack Cloonan reportedly stated that, at a meeting with Pellegrino, the local CIA station chief took out some of the surveillance photos and said, "I'm not supposed to show these photographs, but here. Take a look at these photographs. Know any of these guys?"[9] These are simply not the actions of a person trying to hide information from the Bureau.

Kuala Lumpur station's apparent non-involvement in a plot to withhold information from the Bureau lends some support to the conclusion suggested above that Cofer Black and George Tenet were not aware of what was going on at the time. If the effort to withhold the information was "official" CIA policy blessed by Blee's superiors, why was one of the field stations not on board?

* * *

Alec Station apparently did nothing with the March 5, 2000 cable, did not watchlist the two men, and did not inform the FBI that a pair of top al-Qaeda operatives had entered the US. Watchlisting the men would at least have prevented Almihdhar from re-entering the US in July 2001, and informing the FBI would have led to surveillance of them, which would probably have prevented both the *Cole* bombing and 9/11.

It is unclear who read the cable from Bangkok reporting Alhazmi's and his companion's entry into the US at this time, and who is therefore responsible for these failures. However, Tom Wilshire was a manager involved in the operation, and he did access the cable in May 2001, when very little was done again.

Wilshire commented on this in his statement to the Congressional Inquiry:

> Later, in early March 2000, long after the dust had settled in Malaysia, information surfaced indicating that Almihdhar's partner was named Nawaf Alhazmi. In early March the CIA also received information indicating that Alhazmi had booked a flight

9. Peter Lance, *Triple Cross: How bin Laden's Master Spy Penetrated the CIA, the Green Berets, and the FBI-and Why Patrick Fitzgerald Failed to Stop Him* (New York: Regan, 2006), p. 340. It is unclear which photos Pellegrino saw, and there is no mention of him seeing the video. He was an experienced agent knowledgeable of al-Qaeda and should have been able to identify "Hambali" and KSM.

that terminated in Los Angles on 15 January 2000. Again, the new information on Alhazmi was not disseminated.

There are significant omissions here: the March 5 cable did not just say that Alhazmi had booked a flight, but also said that he had traveled to the US and that he had been accompanied by a companion on the flight.

Wilshire was asked again about this during the questioning. He replied,

It's very difficult to understand what happened with that cable when it came in. I do not know exactly why it was missed. It would appear that it was missed completely.[10]

The reply is strikingly similar to the explanation he gave for failing to pass on the information about Almihdhar's US visa: "Something apparently was dropped somewhere and we don't know where that was."

Given that we know Wilshire and "Michelle" purposefully blocked the passage of information about Almihdhar to the FBI, it appears that the failure to share the information at this time was also deliberate. The alternative would be that Alec Station purposefully withheld information in January, but had forgotten all about the purposeful withholding by March, when it failed to pass on the same information through some unexplained mishap.

* * *

One of the most remarkable aspects of this episode is sworn testimony provided to the Congressional Inquiry by CIA Director Tenet, when he was questioned about this cable by Senator Carl Levin on October 17, 2002 (emphases added):

SEN. LEVIN: ... Now, then we come to March 5th, same year, 2000, and the CIA learns some additional information, very critical information. On March 5th the CIA learns that Alhazmi had actually entered the United States on January 15th, seven

10. For this and the prior quote, see US Congress, The House Permanent Select Committee On Intelligence and the Senate Select Committee On Intelligence, The Intelligence Community's Knowledge of the September 11 Hijackers Prior to September 11, 2001: Hearing before the Joint Inquiry of the Senate Select Committee on Intelligence and the House Permanent Select Committee on Intelligence, September 20, 2002.

days after leaving the al-Qaeda meeting in Malaysia. So now the CIA knows Alhazmi is in the United States, but the CIA still doesn't put Alhazmi or Almihdhar on the watch list and still does not notify the FBI about a very critical fact, a known al-Qaeda operative—we're at war with al-Qaeda—a known al-Qaeda operative got into the United States. My question is do you know specifically why the FBI was not notified of that critical fact at that time?

MR. TENET: The cable that came in from the field at the time, sir, was labeled information only and *I know that nobody read that cable.*

SEN. LEVIN: But my question is do you know why the FBI was not notified of the fact that an al-Qaeda operative now was known in March of the year 2000 to have entered the United States? Why did the CIA not specifically notify the FBI?

MR. TENET: Sir, if we weren't aware of it when it came into headquarters we couldn't have notified them. *Nobody read that cable in the March timeframe.*

SEN. LEVIN: So that the cable that said that Alhazmi had entered the United States came to your headquarters, nobody read it?

MR. TENET: Yes, sir. It was an information only cable from the field and *nobody read that information only cable.*[11]

Here Tenet claimed three times in sworn testimony that nobody read the cable, yet this claim is clearly untrue. According to an extract from the CIA inspector general's report submitted as evidence to the Moussaoui trial (emphasis added):

In early 2000, *numerous* CIA officers in different divisions accessed one or more operational documents that reported Khalid Almihdhar's passport contained a multiple entry visa for the United States and that Nawaf Alhazmi had departed Thailand on a flight bound for Los Angeles. Most of the officers who accessed the documents were in the Counterterrorism Division at that time.[12]

11. "Testimony from the Joint Intelligence Committee," *New York Times*, October 17, 2002, http://www.nytimes.com/2002/10/17/politics/18ITEXT.html?ei=5070&en=9ddb1047607578ac&ex=1227848400&pagewanted=print&position=top.
12. *United States v. Zacarias Moussaoui*, "Substitute for Passage from CIA OIG Report re: Number of CIA persons who reviewed cables after Spring, 2000," July 31, 2006, http://www.vaed.uscourts.

The executive summary of the re-written CIA inspector general's report spells out just how "numerous" these officers were (emphases added):

> In the period January through March 2000, some *50 to 60 individuals* read one or more of six Agency cables containing travel information related to these terrorists. These cables originated in four field locations and Headquarters. They were read by *overseas officers and Headquarters personnel, operations officers and analysts, managers and junior employees, and CIA staff personnel as well as officers on rotation from NSA and FBI.* Over an 18-month period, some of these officers *had opportunities to review the information on multiple occasions,* when they might have recognized its significance and shared it appropriately with other components and agencies.[13]

The claim that "nobody read that cable" was only one of several false statements Tenet and other CIA officers made during the course of the 9/11 investigations. As we will see, most of these statements concerned Khalid Almihdhar and the seemingly botched surveillance of the Malaysia meeting attendees.

The impunity with which Tenet made these false statements is also remarkable. He was under oath before the 9/11 Congressional Inquiry, and the 9/11 Commission must have known he made the statements and must have known they were false, but it issued no public reprimand to Tenet. Indeed, lying under oath is a criminal offense, but no charges have been advanced against Tenet for this or any other of his false statements.

After the 9/11 Commission pointed out in 2004 that Tom Wilshire had actually read the cable,[14] and after the substitute for a passage from the CIA inspector general's report used at the Moussaoui trial in 2006 stated that "numerous officers" had also done so,[15] Tenet offered a different explanation in his 2007 book:

> CIA officers in the field sent this information back to headquarters but included it at the end of a cable that contained routine

gov/notablecases/moussaoui/exhibits/defense/538B.pdf.

13. OIG Report on CIA Accountability With Respect to the 9/11 Attacks, June 2005, p. xiv, http://www.fas.org/irp/cia/product/oig-911.pdf.

14. *9/11 CR*, pp. 267 n63, 537.

15. *United States v. Zacarias Moussaoui*, "Substitute for Passage from CIA OIG Report re: Number of CIA persons who reviewed cables after Spring, 2000," July 31, 2006, http://www.vaed.uscourts. gov/notablecases/moussaoui/exhibits/defense/538B.pdf.

information. The cable was marked as being for "information" rather than "action." Unfortunately, no one—not the CIA officers nor their FBI colleagues detailed to the CTC—connected the name Nawaf Alhazmi with the meeting of eight weeks before.[16]

The claim that nobody connected Alhazmi with the Malaysia summit is ludicrous. For example, the Congressional Inquiry reported,

> The following day, another station [presumably Kuala Lumpur], which had been copied on the cable by the originating station [Bangkok], cabled CTC's bin Laden unit that it had read the cable "with interest," particularly "the information that a member of this group traveled to the U.S. following his visit to Kuala Lumpur."[17]

Tenet offered two erroneous explanations for why nothing was done about this cable. Before doing so, he clearly spent some time personally investigating what went wrong, speaking to the relevant officers, such as "Michelle." There were also weekly meetings at which the CIA review group investigating what went wrong updated Tenet and other CIA leaders about their findings. One of the group's major discoveries was that the CIA might have failed to notify the FBI of Almihdhar and Alhazmi's presence in the US for well over a year, and George Tenet and the other leaders clearly appreciated how damaging this could be for the Agency.[18] Everything suggests that Tenet knew the statements he made were false when he made them.

* * *

The 9/11 Congressional Inquiry was not the only investigation to have this problem with George Tenet. At a private interview with the 9/11 Commission in January 2004, Tenet gave a string of evasive answers, and the Commission doubted he was telling them the full truth. This despite the fact that they took the unusual step of putting Tenet under oath before questioning him, because, according to Philip Shenon, "The CIA's record was full of discrepancies about the facts of its operations against bin Laden before 9/11, and many of the discrepancies were Tenet's." Although Tenet had evidently held all-night cram sessions before the interview, he re-

16. Tenet 2007, p. 197.
17. 9/11 Congressional Inquiry report, p. 147.
18. The meetings are described in Philip Shenon, *The Commission: The Uncensored History of the 9/11 Investigation* (New York: Twelve, 2008), pp. 140-41.

peatedly replied, "I don't remember," "I don't recall," and "Let me go through the documents and get back to you with an answer." Shenon summarized:

> Tenet remembered certain details, especially when he was asked the sorts of questions he was eager to answer ... But on many other questions, his memory was cloudy. The closer the questions came to the events of the spring and summer of 2001 and to the 9/11 attacks themselves, the worse his memory became.

In addition, the memory lapses concerned not only details, but also "entire meetings and key documents." Tenet even said he could not recall what was discussed at his first meeting with President George Bush after his election in 2000, which the Commission found suspicious. Neither could he recall what he told Bush in the morning intelligence briefings in the months leading up to 9/11.

Philip Zelikow, one of the staffers who interviewed Tenet, later said there was no one "a-ha moment" when they realized Tenet was not telling them the full truth, but his constant failure to remember key aspects disturbed them, and in the end "we just didn't believe him." After the meeting, Zelikow allegedly reported to the Commissioners that Tenet perjured himself. The staff and most of the Commissioners came to believe that Tenet was "at best, loose with the facts," and at worst "flirting with a perjury charge." It seems that even Commission Chairman Tom Kean came to believe that Tenet was a witness who would "fudge everything."[19]

One particular thing Tenet failed to recall was a memorandum of notification issued by President Clinton after the African embassy bombings. The memo authorized the CIA to kill Osama bin Laden, using a set of tribal assets that were monitoring him in Afghanistan. Tenet and other CIA leaders repeatedly claimed they had no such authorization, although former National Security Advisor Sandy Berger tipped the Commission off, and the actual document was found.[20] The Commission arranged a final interview of Tenet

---

19. Ibid., pp. 257-60.
20. Clinton issued a series of memos about operations against bin Laden. This memo is the only one that authorized the Agency to kill bin Laden and it only applied to a specific group of tribal CIA assets that were monitoring him. When Clinton was given a draft memo authorizing the CIA to kill bin Laden using other assets, he altered the wording so that the Agency was not so authorized.

in early July 2004, a couple of weeks before *The 9/11 Commission Report* was published, to talk about the memo.

The staff considered the meeting a "final test of Tenet's credibility," but when Philip Zelikow said he wanted to talk about the memo, Tenet replied, "What are you referring to?" Zelikow elaborated, but Tenet said, "I'm not sure what we're talking about." He then claimed to remember an early draft of the memo, which did not authorize the CIA to kill bin Laden. Zelikow explained that the draft Tenet was referring to was an earlier version of the memo, and that a later version, apparently requested by Tenet himself, authorized the CIA to kill bin Laden. Zelikow was unable to bring the actual memo with him, because it was so highly classified, and Tenet still said he did not remember: "Well, as I say, I don't know what you're talking about."

Philip Shenon wrote of this, "Zelikow and [Commission staffer Alexis] Albion looked at each other across the table in disbelief. It was the last straw with Tenet, the final bit of proof they needed to demonstrate that Tenet simply could not tell the truth to the Commission." Zelikow later said he concluded Tenet's memory lapses were not genuine, but "George had decided not to share information on any topic unless we already had documentary proof, and then he would add as little as possible to the record."

Tenet later denied this was the case, and said he could not remember the authorization to kill bin Laden because he had been on vacation when it was signed and transmitted to Afghanistan.[21] However, the 9/11 Commission found that this memo was "given to Tenet." In addition, the final report described the message in which the instructions were communicated to the assets in Afghanistan that were to kill bin Laden as "CIA cable, message from the DCI." DCI, Director of Central Intelligence, was Tenet's official title.[22]

Another false statement of Tenet's, about briefings he gave President Bush in the run-up to 9/11, will also have an important place in the narrative ahead.

We must ask the question: why did Tenet repeatedly make false statements about 9/11? One possible answer is that he genuinely found that the CIA had performed to the best of its ability, but that telling investigators the truth would reveal sensitive informa-

21. Philip Shenon, see note 17, pp. 359-60.
22. *9/11 CR*, pp. 132, 485.

tion. Another is that he was personally involved in the "failures," instructing Richard Blee to withhold information from the FBI, and was covering up for his own wrongdoing. A third is that he realized something bad had gone on, but did not want to look into it for fear of what he might learn, and covered things up deliberately from investigators. The truth is that we do not yet know enough to understand his motivation with certainty.

Finally, we must remark on the 9/11 Commission's treatment of Tenet. They almost certainly thought he had strung together a series of fabrications, but there is not a word about this in the final report. Neither is there anything to suggest they stopped to ask themselves why Tenet had done this.

16

AA 77–3 indiv have been followed since Millennium + Cole

I t seems apparent that the failure of Alec Station to pass on the information about Almihdhar and Alhazmi to the FBI was intentional. The immediate purpose of this must have been to allow people connected to Tom Wilshire and Richard Blee to monitor the two men inside the US undisturbed by the Bureau.

Nawaf Alhazmi and Khalid Almihdhar were not lost, but followed. This was confirmed by a successful FOIA request for notes taken by Principal Deputy Undersecretary of Defense for Policy Stephen Cambone on the afternoon and evening of 9/11. The relevant section of the handwritten notes says,

> AA 77—3 indiv have been followed
> since Millennium + Cole
> 1 guy is assoc of Cole bomber
> 3 entered US in early July
> (2 of 3 pulled aside and interrogated?)[1]

The FOIA request was filed by the blogger Thad Anderson of outragedmoderates.org. Andersen was looking for something else, comments made by Donald Rumsfeld about the response to the attacks and their relation to Saddam Hussein: "Go massive – sweep it all up. Things related and not." However, in its wisdom the Pentagon decided to send him the five lines quoted above as well.

The three individuals who had been followed since the Millennium plot alert are very probably the Alhazmi brothers and Almihdhar, who were monitored in Malaysia and elsewhere at that time. Nawaf Alhazmi and Almihdhar even entered the US at Los Angeles airport, a target of the Millennium plot. Hani Hanjour, the alleged

1. Thad Andersen, "DoD staffer's notes from 9/11 obtained under FOIA," February 16, 2006, http://www.outragedmoderates.org/2006/02/dod-staffers-notes-from-911-obtained.html.

pilot of Flight 77, appeared on the FBI's radar in the mid-1990s during an investigation in Phoenix. Its investigation led to the famous "Phoenix memo,"[2] but Hanjour was gone by the time that was written and was not mentioned in the memo. There are no reports of surveillance of the final Flight 77 hijacker, Majed Moqed, during the Millennium alert and the *Cole* bombing, although a group of trainees he was part of is said to have been briefly detained in Turkey at some point before 9/11.[3]

As we will see, both Alhazmi brothers called the Yemen operations center, which helped coordinate the *Cole* bombing, some time before the attack. However, as set out below, Khalid Almihdhar had numerous links to the attack, and he is the most likely candidate for the "associate of *Cole* bomber." It is hard to determine exactly which *Cole* bomber he was thought to be an associate of, as he associated with several of them, although his ties to Khallad bin Attash seem stronger than they were with the others. Along with Abd al-Rahim al-Nashiri, bin Attash was one of the masterminds of the *Cole* attack, and Almihdhar was photographed standing next to him in Malaysia.

The "3 entered US in early July" is puzzling, as only Almihdhar entered the US in early July, although Salem Alhazmi entered the US on June 29, together with Abdulaziz Alomari, an alleged Flight 11 hijacker.

There are no reports of Almihdhar and Salem Alhazmi being pulled aside and "interrogated"—possibly a reference to a secondary inspection—upon arrival. However, there is information indicating some of the hijackers were questioned with a reasonable degree of thoroughness on arrival. For example, according to the FBI's timeline for the hijackers, on May 2, 2001, the day Moqed and Ahmed Alghamdi entered the US: "INS inspector [name redacted] stated that [name redacted, evidently Alghamdi] commented to him that the media distorts the facts about UBL [Osama bin Laden] and th[at] UBL is a good Muslim."[4]

2. The Phoenix Memo was drafted by FBI agent Ken Williams in July 2001. It reported that a number of suspicious people linked to Sunni extremism were taking flying lessons in the area.
3. Chris Gourlay and Jonathan Calvert, "Al-Qaeda kingpin: I trained 9/11 hijackers," *Sunday Times* (London), November 25, 2007, http://www.timesonline.co.uk/tol/news/world/europe/article2936761.ece.
4. Federal Bureau of Investigation, "Working Draft Chronology of Events for Hijackers," October 2001, p. 139, http://www.historycommons.org/sourcedocuments/2001/pdfs/fbi911time-

One cannot help but wonder what motivated a suicide terrorist determined to attack the US to inform the first American official he met upon arrival of his admiration for bin Laden. This was definitely an unwise move by Alghamdi and a serious error of tradecraft. Did he simply blurt this out, or was it the result of more thorough questioning? According to media reports, at this time Alghamdi was a subject in a customs investigation into terrorism finance,[5] so there certainly would be reason to question him in depth.

The notes' statement that three of the hijackers were actually under surveillance at this time is supported by a response that had been sent by the CIA to an unidentified foreign service over eighteen months earlier, in February 2000. According to the 9/11 Congressional Inquiry:

> [… in February 2000, CIA rejected a request from foreign authorities to become involved [in the hunt for Almihdhar] because CIA was in the middle of an investigation "to determine what the subject is up to]."[6]

The identity of the foreign authorities is not known, although the list of potential candidates would certainly include Saudi Arabia, Yemen, the United Arab Emirates, Malaysia, Thailand, and possibly the NSA's aforementioned four major partners.

According to its post-9/11 claims, the CIA forgot all about Almihdhar and Alhazmi after January 15, 2000, and moved on to other things. Yet here we have a contemporary communication referencing him, and an investigation into him, while he was in the US. Any investigation to determine what he was up to would logically look at his movements and contacts where he was, which was inside the US.

---

line1-105.pdf. According to the Commission's Terrorist Travel report, Moqed and Alghamdi were not referred to a secondary inspector. Alghamdi's customs declaration indicated he had more than $10,000 on him, but the Customs inspector who processed him did not fill out the relevant electronic forms.

5. See, for example, John Mintz and Allan Lengel, "FBI Arrests Kuwaiti Liquor Store Clerk," *Washington Post*, September 21, 2001, http://nucnews.net/nucnews/2001nn/0109nn/010921nn.htm#590; "Chicago's Ties to Terrorism," *ABC 7*, January 31, 2002, http://web.archive.org/web/20020210003327/http://abclocal.go.com/wls/news/013102_ss_tiestoterrorism.html; Tim Golden with Judith Miller, "Bin Laden Operative Is Linked To Suspects," *New York Times*, September 18, 2001, http://www.nytimes.com/2001/09/18/us/a-nation-challenged-the-plot-bin-laden-operative-is-linked-to-suspects.html?scp=1&sq=Bin%20Laden%20Operative%20Is%20Linked%20To%20Suspects.

6. 9/11 Congressional Inquiry report, p. 147.

This string of failures over the twenty months before 9/11 is incredible in its own right. The fact that the failures are attributable to either Tom Wilshire or his associates makes them doubly so. The Cambone notes can only act to further increase our skepticism of the official history. It seems unbelievable that the CIA picked some of the hijackers up, lost them in bizarre circumstances, missed multiple opportunities to inform the FBI, lied about this repeatedly, and then, hours after the 9/11 attacks, somehow was able to tell the Principal Deputy Undersecretary of Defense for Policy that some of the plotters had been followed for over a year and a half.

17

The FBI could have potentially linked them through financial records to the other Flight 77 hijackers

Although Tom Wilshire and Richard Blee were primarily withholding information about two of the nineteen hijackers from the Bureau, surveillance of Khalid Almihdhar and Nawaf Alhazmi by the FBI would have led to most or all of the others.

The hijackers' operational security and tradecraft were poor. The teams that would hijack each plane were not kept apart from each other. Neither were the alleged pilots (Mohamed Atta, Marwan Alshehhi, Hani Hanjour and Ziad Jarrah) kept separate from the "muscle" hijackers, whose job it was to subdue the passengers. Rather, members of the various teams intermingled with each other, and the pilots intermingled with the muscle hijackers. This meant that the discovery of one member of the conspiracy by the authorities would enable them to find most or all other members of the plot relatively easily.

For the sake of illustration, here are a few examples of how Almihdhar and Alhazmi were linked to the other hijackers and how the others were interlinked:

- Upon arriving in the US on July 4, 2001, Almihdhar briefly stayed in a hotel in New York and then moved to Paterson, New Jersey, living in the same apartment as some of the other hijackers. These other hijackers included Hani Hanjour, the alleged pilot of Flight 77, which hit the Pentagon, as well as the other three alleged hijackers of that flight, Nawaf and Salem Alhazmi, and Majed Moqed. Also living there were Ahmed Alghamdi, who would hijack Flight 175, the second plane to hit the World Trade Center, and Abdulaziz Alomari, who would hijack Flight 11, the first plane to hit the

World Trade Center.[1] Alomari and Alghamdi flew to Florida on August 7,[2] where they met the main bulk of the hijackers based there.

- Not only did Almihdhar live with the other hijackers, he also obtained documents with them. For example, according to the 9/11 Commission's staff report on Terrorist Travel, on July 10, 2001, Almihdhar, Nawaf Alhazmi, and Alomari obtained USA ID cards in New Jersey (note: these cards were not official government documents, but were issued in a system administered by a private company based in Florida). Salem Alhazmi, Majed Moqed and Ahmed Alghamdi also obtained these ID cards around the same time.[3] According to FBI Director Robert Mueller III, alleged Flight 11 pilot Mohamed Atta also purchased a USA ID card from the same business.[4]

- Another example of mass document acquisition dated from early August 2001. On August 1, Hanjour and Almihdhar obtained Virginia identification cards using a falsely certified local address. The same address was later used by Moqed and Salem Alhazmi to obtain Virginia ID, and by Hanjour when he helped alleged Flight 93 pilot Ziad Jarrah obtain a Virginia ID card later in the month. Alghamdi and Alomari also obtained Virginia ID cards at the same time.[5]

---

1. *9/11 CR*, pp. 230, 240.
2. Ibid., p. 248.
3. For the issue of the cards see the 9/11 Commission's Terrorist Travel report, pp. 27-28. There is some confusion about exactly when, where and how many of these USA ID cards were issued to the hijackers, and the account in the Terrorist Travel report may be incomplete or inaccurate in some ways. Nevertheless, it appears some were issued to them, and one, or perhaps two (accounts differ), were later found in the rubble at the Pentagon.
4. "Statement for the Record, FBI Director Robert S. Mueller III," Joint Intelligence Committee Inquiry, September 26, 2002, http://www.fas.org/irp/congress/2002_hr/092602mueller.html. Atta's USA ID card is not mentioned in the 9/11 Commission's Terrorist Travel report. Mueller's claim that the six hijackers other than Atta obtained New Jersey USA ID cards is partially inaccurate: Almihdhar's card is for New York, not New Jersey, as can be seen from an image of the card reproduced on page 192 of the 9/11 Commission's staff report on Terrorist Travel. Mueller's claim that all the cards were issued by Apollo Travel is also questionable, as Mohamed El-Atriss, a businessman not associated with Apollo travel, was later found guilty of issuing Almihdhar with his USA ID card; see Peter Lance, *Triple Cross* (New York: Regan, 2006), pp. 372-73. The expiration dates on the three cards that have been made public also indicate that they were issued in late December 2000, not in July 2001; see Timothy J. Burger, "Was Mohammed Atta Overlooked?" *Time*, August 21, 2005, http://www.time.com/time/magazine/article/0,9171,1096480,00.html. The whole episode of the USA ID cards is bizarre and confusing.
5. Terrorist Travel report, p. 29.

- While on a trip to Florida, on June 25, Nawaf Alhazmi obtained a Florida driving license, listing the same address as two Florida-based hijackers.[6]

- The hijackers arrived in the US together. Ahmed Alghamdi (Flight 175) arrived with Moqed (Flight 77) on May 2, 2001; Hamza Alghamdi and Mohand Alshehri (both Flight 175) arrived with Ahmed Alnami (Flight 93) on May 28; Ahmed Alhaznawi (Flight 93) arrived with Wail Alshehri (Flight 11) on June 8; Saeed Alghamdi (Flight 93) arrived with Fayez Ahmed Banihammad (Flight 175) on June 27; and Salem Alhazmi (Flight 77) arrived with Alomari (Flight 11) on June 29.[7]

- The hijackers banked together. For example, Ahmed Alghamdi (Flight 175), Nawaf Alhazmi and Moqed (both Flight 77) all opened accounts with the Dime Savings Bank on July 9, 2001; Hanjour, Almihdhar, Salem Alhazmi (all Flight 77) and Alomari (Flight 11) also opened accounts with the Hudson United Bank around the same time; Almihdhar and Hanjour opened accounts with the First Union National Bank around the same time.[8]

Regarding the links among the hijackers shown by the banking transactions, the 9/11 Commission noted,

Among other things [the hijackers] used the debit cards to pay for hotel rooms—activity that would have enabled the FBI to locate them, had the FBI been able to get the transaction records fast enough. Moreover, [Nawaf] Alhazmi used his debit card on August 27 to buy tickets for himself ... and fellow Flight 77 hijacker Salem Alhazmi. If the FBI had found either Almihdhar or Nawaf Alhazmi, it could have found the other. They not only shared a common bank but frequently were together when conducting transactions. After locating Almihdhar and Alhazmi, the FBI could have potentially linked them through financial records to

6. Ibid., p. 26; Steve Bousquet and Alisa Ulferts, "Hijackers Got State IDs Legally," *St. Petersburg Times*, September 16, 2001.
7. *9/11 CR*, pp. 527-28 n114.
8. *United States v. Zacarias Moussaoui*, "Hijackers' True Name Usage Chart," July 31, 2006, http://www.vaed.uscourts.gov/notablecases/moussaoui/exhibits/prosecution/OG00013.pdf; *United States v. Zacarias Moussaoui*, "Chronology of Events for Hijackers, 8/16/01 – 9/11/01, Khalid al-Mihdhar," http://www.vaed.uscourts.gov/notablecases/moussaoui/exhibits/prosecution/OG00020-11.pdf; *United States v. Zacarias Moussaoui*, "Chronology of Events for Hijackers, 8/16/01 – 9/11/01, Hani Hanjour," http://www.vaed.uscourts.gov/notablecases/moussaoui/exhibits/prosecution/OG00020-09.pdf.

the other Flight 77 hijackers ... Nawaf Alhazmi and Flight 77 pilot Hani Hanjour had opened separate savings accounts at the same small New Jersey bank at the same time and both gave the same address. On July 9, 2001, the other Flight 77 muscle hijacker, Majed Moqed, opened an account at another small New Jersey bank at the same time as Nawaf Alhazmi, and used the same address. Given timely access to the relevant records and sufficient time to conduct a follow-up investigation, the FBI could have shown that Hani Hanjour, Majed Moqed, and Salem Alhazmi were connected to potential terrorist operatives Almihdhar and Nawaf Alhazmi.[9]

This is an understatement by the 9/11 Commission. Almihdhar and Nawaf Alhazmi could not only have been tied to the other three Pentagon hijackers, but also Alomari and Alghamdi, who would go on to hijack the two planes that hit the World Trade Center. In addition, they could be linked to other plotters such as Jarrah and Atta.

In this context it is worth noting that Global Objectives, a British banking compliance company, identified fifteen of the nineteen hijackers as high-risk individuals and established database profiles for them before the attacks. According to the Associated Press, the hijackers in the database were suspicious because they were "identified as people linked to Osama bin Laden, suspected terrorists or associates of terrorists." The list of high-risk people maintained by Global Objectives was available to dozens of banks, and the hijackers' files contain their dates and places of birth, aliases, and associates. It is unclear which fifteen hijackers were considered high-risk.[10]

There were obviously more connections between the hijackers than contained in this brief summary, for example they lived together in Florida, banked together there, met in Las Vegas, and, of course, booked tickets for the same flights on 9/11, sometimes in pairs.

* * *

These connections are of dual significance. First, they show that if the FBI had been informed of Almihdhar's and Alhazmi's presence

9. National Commission on Terrorist Attacks upon the United States, Monograph on Terrorist Financing, Staff Report to the Commission, pp. 58-59, 141, http://govinfo.library.unt.edu/911/staff_statements/911_TerrFin_Monograph.pdf.
10. Catherine Wilson, "British Banking Database Listed 15 of 19 Hijackers before Attack," Associated Press, February 21, 2002.

in the US at the right time, they could have found the other hijackers, or at least some of them, and stopped the plot.

Second, occasions when the Alec station group failed to share information with the FBI about Alhazmi and Almihdhar are highlighted throughout this book. It is reasonable to conclude that the information was withheld for a purpose that included uninterrupted monitoring of the hijackers, with some end in mind. This conclusion is supported by the hijackers' claims they were followed, the February 2000 e-mail that said the CIA was in the middle of an investigation to determine what Almihdhar was up to, and Stephen Cambone's notes, which stated that three of the Pentagon hijackers were followed.

Such surveillance must have uncovered the other operatives connected to Alhazmi and Almihdhar, and it is hard to imagine that it could have missed their immediately suspicious multiple plane ticket purchases for 9/11. However, the presumed off-the-books surveillance linked to Richard Blee clearly did not prevent 9/11, and no known action was taken against the hijackers based on this surveillance.

If the activities of the Alec Station group are viewed as being directed by people who wanted to protect the US, then this inaction makes no sense. Later, we will see that Tom Wilshire, one of the key officers in the concealment of the information, was almost certainly aware of an impending attack before 9/11 and aware Almihdhar might be part of it, but continued to hamper the FBI's efforts. It is highly likely that Blee was aware of the same information.

We have a period of high threat in the summer of 2001, a group of terrorists under surveillance known to be linked to the threat, and suspicious activity—flight training, the mass ticket purchase for 9/11—by these terrorists. Yet we have inaction by those performing the surveillance. How should we interpret this inaction?

The initial reaction to learning of the first failure—to pass on the information about Almihdhar's visa in January 2000—may be to presume that it must simply have been a genuine failure. The initial reaction to learning that the multiple failures were made by a group of people all linked to Wilshire may be to presume that somebody linked to Alec Station was simply having the hijackers monitored in the hopes of penetrating al-Qaeda. However, this presumption is highly questionable: it is hard to imagine circumstances under which these hijackers, under surveillance by people wishing to prevent the attacks, could successfully have carried out their mission.

Given the high-threat alert and the fact that Wilshire and apparently Blee were aware Almihdhar was of "very high interest" in connection with threatened attacks, it is highly unlikely that surveillance of the hijackers would be terminated or downgraded over the summer of 2001. If anything, it should have been further increased because of the threat and because of the illegal nature of what the Alec Station group was doing—keeping the information from the FBI and probably running an off-the-books operation inside the US itself.

However, if we view the actions of the group of people around Wilshire and Blee as actions with the aim of enabling attacks, then they make perfect sense. They hide the hijackers from the FBI, put them under surveillance, realize an attack is coming, watch the nineteen buying tickets and sit back to see what happens.

Any claim that at least one of the Alec Station group did not desire the actual outcome should explain why the surveillance operation was not shut down and the hijackers thrown out of the country during the threat alert for reasons of prudence, and how the surveillance missed the rather obvious clues to the operation that was carried out. I am unable to construct credible scenarios in which the group let the surveillance run during the threat alert and also missed the clues to the plot.

Part 3: San Diego

| 740 | 3/20/2000 | TEL | Khalid Al-Mihdhar | The San Diego telephone number associated with NAWAF AL- HAZMI [redacted] made a call which lasted 16 minutes to Yemen [redacted] This is the telephone number subscribed to by AHMED [redacted] AL-MIHDHAR's father-in-law, who is associated with the |

Enlarged portion of Hijackers Timeline document below (rotated upper left), showing monitored call on March 20, 2000 from known al-Qaeda operative Nawaf Alhazmi's phone in San Diego to the organization's Yemen communications hub.

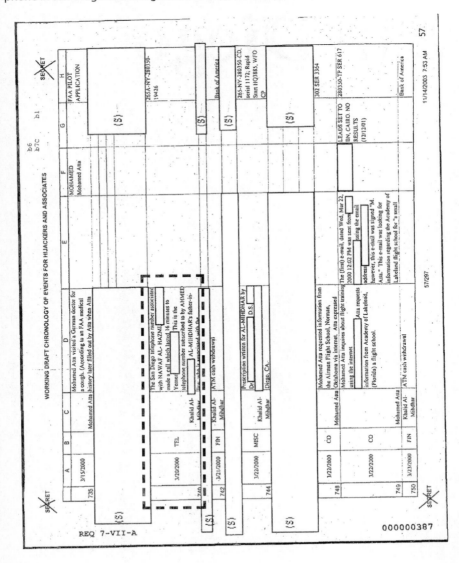

18

Two al-Qaeda guys living in California—are you kidding me?

Khalid Almihdhar and Nawaf Alhazmi had arrived in California on January 15, 2000. Some accounts say they stayed briefly in Los Angeles and then moved to San Diego; some evidence indicates they went straight to San Diego. When they got there, they began associating with known extremists, alleged agents of the Saudi government, and a contact of the "Blind Sheikh," Sheikh Omar Abdul-Rahman. By this point the Yemen hub had been under surveillance by the NSA and CIA for some time, and Almihdhar had just been put on the NSA's watch list.[1]

Perhaps the most important thing they did in their year in southern California was to make a few calls. The calls were back to the Yemen hub, the operations center run by Almihdhar's father-in-law, Ahmed al-Hada. As President Bush admitted in the President's Radio Address of December 17, 2005,

> Two of the terrorist hijackers who flew a jet into the Pentagon, Nawaf Alhazmi and Khalid Almihdhar, communicated while they were in the United States to other members of al-Qaeda who were overseas.

First of all, some basic questions: Who made the calls? How many were there? When were they made? What was said? What exactly did the NSA do with the intercepts? And what information was disseminated to other agencies?

---

1. 9/11 Commission Staff Statement No. 2, "Three Hijackers: Identification, Watchlisting and Tracking," http://www.9-11commission.gov/staff_statements/staff_statement_2.pdf. The Commission states that this watchlisting by the NSA had "limited effectiveness," although it is unclear what this means. The 9/11 Congressional Inquiry report has an extremely cryptic, but possibly related, redacted passage on page 157: "[In mid-January 2000, NSA queried its databases for information concerning Khalid [... ... ...]. These queries remained active until May 2000, but did not uncover any information]." The phrase "queries remained active" may be redacted-speak for watchlisting.

Most importantly, why did the NSA not wrap up the plot based on these intercepts? The NSA intercepted them. The NSA knew the calls were between the Yemen hub and the US. The NSA had the technical capability to trace the calls inside the US. By this point it knew that both Alhazmi and Almihdhar were al-Qaeda terrorists and associated them with the operations center in Yemen they were calling. Yet the NSA later said that it failed to trace the calls. It certainly should have done so and informed the FBI, but why did this not happen?

Who made the calls? The hijacker most frequently said to have made the calls is Almihdhar, although, as we can see from the above statement by Bush, Alhazmi also made or received some of the calls. In addition, according to Tom Brokaw of MSNBC, "Investigators say that phone numbers in Yemen called by associates of the hijackers in the weeks before the attacks also show up in the phone records of bin Laden recruits who were involved in the bombing of those US Embassies in Africa in 1998."[2] The names of the associates are not known, but Khallad bin Attash is thought to have made calls to the hub, and Ramzi bin al-Shibh, coordinator of the 9/11 attacks and reportedly a cousin of Almihdhar's wife,[3] is another candidate.

Some calls were made from mobile phones,[4] others were made from the apartment phone.[5] Incredibly, this phone was registered to Alhazmi in his real name.[6] The NSA intercepted these calls, knew Alhazmi was an al-Qaeda operative and associated him with the Yemen hub, as it had previously intercepted calls he made to it. Had the NSA traced the calls and learned the subscriber's name, it would have had no trouble realizing their importance.

The question of how many calls were made is murkier. The Congressional Inquiry report just says "communications," although it later says information from "some" of the communications was

---

2. "Phone records show links to Osama bin Laden," MSNBC, October 3, 2001.
3. For the claim that Almihdhar and bin al-Shibh were related see Oliver Schröm, "Deadly Mistakes," Die Zeit, October 2, 2002, http://www.antiwar.com/article.php?articleid=2305.
4. Bamford 2008, p. 25; Terry McDermott, Perfect Soldiers: The 9/11 Hijackers, Who They Were, Why They Did It (London: Pontico's, 2005), p. 296.
5. See, for example, Justice Department IG report, p. 259; also 9/11 CR, p. 222.
6. Michael Isikoff and Daniel Klaidman, "The Hijackers We Let Escape," Newsweek, June 2, 2002, http://holtz.org/Library/ToFile/The%20Hijackers%20We%20Let%20Escape.htm.

disseminated,[7] presumably meaning there were at least three. Most media accounts simply refer to multiple calls, although Lawrence Wright wrote that there were eight made by Almihdhar from San Diego, where he lived from January or February 2000 to June of the same year.[8] A senior US counterterrorism official told the *Los Angeles Times* that there were "half a dozen" calls,[9] and MSNBC opted for "a dozen calls."[10]

When were they made? According to MSNBC, the first call was "early 2000, days after the two hijackers settle into [a] San Diego apartment." The hijackers are generally thought to have arrived in San Diego in early February, although it may have been earlier. One of the calls was placed from San Diego to Yemen on March 20, 2000, and lasted sixteen and a half minutes.[11] According to MSNBC, "The final call from Yemen to the hijackers came only weeks before 9/11." The fact of this last call is most remarkable, as this was after the bombing of the USS *Cole* in Yemen, an attack reportedly coordinated from the Yemen hub, and came at a time the threat level in the US was very high.

What was said? One version is that Almihdhar was merely talking to his wife, who lived at the operations center with her father. For example, in 2006 Lawrence Wright wrote that the calls Almihdhar made from San Diego were "to talk to his wife, who was about to give birth."[12] In 2008 James Bamford wrote that the March 20 call was "probably to check on his then pregnant wife."

The first known version of this story was in *The 9/11 Commission Report*, which said, "Almihdhar's mind seems to have been with his family back in Yemen, as evidenced by calls he made from the apartment telephone."[13] The 9/11 Commission's account of the

7. Congressional Inquiry report, p. 157.

8. Lawrence Wright, "The Agent: Did the C.I.A. stop an F.B.I. Detective from Preventing 9/11?" *New Yorker*, July 10 and 17, 2006, http://www.lawrencewright.com/WrightSoufan.pdf.

9. Josh Meyer, "Officials Fault Case Bush Cited; Internal breakdowns, not shortcomings in spy laws, were at play before Sept. 11, they say," *Los Angeles Times*, December 21, 2005, http://articles.latimes.com/2005/dec/21/nation/na-targets21.

10. *Hardball Special Edition for July 24, 2004*, MSNBC, transcript.

11. Justice Department IG report, p. 259; Federal Bureau of Investigation, "Working Draft Chronology of Events for Hijackers," October 2001, p. 57, http://www.historycommons.org/sourcedocuments/2001/pdfs/fbi911timeline1-105.pdf.

12. Lawrence Wright, see note 8.

13. *9/11 CR*, p. 222.

Yemen hub calls is intensely problematic and will be examined in depth below.

In the simplistic code used by al-Qaeda mentioned in Chapter One, being heavily pregnant had another, more sinister meaning. A presidential daily brief item provided to President Clinton on December 4, 1998 stated,

> Bin Laden associates last month discussed picking up a package in Malaysia. One told his colleague in Malaysia that "they" were in the "ninth month [of pregnancy]."[14]

Of course, it is more likely for a married woman to be pregnant than a group of men, but if pregnancy was mentioned on the calls, there is reason to withhold judgment about what the parties were really talking about. This is especially true as the two occasions on which Almihdhar reportedly returned home to Yemen to see his wife preceded the attacks on *The Sullivans* and the *Cole*, attacks in which he seems to have been involved.

There are other good reasons to doubt that all the calls were simply marital chit-chat. It is certainly possible that Almihdhar may have spent some time on the phone talking to his wife, but, given that the Yemen hub was al-Qaeda's operations center and that Almihdhar and Alhazmi were leading operatives in the organization's signature mission, there are certainly grounds to speculate that operational information was passed on in the phone calls, and overheard by the NSA. Indeed, the Congressional Inquiry report explicitly states that some of the information the NSA learned from the calls met NSA reporting thresholds and was disseminated to other agencies.[15]

Further, some of the calls are said to have been made by Nawaf Alhazmi, who was reportedly in the US without Almihdhar from June 2000 until July 2001. It is highly unlikely he would have spoken solely to Almihdhar's wife. Additionally, according to a press release issued by the Yemeni embassy in the US, "U.S. intelligence officials, speaking on condition of anonymity, said that intercepts of al-Qaeda communications indicate that the al-Hada family phone was used to relay messages both to the embassy bombers and the

14. Ibid., p. 129.
15. 9/11 Congressional Inquiry report, p. 157.

Sept. 11 hijackers."[16] Other reasons for doubting the primarily personal nature of these calls will be pointed out in the chapter on their treatment by the 9/11 Commission.

Even less is known about what exactly the NSA did with the intercepts and what information was disseminated to other agencies. The main source for this is the Congressional Inquiry report, which simply says, "Some of these communications met NSA reporting thresholds and were reported to FBI, CIA, and other customers, but some did not."[17] However, we also know that after 9/11, FBI investigators discovered "several key NSA dispatches" related to the hub and asked Dan Coleman, a leading FBI expert on al-Qaeda, about them.[18] Where the dispatches were discovered, what had been done with them before 9/11, and what was in them is not known.

Investigative reporters Joe and Susan Trento also found the CIA began cutting the FBI off from NSA material in early 2001:

> Another bizarre move by the CIA began in early 2001, shortly after George Bush's inauguration. At that point STATION ALEC ... began to cut the FBI off from NSA material tracking al-Qaeda members. By withholding from the FBI the identities of al-Qaeda members, as well as message traffic, the CIA effectively ended any chance in the months leading up to 9/11 of discovering that these Saudi nationals were actually al-Qaeda agents destined to play major roles in the 9/11 attacks.[19]

Presumably, the dispatches were sent to the CIA, where they would logically be routed to Alec Station. We do not know who read them there or what was done with them, although we do know that Tom Wilshire was aware of the December 1999 report of the intercept from the Yemen hub that said Almihdhar and Alhazmi were to travel to Kuala Lumpur.

* * *

16. Embassy of Yemen in Washington, DC, "Yemen Cracks Major Terrorist Super Cell," February 13, 2002, http://www.scoop.co.nz/stories/HL0310/S00257.htm.
17. 9/11 Congressional Inquiry report, p. 157.
18. Ron Suskind, *The One Percent Doctrine: Deep Inside America's Pursuit of its Enemies Since 9/11* (New York: Simon & Schuster, 2006), p. 94.
19. Susan Trento and Joseph Trento, *Unsafe at Any Altitude: Failed Terrorism Investigations, Scapegoating 9/11, and the Shocking Truth about Aviation Security Today* (Hanover, New Hampshire: Steerforth Press, 2006), p. 194.

The information that the Yemen hub was communicating with a phone number in the US was very important, and this was known at the time. FBI al-Qaeda expert Dan Coleman said that "anyone who called the Yemen number is white-hot, a top suspect."[20]

Wright described the number as "one of the most important pieces of information the FBI would ever discover" and an "intelligence bonanza."[21]

FBI supervisor Kenneth Maxwell said, "Two al-Qaeda guys living in California—are you kidding me? We would have been on them like white on snow: physical surveillance, electronic surveillance, a special unit devoted entirely to them."[22]

Mark Rossini agreed:

> So they come in, we follow them and find out where they're going, listen to their homes, listen to their conversations at their home, or cell phone, whatever. E-mails. The possibilities are endless once you're able to peer into someone's life … You could link back who they were, their connection to bin Laden, the connection to the Yemeni house, etc. You could have gone to any court and any judge in the FISA court and say, "We want a FISA [warrant]on that residence in San Diego." It would have been easy and we would have surveilled them. And we would have learned more information.[23]

Lawrence Wright underlined the point:

> You know, this is the key. The NSA is all over this phone. And everybody, you know, that has any connection with it is drawing links from that phone. Now imagine eight lines from Yemen to San Diego. How obvious would it be that al-Qaeda is in America?[24]

Given the multiple links described above between the hijackers, surveillance by the FBI of Alhazmi and Almihdhar would have led to the rest of them.

20. Ron Suskind, see note 18.
21. Wright 2006, p. 343.
22. Lawrence Wright, see note 8.
23. PBS, *NOVA*, "The Spy Factory," February 3, 2009, http://www.pbs.org/wgbh/nova/transcripts/3602_spyfactory.html.
24. Lawrence Wright, "Inside the Terrorist Plot," *Federal News Service* , October 5, 2006, http://www.cfr.org/publication/11705/.

There are two key questions. Why did the NSA not alert the FBI to the fact the hijackers were in the US? And is there any connection between the NSA's withholding of the information and Alec Station's parallel conduct?

19

CTC sent one officer to NSA for a brief period of time in 2000, but failed to send others, citing resource constraints

Before moving on to the contradictory explanations offered for this failure by the NSA, a brief look at what the CIA was doing is in order.

In 2000, the CIA finally got what it had been battling for with the NSA for years: access to raw transcripts of calls to and from al-Qaeda operatives, including the Yemen hub. We have seen how Alec Station had discovered the hub, had fought with the NSA over it, built its own ground station in the Indian Ocean, got access to the transcripts of calls to the hub just after the embassy bombings, but had then been cut off in short order. Then, it got access to the transcripts again. The CIA's inspector general found:

> In the late 1990s ... NSA managers offered to allow a CTC [Counterterrorist Center] officer to be detailed to NSA to cull the transcripts for useful information. CTC sent one officer to NSA for a brief period of time in 2000, but failed to send others, citing resource constraints.[1]

Bizarre as this may seem, the brief detailing of one CTC officer to the NSA was confirmed by a 9/11 Commission memo about an NSA briefing. It adds:

> When her tour was over they [the NSA] did not get another integree and the computer link was taken out. They were told CTC

---

1. OIG Report on CIA Accountability With Respect to the 9/11 Attacks, June 2005, p. xxiii, http://www.fas.org/irp/cia/product/oig-911.pdf. The main bone of contention between Alec Station and the NSA had been transcripts of calls from the Yemen hub, but the language quoted from of the CIA inspector general's report indicates that the CIA detailee would have access to all al-Qaeda transcripts, not just those of calls to and from the hub.

was short of resources and no one would volunteer to travel to NSA. Some other offices at NSA do have CIA integrees.[2]

This makes no sense. Alec Station had been desperate for access to the intercepts for four years, there were repeated arguments with the NSA, access to them was the thing Michael Scheuer most desired after the embassy bombings, yet, upon being granted its dearest wish, the Counterterrorist Center turned round and said it could not really be bothered.

The importance of these calls to the work of Alec Station cannot be overstated. The material included all calls to and from al-Qaeda's operations center and, once the simplistic code had been cracked, offered a full picture of what the organization was doing and where its operatives were.

Yet, we are led to believe, after a "brief period," the Counterterrorist Center voluntarily renounced all this, saying it could not spare a single officer to go to the NSA, check the intercepts and learn al-Qaeda's plans.

The renunciation was so bizarre that even the rewritten CIA inspector general's report found it hard to stomach, recommending that "an Accountability Board review the performance of the Chiefs of CTC for their failure to detail officers to NSA on a consistent, full-time basis to exploit this material in the years before 9/11."[3]

This is all the stranger because, as the 9/11 Congressional Inquiry found, "An NSA counterterrorism supervisor noted that the productivity of NSA analysts was substantially increased when a CIA analyst with access to Directorate of Operations cables was detailed to NSA."[4]

Here is an alternative explanation: although the CIA had been unable to obtain the intercepts independently at the start, it had by now managed to acquire them somehow. For example, it was reported that the CIA had bugged the house, and it would hardly have been a difficult matter to obtain access to the phone locally,

2. 9/11 Commission, "Memo of NSA Briefing for 9/11 Commission on Interactions with CIA," May 19, 2004, http://www.scribd.com/doc/23252628/Memo-of-NSA-Briefing-for-9-11-Commission-on-Interctions-with-CIA.

3. OIG Report on CIA Accountability With Respect to the 9/11 Attacks, June 2005, p. xxiii, http://www.fas.org/irp/cia/product/oig-911.pdf. A list of officials whose performances the OIG recommended be reviewed by accounatability boards is provided on pages 68-69 herein.

4. 9/11 Congressional Inquiry report, p. 356.

for example by asking Yemen's security services to arrange it, or simply bribing a telecom engineer.

What is important in this context is the difference between Scheuer and Blee. While Scheuer is perceived as a tough-guy character by the media due to his support for policy positions such as the permissibility of torture, he was an analyst. But Blee was a real case officer, trained in the arts that the public usually associates with CIA officers. In addition, he had served in unglamorous postings in Bangui, Central African Republic, and Niamey, Niger, as well in the dangerous environment of Algeria during the bloody civil war there, and would naturally have had a standing different from Scheuer's in the eyes of CIA case agents in postings where the comfort level was not so high.

We will see below that someone at Alec Station was in close contact with one of the CIA officers stationed in Yemen, and that the station there withheld information about Almihdhar from the FBI agents investigating the USS *Cole* bombing.

We should also consider what the local services were doing in Yemen. The Yemeni government had an uneasy relationship with the Islamic militants it harbored, and it sometimes clashed with them, such as after the kidnapping of western tourists in late 1998. The government certainly would have had reason to monitor al-Hada's calls itself, and the local CIA station could have got its information from the Yemenis.

20

[... NSA regularly provided information about these targets to the FBI ...]

Varying explanations have been advanced to explain why the NSA did not trace the US end of the calls and alert the FBI, which would then have placed the hijackers under surveillance and stopped the plot. The intercepts were first revealed by the 9/11 Congressional Inquiry, which also offered the first excuse about why the calls were not exploited. This explanation was largely based on statements made to it by NSA Director Michael Hayden.

As this is one of the key issues, this section of its report will be quoted at length:

> [There were also gaps between NSA's coverage of foreign communications and the FBI's coverage of domestic communications that suggest a lack of sufficient attention to the domestic threat. Prior to September 11, neither agency focused on the importance of identifying and then ensuring coverage of communications between the United States and suspected terrorist-associated facilities abroad [... ... ...]. Consistent with its focus on communications abroad, NSA adopted a policy that avoided intercepting the communications between individuals in the United States and foreign countries].
>
> NSA adopted this policy even though the collection of such communications is within its mission and it would have been possible for NSA to obtain FISA Court authorization for such collection. NSA Director Hayden testified to the Joint Inquiry that NSA did not want to be perceived as targeting individuals in the United States and believed that the FBI was instead responsible for conducting such surveillance. NSA did not, however, develop a plan with the FBI to collect and to ensure the dissemination of any relevant foreign intelligence to appropriate domestic agencies....

Disconnecting the Dots

[The Joint Inquiry has learned that one of the future hijackers communicated with a known terrorist facility in the Middle East while he was living in the United States. The Intelligence Community did not identify the domestic origin of those communications prior to September 11, 2001 so that additional FBI investigative efforts could be coordinated....].[1]

Note the difference between what Hayden told the Congressional Inquiry, where it was only "one of the future hijackers," Almihdhar, who called the Yemen hub from the US, and what President Bush and other officials said after the warrantless wiretapping story ran, that it was two of them, Almihdhar and Alhazmi. Later in its report, the Congressional Inquiry added,

Both the NSA and the FBI have the authority, in certain circumstances, to intercept international communications, to include communications that have one communicant in the United States and one in a foreign country, for foreign intelligence purposes. While those authorities were intended to insure a seamless transition between U.S. foreign and domestic intelligence capabilities, significant gaps between those two spheres of intelligence coverage persisted and impeded domestic counterterrorist efforts.

Before September 11, it was NSA policy not to target terrorists in the United States, even though it could have obtained a Foreign Intelligence Surveillance Court order authorizing such collection....

[As a result, NSA regularly provided information about these targets to the FBI – both in its regular reporting and in response to specific requests from the FBI – [... ... ...] that NSA acquired in the course of its collection operations. The FBI used this information in its investigations and obtained FISA Court authorization for electronic surveillance [... ... ...] when FBI officials determined that such surveillance was necessary to assist one of its intelligence or law enforcement investigations].[2]

In a nutshell, the NSA intercepted the communications between the hijackers in the US and the Yemen hub, analyzed them and disseminated the reports to other intelligence agencies. However, it

---

1. 9/11 Congressional Inquiry report, p. 36.
2. Ibid., pp. 73-75.

did not trace the identity of the party in the US, as it was focused on foreign intelligence. This means that it must have been aware that one end of the calls was in the US. Essentially, what we are being told is that NSA employees knew that the people who bombed the US embassies in East Africa and, later, the USS *Cole* were calling the US, but declined to trace these calls so their associates might be monitored and apprehended. All this at the same time that the CIA was also withholding related information from the FBI.

One way of summarizing this is that the NSA could have got a warrant to trace the US end, but did not, thinking this was the FBI's job. But the FBI could not get a warrant because it did not know about the calls, and this was because the NSA had not told it about them. A real-life Catch-22 situation.

Unfortunately for Hayden, the NSA did sometimes provide the FBI with precisely the information it did not provide in the case of Almihdhar. The section of the report quoted above says, "Before September 11, it was NSA policy not to target terrorists in the United States," but then adds in the next paragraph that "NSA regularly provided information about these targets to the FBI – both in its regular reporting and in response to specific requests from the FBI – [... ... ...] that NSA acquired in the course of its collection operations."

The phrase "these targets" means "terrorists in the United States." Substitute this and we have, "NSA regularly provided information about [terrorists in the United States] to the FBI – both in its regular reporting and in response to specific requests." This is where the alleged "gap" in coverage is supposed to be. On closer inspection, there seems to be no gap. Even if there was no specific plan aimed at getting information on foreign-domestic connections and informing the FBI, this was actually done, albeit on an ad hoc basis.

In addition, the FBI had specifically asked the NSA to report to it all calls between the Yemen hub and the US. Author Ron Suskind wrote, "In fact, [FBI agent Dan] Coleman and other FBI al-Qaeda specialists had even placed an order with the NSA back in 1998— that any calls between the Yemen line and the US be passed to the bureau—that the NSA didn't fill."[3] Clearly, the FBI thought that the

---

3. Ron Suskind, *The One Percent Doctrine: Deep Inside America's Pursuit of its Enemies Since 9/11* (New York: Simon & Schuster, 2006), p. 94.

NSA could and would trace calls between the Yemen hub and the US, otherwise it would not have asked the NSA for the information.

* * *

There is another problem for this explanation of the failure: at the same time as the NSA was allegedly not tracing the US end of calls to and from the Yemen hub due to privacy concerns, it was obtaining data from US telecoms about US citizens in an operation that was illegal. The operation was revealed by Joe Nacchio, chief executive officer of the US telecommunications firm Qwest. James Bamford set out how Nacchio learned of what was going on:

> On February 27, 2001 ... Nacchio and the new head of Qwest's government business unit, James F.X. Payne, arrived at the NSA. They had come to present their proposal to become part of the Groundbreaker project. Although the company was on the list of potential subcontractors, Nacchio was looking to up the ante by outlining a much larger role for the company. Neither, however, was prepared for the agency's counteroffer: to give the NSA secret, warrantless access to Qwest's database containing the calling records of its millions of American customers. And possibly later, to give Nacchio's blessing to install monitoring equipment on the company's Class 5 switching facilities, the system over which most of the company's domestic traffic flows.[4]

Qwest basically rejected the counteroffer due to legal concerns, as the NSA was not entitled to get such information about communications without a warrant. Nacchio alleges that the NSA victimized Qwest as a result of this rejection. Despite this, other US telecoms worked with the NSA on the program, allowing the NSA to access information about US persons without warrants.[5]

---

4. Bamford 2008, pp. 172-73.

5. James Bamford was asked about the contradiction between the NSA's alleged reluctance to get involved in domestic operations in the case of Almihdhar and its attempt to obtain data on US persons without a warrant at the same time. He replied, "It would've been nice if everything fit into a nice little package, but it didn't. That was one of the outlying issues. The time line seemed to be off. You know, I could see [Hayden] doing that after 9/11, but before 9/11 he was very careful. It's hard to say. Again, I'm just one guy trying to write this book. But that's why there really needs to be a congressional investigation into what went on at NSA. The only thing I can think of is that [Hayden] may not have been trying to get access to the actual voice conversations. What he may have been trying to get from Qwest was their database of subscribers — subscriber names, subscriber telephone numbers. It's one of the things that NSA has always tried to get. I mean, going back to the early days, they had the world's largest collection of telephone books. Hayden would've known that was at least questionable, if not illegal, because I think he made a

During his tenure at the NSA, Michael Hayden was never forth-coming about the extent of the NSA's spying on Americans. Why should anyone believe him when he says the calls between the US and the Yemen hub were not traced due to privacy concerns? Especially when all the evidence suggests he does not much care for Americans' privacy?

The entire explanation seems absurd on its face—the NSA intercepted, but failed to trace, calls between the US and al-Qaeda's logistics hub, which was involved in the African embassy and *Cole* bombings. On top of that are the facts that the FBI had specifically asked the NSA to do so, that it had intercepted these types of calls and then told the FBI about them, and that Hayden's excuse, that the NSA was reluctant to undertake domestic operations, is contradicted by his desire to get access to Qwest's information.

Perhaps this is why the explanation changed in early 2004.

---

comment about that very kind of access before 9/11." Bamford is quoted in Noah Shachtman, "Top NSA Scribe Takes Us Inside *The Shadow Factory," Wired,* October 14, 2008, http://blog.wired.com/defense/2008/10/bamford-intervi.html.

21

Neither the contents of the calls nor the physics ... allowed us to determine that one end of the calls was in the United States

The putative explanation for the non-exploitation of the calls between the hijackers in the US and the Yemen hub changed in an article for *US News and World Report*, published in March 2004. This was a few months after the redacted version of the Congressional Inquiry report had been published, and a few months before the 9/11 Commission would publish its final report.

The article, entitled "Pieces of the 9/11 Puzzle: U.S. spies knew about 'Khalid'—but they didn't know he was here" by David E. Kaplan and Kevin Whitelaw,[1] bears the marks of a certain type of article placed by government officials whose purpose is to shape the public perception of a story before an alternative, generally truer, account takes hold. Here, the purpose was to play down the NSA's culpability in not passing on information about the calls.

After a description of the Yemen hub, the article delivers its main message: "And what no one knew back in early 2000 was that Almihdhar was in the United States when he called the house in Yemen." It adds, "Surprisingly, government agencies often did not—or could not—trace the location of all calls made to and from targeted sites, even such high-value ones as the Yemeni house." An anonymous "senior intelligence official" is then quoted as saying, "Neither the contents of the calls nor the physics of the intercepts allowed us to determine that one end of the calls was in the United States."

This does not square with generally known information about the NSA. It is the largest spy organization the US has ever known, currently dwarfing even the CIA. Tracing calls is a relatively basic

1. David E. Kaplan and Kevin Whitelaw, "Pieces of the 9/11 Puzzle," *US News and World Report*, March 7, 2004, http://www.usnews.com/usnews/news/articles/040315/15nine11.htm.

activity, and tracing calls from the Yemen hub would be a high priority, as it was the nerve center of al-Qaeda, an organization that had blown up two US embassies in 1998 and the USS *Cole* in 2000.

Indeed, this does not square with that map of al-Qaeda's global network on the wall of the FBI's New York office. The map was made by intercepting calls between the Yemen hub and al-Qaeda operatives elsewhere. If the US could not trace the calls, how was the map made?

Neither does it square with the claim that the NSA did not trace the calls in the US because of privacy concerns. For the NSA to have decided not to trace a call due to privacy concerns, it must have realized that one end of the call was in the US. Otherwise, domestic privacy concerns would not have prevented tracing it.

As we will see, evidence submitted at the embassy bombings trial in early 2001 included information about calls between the Yemen hub and locations in Afghanistan and Kenya. Both ends of the calls were determined by the US after the bombings, so the US clearly did have the capability to trace calls to and from the hub.

And to cap it all, we have the Hijackers Timeline document (see p. 138), which clearly shows a monitored call on March 20, 2000 from Nawaf Alhazmi's phone in San Diego to the Yemen hub. The NSA claimed both that it was unable to trace the calls and that it decided not to trace the calls because it knew one end was in the US. We have been given two accounts, and we can't believe either of them.

22

For the commission's staff, Fort Meade might as well have been Kabul

The casual reader of *The 9/11 Commission Report* might think that the NSA intercepts of the calls between the hijackers in the US and the Yemen hub were entirely omitted from the report. However, this is not quite the case. The report, and the Commission's preceding documentation, does reference them, but in an extremely roundabout way.

The 9/11 Commission was designed as a follow-on to the Congressional Inquiry, and all the Commissioners read the Inquiry's report, in the classified, unredacted version, as the basis of their own research. As mentioned above, one of the Commissioners, Tim Roemer, had also been on the House Intelligence Committee at the time it was working on the Congressional Inquiry report. The Inquiry report mentions the calls to and from the hub, so the Commissioners must have been aware of them.

The intercepts are mentioned in the Commission's second staff statement, "Three 9/11 Hijackers: Identification, Watchlisting and Tracking," which says that after Almihdhar and Alhazmi entered the US,

> weeks passed. Meanwhile, NSA would occasionally pass new information generally of a personal nature, associated with Khalid, Salem, Salem's brother (Nawaf), and perhaps Khallad [bin Attash] as well. At this time, though the Intelligence Community did not know it, Almihdhar was in San Diego, California.[1]

This is clearly a reference to the NSA intercepts of the hijackers' calls between San Diego and Yemen, as detailed on page 157 of the

---

1. 9/11 Commission Staff Statement No. 2, "Three Hijackers: Identification, Watchlisting, and Tracking," http://www.9-11commission.gov/staff_statements/staff_statement_2.pdf.

Congressional Inquiry report, as well as to other intercepts of calls to and from the Yemen hub.

However, this reference to the NSA intercepts is extremely problematic. A person who simply reads the sentence, "Meanwhile, NSA would occasionally pass new information generally of a personal nature, associated with Khalid, Salem, Salem's brother (Nawaf), and perhaps Khallad as well," would not necessarily take it to mean that the NSA was intercepting calls between one of the hijackers and al-Qaeda's operations center. For example, the reader may attribute the NSA's acquisition of this information to a search of its databases, to processing information from partner foreign intelligence agencies, or to intercepting calls from operatives other than those based in the US (such as Salem Alhazmi and Khallad bin Attash at this time).

The non-specification of the source of the information was clearly a serious error of omission. However, it was not the only such error by the Commission.

The role of Commission staffer Barbara Grewe in the Commission's work on information sharing between the CIA and FBI has been discussed, and we should bear in mind that, according to a stub biography about her for a speaking event, she was a "key drafter of two staff statements regarding what the intelligence community knew about the hijackers and possible threats prior to the attacks."[2] One of these was staff statement ten, part of which she read in public. The other was presumably the staff statement cited earlier, number two.

Grewe clearly was involved in NSA-related aspects of the Commission's investigation. A staff monograph she drafted repeatedly mentions the December 1999 intercept of the call between Khalid Almihdhar and Khallad bin Attash.[3] In addition, an outline for a monograph about law enforcement and domestic intelligence, prepared by the Commission's Team 6 shortly after Grewe was moved to Special Projects, contains the headlines of sections that were to cover the alleged non-tracing of the calls. The outline says the

2. "Barbara A. Grewe," Center for American Progress, http://www.americanprogressaction.org/events/2008/inf/GreweBarbara.html.
3. 9/11 Commission, Barbara Grewe, "Legal Barriers to Information Sharing: The Erection of a Wall Between Intelligence and Law Enforcement," August 20, 2004, http://www.scribd.com/doc/22564583/FAS-911C-2004-08-20-Staff-Monograph-Legal-Barriers-to-Info-Sharing-Grewe.

monograph, which appears never to have been drafted, would contain sections about "the NSA and the issue of U.S. persons" before 9/11, and "the NSA and the continuing issue of U.S. persons" after 9/11.[4]

However, internal Commission documents make it clear that Barbara Grewe was not the only Commission staffer investigating the NSA. For example, the Commission's Team 2, which investigated the US intelligence community, also looked at the NSA.

Although a good deal of what was written in the Commission's staff statements was reprinted verbatim in the final report, and some material was accepted with only minor alterations, the "weeks passed" paragraph saying the NSA disseminated information about Almihdhar and others to partner agencies was omitted from the final report.[5] Despite this, the intercepted calls were mentioned elsewhere. On page 222, the Commission writes,

> Almihdhar's mind seems to have been with his family back in Yemen, as evidenced by calls he made from the apartment telephone. When news of the birth of his first child arrived, he could stand life in California no longer.

These two sentences are startling for a number of reasons. First, we encounter the same problem as we saw in the staff statement. These calls were intercepted by the NSA, and the Commission must have been aware of this. The casual reader of this passage would not know that these calls were intercepted by the NSA, as there is no mention whatsoever of such intercepts in the passage. Consequently, one would not look for an explanation of why the NSA failed to take advantage of the intercepts to roll up the plot.

Second, as discussed above, the Commission is making an implied claim here: that the calls between Almihdhar and the Yemen hub were merely about keeping in touch with his wife. Given that we are talking about calls involving a top al-Qaeda operative on a signature mission for the organization, might he have had another reason to make calls to its operations center? It would certainly be

---

4. 9/11 Commission, "Team 6 Monograph Outline: Law Enforcement and Domestic Intelligence," undated, http://www.scribd.com/doc/14863646/Outline-for-911-Commission-Monograph-on-Domestic-Intelligence-with-Staffers-Comments.
5. Some of the other surrounding paragraphs from the second staff statement appear on page 181 of *9/11 CR*.

amazing if no details of the mission were ever mentioned, especially because, as we have seen, some of the calls were made by Nawaf Alhazmi. He can hardly have been discussing family matters with Almihdhar's wife.

The claim that Almihdhar was only talking to his wife and only about family matters is made by implication. Given that the claim is unusual on its face, one would expect that anyone making such a claim would research it carefully and set out the reasons for his conclusions in full. For example, in this case it would be appropriate to review recordings or transcripts of the calls themselves and vet them for possible hidden references to flying aircraft into large buildings. However, in the report there is no hint that the Commission did any of this. It just implies he was talking to his wife, as though he could not have had any other reason for making the calls.

The sourcing for this passage in the report is contained in the relevant endnote,[6] which reads,

> On Almihdhar's phone calls, see, e.g., FBI report, "Hijackers Timeline," Nov. 14, 2003 (Mar. 20, 2000, entry, citing 265A-NY-280350-19426).

I obtained the Hijackers Timeline document from the FBI under the Freedom of Information Act. The relevant entry, for March 20, 2000 reads,

> The San Diego telephone number associated with NAWAF AL-HAZMI, [redacted] made a call which lasted 16 minutes to Yemen [redacted] This is the telephone number subscribed to by AHMED [redacted] ALMIHDHAR's father-in-law, who is associated with the[7]

The entry in the copy of the timeline ends there. Presumably, the first redaction is Alhazmi's phone number in San Diego, the second al-Hada's phone number in Yemen and the third his surname. What he is "associated with" may be the embassy bombings and/or the *Cole* attack.

---

6. *9/11 CR*, p. 518 n39.
7. Federal Bureau of Investigation, "Working Draft Chronology of Events for Hijackers," October 2001, p. 57, http://www.historycommons.org/sourcedocuments/2001/pdfs/fbi911timeline1-105.pdf. See page 138 herein.

This sourcing is deficient. It does not say anything about the content of the calls, and there is no particular reason, based on this, to suppose that Almihdhar spoke to his wife at all, or about any particular topic—although his wife did live at the number, and the birth of his child, if it occurred at that time, would clearly be an event worthy of mention. But there is no reason, based on this, to assume he did not discuss operational matters in the calls.

The use of the abbreviation "e.g." to introduce the FBI timeline as a source should also be highlighted. It indicates that the Commission had other sources for these calls, but declined to cite them in this instance. What were they, and why did the Commission not mention them?

The Commission *did* cite NSA intelligence reports as sources in its final report, but *did not* attribute them to the NSA. For example, the sourcing for its passage about the NSA's December 29, 1999 intercept between Almihdhar and bin Attash mentions three reports. One of them is by the CIA, but the agency that produced the other two reports is not named. The sources are simply called, "Intelligence report, activities of bin Laden associates, Dec. 29, 1999; intelligence report, review of 9/11 hijackers' activities, Sept. 23, 2002."[8] As we will see later in this chapter, the Commission found evidence linking the hijackers to Iran in the NSA files. However, the report's main text does not mention that the information came from the NSA, and the endnotes containing the sources frequently cite intelligence reports without specifying which agency they came from.[9]

Although the Commission did not mention that the NSA intercepted the hijackers' calls in the US in this passage, or anywhere else, it did provide an explanation for why the NSA failed to exploit the calls. However, that explanation is found on pages 87 and 88 of its report, and there is no explicit link between it and the mention of the calls on page 222, where they were supposedly evidence that Almihdhar's mind was on his family. It would take the reader some time spent on analysis to realize that the two passages are related.

The explanation reads,

> The law requires the NSA to not deliberately collect data on U.S. citizens or on persons in the United States without a warrant

8. *9/11 CR* pp. 181, 502 n41.
9. The section about Iran in *9/11 CR* is in pp. 240-41; the related endnotes are on p. 529.

160

based on foreign intelligence requirements. Also, the NSA was supposed to let the FBI know of any indication of crime, espionage, or "terrorist enterprise" so that the FBI could obtain the appropriate warrant. Later in this story, we will learn that while the NSA had the technical capability to report on communications with suspected terrorist facilities in the Middle East, the NSA did not seek FISA Court warrants to collect communications between individuals in the United States and foreign countries, because it believed that this was an FBI role. It also did not want to be viewed as targeting persons in the United States and possibly violating laws that governed NSA's collection of foreign intelligence.

An almost obsessive protection of sources and methods by the NSA, and its focus on foreign intelligence, and its avoidance of anything domestic would, as will be seen, be important elements in the story of 9/11.

This explanation comes in the middle of several paragraphs about the general development of the NSA and its role in the Cold War. Again, there is no mention that the NSA was intercepting the hijackers' calls inside the US but somehow failed to roll the plot up. The ordinary reader cannot therefore divine what this is supposed to explain.

This explanation flatly contradicts the one offered in the *US News and World Report* article noted in the last chapter. That article quoted an anonymous senior official saying, "Neither the contents of the calls nor the physics of the intercepts allowed us to determine that one end of the calls was in the United States," but the 9/11 Commission says, "the NSA had the technical capability to report on communications with suspected terrorist facilities in the Middle East."

The relevant endnote for the explanation reads, "Michael Hayden interview, (Dec 10, 2003)."[10] There must be numerous internal NSA memos on this issue. However, there is no indication that the Commission, or the Congressional Inquiry before it, obtained these memos. Instead, it looks as if the Commission, behind closed doors, just asked the director of the agency in question what happened, chose to believe whatever he said, and then removed all traces of the NSA's failure from its report.

10. Endnote 68 on page 477.

One sentence in the quoted section states that "later in this story, we will learn" and another says "as will be seen." However, the only other reference in the report to the NSA intercepts of the hijackers' calls in the US is the one found on page 222 regarding Almihdhar's familial concerns. We do not learn anything more about the NSA's technical capability or its lack of desire to obtain FISA warrants. Nor do we see that its avoidance of anything domestic would be one of the "important elements in the story of 9/11."

These curious omissions indicate that there was a passage discussing the NSA intercepts in a draft version of the report, but that this passage was deleted. If this is what occurred, the deletion remains a mystery.

The *US News and World Report* article also said that the failure to discover Almihdhar's presence in the US "is also now a central focus of the independent 9/11 commission, which plans to address the larger problem in the handoff of information from the NSA to the FBI in an upcoming public hearing."[11] I am unable to find such material in the transcripts of the Commission's subsequent hearings or anywhere else. If it did ever plan to address the issue, this plan was abandoned. The only NSA official to testify at a public Commission hearing was Stewart Baker, who worked for the agency for a mere two years, leaving in 1994.[12] When he testified in December 2003, he mentioned the agency one time in his prepared statement, saying that he had previously worked there, and one time in his actual testimony, to the same effect.

* * *

The Commission's treatment of the issue is made even more bizarre by its general attitude toward the NSA. Essentially, the Commission ignored the NSA publicly, spending very little time on NSA material in its presentations. Michael Hayden did not testify publicly, although he had testified four times before the Congressional Inquiry, once in open session and three times behind closed doors.

11. David E. Kaplan and Kevin Whitelaw, "Pieces of the 9/11 Puzzle," *US News and World Report*, March 15, 2004, http://www.usnews.com/usnews/news/articles/040315/15nine11.htm.
12. 9/11 Commission, "Testimony of Stewart Baker before the National Commission on Terrorist Attacks upon the United States," December 8, 2003, http://www.9-11commission.gov/hearings/hearing6/witness_baker.pdf; "Transcript of 9/11 Commission hearing on December 8, 2003," http://govinfo.library.unt.edu/911/archive/hearing6/9-11Commission_Hearing_2003-12-08.htm.

Perhaps as a result of this, Hayden was not mentioned even once by name in the main text of *The 9/11 Commission Report*, but relegated to a mere four mentions in the small-type endnotes. In contrast, George Tenet testified twice publicly, was questioned repeatedly in private, and got over a hundred mentions in the main text (excluding endnotes). In its final report, the Commission mentions the NSA 31 times in the main text, whereas both the CIA and the FBI have over ten times more mentions.

In his 2008 book, Philip Shenon gave an account of the Commission's dealings with the NSA. He argued the Commission had not paid much attention to the agency at all, and had very probably missed some key things as a result.

In Shenon's telling, Philip Zelikow was in full charge of the Commission and was focused on the CIA and FBI, to the exclusion of the NSA. No explanation of exactly why he ignored the NSA is offered. One of the staffers, an Air Force intelligence officer named Lorry Fenner, realized that the Commission was ignoring NSA material related to the 9/11 plot, even though she was assigned to a different part of the Commission's work. She apparently thought that it could be important, a "treasure trove" of information about al-Qaeda and "helpful to the teams that would be investigating the September 11 plot."[13]

Fenner asked around to see what the Commission would do with the NSA's material and "was dumfounded by what she was hearing" because, "No one from the commission—no one—would drive the twenty-seven miles from downtown Washington north to the headquarters of the NSA, in Fort Meade, Maryland, to review its vast archives of material on al-Qaeda and terrorist threats." The NSA was actually closer than the CIA in Langley, Virginia, "But for the commission's staff, Fort Meade might as well have been Kabul, it seemed so distant."

Shenon then writes,

> It was all the more frustrating to Fenner given the obvious willingness of the NSA, unlike so many other parts of the government, to cooperate with the 9/11 commission. The NSA's director, General Michael Hayden, had thrown open its archives on

---

13. Philip Shenon, *The Commission: The Uncensored History of the 9/11 Investigation* (New York: Twelve, 2008), pp. 87-88.

al-Qaeda; Zelikow and others were impressed by his eagerness to help. But perversely, the more eager General Hayden was to cooperate, the less interested Zelikow and others at the commission seemed to be in what was buried in the NSA files.[14]

Fenner then contacted the NSA and had them transfer parts of their files to a special reading room in an NSA office in Washington so the Commission's staff could have easier access to them. This happened at the end of 2003, months before the Commission was due to report. Interestingly, Hayden's interview by the Commission was on December 10, and Fenner's team leader, Kevin Scheid, was present at that interview,[15] suggesting the interview and the file transfer might be related. However, Shenon does not mention any such link.

Nevertheless, nobody went to review the NSA files for weeks, so Fenner took the job on herself. However, in the reading room, "The cabinet bulged with tens of thousands of pages of documents about the NSA's efforts to track bin Laden and al-Qaeda since the mid-1990s … It would take several days of reading to get through even a small portion of it."

What Fenner did find was a series of NSA reports indicating that some of the hijackers-to-be might have coordinated their travel with the Iranian terrorist proxy Hezbollah. Shenon says that she spent "several days" between December 2003 and June 2004 reading the material, taking "two or three hours" over every visit.

Alarmed by the Iranian connection, Fenner asked for a second opinion and turned to fellow staffer and CIA employee Lloyd Salvetti. Salvetti thought it was interesting, and they got a third opinion, that of Doug MacEachin, a veteran CIA analyst also on the Commission's staff. MacEachin confirmed what they thought, and they went to see Zelikow, who saw the importance of what they had uncovered.[16]

In the end, a group of staffers also spent one day at NSA headquarters just before the Commission reported, although by then they were mostly focused on the possible Iran link. The link made it into the final report, getting a page and a half there.[17]

---

14. For this and subsequent paragraphs see ibid. pp. 155-57.
15. E-mail to the author from Kirsten Wilhelm of the National Archives, February 3, 2009. Neither Zelikow nor any Commissioner was present at this interview, which was headed by Zelikow's deputy Chris Kojm.
16. Philip Shenon, see note 13, pp. 370-73.
17. *9/11 CR*, pp. 240-41.

Shenon ends his section on this issue as follows:

> What was left unsaid in the report, although the staff knew it perfectly well, was that the NSA archives almost certainly contained other vital information about al-Qaeda and its history. But there was no time left to search for it. Zelikow would later admit he too was worried that important classified information had never been reviewed at the NSA and elsewhere in the government before the 9/11 commission shut its doors, that critical evidence about bin Laden's terrorist network sat buried in government files, unread to this day. By July 2004, it was just too late to keep digging.

Lloyd Salvetti, one of the colleagues Fenner turned to, was present at the Commission's interview of Hayden in December 2003,[18] at which the monitoring of the hijackers' calls from the US was discussed. Kevin Scheid was also present, and Fenner discussed her work on the NSA archives with Scheid repeatedly. Both Salvetti and Scheid must have known of the Yemen calls, yet we are left with a string of unanswered questions. Did Scheid and Salvetti tell Fenner about the calls? Did they look for them in the NSA archives? If not, why not? If so, did they find the calls, and what did they do with them? Or were the calls perhaps already well known to the Commission, despite their near-total absence from its final report?

* * *

In contrast to the outward lack of interest in the NSA, and Shenon's account that some NSA material was missed, the Commission's files tell a somewhat different story. They contain a substantial number of interviews of NSA personnel, document requests to the NSA and mentions of documents that the NSA sent to the Commission. Given their importance to the Commission's work, it must have obtained information from the NSA about the intercepts of the calls between the hijackers in the US and the Yemen hub.

The recordings, transcripts, and reports of Almihdhar and Alhazmi talking to al-Qaeda's main operations center would be of huge value as historical source material. They would have taken on an added significance given the poor quality of some of the other sources on which the Commission was forced to rely. For example, the Commission was extremely frustrated by its lack of access to

---

18. E-mail to the author from Kirsten Wilhelm of the National Archives, February 3, 2009.

CIA detainees, such as the alleged 9/11 mastermind Khalid Shaikh Mohammed, whom it wanted to question.

But the CIA did not allow such questioning, as the detainees were being held at "black sites," and a Commission staffer who met a detainee who had been tortured might thus have represented a security risk. This meant that the Commission derived a lot of its information about the plot from tortured detainees it never met, and it was suitably skeptical of this information. For example, historian Ernest May, a senior advisor to the 9/11 Commission, later wrote, "We never had full confidence in the interrogation reports as historical sources. Often we found more reliable the testimony that had been given in open court by those prosecuted for the East African embassy bombings and other crimes."[19]

The way this looks is that the Commission found some—perhaps not all—NSA material, but that the NSA pressured it to leave out certain things from the report. This would explain the missing references to the NSA in the relevant endnotes, the apparently deleted section about NSA-FBI problems concerning the calls to the Yemen hub, and the Commission's apparent lack of interest in the NSA—the Commission was geared toward producing its final report, if something could not be mentioned in that report anyway, then why spend much time investigating it?

The Commission clearly was pressured successfully to omit information about the Department of Defense, of which the NSA was part, from its report. For example, in his 2009 book *The Ground Truth*, Commission team leader John Farmer mentioned an E-4B "Doomsday Plane" that was seen over Washington around the time the Pentagon was hit.[20] Farmer and his team were aware of the plane, but had failed to mention it in their section of the report. According to Farmer: "The reason for the omission was that the administration deemed any information regarding the plane or its flight path highly confidential. Like other omissions, however, it has led some to believe that the plane played a significant role in the events of that morning. It did not. In that respect the omission of it was regrettable."[21]

---

19. Ernest R. May, "When Government Writes History: The 9/11 Commission Report," *History News Network*, June 27, 2005, http://hnn.us/articles/11972.html.

20. The E-4B "Doomsday Plane" is a command-and-control center, also known as a "Flying Pentagon." There were four in service on September 11, 2001.

21. John Farmer, *The Ground Truth: The Untold Story of America under Attack on 9/11* (New York: Riverhead Books), 2009, p. 372.

Farmer's admission about the E-4B cover-up came a year after researcher Mark Gaffney had published *The 9/11 Mystery Plane and the Vanishing of America*, clearly demonstrating the plane's existence and highlighting its probable relevance to the day's events.[22] Had Gaffney not put in the work, it is quite possible that Farmer would not have admitted anything. In any case, no additional documentation followed Farmer's admission, and we only have Farmer's word that the plane did not play a "significant" role in events.

In summary, the Commission's investigation of the Yemen calls answered no questions and raised several. What did the Commission know? How did it know what it knew? Why was so much left out? And how can the public believe that the Commission conducted a full investigation?

---

22. Mark H. Gaffney, *The 9/11 Mystery Plane and the Vanishing of America* (Walterville, Oregon: TrineDay, 2008). Much of Gaffney's data is hard sledding for the non-technical reader, but his account once again shows that there was far more to 9/11 than met the eye.

SOCOM lawyers would not permit the sharing of the U.S. person information regarding terrorists located domestically due to "fear of potential blowback"

While the CIA and NSA were failing to provide information on the future hijackers to the FBI, a US Army unit was also prevented from sharing information about al-Qaeda with the Bureau. Members of the unit, a data-mining program known as Able Danger, later claimed that they had linked four of the hijackers—Almihdhar, Alhazmi, Mohamed Atta and Marwan Alshehhi—to the terrorist organization. But the information was not utilized, and the program was shut down. Although there is no known direct connection between this failure and the ones related to the Alec Station group, the nature of the failure—withholding information about the hijackers—suggests that the same controlling forces may have been involved.

Able Danger started in the late 1990s at the US military's Special Operations Command (SOCOM) with the aim of using data-mining techniques to track persons the US government was interested in, including al-Qaeda operatives.[1] It began to gather information from sources such as al-Qaeda Internet chat rooms, news accounts, websites, and financial records, as well as government documents such as visa applications by foreign tourists[2] and information about mosque attendance. Despite the clear usefulness of the project, the CIA refused to come on board, and said it would not share information it had on al-Qaeda with the effort. The unit

1. Jacob Goodwin, "Inside Able Danger—the Secret Birth, Extraordinary Life and Untimely Death of a U.S. Military Intelligence Program," *Government Security News*, September 2005, http://web.archive.org/web/20050924164439/http://www.gsnmagazine.com/sep_05/shaffer_interview.html.
2. Mike Kelly, "Deadly Tale of Incompetence," *Bergen (NJ) Record*, August 14, 2005, http://newsgroups.derkeiler.com/Archive/Alt/alt.religion.islam/2005-08/msg00949.html.

worked up its information into charts showing linkages between people it thought were connected to al-Qaeda operations.[3]

Around January or February of 2000, Able Danger officials say they identified the four hijackers as being linked to al-Qaeda. They were allegedly connected through ties to a Brooklyn cell centered on the "Blind Sheikh," then in jail for his part in the Day of Terror plot.[4]

Shortly after the connection was reportedly made, Able Danger began running into trouble. First, SOCOM lawyers reviewed the data and said that any terrorist suspects living and working in the US were "off limits" to Able Danger, because they were US persons.[5] As a result, yellow stickers were placed over the faces of some suspects on one of the charts.

Federal agents then confiscated much of the data assembled by an Able Danger contractor, Orion Scientific Systems. Orion employee James D. Smith later commented on this: "All information that we have ever produced, which was all unclassified, was confiscated, and to this day we don't know by whom."[6]

Subsequently, the army's Land Information Warfare Unit was ordered to cease its analytical support for the program and some information, reportedly 2.5 trillion bytes, was destroyed.[7] The program resumed in August 2000[8] and reportedly linked Mohamed Atta to al-Qaeda again,[9] but it was shut down for a second time in early 2001.[10]

Some of the Able Danger team members say that after 9/11 they realized they had identified Atta,[11] and a chart with a photo of him

3. Jacob Goodwin, see note 1.

4. Ibid.; Douglas Jehl, "Four in 9/11 Plot Are Called Tied to Qaeda in '00," *New York Times,* August 9, 2005, http://www.nytimes.com/2005/08/09/politics/09intel.html?_r=1.

5. US Congress, "Prepared Statement of Anthony A. Shaffer, Lt Col, US Army Reserve, Senior Intelligence Officer before the House Armed Services Committee (HASC)," February 15, 2006, http://www.investigativeproject.org/documents/testimony/251.pdf.

6. US House of Representatives, Armed Services Committee, Hearing of Subcommittee on Strategic Forces and Subcommittee on Terrorism, Unconventional Threats and Capabilities, 109th Cong., 2d sess., February 15, 2006.

7. Bill Gertz, "Atta Files Destroyed by Pentagon," *Washington Times*, September 21, 2005, http://washingtontimes.com/news/2005/sep/21/20050921-102450-4688r/.

8. US Senate, Committee on the Judiciary, Hearing on Able Danger and Intelligence Sharing, 109th Cong., 1st sess., September 21, 2005, http://www.fas.org/irp/congress/2005_hr/shrg109-311.pdf.

9. Keith Phucas, "Weldon Pushes 'Able Danger' Criminal Probe," *Times Herald*, November 11, 2005, http://www.yourbbsucks.com/forum/showthread.php?t=6185.

10. U.S. House of Representatives, Armed Services Committee, see note 6.

11. US Congress, "Prepared Statement of Anthony A. Shaffer ...," see note 5.

may have been shown to Deputy National Security Advisor Stephen Hadley.[12] Two of the officers involved, Lt. Col. Anthony Shaffer[13] and Captain Scott Phillpott,[14] also briefed 9/11 Commission staff on the effort. Despite this, the Commission evidently concluded that Able Danger had not identified the four hijackers and did not mention the effort at all in its final report or any other public release.

Thanks to efforts by Congressman Curt Weldon, the veil of secrecy was pierced in August 2005, and the *New York Times* ran a page-one story containing a history of the program and the allegation that it had identified four of the hijackers.[15] The affair rumbled on for a while with various Congressional hearings and media statements, until the Defense Department inspector general produced a report in September 2006 saying the program had not identified Atta,[16] and media interest in it tailed off.

Several people involved in Able Danger say they *did* identify Atta and the other three; other authorities say they did not. As the data has been destroyed, the issue cannot be resolved definitively. However, there were multiple connections between several hijackers and the Brooklyn cell of the imprisoned "Blind Sheikh," Sheikh Omar Abdul-Rahman.

The names of Alhazmi and Almihdhar were in US government databases by January-February 2000, as they had applied for visas in Jeddah the previous year using passports with the indicator of terrorist affiliation, they had recently traveled to the US, their calls had been monitored by the NSA—also a Defense Department component—for some time, and they had recently been followed in Malaysia. In addition, they could clearly be linked to the Blind Sheikh by data mining, as in San Diego they were connected to a Saudi

---

12. "Will There Be Senate Hearings on 'Able Danger' Findings," *Fox News*, August 22, 2005, http://www.foxnews.com/printer_friendly_story/0,3566,166413,00.html.

13. "Officer: 9/11 panel didn't receive key information," CNN, August 17, 2005 http://edition.cnn.com/2005/POLITICS/08/17/sept.11.hijackers/.

14. Philip Shenon, "Navy Officer Affirms Assertions About Pre-9/11 Data on Atta," *New York Times*, August 22, 2005, http://www.nytimes.com/2005/08/22/politics/23cnd-intel.html?pagewanted=print.

15. Douglas Jehl, see note 4.

16. Department of Defense, Office of the Inspector Genera l, "Alleged Misconduct by Senior DOD Officials Concerning the Able Danger Program and Lieutenant Colonel Anthony A. Shaffer, U.S. Army Reserve," September 18, 2006, http://msnbcmedia.msn.com/i/msnbc/sections/news/Able_Danger_report.pdf.

named Osama Basnan, who US intelligence believed had hosted a party attended by the Blind Sheikh in the early '90s.[17] Both Basnan and the two hijackers were closely linked to a suspected Saudi intelligence agent, Omar al-Bayoumi, who assisted the hijackers and was friendly with Basnan. The hijackers also lived on the same street as Basnan and Bayoumi, and Basnan attended the same mosque as the hijackers—recall that mosque attendance was one of the methods Able Danger personnel said they used to make linkages. In addition, a close associate of the Blind Sheikh who was under FBI surveillance visited the mosque around this time.

Atta and Alshehhi's names were also in US government databases by this time, as Atta twice entered a green card lottery in late 1999[18] and Alshehhi received a US visa in mid-January 2000.[19] The two, along with the rest of the Hamburg cell and their associates, were under surveillance in Germany, operations carried out in co-operation with the CIA. They were also known attendees of at least one radical mosque in Germany.

While in the US, Atta and Alshehhi attended a Florida mosque run by Gulshair El-Shukrijumah,[20] a cleric who had previously worked with the Blind Sheikh in Brooklyn before moving south. El-Shukrijumah had translated for the Blind Sheikh and had even appeared as a witness for the defense at the Day of Terror trial that followed the 1993 World Trade Center bombing.[21] Presumably, Atta and Alshehhi first attended this mosque after they entered the US using their own names in mid-2000, although previous attendance after entering the US under name variants cannot be excluded. Therefore, physical attendance at the mosque probably was not the reason for the linkage made by Able Danger. Nevertheless, Gulshair El-Shukrijumah's son Adnan was a known, senior al-Qaeda operative and was seen with Atta in Miami on May 2, 2001. It is highly unlikely that Atta and the El-Shukrijumahs met through

---

17. 9/11 Congressional Inquiry report, pp. 175-77.
18. *United States v. Zacarias Moussaoui*, "Stipulation [Regarding flights hijacked on September 11, 2001; September 11, 2001 deaths; al Qaeda; chronology of hijackers' activities; Zacarias Moussaoui; and the Computer Assisted Passenger Pre-screening System (CAPPS)]," Part A, p. 35, http://www.vaed.uscourts.gov/notablecases/moussaoui/exhibits/prosecution/ST00001.html.
19. Terrorist Travel report, p. 10.
20. Brian Ross and Vic Walter, "FBI Informant Says Agents Missed Chance to Stop 9/11 Ringleader Mohammed Atta," ABC, September 10, 2009, http://abcnews.go.com/Blotter/Whistleblowers/911-ringleader-mohammed-atta-stopped-fbi-informant/Story?id=8540605.
21. 9/11 Commission, see note 19, pp. 40-41.

mere coincidence, and some prior communications must have occurred; such communications may have been uncovered, and Able Danger may have learned of them.

Had the Able Danger program been allowed to continue, it could have picked up further links between the Blind Sheikh and the hijackers. For example, several of the hijackers rented mailboxes from a company called Sphinx Trading in Jersey City, New Jersey. The Blind Sheikh and at least one of his associates had previously used the same mailing address—it was four doors down from one of the mosques the Sheikh had preached at. Sphinx Trading was even owned by Waleed al-Noor, an unindicted co-conspirator in the Day of Terror plot for which the Sheikh was sent to prison. Al-Noor's business partner Mohammed el-Atriss also provided at least two of the hijackers, Almihdhar and Abdulaziz Alomari, with fake IDs, and interacted with a third hijacker, Hani Hanjour.[22]

What is remarkable about the El-Shukrijumah connection is the way it was ignored by all the investigations. Investigators certainly appear to have known of it, as the final Congressional Inquiry report states that "Almihdhar, Alhazmi, Hanjour, Atta, Alshehhi, and possibly other hijackers attended at least seven mosques in California, Florida, Virginia, Arizona, and Maryland, some of which were also attended by persons of interest to the FBI."[23] While some of the other mosques attended by the hijackers, such as the King Fahd mosque in Los Angeles, the Rabat mosque in San Diego, and the Dar al Hijra mosque in Virginia, are named repeatedly in media and official documents, the hijackers' attendance at the El-Shukrijumah mosque was first revealed in full in a 2009 ABC report.[24]

The Commission did mention a link between Atta and Adnan El-Shukrijumah, but this was relegated to an endnote in a subsidiary document, its Terrorist Travel staff report, which was published on

22. Lance 2006, pp. 372-74; Robert Hanley and Jonathan Miller, "4 Transcripts Are Released in Case Tied to 9/11 Hijackers," *New York Times*, June 25, 2003, http://www.nytimes.com/2003/06/25/nyregion/4-transcripts-are-released-in-case-tied-to-9-11-hijackers.html; Robert Schwaneberg, "Six months in jail on a false assumption," *Newark (NJ) Star-Ledger*, October 20, 2003, http://www.nj.com/specialprojects/index.ssf?/specialprojects/court/court2.html; Mike Kelly, "Remains of the day: Lives 'stuck' at Ground Zero," *Bergen (NJ) Record*, September 11, 2006; "Analysis: Mohamed El Atriss arrested on charges he sold fake IDs to two of the 9/11 terrorists," National Public Radio, August 20, 2002, http://www.highbeam.com/doc/1P1-55389534.html.
23. 9/11 Congressional Inquiry report, p. 169.
24. Brian Ross and Vic Walter, see note 20.

a Saturday in August.[25] This link was of huge importance, because it connected the lead 9/11 hijacker to a domestic terrorist, yet the Commission declined to pursue this.

Unraveling the El-Shukrijumah connection had the potential to substantiate the Able Danger allegations, but covering it up may have been motivated by additional factors. For example, the FBI had Atta and Adnan El-Shukrijumah under surveillance at the mosque, but failed to stop the 9/11 plot, something that would immensely embarrass the FBI if revealed. In addition, Gulshair El-Shukrijumah was in receipt of monies from the Saudi embassy in Washington,[26] and it is also possible there was some involvement with a terrorist finance investigation that may have been ongoing.

Although the Able Danger allegations were dismissed by the Defense Department's inspector general, they still appear persuasive. The allegation that Atta and others were identified was made not by one person, but by several, yet the inspector general's report failed to consider any of the open-source information outlined here linking the hijackers to the Blind Sheikh, rendering its conclusions problematic. Despite this, it is unclear how Able Danger fits in with the larger pattern of withheld information described in this book. While it is certainly possible that notification to the FBI of the terrorists that Able Danger found in the US was stymied by the Alec Station group in order to protect the hijackers, there is as yet no reliable evidence indicating Alec Station involvement in hampering that program.

25. August 21, 2004.
26. Michael Isikoff, "Tangled Ties," *Newsweek*, April 7, 2003, http://www.newsweek.com/2004/04/06/terror-watch-tangled-ties.html.

Part 4:
Aden, Yemen

RET

VP report:

1) CIA - Intercept

9:53 EST

N.R.
(b)(1)

2) AA 77 - 3 indiv have been followed
since Millenium + Cole
1 guy is assoc of Cole bomber
2 Entered US in early July
(2 of 3 pulled aside & interrogated?)

3) No M.O.

N.R.

TOP SECRET

(9)

A FOIA request yielded the redacted notes of Principal Deputy Under Secretary of Defense for Policy Stephen Cambone, taken on the afternoon and evening of 9/11.

24

Further connections had been made between Almihdhar and al-Qaeda

Khalid Almihdhar left the US on June 10, 2000, flying from
Los Angeles to Frankfurt and then to Oman; from there he
continued to Yemen. The 9/11 Commission commented
that "he … abandoned Alhazmi in San Diego in June 2000 and returned to his family in Yemen."[1]

Returning to his family—his wife and, reportedly, one daughter—meant returning to al-Qaeda's global operations center in
Sana'a, which had been under surveillance for about four years.
This was the home of his father-in-law, Ahmed al-Hada, veteran of
the famous "C" formation battle. As we have seen, a call to or from
Almihdhar at the hub had been intercepted by the NSA in 1999
and had led to the surveillance of al-Qaeda's Malaysia summit. In
addition, calls between the hub and Almihdhar in the US were intercepted by the NSA, but not fully exploited, allegedly due to some
mix-up that was never properly explained.

After returning home, Almihdhar was then involved in new calls
that the NSA picked up. The 9/11 Congressional Inquiry discussion
of these calls was redacted:

> [NSA analyzed additional communications in the summer of
> 2000 that were associated with a suspected terrorist facility in
> the Middle East, Salem and Khalid. [… … … … … … … … … …
> …]. NSA did
> not believe this provided any new information, and there was no
> dissemination].[2]

Not surprisingly, the 9/11 Commission entirely ignored these
calls in its public output.

---

1. 9/11 Congressional Inquiry report, p. 135; *9/11 CR*, p. 237.
2. 9/11 Congressional Inquiry report, p. 157.

The NSA's non-dissemination of the calls is certainly disturbing. As we will see in the next few chapters, the operations hub and Almihdhar were involved in the bombing of the USS *Cole*, so they should also have been re-scrutinized after that bombing. In addition, the NSA's explanation for its non-exploitation of the calls between the US and the hub does not hold much water, so why should we believe there was nothing in the calls that provided new information here?

As we have seen, the hub was not just under surveillance through the interception of its calls, but also by satellite and possibly through bugs placed inside it. Even if Almihdhar was careful not to say anything incriminating on the phone, it is likely that he would have mentioned his time in the US several times in the company of his family.

Interestingly, a CIA cable sent in the second half of December 2000 noted that, according to the Justice Department's inspector general, "further connections had been made between Almihdhar and al-Qaeda."[3] The cable appears to have been sent by the CIA station in Sana'a, Yemen. The nature of these further connections is unclear, although by this time the CIA should have made such connections due to additional calls involving Almihdhar to and from the Yemen hub, as well as possible investigation of him in Yemen.

Under interrogation, Khalid Shaikh Mohammed said that after staying in Yemen for a month, Almihdhar traveled to Afghanistan, where the two men met. Almihdhar was summoned there not by KSM himself, but by Khallad bin Attash.[4] In December 1999 bin Attash had summoned Almihdhar to Malaysia by calling him at the Yemen hub, but we do not know how he contacted Almihdhar at this time. The caveat on KSM's confessions applies here, although this travel could potentially be confirmed by other detainees, such as bin Attash, airline records and, of course, the NSA's archives.

Although information about Almihdhar's travels during his thirteen months outside the US from June 2000 to July 2001 is incomplete, interrogations of bin Attash and KSM indicate he returned to Yemen at least one more time, in February 2001.[5] It is unclear how

---

3. Justice Department IG report, p. 269.
4. *9/11 CR*, p. 237; *United States v. Zacarias Moussaoui*, "Substitution for the Testimony of Khalid Shaikh Mohammed," July 31, 2006, pp. 20-21, http://www.vaed.uscourts.gov/notablecases/moussaoui/exhibits/defense/941.pdf.
5. *9/11 CR*, p. 237.

long Almihdhar stayed, but it could not have been much more than two or three months.

The same points apply to this visit to Yemen as they do to the previous one: Almihdhar was under surveillance, the NSA was intercepting his calls. What did he say in them? What did the NSA do with them? Did it disseminate anything? If so, what?

One unresolved issue is what Almihdhar was doing outside the US for a year. Allegedly, he returned to see his family, but then spent a large portion of that time away from Yemen: in Malaysia, Afghanistan and Saudi Arabia. FBI Director Robert Mueller speculated on this for the 9/11 Congressional Inquiry:

> Almihdhar's role in the September 11 plot between June 2000 and July 2001 – before his re-entry into the United States – may well have been that of the coordinator and organizer of the movements of the non-pilot hijackers. This is supported by his apparent lengthy stay in Saudi Arabia and his arriving back in the United States only after the arrival of all the hijackers.[6]

It is likely, although there is no proof of this, that Almihdhar was involved in organizing the rest of the muscle in some way. This makes the NSA's inaction all the more incredible. NSA officials may well have listened to him discuss the deployment of the other hijackers to the US on the Yemen hub phone.

Almihdhar presumably made calls home from Saudi Arabia and the other locations he visited, and these calls would also have been intercepted. Such intercepts could be traced and Almihdhar's phone numbers outside Yemen then exploited.

Regarding the intelligence Almihdhar's return to Yemen must have generated, the silence is deafening. How many calls can he have made to and from the hub in the thirteen months he was outside the US? Dozens? Hundreds? Yet all we know about them is contained in two semi-redacted sentences in the Congressional Inquiry report and a cryptic mention in the Justice Department inspector general's report.

---

6. Joint Intelligence Committee Inquiry, "Statement for the Record, FBI Director Robert S. Mueller III," September 26, 2002, http://www.fas.org/irp/congress/2002_hr/092602mueller.html.

25

As far as the Cole bombing, a U.S. investigator said the phone was used by the bombers to "put everything together"

After the embassy bombings, the US intelligence community must have taken a decision to let the Yemen hub continue to operate. The US could have tried to shut it down, as there was enough evidence against Ahmed al-Hada to charge him in connection with the attacks. Despite this, the hub continued to operate, and the FBI was able to map al-Qaeda's entire global network.

The chickens came home to roost on October 12, 2000, when al-Qaeda attacked the USS *Cole* in Aden, Yemen, killing seventeen of the sailors on board.

Numerous sources report that the Yemen hub, al-Qaeda's main center in the country of the bombing, was involved in this attack. For example, in sworn testimony at a public 9/11 Commission hearing, former FBI Director Louis Freeh said (emphasis added),

> If that information and the initiation for that surveillance [of Al-hazmi, Almihdhar and the others in Malaysia], which were phone calls to a central number, *which you're well aware of,* which plays a integral role not only in the East African bombings case but also in the *Cole* investigation ...[1]

Confirmation of this was provided by an FBI document sent to the Commission (emphases added):

> UBL [Osama bin Laden] can be directly connected to the attack on the USS *Cole* in October 12, 2000 (ADENBOM 265A-

---

1. National Commission on Terrorist Attacks Upon the United States, Tenth Public Hearing, April 13, 2004, http://govinfo.library.unt.edu/911/archive/hearing10/9-11Commission_Hearing_2004-04-13.htm.

NY-277013). *The 200578 telephone number* which was originally identified as significant through the KENBOM/TANBOM investigation *was also used during the planning of the attack on USS* Cole. *FBI investigators have learned the 200578 telephone number is subscribed to by AHMED AL-HADDA,* whose daughter is married to KHALID AL-MIHDHAR (Flight 77). The ADENBOM investigation has also linked ALMIHDHAR to both NAWAF AL-HAZMI (Flight 77) and KHALLAD, now identified as TAWFIQ MOHAMED BIN SALEH BIN ROSHAYED BIN ATTASH.[2]

Links between the Yemen hub and the *Cole* bombing have also been reported several times in the media. The first was in mid-February 2002, after Samir al-Hada killed himself as he was being pursued by Yemeni security forces. MSNBC reported that his phone was "used to relay orders to the Sept. 11 hijackers and the terrorist cells responsible for the bombings of two U.S. embassies in East Africa and the USS *Cole*." It added, "U.S. intelligence officials, speaking on condition of anonymity, said that intercepts of al-Qaeda communications indicate that the al-Hada family phone was used to relay messages to the embassy bombers, the USS *Cole* bombers, and the Sept. 11 hijackers ... U.S. officials say they can link the clan to the Sept. 11 attacks, the August 1998 bombing of U.S. embassies in Kenya and Tanzania, and the October 2000 bombing attack on the destroyer USS *Cole* in Aden harbor." The report even went so far as to say, "As far as the *Cole* bombing, a U.S. investigator said the phone was used by the bombers to 'put everything together.'"[3]

MSNBC confirmed the Yemen hub's role in the *Cole* bombing in May 2005, reporting:

> [Ahmed] Al-Hada, who fought with bin Laden in Afghanistan, is the patriarch of a family whose members played key roles in both the bombing of the *Cole* and the Sept. 11 attacks ... Moreover, al-Hada operated al-Qaeda's so-called "Yemeni Switchboard" used by bin Laden and others to pass messages during the run-ups to both the *Cole* bombing and the Sept. 11 attacks.[4]

---

2. Federal Bureau of Investigation, "PENTTBOM Case Summary as of 1/11/2002," January 11, 2002, http://www.scribd.com/doc/13120344/FBI-Case-Summary-for-911-from-the-911-Commission-Files.

3. Robert Windrem, "U.S. links Yemen clan to Sept. 11 and East Africa attacks," MSNBC, February 14, 2002.

4. Robert Windrem, "Al-Qaida leaders, associates," MSNBC, May 2005, http://www.msnbc.msn.com/id/4686491/.

The *US News and World Report* article discussed in detail earlier included this claim: "The home [Yemen hub] also served as a planning center for the 2000 attack on the USS *Cole* in Yemen."[5] The authors of the 2003 book *The Cell* also wrote, "Telephone records in Yemen showed that suspects in the *Cole* bombing had been in touch with suspects from the 1998 embassy bombings in East Africa."[6]

Newsweek reported that al-Hada interacted with Abd al-Rahim al-Nashiri, one of the *Cole* bombing's alleged masterminds, before the attack: "Visiting Yemen before the *Cole* attack, Nashiri came into contact with Ahmed Al-Hada, father-in-law of 9-11 hijacker Khalid Almihdhar, intelligence sources say."[7] As we will see in the next chapter, there is also a large amount of evidence linking Almihdhar himself to the *Cole* bombing.

At the outset of this investigation, we saw that embassy bomber Mohamed al-Owhali called the Yemen hub shortly before he went on his suicide mission. He called it once on August 5, 1998, twice on August 6, and once again on the morning of the bombing. The contents of these conversations are not known, but it is certainly possible that he became emotional with his old friend at the prospect of his impending martyrdom, or that he asked al-Hada to pass on a last message to his family. In any case, there may well have been a clue to an impending attack in the calls. Such clues could have been exploited to thwart the attack, for example by the NSA telephoning the US embassy in Nairobi and informing it that a suicide bomber had just ended his last call and was en route to destroy the building.

By the time of the embassy bombings, the Yemen hub had been Osama bin Laden's operations center for around two years. It is hard to imagine that the calls to and from it, or at least some of them, were not monitored in real time or near real time. It is also hard to understand why this intelligence was not exploited to prevent the bombings. Circumstances that excuse the NSA of negli-

5. David E. Kaplan and Kevin Whitelaw, "Pieces of the 9/11 Puzzle," *US News and World Report*, March 7, 2004, http://www.usnews.com/usnews/news/articles/040315/15nine11.htm.
6. John Miller and Michael Stone with Chris Mitchell, *The Cell: Inside the 9/11 Plot and Why the FBI and CIA Failed to Stop It* (New York: Hyperion, 2002), p. 237.
7. Mark Hosenball, "Terrorism: Score One For The United States," *Newsweek*, December 2, 2002, http://www.newsweek.com/id/66647.

gence or worse before the bombings can be postulated, but, given the lack of facts about what the NSA was doing with the hub, it is hard to make a firm judgment. At the very least, the NSA should be asked to explain this failure.

Even if we were to assume that the NSA had somehow missed the hub's importance before the embassy bombings, the situation after the bombings was completely different. The NSA must have been aware of the Yemen hub's importance to al-Qaeda, that it was involved in the embassy bombings, and that the intelligence that either was or could have been generated around the embassy bombings should have thwarted the terrorists. This would have made the hub a top priority for the NSA.

Then, the *Cole* bombers used the Yemen hub to "put everything together" before the attack, and the NSA missed it. How could that possibly have happened?

The above accounts of the Yemen hub's involvement in the *Cole* bombing appear to be contradicted by a CBS interview of NSA Director Michael Hayden, who said,

> When the *Cole* disaster took place I had brought to my desk in, in this office, every stitch of NSA reporting on the—that could in any way be related to this. And I went through it report by report and I sent a letter out to our entire work force, which was essentially, you performed well. Keep up the good work.[8]

There are a number of problems with Hayden's statement. First, immediately prior to the quote from Hayden, the CBS account said,

> Last year we asked him if NSA had overlooked any warnings of another al-Qaeda attack – the bombing of the USS *Cole* in Yemen, killing 17 Americans. He told us he personally checked and NSA hadn't missed a thing. It just wasn't there.

It is unclear what CBS's claim—Hayden said he had "personally checked and NSA hadn't missed a thing. It just wasn't there"—was based on. Possibly Hayden told them straight out that the NSA did not miss anything, and this quote was not included in the report. Possibly CBS interpreted Hayden's statement quoted above

---

8. "National Security Meltdown," CBS, June 19, 2002, http://www.cbsnews.com/stories/2001/01/24/60II/main266857.shtml.

to mean, "NSA hadn't missed a thing. It just wasn't there." In any event, accepting the judgment on its face requires us to believe that terrorists known to be involved in the *Cole* attack spoke to each other repeatedly, but never once discussed the bombing on the Yemen phone.

Let's look at the quote again: "And I went through it report by report and I sent a letter out to our entire work force, which was essentially, you performed well."

There is a way of saying one thing, but having your listeners believe you said something different. It involves leaving out a key piece of information which the listeners then make an assumption about, based on the other things you said and what they think of you generally. The statements you made were true, but your listeners now believe something that is not true. In some contexts this is referred to as a "non-denial denial."

First, Hayden said that he went through the reports, then he said that he sent out a letter telling the workforce they performed well. The listener assumes that the NSA would have prevented the attack if it could, that all the relevant information was contained in the reports and there was no need to review transcripts or recordings, and that Hayden did not find any errors in the reports. However, Hayden does not say any of this, he simply leaves us to presume it.

His statement is also consistent with several other scenarios: A) the NSA desired an attack and let it happen; B) the reports did not highlight any errors because the reports themselves were faulty, and additional relevant information in fact was contained in the transcripts or recordings of the intercepts; and C) Hayden found errors in the reports, but decided to praise his staff anyway. The possibility that the reports were incomplete must be taken seriously. Based on Michael Scheuer's discussion of them, we know that the reports were incomplete from 1996 to spring 1999.

Another alternative is that Hayden was simply lying. As we will see, he certainly did make at least one false statement about 9/11.

In addition, we are not told whether there was another investigation into the failings and what conclusion this investigation came to. Certainly, a possible failure of this magnitude should be officially investigated by the appropriate body, the NSA's inspector general. Asked whether the NSA's inspector general had written reports about the embassy bombings, the *Cole* attack and 9/11, James Bamford replied, "I know of no IG reports written on those incidents. In the past, most of the IG reports have dealt with employee complaints and not about failed policies."[9] Hayden's statement makes no mention of the NSA's inspector general.

Indeed, it seems that Michael Hayden simply usurped its function, conducted a cursory review, and issued a no-fault finding.

9. PBS, *NOVA*, "Ask the Expert," February 9, 2008, http://www.pbs.org/wgbh/nova/spyfactory/ask.html.

26

One has also been identified as playing key roles in both the East African Embassy attacks and the USS Cole attack

S ome of the links between the Yemen hub and the *Cole* bombers were highlighted in the previous chapter. However, there are additional links between Khalid Almihdhar and the other *Cole* plotters, and they will be set out here. Almihdhar's exact connection to the bombing is not known, although there is a wealth of circumstantial evidence indicating his involvement.

The claim that Almihdhar was involved in the *Cole* bombing was first made in public by British Prime Minister Tony Blair in a key speech, on October 4, 2001, which held al-Qaeda responsible for 9/11. Blair said that one of the nineteen hijackers "has also been identified as playing key roles in both the East African Embassy attacks and the USS *Cole* attack."[1] Two days later, the *New York Times* identified the mystery hijacker as "Mr. Almihdhar," adding, "United States investigators said they had clearly linked Mr. Almihdhar to the *Cole* attack and 'possibly' to the embassy bombings."[2]

Given Blair's record of not telling the truth, in particular in relation to the issue of Iraq's non-existent weapons of mass destruction, it is wise to take his claim that Almihdhar played a key role in the *Cole* bombing with a grain of salt, especially as the statement came so close to 9/11 and the invasion of Afghanistan, which the US and Britain needed to justify in the eyes of the their citizens.

However, Blair was supported by Abd al-Karim al-Iryani, Yemen's prime minister at the time of the bombing. "Khalid Almihd-

1. Tony Blair, "Statement to Parliament (US terror attacks)," October 4, 2001, http://webarchive. nationalarchives.gov.uk/+/http://www.number10.gov.uk/Page1606.
2. Jeff Gerth and Don Van Natta Jr., "US Traces path of Hijacker Tied to Other Attacks," *New York Times*, October 6, 2001, http://www.nytimes.com/2001/10/06/national/06INQU.html?pagewanted=1.

har was one of the *Cole* perpetrators, involved in preparations," he said. "He was in Yemen at the time and stayed after the *Cole* bombing for a while, then he left."[3]

Here is the evidence linking Almihdhar to the *Cole* attack:

(1) As we saw above, a passage in the Congressional Inquiry report indicates Almihdhar spoke to Khallad bin Attash, one of the two alleged masterminds of the *Cole* bombing, in mid-1999. This call was monitored by the NSA.[4]

(2) According to a detainee, Almihdhar was aware of a ship-bombing operation by December 1999 and knew the plan had been conceived by *Cole* bombing mastermind Abd al-Rahim al-Nashiri. *The 9/11 Commission Report* says, "A detainee says that 9/11 hijacker Khalid Almihdhar told him about the maritime operation sometime in late 1999 and credited al-Nashiri as its originator."

The plot at this point was not to attack the *Cole*, but the USS *The Sullivans*. This attack was attempted in early January 2000 and failed. The 9/11 Commission sources the claim of Almihdhar's prior knowledge of the ship bombing to "intelligence report, interrogation of detainee, Dec. 2, 2001." The methods used to extract information from detainees may make this information unreliable.[5]

(3) In late 1999, Almihdhar attended, or at least began, a training course for al-Qaeda operatives in Afghanistan. The course was also attended by fellow Pentagon hijacker Nawaf Alhazmi, Khallad bin Attash, and one of the eventual *Cole* bombers, Ibrahim al-Thawar. Although the caveat on detainee information applies, the existence of the training course was confirmed by Khalid Shaikh Mohammed, bin Attash, and Abu Jandal, a militant held by authorities in Yemen, where he was questioned by the FBI.[6]

(4) About a month before the failed attack on *The Sullivans*, Almihdhar traveled to Yemen. Although Almihdhar was a Saudi national, he lived in Yemen with his family, so there may be an innocent explanation for this. However, when detainees were asked to explain why Almihdhar went to Yemen at this time instead of attending/finishing the scheduled training course in Afghani-

3. Brian Whitaker, "Piecing together the terrorist jigsaw," *Guardian* (London), October 15, 2001, http://www.guardian.co.uk/Archive/Article/0,4273,4277367,00.html.
4. 9/11 Congressional Inquiry report, pp. 155-56.
5. *9/11 CR*, p. 491.
6. Ibid., pp. 156-57, 493.

stan, they gave differing explanations. KSM claimed that Almihdhar could not handle the course and quit after a week, bin Attash
claimed both that Almihdhar was pulled out early by bin Laden and
that he completed the course, and Abu Jandal claimed that Almihd-
dhar completed the course.[7] These differing accounts may suggest
that the operatives were trying to hide something. It is possible that
they were aware that Almihdhar's participation in the failed attack
on *The Sullivans* would implicate someone else, such as Ahmed al-
Hada, and they wanted to protect that someone else.

(5) While in Yemen in late 1999, Almihdhar spent some time
with his family in Sana'a, at the communications hub that was used
to "put everything together" before the *Cole* bombing. Given that
the hub was used for the *Cole* bombing, it may well have been used
for the failed *The Sullivans* bombing as well.

(6) Bin Attash, an alleged mastermind of the *Cole* operation,
telephoned Almihdhar shortly before the attempted bombing of
The Sullivans.[8] This call was monitored by the NSA, and the two
are reported to have talked about meeting in Malaysia.

(7) The attempt to bomb *The Sullivans* failed on January 3, 2000,
and Almihdhar left Yemen the next day, tracked by the CIA and
foreign intelligence agencies.

(8) In Malaysia, Almihdhar then met numerous other al-Qaeda
operatives involved in the failed attack on *The Sullivans* and the
subsequent attack on the *Cole*. As we have seen, the summit's attendees included bin Attash and al-Nashiri, the two operatives
credited with being the *Cole* operation's masterminds. Three other
operatives allegedly involved in the operation are also said to have
been present: KSM, Ramzi bin al-Shibh, and Fahad al-Quso.

(9) After leaving the summit, Almihdhar traveled with Alhazmi
and bin Attash to Thailand, where bin Attash, and possibly Almihdhar and Alhazmi, met al-Quso and Ibrahim al-Thawar.[9]

(10) After arriving in the US, Almihdhar continued to call the
communications hub in Yemen, where his family lived, and which
was used to "put everything together" before the *Cole* bombing.

7. Ibid., p. 493 n50.
8. Wright 2006, p. 310.
9. *9/11 CR*, p. 159.

188

(11) In June 2000, Almihdhar left the US and returned to the communications hub in Yemen. According to the 9/11 Commission, this was because he wanted to see his child, although, as set out above, there are reasons to be skeptical of this.[10] He may have simply been needed for the ship-bombing operation.

(12) Almihdhar was then contacted by bin Attash and went to see KSM in Afghanistan.[11] This information is based on detainee interrogations, so the caveat about such sources applies, although there is other information to suggest Almihdhar was traveling in Asia at this time.

(13) When the *Cole* was bombed, Almihdhar was in Yemen, and he left shortly after. Author Terry McDermott wrote in 2005, "At least one of the men who had been with [bin Attash] at the Kuala Lumpur meeting, Khalid Almihdhar, was back in Yemen with him in the fall … [Bin Attash] and Almihdhar escaped without notice."[12]

(14) Almihdhar visited Malaysia in October 2000 to discuss a third ship-bombing operation, to be carried out in Singapore with a local operative.

(15) He visited Malaysia again for the same purpose in June 2001.[13]

Whether this constitutes proof of Almihdhar's involvement in the ship-bombing operations may depend upon how high the bar is set. However, his repeated contacts with the other bombers and his presence in Yemen at the time of both *The Sullivans* and *Cole* operations strongly suggest that he was involved.

10. Ibid., p. 222.
11. Ibid., p. 237; *United States v. Zacarias Moussaoui*, "Substitution for the Testimony of Khalid Shaikh Mohammed," July 31, 2006, pp. 20-21, http://www.vaed.uscourts.gov/notablecases/moussaoui/exhibits/defense/941.pdf.
12. Terry McDermott, *Perfect Soldiers: The 9/11 Hijackers, Who They Were, Why They Did It* (London: Pontico's, 2005), p. 209.
13. *United States v. Zacarias Moussaoui*, trial transcript for March 8, 2006, morning session, http://cryptome.org/usa-v-zm-030806-01.htm; *United States v. Zacarias Moussaoui*, trial transcript for March 8, 2006, afternoon session, http://cryptome.org/usa-v-zm-030806-02.htm.

27

This is a high threshold to cross

T he response to the *Cole* bombing by the Clinton administration and the US intelligence community was even more
inexplicable than the NSA's performance in the run-up to
it. The list of terrorist organizations that could pull off an operation of this magnitude and were known to be active in Yemen was
extremely short, and it was clear from the start that al-Qaeda was
the lead suspect.

However, it appears that the administration did not want to respond. CIA Director George Tenet later wrote,

> In the aftermath of the attack, it was clear that known al-Qaeda
> operatives were involved, but neither our intelligence nor the FBI's
> criminal investigation could conclusively prove that Osama bin
> Laden and his leadership had had authority, direction, and con-
> trol over the attack. This is a high threshold to cross. The ultimate
> question policy makers have to determine is what standard of proof
> should be used before the United States decides to deploy force? It
> must always be a standard set by policy makers because ultimately
> it is they who bear the responsibility for actions taken.[1]

There has been some speculation about why the Clinton administration set the bar so high. Tenet himself suggested that it may
have been because of the arguments over the disputed Bush-Gore
election. Another version attributes the inaction to not wanting to
disrupt the Israeli-Palestinian peace process. Whatever the case, it
appears that the decision not to retaliate—in any form—was influenced by outside political considerations.

Deputy CIA director John McLaughlin explained to the 9/11
Commission what the high threshold meant for investigators: "It
was not enough for the attack to smell, look, and taste like an al-
Qaeda operation. To make a case, the CIA needed not just to guess
a link to someone known to be an al-Qaeda operative."[2]

1. Tenet 2007, p. 128.
2. *9/11 CR*, p. 192.

Nevertheless, links to al-Qaeda were turned up by the investigation within weeks. According to *The 9/11 Commission Report*:

> The Yemenis provided strong evidence connecting the *Cole* attack to al-Qaeda during the second half of November, identifying individual operatives whom the United States knew were part of al-Qaeda [bin Attash and al-Nashiri]. During December the United States was able to corroborate this evidence. But the United States did not have evidence about bin Laden's personal involvement in the attacks until al-Nashiri and [bin Attash] were captured in 2002 and 2003.[3]

In 1998, the connections to Abd al-Rahim al-Nashiri and Khallad bin Attash were some of the links to al-Qaeda that had allowed responsibility for the embassy bombings to be attributed to Osama bin Laden, and missiles were launched against targets in Afghanistan and Somalia. Yet this time these connections were not considered enough to establish a link to al-Qaeda, although it was clear that the two men, both known al-Qaeda operatives, had run the operation?

The case for al-Qaeda responsibility for the embassy bombings had another clue: at least one of the bombers had repeatedly called the Yemen hub, al-Qaeda's operations center, and it had received calls from bin Laden's phone. A series of calls to al-Qaeda's operations center would clearly indicate that the bombers were linked to al-Qaeda. Despite this, the reports of briefings on responsibility for the *Cole* bombing contain no mention of the Yemen hub. As we have seen, there is nonetheless good reason to believe that the hub and operatives linked to it, in particular Almihdhar, were involved in the *Cole* bombing.

Either the Yemen hub was mentioned in documents about responsibility for the bombing, which means policy makers insisted on even more proof of al-Qaeda's responsibility than its operations center being used to "put everything together" before the bombing, or the intelligence community withheld its involvement from policy makers. The lack of references to the hub, whose existence was first publicly revealed in Egypt in 1999, in reports of the briefings would seem to indicate the latter.

Whatever the reason, the hub's operations were allowed to continue. The decision to allow it to operate after the embassy bombings was, at minimum, questionable. But the attack on the *Cole* with its

---

3. *9/11 CR*, p. 193.

seventeen lives lost showed this policy to have been a failure. Whatever intelligence had been learned, and whatever plots prevented, it would be hard to argue that it was worth the victims of the *Cole* attack. This applies doubly to the NSA as part of the Department of Defense, the department that oversees the Navy and had employed the murdered sailors.

In any case, as we will see, the fact that the US government was aware of the hub was disclosed in February 2001 during the embassy bombings trial. Ahmed Al-Hada was named repeatedly and his phone number read out in open court during the trial, allowing al-Qaeda to discover that the US was aware of the hub. After US knowledge of al-Hada was revealed, what then was the point of concealing his involvement in the *Cole* bombing?

Let's restate this: the NSA discovered a terrorist facility, al-Hada's Yemen hub, before the embassy bombings; two US embassies were bombed with the assistance of the facility and al-Hada; the US decided not to shut the facility down, but to monitor it to gain intelligence; the facility assisted the bombing of the USS *Cole*; the US seemingly ignored its role in the *Cole* bombing and claimed it did not really know who had attacked the ship; and it continued to monitor the facility, which went on to play a role in the 9/11 attacks.

The same problem that applies to the hub and al-Hada also applies to Khalid Almihdhar, but much more so. The CIA's hiding of information about him from the FBI had allowed him to operate unchecked, except possibly by still-secret CIA surveillance. There is evidence suggesting Almihdhar was involved in the *Cole* operation. The CIA was aware of Almihdhar's possible links to the *Cole* no later than December 2000, when an overseas station pointed out in a cable that Almihdhar may have met one of the *Cole* bombers in Thailand in mid-January 2000.[4]

Some CIA officers must have known that a terrorist operative they had shielded from the FBI had just helped blow up a US destroyer, killing seventeen US sailors. It is hard to imagine how much more badly an operation could go. Yet their reaction, as we will see, was that they continued to conceal Almihdhar. What could possibly have motivated this continued patronage?

4. Justice Department IG report, p. 269.

28

Hampered the pursuit of justice in the death of seventeen American sailors

T he FBI team that arrived in Yemen in the autumn of 2000 to investigate the *Cole* bombing was headed by one of the Bureau's top counterterrorism managers, John O'Neill, and lead investigator Ali Soufan.[1]

In late October 2000, Fahad al-Quso, the operative who had stayed at the same Bangkok hotel as Khalid Almihdhar, Nawaf Alhazmi and Khallad bin Attash in January 2000, was arrested and interrogated by authorities in Yemen. Al-Quso admitted that he and one of the two *Cole* suicide bombers, Ibrahim al-Thawar, went to Bangkok and gave several thousand dollars to bin Attash. He said the money was to buy a new artificial leg for bin Attash.

The FBI got a transcript of the interrogation a month later, and Soufan remembered a source he recruited in Afghanistan who had mentioned bin Attash. Soufan got a photo of bin Attash from the Yemenis and sent it to Islamabad for the source to identify. This set in motion a complex chain of events that will be described in the next chapter. Upon learning that al-Quso had given bin Attash cash in Thailand, Soufan wondered why money was being sent away from the *Cole* plotters and away from Yemen prior to a major planned attack there. He speculated that it might mean another al-Qaeda operation was being planned elsewhere.

After these links to bin Attash and links to al-Nashiri were uncovered, Soufan managed to deduce, based on the *Cole* bombers' movements, that there might have been an important al-Qaeda meeting in Southeast Asia in January 2000. Soufan filed a series of

---

1. This chapter is based on Lawrence Wright, "The Agent : Did the C.I.A. stop an F.B.I. Detective from Preventing 9/11?" *New Yorker*, July 10 and 17, 2006 , http://www.lawrencewright.com/WrightSoufan.pdf; also Wright 2006, pp. 321-22, 325-27, 329-31.

three requests with the CIA, in November 2000, and April and July 2001, asking for information about such a possible meeting. He was right, there had been such a meeting—the Malaysia summit—and the CIA was highly aware of it. CIA headquarters had the NSA intercepts, the tracking of the meeting's attendees, the Malaysian surveillance, and numerous internal cables. However, it repeatedly denied knowing anything about any such meeting.

The first request, filed in November 2000, was spurred by information Soufan obtained from his questioning of al-Quso, who, again, had stayed at the same Bangkok hotel as Almihdhar and Alhazmi in January 2000. The CIA responded by saying it knew nothing about the meeting. Author Lawrence Wright wasn't buying this:

> The fact that the CIA withheld information about the master-mind of the *Cole* bombing and the meeting in Malaysia, when directly asked by the FBI, hampered the pursuit of justice in the death of seventeen American sailors. Much more tragic consequences were on the horizon.[2]

The CIA station in Yemen that was working with the FBI investigators was well aware of the Malaysia summit. The CIA had employed officers from eight stations to help monitor the summit, and, as Almihdhar had flown there from Yemen, it is highly likely the station in Yemen was involved in this work.

Further, in early 2001 the Yemeni authorities were shown photos of Almihdhar and Alhazmi taken at the summit and passed by the Malaysian authorities to the CIA.[3] It is highly likely these photos were shown to the Yemenis by a CIA officer. Around the same time, a CIA officer in Islamabad showed two of the Kuala Lumpur photos to an asset for identification purposes. It appears he got these photos from his colleagues in Yemen. Whatever the case, he reported back what the asset said to the Agency's Yemen station.[4]

---

2. Wright 2006, p. 329. Interestingly, early printings of Wright's book contain the phrase "amounted to obstruction of justice" instead of "hampered the pursuit of justice" in the investigation; see Peter Dale Scott, "The JFK Assassination and 9/11: the Designated Suspects in Both Cases," *Global Research*, July 5, 2008, http://www.globalresearch.ca/index.php?context=va&aid=9511. The passage is quoted at note 19.

3. The Yemenis were shown the photographs on January 3, 2001; see Justice Department IG report, p. 268.

4. For the report on the identification being sent to the CIA station in Yemen, see untitled CIA memo to 9/11 Commission commenting on draft commission staff statement, April 9, 2004, http://www.scribd.com/doc/14579489/CIA-Comments-on-911-Commission-Staff-Statement-about-Khallad-

In addition, as will be discussed later, on September 12, 2001, the CIA station chief in Yemen would hand Soufan a manila envelope containing the three photos and a report about the Malaysia summit. Why wasn't this available on September 10?

Wright's *New Yorker* article makes it clear that the FBI director knew of Soufan's request: "On Soufan's behalf, the director of the FBI sent a letter to the director of the CIA, formally asking for information about [bin Attash], and whether there might have been an al-Qaeda meeting somewhere in Southeast Asia before the bombing."

But, as we saw in Part 2, FBI director Louis Freeh and other Bureau officials were aware of the meeting, as they had been briefed by the CIA at the time. These other officials included Thomas Pickard, deputy director of the Bureau when the *Cole* investigation started, but acting director in the summer of 2001, and Dale Watson, assistant director of the Counterterrorism Division.[5] Nevertheless, they failed to point this out to Ali Soufan. Had they done so, Soufan would have discovered the meeting, and worked out that the CIA was lying to him. Pickard later told the 9/11 Commission that he had not told Attorney General John Ashcroft of the meeting in 2001 because the CIA had placed a "close hold" on the information, meaning the FBI officials who knew of it could not tell anyone else. Presumably, this is the reason Soufan was not told. How hard these officials tried to get the information to Soufan is unclear.

In early December, after the first of the three requests had been filed, Soufan was given the chance to interrogate al-Quso directly. Al-Quso admitted to meeting bin Attash and al-Thawar in Bangkok, but said he gave bin Attash $36,000, not the $5,000 for medical expenses that he had claimed when talking to the Yemenis the month before. Al-Quso also said they stayed in the Washington Hotel in Bangkok, so Soufan checked telephone records, finding calls between the hotel and al-Quso's house in Yemen, as well as calls to both places from a pay phone in Kuala Lumpur. The pay phone was the one mentioned in the discussion of the Malaysia summit; it was directly outside the condominium where the summit was held.

Identification.
5. Thomas Pickard, "Letter from Former FBI Director to 9/11 Commission about AG Ashcroft's Non-Interest in Terrorism," June 24, 2004, http://www.scribd.com/doc/15644704/Letter-from-Former-FBI-Director-to-911-Commission-about-AG-Ashcrofts-NonInterest-in-Terrorism.

John O'Neill believed that al-Quso was still holding back important information. He was right, as al-Quso had met Almihdhar and Alhazmi in January 2000, but was still keeping this to himself.[6] However, O'Neill left Yemen in late November and was prohibited from returning by the US ambassador to Yemen, Barbara Bodine, in January 2001.[7] Without his influential presence, the Yemeni government would not allow any more interrogations, perhaps for fear the FBI would uncover some of the numerous links between it and radical Islamists.

Because of this newly discovered information, the second request in April 2001 was more specific than the first. Again, the CIA kept what it knew from Soufan, falsely claiming it knew nothing of the meeting. Wright commented in *The Looming Tower*:

> If the CIA had responded to Soufan by supplying him with the intelligence he requested, the FBI would have learned of the Malaysia summit and of the connection to Almihdhar and Alhazmi. The bureau would have learned—as the [CIA] already knew— that the al-Qaeda operatives were in America and had been there for more than a year. Because there was a preexisting indictment for bin Laden in New York, and Almihdhar and Alhazmi were his associates, the bureau already had the authority to follow the suspects, wiretap their apartment, intercept their communications, clone their computer, investigate their contacts—all the essential steps that might have prevented 9/11.[8]

The third request, sent in July, was even more specific, but again the CIA denied it knew anything.

By this point, the *Cole* investigation, which had been limping along for months, had been further hampered because all the investigators had to leave Yemen due to an alleged threat of an attack against the US embassy there. Although the *Cole* attack occurred in Aden, some way from the capital, the investigators had left the scene and holed up in the US embassy in Sana'a in early 2001. In June, the Yemeni authorities said they had arrested eight men who were part of a plot to blow up the embassy. Although the FBI was on the verge of being granted

6. Jim Gilmore, PBS, *Frontline*, "What if …," October 3, 2002, http://www.pbs.org/wgbh/pages/frontline/shows/knew/could/.
7. Bodine was elevated to the board of the American Foreign Service Association in 2008, at the same time as Shayna Steinger, the consular officer who issued the hijackers with twelve visas.
8. Wright 2006, pp. 330-31.

access to a group of people who might have had further information about the bombing, O'Neill and FBI Director Freeh agreed that the team should be pulled out, and they all flew home on June 17.[9]

The information Ali Soufan requested about the *Cole* bombers, bin Attash, and the Malaysia summit would have led to Alhazmi and Almihdhar, who were known to have been in Malaysia with bin Attash. Their subsequent travel to the US would have been of great interest to the FBI, which could have easily found them—at the time of the first request in November 2000, Alhazmi was actually living with the FBI informer Abdussattar Shaikh in San Diego. When one of Soufan's assistants, Steve Bongardt, was allowed to join the search for Almihdhar after 9/11, he turned up information leading to Alhazmi's whereabouts within a few hours. Given that the two men used their own names for bank accounts, credit cards and identification documents in the US, this was not difficult.

The major question here: *why* did the CIA repeatedly lie to the FBI? A secondary question: *who* at the CIA repeatedly lied to the FBI? Wright does not identify the CIA component that falsely claimed the Agency knew nothing of the summit, but the logical place to route such a request was Alec Station. Some of the officers there, including "Michelle" and Tom Wilshire, had previously deliberately withheld information from the FBI about Almihdhar and his US visa. Therefore, it seems extremely likely that the CIA knew that its claims of ignorance about the requests were false and that they were part of a pattern to withhold information from the Bureau.

* * *

Despite their clear relevance to the 9/11 investigations, there is not a word about Ali Soufan's three requests in the 9/11 Congressional Inquiry report, *The 9/11 Commission Report*, or the Justice Department inspector general's report.

Although the inspector general's report does not mention Soufan by any name or alias, there are what appear to be references to him in the report, for example:

> On January 9, 2001, a New York FBI agent who was the FBI's lead case agent on the *Cole* investigation sent Max [the FBI's represen-

---

9. Lawrence Wright, "The Agent ...," see note 1.

tative in Pakistan][10] an e-mail stating that he and his co-case agent wanted to meet with the source [who had identified bin Attash in a photograph] to talk about some of the *Cole* suspects, including [bin Attash].[11]

The report goes on to discuss the meeting, which will be dealt with in greater detail in the next chapter. The lead case agent on the *Cole* investigation would be Soufan, and the Justice Department inspector general's report clearly states that this agent had been interviewed.[12] It is therefore hard to believe that the Justice Department inspector general could have remained unaware of the CIA's three false responses to Soufan's requests, especially as its report spent dozens of pages discussing the investigation into the *Cole* bombing.

The key staffer on the Justice Department inspector general's probe was Barbara Grewe, who, according to a 9/11 Commission document quoted above, was responsible for "examin[ing] intelligence sharing between the FBI and CIA." Grewe interviewed Ali Soufan twice in the late summer and fall of 2003. Although she had moved to the Commission by then, she was still interacting with the inspector general's investigators.

The case to be built against the Alec Station group involves not just one or two key events where something went wrong, but an incredible string of failures. Recall what Tom Wilshire himself said, "Every place that something could have gone wrong in this over a year and a half, it went wrong."

Here, the three wrongly denied requests from the FBI are three dots that needed to be connected to obtain the full picture. However, instead of connecting them, the Justice Department inspector general simply removed them from the picture.

The situation of the 9/11 Commission is similar. Ali Soufan, referred to by the alias "Al S." in the Commission's report, was interviewed three times by the Commission, on August 26, September

---

10. Max is the agent identified as "Michael D" in *9/11 CR*. Tracking individuals in the reports through their aliases is rendered more problematic by the use of "warning quotes" on aliases in *9/11 CR*— "John," "Jane," etc.—and their general absence in the Justice Department IG report, as here. To avoid confusion, this individual is identified as "Michael D" in my text.
11. Justice Department IG report, p. 273.
12. Ibid., p. 276: "Both FBI agents who participated in the February 1 debriefing of the source told the OIG …"

15 and November 12, 2003.[13] Yet its report fails to mention his three requests for information to which the CIA falsely responded that it knew nothing of al-Qaeda's Malaysia summit. Barbara Grewe was present for the first two of these interviews, and drafted the memorandum for the record about them. It was Grewe who also conducted the Commission's interviews of Wilshire and Dina Corsi, but failed to draft a memo about them, and omitted or glossed over the errors they made.

Although Soufan's requests were revealed in full detail in 2006 by Lawrence Wright in an article for the *New Yorker* and his book, they were first mentioned publicly in a *New York Times* article in April 2004.[14]

The *Times* article said that a few weeks into the *Cole* investigation, the FBI "turned to the CIA for help and sent a formal query in November 2000." It gave details of the first request:

> The FBI investigators gave the CIA [bin Attash]'s Yemeni passport picture and a phone number at a Bangkok hotel that seemed connected with the meeting with Mr. Quso, one of two men indicted in New York in the *Cole* bombing. In an interview, CIA officials acknowledged that they had received the request from the FBI.

The second request was also described:

> In April 2001, the FBI sent another query to the CIA asking about a phone number in Kuala Lumpur and passing along information about the Washington Hotel in Bangkok, which investigators had determined was the site of Mr. Quso's meeting with [bin Attash].

Although the sources for the article are anonymous, it his highly likely one or more of them were members of the FBI's *Cole* investigation team, perhaps Soufan or Steve Bongardt.

The *Times* article shows the omission of the three requests from the two reports to be even more unconscionable. Both the Justice Department's inspector general and the 9/11 Commission inter-

---

13. "Al S." is mentioned in the endnotes to *9/11 CR*: p. 507 n122, n128, n132; p, 536 n56; and pp. 536-537 n60. These endnotes are sources for passages in the main text about the *Cole* bombing. The third interview was mentioned in an e-mail to this author from Kirsten Wilhelm of the National Archives, February 3, 2009.

14. David Johnston and James Risen, "Inquiry Into Attack on the Cole in 2000 Missed 9/11 Clues," *New York Times*, April 11, 2004, http://www.nytimes.com/2004/04/11/politics/11COLE.html?hp?pagewanted=1.

viewed people who knew about these requests, and a focus of those interviews was the investigation of the *Cole* bombing—regarding which the requests had been made.

29

The "Khallad" mentioned by al-Quso could actually be Khalid Almihdhar or one of his associates

B etween the submission of Ali Soufan's first and second requests, an informer in Osama bin Laden's organization identified Khallad bin Attash as a person who attended the Malaysia summit. Both the way the identification was made and its subsequent non-dissemination to the FBI show that the CIA was still withholding information about the Malaysia summit and, in particular, about Khalid Almihdhar and Nawaf Alhazmi.

A few weeks after the *Cole* investigation started, the FBI obtained a photo from the Yemenis of a man they thought was bin Attash and sent it for confirmation to Islamabad, Pakistan. The confirmation was to be provided by an informer, whom we will call "Omar," handled as a joint FBI-CIA source out of the Pakistani capital. However, his FBI handler, "Michael D," could not speak his language and relied on his CIA counterpart, "Chris," for translation. In this case, the CIA officer had Omar identify the photo, which he recognized as being of bin Attash, for his FBI colleague, who properly documented the identification and sent it to the *Cole* investigators.[1]

A CIA officer at an overseas station, presumably in Yemen, then wrote a cable saying that further connections had been made between Almihdhar and al-Qaeda. It is unclear exactly what these connections were, but, as detailed above, over the prior few months Almihdhar had spent some time at his home, al-Qaeda's operations center, which was under surveillance by the US. In these circumstances it would hardly be difficult to make further connections between him and bin Laden's organization. The station noted Almihdhar might be linked to the *Cole* plotters, and asked for the Malaysia photos.

---

1. Much of the material in this chapter is taken from the relevant sections of the Justice Department IG report, pp. 262-78.

After the photos were received, an officer at the station speculated that Almihdhar and bin Attash might be the same person. The Justice Department inspector general summarized:

> The CIA office reported in the December 2000 cable that it had learned that Fahad al-Quso, who was in Yemeni custody for his participation in the *Cole* attack, had received $7,000 from someone named Ibrahim [al-Thawar], which al-Quso had taken to Bangkok, Thailand, on January 6, 2000, to deliver to "Khallad," [bin Attash] a friend of Ibrahim's. It was noted in the cable that because Almihdhar had departed Kuala Lumpur around that same time to travel to Bangkok, the CIA suspected that the "Khallad" mentioned by al-Quso could actually be Khalid Almihdhar or one of his associates. It was noted further that this information had "added significance" because Khallad had been identified as a "key operative likely serving as an intermediary between Osama Bin Laden and the [*Cole*] perpetrators."

It is unclear how anyone at the CIA could have thought Almihdhar might be bin Attash, as the Agency had photographs of the two men by this time and, although they were both Arab males of a similar age, their facial features were dissimilar. In addition, bin Attash had only one leg, having lost the other in Afghanistan, and this may well have been apparent on the video provided by the Malaysians of the al-Qaeda summit in Kuala Lumpur. Further, before traveling to Southeast Asia around January 4, both al-Quso and Almihdhar were in Yemen. If al-Quso had wanted to give the money to Almihdhar, he could have done so before Almihdhar's departure to Kuala Lumpur.

In one version of these events, the version implicitly endorsed by the Justice Department inspector general and 9/11 Commission, the CIA officers were doing their level best, and the problems simply arose from systemic communication barriers with the FBI. In the alternative narrative, one supported by evidence that Doug Miller and Mark Rossini were directed to hide information from the FBI in January 2000 and then pressured to conceal this from the Justice Department inspector general after 9/11, the CIA officers were deliberately concealing information about Almihdhar and Alhazmi from the Bureau. This alternative narrative provides us with a different perspective.

The speculation that Almihdhar and bin Attash were the same person ultimately led Chris, the CIA officer in Islamabad, to show photos of Almihdhar and Alhazmi to Omar, who had just identified bin Attash in the photo provided by the Yemenis. The alternative narrative accounts for this as a ruse, developed because the Alec Station group discovered that the FBI was aware of bin Attash's role in the *Cole* bombing, and that a source inside al-Qaeda had identified him in a photo, and they had become worried. Possibly, they were worried that whatever operation they had going involving Almihdhar and Alhazmi, close associates of bin Attash, would be blown by the FBI. They may have been concerned that Omar could also identify Almihdhar and Alhazmi for the FBI, and perhaps provide it with additional information about the two men.

So, to find out how worried they should be about information Omar might have, they engineered a test to see whether he recognized Almihdhar and Alhazmi. The test was to show him photos of the two men and see what his reaction was. However, the photos needed to be passed officially, and a reason had to be found for this. The solution was to have somebody speculate that Almihdhar and bin Attash were the same person, and put this in a cable that both the sender and the recipient knew did not contain genuine speculation, but was merely generated to provide an excuse for some other purpose. Alec Station would then simply respond to the cable and send the photos for Omar to look at. This is not the first time such a tactic of false cables had been used—recall the January 2000 cable drafted by "Michelle" that said the FBI had been informed of Almihdhar's US visa. Nor would it be the last time, as we shall see.

None of the speculation that Almihdhar was bin Attash was shared with the FBI, despite the fact that the two agencies were supposed to be conducting a joint investigation into the *Cole* bombing. In fact, some CIA cables drafted at this time contain both information about bin Attash and information not related to bin Attash; CIA officers were instructed to share the information not related to bin Attash with the FBI, but were not instructed to share the information about bin Attash and al-Qaeda's Malaysia summit.

The CIA's Counterterrorist Center said that it thought the overseas officer's speculation was interesting, and agreed to send a photo of Almihdhar taken at the Malaysia summit to Omar's handler, Chris, in Islamabad "to confirm/rule out this particular Khalid [Almihdhar] as a match for [bin Attash]." The identity of the CIA officer who sent this cable to Islamabad is unknown. Omar would be shown the photo and would say whether he recognized it as being bin Attash, thus confirming or refuting the theory.

When the photo arrived in Islamabad, it was accompanied by another one, showing Alhazmi at the Malaysia summit. This supports the alternative theory in which the purpose of showing Omar the photos was to determine whether he recognized Almihdhar and Alhazmi—if the purpose was just to confirm Almihdhar as a match for bin Attash, why send a photo of somebody else as well?

While Michael D, the FBI representative, was out of the room, Chris showed Omar the two photos, and Omar said he did not know Almihdhar, but wrongly identified Alhazmi as bin Attash—the two men had similar facial features. The Agency had other photos of bin Attash at the meeting, but they were not shown to Omar.

Omar was not re-shown the photograph the Yemenis had provided, the one that he had already correctly identified as bin Attash. If Alec Station really had wanted to know if Almihdhar was bin Attash, then it certainly would have been a good idea to show him the Yemeni photograph at the same time as the one of Almihdhar, but this was not done. If they had done this he would probably have expressed his surprise that anybody could have thought that bin Attash and Almihdhar were the same person.

If the purpose of showing the photographs was really to assess what Omar might tell the FBI about Almihdhar and Alhazmi, then the test had been a great success, as he was unable to correctly identify photographs of the two men. However, the Alec Station group had created another problem for itself: Chris put the identification of the photo of Alhazmi as bin Attash in an official cable. This meant that Alec Station now officially thought bin Attash had been at the Malaysia meeting. It is hard to imagine that Richard Blee and Tom Wilshire had not known this before, but they had managed to keep it out of cable traffic and other documents, meaning they could later plausibly claim not to have known it. Now, that recourse was denied them.

Putting bin Attash at the meeting would have been highly significant to the FBI, as it would have connected fellow Malaysia summit attendees Almihdhar and Alhazmi to one of the *Cole* bombing's masterminds, and put them, especially given their presence in the US, firmly at the center of the *Cole* investigation. However, the FBI did not learn of the identification at the time, as it was made when Michael D was absent and, diverging from his action with the previous photograph, Chris did not have it repeated when Michael D returned.

After the attacks, numerous commentators criticized the apparent inability of the rival CIA and FBI to cooperate, yet in the case of the first identification of bin Attash in the Yemeni-provided photograph we again see that the CIA and FBI often shared information in a problem-free way. It was only when the information to be shared touched on Khalid Almihdhar or something related to him that it did not get passed.

Chris then drafted three cables about the meeting with Omar, but the cable shared with other agencies such as the FBI failed to mention the identification of bin Attash in the Malaysia summit photo. The identification was only mentioned in an internal cable for the CIA. The cable he sent after Omar's identification of bin Attash in the Yemeni-provided photograph highlighted the fact the photo identification had been repeated for Michael D, but now he made no such claim. Naturally, "Chris" later denied remembering anything of the incident.

In addition, the CIA again failed to watchlist Almihdhar, Alhazmi, or bin Attash. Almihdhar was out of the US at this time, and, at the very least, his watchlisting would have deprived the hijackers of one of their most experienced operatives.

Despite not informing the FBI, the CIA later repeatedly claimed it had done so. For example, Counterterrorist Center chief Cofer Black told the Congressional Inquiry:

> Our records establish that the Special Agents from the FBI's New York Field Office who were investigating the USS *Cole* attack reviewed the information about the Kuala Lumpur photo in late January 2001.

This is a reference to a meeting held in preparation for a trip by Ali Soufan to Islamabad where he would meet Omar, who was to formally identify the first photograph provided by the Yemenis so the FBI could then use this in a prosecution of bin Attash. The meeting before the trip was proposed by Chris, and in his cable to headquarters suggesting the meeting he made sure to point out that the source was "currently of very high interest to our [FBI] colleagues." It is unclear who represented the CIA at the meeting or why the FBI was not told of the identification of bin Attash in the Malaysia photograph, but it is clear that this information was not shared. This was an evident benefit to Chris in Pakistan, as he would not now be the only one to have failed to share the information, and blame shared is blame halved.

At the start of February, Ali Soufan and another FBI agent flew to Islamabad and met Omar, who confirmed his identification of bin Attash in the original photo from the Yemenis. Chris was present at the meeting, but, although the entire point of the meeting was to identify bin Attash due to his role in the *Cole* bombing, Chris never once mentioned Omar's prior identification, just a few weeks back, of bin Attash in the Malaysia summit photograph.

* * *

Tom Wilshire was asked about this incident in his testimony to the Congressional Inquiry as a part of a discussion with Congressman Richard Burr and FBI agent Steve Bongardt. The transcript shows that he shut the discussion down, claiming the matter was classified (emphases added):

> REP. BURR: In January 2001 the photographs from the January 2000 Malaysian meeting were shown to an individual who was frequented by the CIA and also by the FBI for their help. The – this individual identified one of the people in the photograph as in fact Khallad bin Attash, an individual that is now tied to playing a large orchestrating role in the *Cole* bombing. To the FBI agent, is that correct?
> BONGARDT: Sir, I don't know about that – those photographs. We had two photographs of [bin Attash]. One was a photograph that we had derived from investigation. And I understand your concerns – and I can hear it in your voice – trying to protect certain things about this with regards to source information. But that photograph, that – which was an identification photograph, was shown to the source, and he identified the individual as [bin

Attash]. But the two photographs – the other two photographs are the photographs taken from prior meetings –

REP. BURR: You're in fact correct.

BONGARDT: – we do not – I had not – I'm unaware of that, if those photographs –

REP. BURR: Let me ask our CIA officer if in fact that identification was made.

WILSHIRE: *I don't believe this has been declassified, sir, and I have a hard time talking about this in public. I would be happy to talk about it in closed session in detail.*

REP. BURR: Well, I will trust that you're accurate on that.

WILSHIRE: As I said in my statement – maybe I can help with the answer a bit. As I said in my statement, we had intelligence that supported the hypothesis. It was not a confirmation, it supported the hypothesis. And in fact I would prefer to answer the rest of it –

REP. BURR: Is it in fact factual that we now have a photographs – photograph, that we know one of the individuals is Attash or an individual who orchestrated, we think, the *Cole* bombings?

WILSHIRE: That was a different photograph.

REP. BURR: I realize that. I'm talking about –

WILSHIRE: A different individual.

REP. BURR: We have a – we have photographs that show Khallad bin Attash, as well as Almihdhar and Alhazmi. Am I correct that there's a photograph with all three?

WILSHIRE: Yes, sir. Yeah.

REP. BURR: Did any of these three go on the watch list at that time? Connections to the East African bombing by two of them and connections to the *Cole* bombing by a third. Did any of the three go on the watch list?

BONGARDT: From what occurred, there actually – it turns out there's – and I'm – I know my CIA colleague doesn't want to get into it too much – there's a little bit of confusion. There were four photographs that were taken out of a certain operation.

WILSHIRE: *Sir, this shouldn't be talked about in public. I'm sorry. It should not be. It's not – we can't go there.*

REP. BURR: I will move on, then.

WILSHIRE: *I apologize, but we just can't –*[2]

2. US Congress, The House Permanent Select Committee On Intelligence and the Senate Select Committee On Intelligence, The Intelligence Community's Knowledge of the September 11 Hijackers Prior to September 11, 2001: Hearing before the Joint Inquiry of the Senate Select Committee on Intelligence and the House Permanent Select Committee on Intelligence, September 20, 2002.

An outline of this information—that the CIA had in January 2001 acquired information indicating bin Attash had been in Kuala Lumpur a year earlier—was not classified, although the staff summary read at the start of the session did not mention that this information had come from a source inside al-Qaeda. And the answer to Burr's question about whether the terrorists were watchlisted at this time, which is the question after which Wilshire stopped the discussion, was certainly not classified. A truthful answer would have been highly embarrassing to Alec Station.

In Tom Wilshire's very first remarks to the Inquiry, he had urged it not to uncover much publicly. First he warned that al-Qaeda "remains poised to strike again," and then commented, "What we say in this venue over the coming weeks will be closely followed by the very people who are just trying to destroy you, me, our families and our way of life." The subtext was clear: the Inquiry should not say much at all publicly. This would obviously benefit Wilshire by limiting public discussion of his actions.

* * *

This episode once again represents not just one failure, but a string of them. The CIA discussed Almihdhar in December 2000, but failed to notify the FBI of these discussions. Chris failed to inform his FBI counterpart, Michael D, that Omar saw bin Attash in one of the Malaysia photographs. Chris then failed to inform the FBI of this in a formal report on the interview, and it was not mentioned at the meeting between the CIA and the FBI's New York Field Office in late January. Then Chris forgot to mention it in the meeting with Ali Soufan and the source in February. And to cap it all, neither Alhazmi nor Almihdhar nor, apparently, bin Attash was watchlisted at this time.

As usual, it is the Congressional Inquiry's conclusions that contain the least spin. Its report briefly explains the events and then concludes that the CIA did not inform the FBI of the identification, laying out the evidence for this.

The Justice Department inspector general's report, researched and originally drafted by Barbara Grewe, recounts these events over several pages in a dry style. In its conclusion, it merely states that there were "significant problems in communication between the FBI and CIA," which it only partially attributes to a spurious systemic issue. Otherwise, it just says it is "unable to fully examine why the CIA did not inform [Michael D, Soufan and his colleague] that the source had identified [bin Attash] in the Kuala Lumpur photographs."

In *The 9/11 Commission Report*, on the other hand, Grewe felt the need to add some cheerful commentary: "This incident is an example of how day-to-day gaps in information sharing can emerge even when there is mutual goodwill." She added that Chris, who had no recollection of any of these events, "might not have understood the possible significance of the new identification."[3] How exactly he could have failed to appreciate the identification of the mastermind of a recent attack that killed seventeen Americans is not explained.

This odd comment had also been in one of the Commission's staff statements. After a draft of that staff statement was circulated to the CIA, an Agency officer faxed the Commission a response: "In fact, the whole purpose of showing the photo to the asset was, in the words of the message to the case officer, 'to confirm/rule out this particular Khalid (in the KL photo) as a match for Muhammad Bin 'Atash [*sic*] (Khallad the *Cole* bombing suspect)'. The purpose was to support the *Cole* bombing investigation." The officer added that Chris then sent the cable with the identification to Yemen station and that "the only purpose of dissemination to Aden would have been to aid the *Cole* investigation." Therefore, "The record indicates that CIA officers fully understood the significance of [bin Attash] in the *Cole* investigation."[4]

The ubiquitous staffer Barbara Grewe apparently took no notice of this, and the comment about "Chris" possibly not understanding the significance of the identification remained in the staff statement. It was later transferred to the final report.

---

3. *9/11 CR*, p. 267.
4. Untitled CIA memo to 9/11 Commission commenting on draft commission staff statement, April 9, 2004, http://www.scribd.com/doc/14579489/CIA-Comments-on-911-Commission-Staff-Statement-about-Khallad-Identification.

30

In addition, the cable identified the third traveler as Salah Saeed Mohammed Bin Yousaf

Before concluding the discussion of the *Cole* bombing, it is worth examining the CIA's other failures regarding Khallad bin Attash. We have already seen that the NSA intercepted at least one, probably several, of his calls to the Yemen hub, that the CIA had him followed in Malaysia, but allegedly let him vanish in Thailand, and that it concealed his identification by the source in Islamabad from the FBI. There is still more to the story.

The first issue is a US visa application bin Attash submitted in Yemen when he was scheduled to be part of the 9/11 plot. He submitted it using the alias "Salah Saeed Mohammed bin Yousaf," but it was denied because he failed to submit sufficient documentation in support.[1]

While bin Attash was waiting for further documentation—confirmation of an appointment at a US clinic where he would get a new leg—he was arrested by the Yemenis as a terrorist. This is said to have been a case of mistaken identity, as the Yemenis had confused him with another one of the *Cole* plotters, whose car he was driving at the time. He was released a few months later, when Osama bin Laden reportedly struck a deal with the Yemenis not to stage attacks in Yemen in exchange for bin Attash's freedom.

Bin Attash's visa application is significant in another way. It is alleged, for example in *The 9/11 Commission Report*, that Almihdhar and Alhazmi obtained their US visas in April 1999 not as a part of the 9/11 operation, but simply out of a general desire to participate in a suicide operation inside the US. However, this is extremely unlikely, as bin Attash's visa application was made on April 3, 1999. Alhazmi obtained his US visa the same day and Almihdhar obtained his four days later. Given that bin Attash later said that his

---

210   1. *9/11 CR*, pp. 155, 492.

US visa application was made at bin Laden's direction, evidently in furtherance of the 9/11 plot, it is hard to believe that Almihdhar and Alhazmi, unaware of the plot, coincidentally made their applications at the same time.

In addition, the claim that Almihdhar and Alhazmi were not part of the 9/11 operation at that point is based upon something that the 9/11 Commission said that the CIA said that Khalid Shaikh Mohammed said that bin Laden told him, and this after KSM was tortured by the CIA. It is hard to imagine how a piece of information could be less reliable.

Bin Attash was already known to the US intelligence community by April 1999, because Mohamed al-Owhali had told the FBI that bin Attash had helped him make his martyrdom statement before the embassy bombings. However, there is no indication bin Attash's links to terrorism were discovered during the visa application, for which he used an alias, but a real photo of himself.

Salah Saeed Mohammed bin Yousaf is an alias bin Attash used in Malaysia, when he was under surveillance. It is the alias he used for the flight to Thailand on January 8, when he sat next to Almihdhar and Alhazmi. Initially, the alias he used for this flight was reported to be "Salahsae," presumably an eight-letter abbreviation directly from the flight manifest.[2] However, the full alias was discovered by the time of the March 5, 2000 cable from the CIA station in Thailand to Alec Station. The Justice Department inspector general's report tells us, "In addition, the cable identified the third traveler as Salah Saeed Mohammed Bin Yousaf," and points out that the cable also said this person had left Bangkok for Karachi on January 20.[3]

This clearly connected the alias to terrorism—the person using it had just been at a meeting of top al-Qaeda leaders and had left on a plane with two other operatives. However, as well as failing to watchlist Almihdhar and Alhazmi, the CIA also failed to watchlist the alias. Neither was it checked against US visa applications. One of the two men the alias was traveling with was known to have a US visa, so checking to see if the man using the alias had a US visa, or had applied for one, would be a reasonable thing to do. Nevertheless this was not done, at least as far as we know.

---

2. *9/11 CR*, p. 181.
3. Justice Department IG report, p. 248.

As described above, the FBI obtained a passport photo of bin Attash from the Yemenis on November 22, 2000 and passed it on to the CIA for help with the photo's identification by the source in Islamabad. We do not know where this photo was from. It is possible that the Yemenis obtained it when issuing bin Attash with his passport for the alias, in which case the FBI and CIA would have probably linked the alias to bin Attash at this point. It is also possible that it was from some other passport issued to bin Attash, and that not even the Yemenis knew of the Salah Saeed alias at this point.

Whatever the case, the passport photo increased the discoverability of the alias. In addition to being able to match this photo with one of the set of photos in Malaysia, it could also be matched with the one used for the US visa application under the Salah Saeed alias. However, this was not done. Neither are there any reports of the CIA going back and examining the Malaysia photos in detail. If there were photos of the three men on the way to the airport on January 8, 2000, it may have been possible to link the alias to bin Attash that way.

The identification of bin Attash by the source in early January 2001 also failed to prompt any action that connected bin Attash to his alias. There are no reports of his being watchlisted at this time either, although he may have been, with this information simply not made public.

As we will see, the US watchlisted Khalid Almihdhar and Nawaf Alhazmi in late August 2001, and "Salah Saeed Mohammed bin Yousaf" was watchlisted along with them. This was another opportunity to go back and examine the data—checking if the alias had ever applied for a US visa, a check that could have revealed that bin Attash was really Salah Saeed through a photo comparison. Given that the primary concern by that point was that Almihdhar and Alhazmi had used their US visas to enter the US, this would have been a logical move.

Although a connection between bin Attash and the two hijackers was already known by then, the knowledge that the two had applied for their US visas at the same time as one of the masterminds of the *Cole* bombing and had later taken a flight with him, a flight he took to meet other al-Qaeda operatives, would have further increased the FBI's interest in them. Yet we again have a case where the appropriate action was not taken.

31

The number that he called in Yemen to reach Ahmed al-Hada was 9671200578

O ne of the world's greatest intelligence blunders may have taken place during the embassy bombings trial in a New York courtroom on March 7, 2001. On that day the US revealed to the world, and to al-Qaeda, that it was aware of the Yemen hub.

Here is the first relevant section of the transcript from the embassy bombings trial, concerning Mohamed al-Owhali's trip to Yemen some months before the bombing:

> FBI agent Stephen Gaudin: So al-Owhali did that. Upon arrival al-Owhali stayed with his friend Ahmed al-Hada who he also gave another name of Abdul Aziz. He said this Ahmed al-Hada was someone — was a very good friend of his who was also trained in the bin Laden camps who fought alongside al-Owhali in that famous, as he describe[d] the famous C formation battle. So al-Owhali stayed at this person's house.
>
> Q: What did al-Owhali do while he was in Yemen?
>
> Gaudin: Al-Owhali telephoned his parents, and it was decided, al-Owhali decided it would be too dangerous for him to travel to Saudi Arabia, so his father, it was agreed that his father would travel from Saudi Arabia to Yemen, and he did and he met with al-Owhali and Ahmed al-Hada.
>
> Q: And did Al-Owhali mention anything else he did while he was in Yemen?
>
> Gaudin: While he was in Yemen he did receive the passport that was facilitated by Bilal [al-Nashiri] and he received a Yemen passport in the name of Khalid Salim Saleh Bin Rashid. Al-Owhali also met with Ahmed al-Hada and his father and there was an agreement made that Ahmed al-Hada would be the middleman in between al-Owhali and his father. From this point on if al-

Owhali needed anything from his father, Ahmed al-Hada would be the go between to make any of that happen.[1]

One of the core principles of counterterrorism, or indeed any covert operation, is that it is good to obtain sources the opposition does not know one has. These sources are exploited to obtain valuable information. But if they become public, they immediately lose their value. If the opposition discovers that a communications channel has been compromised, it is shut down. Or, perhaps worse, false information may be fed through the channel.

At least in this case the latter possibility was foreclosed, because that will only work when the opposition believes you don't know that they are aware of the compromise. Nonetheless, it was a very bad idea for an official to stand up in court and inform the world, including the other side—al-Qaeda in this case—that US intelligence was aware of one of its secret facilities. It must have been presumed that the other side would stop using the facility and the intelligence take would be lost, a sizeable loss in any case. In this case, given that the facility in question was actually al-Qaeda's secret operations center, this was a "blunder" of enormous magnitude.

The transcript continues to provide more details, this time for the period just before the bombing:

> Gaudin: Al-Owhali had explained to me that both on the – between the 4th and up to the day of the bombing that he made a series of telephone calls to his friend in Yemen, Ahmed al-Hada, who had fought with him in the C Formation battle I described earlier today.
>
> Al-Owhali explained to me he made these phone calls, they were collect calls that he had made from Harun's house, and the number that he called in Yemen to reach Ahmed al-Hada was 9671200578, he called that number to reach Ahmed al-Hada.
>
> Q: Did he tell you when the last call that he made to that number was?
>
> Gaudin: Al-Owhali explained to me the last phone call he made was approximately an hour before the bomb exploded on Friday, the 7th of August.

---

1. *United States v. Usama bin Laden et al.*, trial transcript of day 14, March 7, 2001. Al-Hada is referred to as al Hazza in the trial transcript, but, for continuity, al-Hada is retained in the extracts reprinted here.

The transcript continues like this for some time, with Gaudin detailing what al-Owhali did, the timing of his calls to al-Hada before and after the bombing, the absence of any extraction plan to get him out of the country, and his fear that somebody was listening in on his calls to al-Hada. He asked al-Hada to send him money, which he received, and to get him travel documents. In addition, he had a coded message passed on: "Tell Khalid I did not travel," meaning that he did not die during the mission. Had al-Owhali been arrested a day or two later, al-Hada might have been with him, as he was preparing to go to Kenya to hand over the travel documents.

This episode is the equivalent of a US official standing up in court at the height of the Cold War and giving details of communications between KGB agents in the field and its secret operations center. Naturally, the KGB would have responded to this by sealing the security breach, and the US would have expected it to do so.

As if this were not enough, US knowledge of the Yemen hub was re-emphasized in another hearing later in March, when a paralegal who had examined phone records gave evidence about charts that had been compiled of calls by the embassy bombers. First, she discussed the calls made from al-Owhali in Kenya to al-Hada in Yemen:

> Q. And reading along the first row, if you could give us the date, local time, and the information provided therein.
> A. The date is August 5th, 1998, local time 11:11 p.m., length of call 6 minutes, 39 seconds, originating caller, Khalid Salim [al-Owhali's alias], number called 1200578, location called Yemen.
> Q. And the next two calls, if you could just tell us what the originating caller is listed.
> A. Khalid Salim.
> Q. And the number that is called?
> A. 1200578.
> Q. And the location where that is, that number is?
> A. Yemen.
> Q. And for the record, those next two calls are on what date?
> A. August 6th, 1998.[2]

Again, the transcript continues like this for some time, describing exactly when the calls were made, between what numbers and

2. *United States v. Usama bin Laden et al.*, trial transcript of day 23, March 27, 2001.

how long they lasted. First the paralegal describes calls between al-Owhali in Kenya and al-Hada in Yemen before and after the bombing, then she describes calls after the bombing between Osama bin Laden's satellite phone in Afghanistan and al-Hada.

On that day, the phone number of al-Qaeda's still-active operations center, at the heart of US attempts to frustrate the organization, was read out in open court a total of thirteen times. Why?

* * *

At this time, US authorities believed that information disclosed in court cases could be of assistance to associates of the radical militants on trial. For example, Michael Mukasey, the judge in the "Day of Terror" plot in which the "Blind Sheikh," Sheikh Omar Abdul-Rahman, was sentenced to life in prison in 1996, made this comment shortly before he was nominated for the position of US Attorney General in 2007: "Terrorism prosecutions in this country have unintentionally provided terrorists with a rich source of intelligence."[3]

Mukasey cited two instances of this. One was the disclosure to defendants in the Day of Terror trial of the list of unindicted co-conspirators. The list included Osama bin Laden's name, and a copy of it soon reached bin Laden in Sudan, "letting him know that his connection to that case had been discovered." The second occurred during the trial of Ramzi Yousef, the mastermind of the 1993 World Trade Center bombing, when "an apparently innocuous bit of testimony in a public courtroom about delivery of a cell phone battery was enough to tip off terrorists still at large that one of their communication links had been compromised." The link had provided "enormously valuable intelligence," but "was immediately shut down, and further information lost."

Mukasey, who repeated these claims at his confirmation hearings,[4] may or may not have been correct about these instances—for example the accuracy of the anecdote about the cell phone battery is not known. However, that is not the issue here. The issue

3. Michael Mukasey, "Jose Padilla Makes Bad Law," *Wall Street Journal*, August 22, 2007, http://www.opinionjournal.com/extra/?id=110010505.
4. "Senate Judiciary Committee Hearing for Nomination of Judge Mukasey as Attorney General, Day Two," *CQ Transcripts Wire*, October 18, 2007, http://www.washingtonpost.com/wp-srv/politics/documents/transcript_mukasey_hearing_day_two_101807.html.

is that at this time US authorities, including those involved in judicial proceedings, were quite aware that information disclosed in court could find its way back to al-Qaeda.

We should also bear in mind that the people in court at the time included hardcore al-Qaeda members—defendants who had blown up the embassies. During the trial or when in prison, they could simply write to one of their associates, tell them what they heard in court and advise them to use different communication channels. The blind Sheikh Omar Abdul-Rahman continued to head the global jihad movement for years from inside a maximum-security prison, with the help of his legal team.[5] Three members of the 1993 WTC bombing team, Mohammed Salameh, Mahmud Abouhalima and Nidal Ayyad, wrote a series of letters after 9/11 from the Supermax prison in Florence, Colorado, encouraging other Muslims around the world to take up jihad. One was even found following the arrest of the leader of a group of Spanish militants plotting to blow up the National Justice Building in Madrid.[6]

What is even more startling is how the paralegal's testimony continued at the embassy bombings trial:

Q. Now, did you have an opportunity to review all of the billing records for the phone number 682505331?
A. Yes, I did.
Q. Can you tell us, aside from these three calls to that number 1200578 that are listed here, were there any other calls from the satellite phone 682505331 to that number in Yemen aside from these three calls listed here?
A. There were no other calls.

The number 682505331 was Osama bin Laden's satellite phone; 1200578 was the Yemen hub. What the paralegal was claiming was that she reviewed all the records for bin Laden's satellite phone and

5. "N.Y. Lawyer Convicted of Aiding Terrorists," Associated Press, February 11, 2005, http://www.foxnews.com/story/0,2933,147027,00.html; "Civil rights attorney convicted in terror trial," CNN, February 14, 2005, http://www.cnn.com/2005/LAW/02/10/terror.trial.lawyer/; Andrew C. McCarthy, "Lynne Stewart Gets 28 Months for Aiding Terrorists," National Review, October 17, 2006, http://article.nationalreview.com/?q=MTUwYjEwM2NkOTNjYThkOWE3NTc3ZWNmOTAxMzZmNDU=.
6. Lisa Myers, "Imprisoned terrorists still advocating terror," MSNBC, March 1, 2005, http://www.msnbc.msn.com/id/7046691; Lisa Myers, "Jihad letters from prison went far, wide," MSNBC, March 9, 2005, http://www.msnbc.msn.com/id/7140883.

that she only found three calls to the Yemen hub, all made shortly after the embassy bombings. As noted earlier, bin Laden used the phone for about two years, from late 1996 until the fall of 1998. She is telling us that bin Laden never called his operations center before the embassy bombing, and made only three calls to it afterwards.

This is contradicted by the *Los Angeles Times* report by Terry Mc-Dermott that said "dozens" of the calls went to the Yemen hub, and by James Bamford.[7] We know that bin Laden used the phone to place over 200 calls to Yemen, so the claim that only three of them went to the Yemen hub seems unusual at best. One possible explanation is that at the trial the authorities were only releasing selected information about calls to and from the hub because only that much was needed for convictions. The rest may have been hidden so the public would not fully realize what the intelligence community knew.

* * *

The trial received a good deal of news coverage at the time, and the existence of al-Qaeda's still active operations center was soon picked up by the international media. On February 13, 2001, UPI reported,

> Just before the Aug. 7 embassy bombings, a suicide bomber, Mohamed Rashed Daoud al-Owhali, contacted an al-Qaeda number in Yemen from a safe house in Nairobi. Al-Owhali called that same number the next day from a hospital clinic and would make a series of phone calls from Nairobi to Yemen.[8]

A report posted at the State Department's website on March 7, 2001 contained many of the important details, including that al-Owhali placed "several calls to his friend in Yemen":

> Several months before the Nairobi bombing, al-Owhali was told to shave his beard, pick out a new passport, and travel to Yemen. Told not to get a hotel room, he instead stayed with a friend from the Kabul battle named Ahmed al-Hada. He also arranged to contact his father through al-Hada and got a Yemen passport in the name of Khalid Saleh.[9]

---

7. See Chapter 1, note 6.

8. Richard Sale, "NSA Listens to bin Laden," United Press International, February 13, 2001, http://s3.amazonaws.com/911timeline/2001/upi021301.html.

9. Judy Aita, "Embassy Bombing Trial Hears of Confession by Accused Terrorist," US Department of

219

Perhaps the most amazing report was carried by the *Observer*, a British weekly. It was printed on Sunday, August 5, 2001—just five weeks before 9/11—and written by Jason Burke, who later authored a book on al-Qaeda. It said,

> Telephone records obtained by the FBI show that at 8:44 pm on the eve of the [embassy] bombing, al-Owhali rang 00 967 1200578, the number of his former comrade in arms, with whom he had stayed in the Yemen. They spoke for a little over seven minutes. At 9.20 the next morning, the day of the attack, he called the Yemen again, speaking this time for three-and-a-half minutes. Azzam called his family in Saudi Arabia. At 9.45 am the pair drove the truck away from the house and headed into Nairobi....
>
> [After the bombing, al-Owhali went to a hotel.] In room seven, he changed, stuffed his old clothes in a drawer and called his friend in the Yemen. He asked him to pass a message to Pakistan. "Tell them," he said, "that I haven't travelled." ...
>
> The FBI traced [a call to a number associated with bin Laden's London office] to Baku in Azerbaijan, and pulled the phone records. They claim these showed a series of calls from 00 873 68505331 – the number of the satellite phone, registered as Kandahar Communications, that the FBI suspected was used by al-Qaeda. So, they got the call records for the Afghan satellite phone. These, as predicted, showed calls to Baku. But they also, the FBI claimed, showed calls to a number in the Yemen, 00 967 1200578, the San'a number of al-Owhali's friend. On the records for that line they could see several calls to and from Nairobi, which could easily be traced to the Ramada Hotel – in the suburb of Iftin in Nairobi, to be exact. The records didn't show the room number. They didn't need to.[10]

This is almost surreal. The number for al-Qaeda's current operations center, which was involved in the organization's signature operation, shortly to come to fruition, was published in a major international weekly. This was also the home phone number of one of the operatives, Khalid Almihdhar, who was to take part in the operation, and it was called by at least two of his fellow hijackers. Any of the *Observer's* readers could have called the number and asked for a message to be forwarded to Osama bin Laden, as could Burke.

State, March 7, 2001.
10. Jason Burke, "Dead Man Walking," *Observer* (UK), August 5, 2001, http://www.guardian.co.uk/theobserver/2001/aug/05/life1.lifemagazine8.

What is even more absurd is that al-Qaeda continued to use the communications center after it was revealed at the trial. As MSNBC's Lisa Myers made clear, "The final call from Yemen to the hijackers came only weeks before 9/11."[11] Clearly, "only weeks before 9/11" is after March, when US knowledge of the calls was first disclosed at the trial. It would also be around the same time as the *Observer* article. Why would al-Qaeda use a communications center it must have known the US was monitoring?

It is also strange that we have heard nothing of the disclosure of the hub's existence and phone number in court since the attacks. Presumably, there must have been some discussion inside the US government about whether to use the Yemen hub information at the trial, as the government must have been aware that giving it out publicly would alert al-Qaeda that the US knew of the hub. One might have expected that this move would have been opposed by the NSA and the CIA, and that they would have used it as a stick to beat the Justice Department and the FBI in the internecine warfare between the agencies that followed the attacks. However, there has been no mention of it.

* * *

This book is about a series of events—intelligence failures—which, when viewed through the everyday prism of intelligence officers doing their utmost to prevent attacks, do not make much sense. However, when they are viewed from a different angle—in which some of the intelligence officers are actually trying to hide some of the hijackers from their colleagues—they make much more sense. It is unclear how the public disclosure of the Yemen hub's existence in court fits into this pattern, or even if it fits at all.[12] Neither is it clear why al-Qaeda continued to use the hub even though it was evident that the US was aware of it.

11. *Hardball Special Edition for July 24, 2004*, MSNBC, transcript, http://www.msnbc.msn.com/id/5486840/.
12. The hub's existence was also apparently mentioned in an Egyptian trial, the "Trial of the Albanian Returnees," in 1999. A couple of months after 9/11, the *New York Times* reported, "Several [defendants] said they had acquired forged passports, including a forged Saudi Arabian passport, from contacts in Damascus and Latakia in Syria during the 1990's. They made frequent reference to Mr. bin Laden as the organization's financier and some spoke of a safe house he financed in Sana, Yemen, the country where the American destroyer *Cole* was rammed by suicide bombers in a boat in October 2000, with 17 sailors killed." See Susan Sachs, "An Investigation in Egypt Illustrates al-Qaeda's Web," *New York Times*, November 21, 2001, http://www.nytimes.com/2001/11/21/international/middleeast/21JIHA.html?pagewanted=1.

At this point, when the US government had already shown its hand and the Yemen hub was publicly acknowledged, there was no reason not to simply arrest al-Hada and his associates and bring them to justice. Al-Qaeda would discover the US knowledge of the hub at any moment, and the logical thing to do would be to shut it down.

The CIA's rendition program had been running since the mid-1990s, and the Agency was also cooperating with Yemeni authorities. Even if the Yemenis had refused to arrest or allow the rendition of al-Hada there, he and the people related to him were known to travel. For example, al-Hada attended a banquet in Afghanistan with bin Laden in 1999,[13] and he could have been snatched when he was traveling. Not only would this have led to the detention of an accomplice in the African embassy and *Cole* attacks, but it would have had the happy coincidence of throwing the 9/11 plot into disarray.

---

13. Mark Hosenball and Daniel Klaidman, "Calling al-Qaeda: Questions about Iran," *Newsweek*, February 18, 2002.

Part 5: Washington and New York

DCI
Update
Terrorist Threat
Review
23 August 2001

1000671

Declassified
on 2-17-06

M-CTR-80000302

M-CTR-80000302

Islamic Extremist Learns to Fly

- Islamic fundamentalist travels to US to learn to fly a 747 in Minnesota
- Pays for training in cash
- Interested to learn that 747 doors don't open in flight
- Wanted training on London-JFK flights
- FBI arrested him based on the fact that he overstayed his 90 day visa
- We are working the case with the FBI

1000675

M-CTR-80000303

M-CTR-80000303

Exhibit at trial: information brief on Zacarias Moussaoui prepared for
George Tenet nineteen days before 9/11. The final item provides one
of the more grimly ironic comments on the run-up to that tragedy.

32

He was focused on Malaysia

I n May 2001, Tom Wilshire moved from his position as deputy chief of Alec Station at the CIA to the FBI's International Terrorism Operations Section (ITOS), which contained the Bureau's bin Laden unit. No specific explanation for this move is offered in *The 9/11 Commission Report* or the Justice Department inspector general's report, although there was a program in which CIA officers and FBI agents were detailed to the other agency to gain experience.[1]

Wilshire's exact position at the Bureau is unclear. *The 9/11 Commission Report* calls him a "CIA official detailed to the International Terrorism Operations Section at the FBI," and the "counterpart" of ITOS chief Michael Rolince.[2] The Justice Department inspector general's report calls him "a CIA manager who was working in ITOS at FBI Headquarters as a 'consultant' on intelligence issues."[3] The inspector general adds,

> [Wilshire] told the [Office of Inspector General] that in this detail to the FBI he acted as the CIA's chief intelligence representative to ITOS Section Chief Michael Rolince. [Wilshire] stated that he did not have line authority over anyone at the FBI and that his primary role was to assist the FBI in exploiting information for intelligence purposes.[4]

On the other hand, when Wilshire testified to Congress about al-Qaeda's global reach on December 18, 2001, he was identified as the deputy section chief at ITOS, not merely a consultant.[5] It is

---

1. *9/11 CR*, p. 267; Justice Department IG report, pp. 151, 282.
2. *9/11 CR*, pp. 267-68.
3. Justice Department IG report, p. 151.
4. Ibid., p. 282. Note that the inspector general employee writing this section does not take responsibility for telling readers what Wilshire's position was; she merely repeats a claim Wilshire made to her without vouching for its accuracy.
5. US Senate, Committee on Foreign Relations, Hearing before the Senate Subcommittee on International Operations and Terrorism on the Global Reach of al-Qaeda, 107th Cong., 1st sess.,

unclear whether Wilshire held this position from May; possibly he was transferred within the FBI after 9/11 but before the subcommittee hearing. If he was deputy section chief from May, then the Justice Department inspector general is inaccurate, and the 9/11 Commission's report omits this significant fact.

Wilshire's move to the FBI came a few weeks after the second request filed by Ali Soufan, the head of the FBI's investigation into the *Cole* bombing, in April 2001, for information about a possible al-Qaeda meeting back in January 2000. This meeting was al-Qaeda's Malaysia summit, during which Wilshire had blocked the passage of information about Khalid Almihdhar to the FBI.

We do not know who read these requests at CIA headquarters and falsely claimed to Soufan that the Agency knew nothing about any such meeting. However, it would have been apparent to anyone who read the two requests that Soufan was closing in on the Malaysia summit. The first request was just a general query about an al-Qaeda meeting somewhere in Southeast Asia. The second request mentioned the Washington Hotel, where the *Cole* bombers, bin Attash, Almihdhar and Alhazmi had stayed in Bangkok, as well as calls between it, Fahad al-Quso's house in Yemen, and a pay phone in front of the apartment where the Malaysia summit had been held.[6]

Whatever the motivation behind his move, Tom Wilshire was to play a key role in everything that went wrong at the FBI in the run-up to 9/11. He was one of the most senior officials involved in the failure to exploit the arrest of Zacarias Moussaoui and the failure to find Khalid Almihdhar when the Bureau did, belatedly, start to search for him.

* * *

On May 15, Wilshire and a female CIA officer reviewed the cables the CIA had written about the Malaysia summit. The reason for

December 18, 2001, http://www.gpo.gov/fdsys/pkg/CHRG-107shrg390/html/CHRG-107shrg390. htm. The transcript spells Wilshire differently, as "Wilshere." Presumably, this spelling is correct and "Wilshire," is wrong. However, as the official in question is known in the media as "Wilshire," I chose to retain this spelling. Wilshire's name was first disclosed in the context of 9/11 in the media by author Lawrence Wright, who may have obtained it from an interview, not a document, leading to the slight misspelling.
6. Lawrence Wright, "The Agent: Did the C.I.A. stop an F.B.I. Detective from Preventing 9/11?" New Yorker, July 10 and 17, 2006, http://www.lawrencewright.com/WrightSoufan.pdf; Wright 2006, p. 330.

the review is not known, nor is the identity of the second CIA officer, who does not even rate an alias in the reports by the Justice Department's inspector general and 9/11 Commission. The cables they accessed said that Almihdhar had a US visa and that Nawaf Alhazmi had traveled to the US with a companion in January 2000. The other officer took no action following the review. Again, we have no idea why not.[7]

Action clearly should have been taken. For example, Wilshire should have checked with the INS to see whether Alhazmi was still in the US, he should have researched the identity of Alhazmi's companion on the flight to Los Angeles, he should have placed both Alhazmi and Almihdhar on the watch list, which would have prevented Almihdhar from re-entering the US in July 2001, and he should have alerted the FBI to the fact that a major terrorist, Alhazmi, was in the US, which would have led the FBI to find him. However, he did none of this.

An explanation for Wilshire's inaction at this point was offered in the section of *The 9/11 Commission Report* drafted by Barbara Grewe:

> Despite the US links evident in this traffic, "John" [Wilshire] made no effort to determine whether any of these individuals was in the United States. He did not raise the possibility with his FBI counterpart. He was focused on Malaysia.[8]

Wilshire thought Almihdhar and Alhazmi might be involved in a future al-Qaeda attack and knew that Alhazmi had traveled with a companion to the US. He failed to appreciate the possibility that the attack might be in the US because of a claimed focus on a possible attack in Malaysia, despite his impending loan to the FBI, an organization that deals with domestic issues.

In addition, he was so uninterested he did not trouble himself to learn the identity of Alhazmi's companion on his flight to the US—it was clear from the context that the companion was likely to be Almihdhar, because they were known associates, had trav-

7. *9/11 CR*, pp. 267 n63, 536; Justice Department IG report, p. 282. The Commission's staff statement No. 10, which deals with this issue, points out of the officer who re-examined the cables with Wilshire: "She cannot recall this work." This sentence is deleted from the final report, although the other parts of this section of the staff statement were accepted almost verbatim.
8. *9/11 CR*, p. 268.

eled together on the first leg of the journey from Kuala Lumpur to Bangkok, and the cable reporting Alhazmi and an associate had arrived in the US was sent in response to a request for information on Almihdhar's whereabouts. However, Wilshire reportedly did not realize Almihdhar had come to the US at this point.

The Justice Department inspector general's report comments on this:

> [Wilshire] also noted to the [Office of Inspector General] that during this period there were heightened concerns in the Intelligence Community about the threat of an imminent terrorist attack in Southeast Asia.[9]

There were certainly heightened concerns about a terrorist attack against US interests in the late spring of 2001. However, public reports of this stress that the US was not aware of where exactly it would be. There are no public reports of which I am aware suggesting that the US thought there was good reason to suppose the attack would be in Southeast Asia or, specifically, Malaysia.

This is the same excuse that "Michelle" used to induce Doug Miller and Mark Rossini not to share the information about Almihdhar's US visa with the FBI back in January 2000. There was reason to question whether this belief was genuinely held then, and there is even more reason to question whether it was genuinely held at this time, primarily because of the *Cole* attack.

Michelle's prediction that the next al-Qaeda attack was going to be in Southeast Asia turned out to be wrong, as the *Cole* was bombed in Aden, Yemen, not in Southeast Asia. If the reason to hide Almihdhar from the FBI was to penetrate the next al-Qaeda plot, which was allegedly thought to threaten Southeast Asia, then the seventeen dead sailors killed in the *Cole* bombing showed that attempt to have been a failure that should be abandoned. If Alec Station did have a means of predicting the location of the next attack, everybody could now see that this means was faulty. It is farcical to suggest that Alec Station staff believed that the next al-Qaeda attack was going to be in Southeast Asia until mid-October 2000, when the *Cole* was bombed, and then turned round after that attack and convinced themselves that, OK, they had got this one

---

9. Justice Department IG report, p. 282.

wrong, but *now* the next attack, whatever it might be, really was going to be in Southeast Asia.

In addition, accepting Tom Wilshire's excuse that he was "focused on Malaysia" would require us to forget that it was Wilshire who blocked the notification to the FBI about Almihdhar's visa in the first place. Are we to believe that Wilshire intentionally blocked notification to the FBI and then, on a subsequent occasion when he committed essentially the same failure, simply made an honest mistake?

"John" asked her to do the research in her free time

Instead of taking any positive action based on his review of the Malaysia summit cables, Tom Wilshire had them reviewed again. The review was conducted by Margaret Gillespie, the fourth FBI detailee to Alec Station, after Doug Miller, Mark Rossini and the deputy unit/group chief. As we will see, it took Gillespie three months to complete the review and alert the FBI to the fact that Almihdhar was in the US and that Alhazmi had also entered the country.

This review raises a number of key issues, but the first thing to point out is that Wilshire, the officer who initially had "Michelle" block the notification to the FBI about Almihdhar's US visa, received praise for it. The relevant section of the 9/11 Commission's final report drafted by Barbara Grewe says that he started the review "following a good instinct but not part of any formal review."[1] The Commission's second staff statement calls him a "thoughtful CIA official" in this context.[2]

At the Congressional Inquiry hearing with Wilshire on September 20, 2002, Congressman Richard Burr said,

> On July the 13th, I think it was an important day because in fact our CIA officer [Wilshire] began to put some of the pieces together that had bugged him. And that led to finding some of the lost cables or the misfiled cables. That led to decisions, decisions that did put people on watch lists, decisions that did begin the ball rolling towards an all-out press by the Bureau to look for individuals that, for numerous reasons, we had not been able to raise to this profile at that time.[3]

1. *9/11 CR*, p. 269.
2. 9/11 Commission, Staff Statement No. 2, "Three 9/11 Hijackers: Identification, Watchlisting, and Tracking," p. 7, http://govinfo.library.unt.edu/911/staff_statements/staff_statement_2.pdf.
3. US Congress, The House Permanent Select Committee On Intelligence and the Senate Select

As it was Wilshire who withheld the information in the first place, it would be natural to suspect him of possible wrongdoing. However, because he was the officer who initiated the review, this makes any error he may have made before, or even after, appear unintentional. If he had deliberately withheld the information in January 2000, then why would he initiate a review that led to its being found sixteen months later? Especially as the review was conducted by an FBI agent detailed to the CIA.

However, the review did not turn up any new cables—Gillespie merely took three months to find the cables Wilshire already had, but did not give to her, when he told her to start work. Further, he deliberately allocated a low priority to the review; the conduct of the review suggests that Gillespie, as well as Rossini, Miller, Michelle, Blee and others, may have been in league with Wilshire; and the FBI's search for Almihdhar that followed the review was essentially sabotaged by Wilshire and one of his associates.

Nevertheless, we are left with a question: if he was acting in bad faith, why start the review at all? The answer to this may involve a character met in the previous chapter. The CIA officer who, together with Wilshire, read the cables on May 15 then took no action on them. One could explain her inaction if Wilshire told her that he would have a more wide-ranging review initiated, so there was no need for her to do anything. The formal act of initiating a review would then be needed to induce this officer's passivity.

Before examining the review in detail, let us recall that CIA Director George Tenet, in sworn testimony to the Congressional Inquiry in 2002, claimed that he had initiated it:

> During August 2001, CIA had become increasingly concerned about a major terrorist attack on U.S. interests, and I directed a review of our files to identify potential threats. In the course of that review, the Counterterroris[t] Center found that these two individuals had entered the United States.[4]

Committee On Intelligence, The Intelligence Community's Knowledge of the September 11 Hijackers Prior to September 11, 2001: Hearing before the Joint Inquiry of the Senate Select Committee on Intelligence and the House Permanent Select Committee on Intelligence, September 20, 2002.

4. "Testimony From the Joint Intelligence Committee," *New York Times*, October 17, 2002, http://www.nytimes.com/2002/10/17/politics/18ITEXT.html?pagewanted=1. This is apparently another instance of Tenet's calling the CTC the "Counterterrorism" Center.

This is not true; the review was initiated by Tom Wilshire. It is hard to believe Tenet could have been unaware of this at the time of his testimony. He gave a more accurate version of events in his 2007 book:

> By July 2001, indications were everywhere that a major terrorist attack was about to occur. As I later told the 9/11 Commission, "the system was blinking red." I instructed the people in CTC [the Counterterrorist Center] to review everything in their files to search for any clue that might suggest what was coming. The request, though, was redundant. Everyone in CTC felt as strongly as I did that something catastrophic was about to happen, and they had already begun such a review.[5]

Again, the review did not come up with any new information. Margaret Gillespie did not find anything—any cables, e-mails or other communications—that had not been previously read by dozens of other officers, including Wilshire. The allegedly important thing that she found, after a three-month search, was the March 5, 2000 cable that said Alhazmi and a companion had entered the US. Learning that the companion was Almihdhar, she then checked with the INS, found Almihdhar had left the US in June 2000 and re-entered in July 2001, and alerted the FBI. Several CIA officers had read this cable before Gillespie, including Wilshire just before asking her to start work, but none of them had apparently checked with the INS and alerted the FBI. As we saw in the last chapter, Wilshire's excuse for not doing this was that he was "focused on Malaysia." Wilshire could simply have given Gillespie the relevant cables at the start of the review, but did not.

Further, the review was allocated a low priority. *The 9/11 Commission Report* says, "'John' [Tom Wilshire] asked her ['Mary,' i.e., Margaret Gillespie] to do the research in her free time."[6] The low priority is certainly problematic. She was examining what Wilshire purportedly believed were cables that could give the CIA a clue to where the next major al-Qaeda attack would take place. Although the CIA clearly had other important tasks at this time, predicting the location of the next attack must have been quite high on the Counterterrorist Center's to-do list.

The main discussion of these events in the Justice Department inspector general's report clouds the entire picture:

5. Tenet 2007, p. 198.
6. *9/11 CR*, p. 270.

Shortly before assuming his duties at the FBI, John had asked CTC [Counterterrorist Center] management to assign a CTC desk officer with "getting up to speed" on the Malaysia meetings and determining any potential connections between the Malaysia meetings and the *Cole* attack. This assignment was given to Mary. She told the [Office of Inspector General] that "getting up to speed" meant she would have to research and read the pertinent cable traffic as her schedule permitted. She emphasized that her priority assignment during this period was the credible threats of an imminent attack on U.S. personnel in Yemen, and she said that she worked the Malaysia meetings connections to the *Cole* attack whenever she had an opportunity.[7]

"This assignment was given to Mary" suggests that its source was someone in "CTC management" other than the same CIA officer who had requested the review and would soon be "assuming his duties at the FBI." Also, "as her schedule permitted" and "whenever she had an opportunity" are open to various interpretations.

To be fair, the Justice Department inspector general does elsewhere mention that the review was to be done in her spare time, but *does not* attribute this instruction to anyone in particular:

Mary told the [Office of Inspector General] she had recently been given the assignment by CTC management of "getting up to speed" in her spare time on the Malaysia meetings and determining any potential connections between the Malaysia meetings and the *Cole* attack.[8]

And:

In May 2001, one detailee to the CTC was assigned to "get up to speed" on the Malaysian matter in her spare time but said she had been unable to focus on the matter until August 2001.[9]

The 9/11 Commission's claim that it was "John" who asked "Mary" to do the review in her free time was sourced to her interview by the Justice Department inspector general,[10] so the Justice Department inspector general must have been aware that this was his idea. However, the fact that "Mary" was told to do the review

7. Justice Department IG report, pp. 297-98.
8. Ibid., p. 288.
9. Ibid., p. 313.
10. *9/11 CR*, p. 538 n73..

in her spare time was not mentioned in the Justice Department inspector general's report during its discussion of the initiation of the
review, but in two asides, one ten pages before the relevant section,
the other fifteen pages after it and without even an alias to identify
the "detailee to the CTC." In no case was the "spare time" instruction attributed to "John"—a fine textbook example of how to disconnect dots. This was not the first place where the Justice Department inspector general's report omitted information detrimental
to Tom Wilshire, and neither would it be the last.

The whole course of the review is bizarre. It began in May, or
perhaps early June. In a passage that appears to relate to a period
shortly before June 11, Lawrence Wright states,

> Meantime, Maggie Gillespie researched the Intelink database
> about the Malaysia meeting, but the agency had not posted any
> reports about Almihdhar's visa or Alhazmi's arrival in the coun-
> try. There was NSA coverage of the events leading up to the Ma-
> laysia meeting, but Intelink advised her that such information
> was not to be shared with criminal investigators.[11]

In his endnotes Wright adds a significant fact:

> Intelink is a handicapped system available to other intelligence
> agencies. It would have shown Gillespie only what was avail-
> able to FBI intelligence. Had she looked on the Hercules sys-
> tem, the powerful CIA database that contained all the cables
> and NSA traffic and was available to her, she would have gotten
> a complete picture of the agency's knowledge of Almihdhar and
> Alhazmi.[12]

Why would Gillespie look for information in the non-CIA database—where a person familiar with the case would know it was not
present—but not look for it at the same time in the CIA database?

In the second half of July, Gillespie drafted a cable to another
CIA station asking for information about the Malaysia summit that
referenced Omar's January identification of Khallad bin Attash in
the Kuala Lumpur photographs and the fact that bin Attash and
Almihdhar had been in Malaysia at the same time. On the same
day, she found the cable that said Almihdhar had a US visa as well

11. Wright 2006, p. 340.
12. Ibid., p. 425. It is to the detriment of Wright's account that this information was relegated to
the endnotes.

as "Michelle's" cable that falsely said this information had been passed on to the FBI.[13]

It then took Gillespie until August 21 to discover the March 5, 2000 cable that said Alhazmi and a companion had entered the US, which is what triggered her to contact the INS and then the FBI.

Gillespie had already been told back in May that Alhazmi had entered the US, when she was copied on an e-mail between Wilshire and Clark Shannon, another CIA officer involved in the case, stating that Alhazmi had traveled to Los Angeles from Hong Kong with a companion. Gillespie later said she did not understand the significance of this when she read it in May, but that in late August, three weeks before 9/11, "it all clicks for me."[14]

This leaves us with several questions about Margaret Gillespie's conduct of the review. Why did it take so long? Why didn't she search the CIA database straight away? And, after she found some of the cables in July, why did it take her another month to find the other ones?

* * *

There are other reasons to question Gillespie's genuineness. In January 2000, Gillespie accessed three of the relevant Malaysia summit cables at the CIA: "Michelle's" cable that falsely said Almihdhar's visa information had been passed to the FBI, one that stated he had arrived in Kuala Lumpur, and one that said surveillance photographs showed him meeting with others in Malaysia.[15] She was also copied on the e-mail from "James" about the briefings of "Bob" and "Ted" at the FBI.

As we saw, the two FBI agents involved in the withholding of Almihdhar's visa information, Doug Miller and Mark Rossini, later claimed to the Justice Department inspector general that they could not recall the withheld cable. Gillespie went one better. Not only could she not recall reading the cables when asked about them by the Justice Department inspector general, but "she did not recall even being contemporaneously aware of the Malaysia meetings." The matter was assigned to "Michelle," so why would she know

---

13. Justice Department IG report, p. 299. The cable Gillespie drafted was held up for ten days, for three of these days it was with Wilshire.
14. Ibid., pp. 300-01.
15. Ibid., p. 253.

anything about it? When she was shown a copy of the e-mail she received from "James," she claimed to have no recollection of it.[16]

This was not the only thing Gillespie, who had been detailed to the CIA in 1998,[17] could not recall. Her memory was a blank about an apparent meeting she had on May 29 with another FBI analyst and Clark Shannon, although an e-mail from Shannon to her mentioned a meeting they had that day.[18] She also wrongly claimed to the Justice Department inspector general that neither she nor Shannon were asked any questions at a highly contentious meeting on June 11, which will be the subject of another chapter.[19]

A telling episode occurred in response to an e-mail from Wilshire on July 13, which will be discussed in more detail below. Wilshire e-mailed the CTC claiming he had just found the cable that stated Khallad bin Attash had been identified in January 2001 by Omar in the Kuala Lumpur photographs; he urged CTC officers to re-examine the Malaysia summit for information related to bin Attash.

After this, a reply dated the same day from a "CTC bin Laden unit supervisor"—presumably Richard Blee—stated that Gillespie had been assigned to handle the review of the Malaysia summit and that Doug Miller, who was out of the office, would be detailed to help her when he returned.[20] However, it is unclear whether Miller was actually given this assignment on his return.

This is a highly curious move. What would be the point of assigning Miller, an officer who was aware of the intentional withholding of the information from the Bureau, to search for information some of which he already knew, but had been instructed to withhold?

Tom Wilshire spoke about the review during his public testimony to the Congressional Inquiry. In his opening statement he said (emphasis added),

> In midsummer 2001, although the presence of the key planner [bin Attash] in Malaysia had yet to be confirmed, *while burrowing through intelligence related to other terrorist activity in Malaysia, the data from January 2000 and January 2001 was put together in a different way*, and both the FBI and the CIA began to work

16. Ibid., p. 254.
17. Ibid., p. 320.
18. Ibid., p. 285.
19. Ibid., p. 292.
20. Ibid., pp. 299-300.

to flesh out their understanding of all the people linked to the key planner of the *Cole* attack, of all the people linked to Khallad [bin Attash].

He added this during the questioning (emphasis added):

There was a miss in January, there was a miss in March. We acknowledge that. What happened after that was I think in part a function – stuff like that should normally emerge during the course of a file review, if something provokes the final review. *Once that file review is provoked, the information is readily recoverable. That's how I found what I found when I found it kind of thing. But the story kind of emerged in dribs and drabs, because there was no one person who reconstructed the whole file.* And –

These statements are, at best, misleading. There is no mention that he was the officer who suggested the file review, that he had all the relevant cables before he "provoked" the review, that he told Gillespie to do it in her free time, that he failed to give her the relevant cables at the start, or that it took her three months to find a handful of cables readily available in the database.

Finally, the timing of the discovery raises questions. Gillespie first alerted the FBI to the presence of Almihdhar and Alhazmi in the US on August 21, when she telephoned Dina Corsi at the FBI, leaving a message for her. Corsi was apparently on holiday and did not return until the next day, when they met and started to take the actions that will be described in detail as we approach 9/11.[21]

* * *

The time around August 21 and 22 is significant for a number of reasons. Primarily, this is when the hijackers decided to attack on or about September 11. There is no clear explanation of why the decision was taken at this point. However, one of the people known as the "20th hijacker," Mohamed al Kahtani, failed to gain entry to the US on August 4; he seemed suspicious to an immigration inspector, who thought his true intention might have been immigration rather than tourism.

It would have taken the plotters a couple of days to decide that al Kahtani would not try to enter again and that no replacement would be sent. In addition, in the first part of August there had

21. Ibid., pp. 300-01.

237

been ongoing discussions between lead hijacker Mohamed Atta and coordinator Ramzi bin al-Shibh (and through him presumably others including Khalid Shaikh Mohammed and Osama bin Laden) about which targets to attack. These discussions reportedly focused on whether the White House should be a target. According to the 9/11 Commission, Atta wanted to attack the Capitol building, and therefore to wait until Congress was in session in September.[22]

According to bin al-Shibh, Atta informed him of the approximate date of the attack three weeks before 9/11, in an e-mail written in their simplistic code. "The first term starts in three weeks ... There are 19 certificates for private studies and four exams," Atta told bin al-Shibh. Bin al-Shibh made this claim while still free, in an interview with Al Jazeera's Yosri Fouda given to mark the first anniversary of 9/11.[23] The Commission asserted that similar e-mails between Atta and bin al-Shibh were recovered from KSM's computer when he was captured in March 2003, although its final report does not mention this specific communication.[24]

The claim that the decision on the attack's date was taken around this time seems credible, as on August 24 Almihdhar logged into the American Airlines website and established a profile in order to facilitate ticket purchases.[25] The hijackers then began purchasing their 9/11 tickets the next day.[26]

Three weeks before 9/11 would be August 21, the date Gillespie allegedly happened to find the March 5 cable and realize the import of the materials she had had for some time. As we have seen, the immediate purpose for the Alec Station group's withholding of the information from the FBI must have been to enable surveillance of Almihdhar and Alhazmi, which would have led to their associates, including Atta. In addition, in the run-up to 9/11 bin al-Shibh had fallen under surveillance by British, Spanish and German intelligence services, and, as we will see in a later chapter, the NSA was

---

22. *9/11 CR*, p. 248-49.
23. Giles Tremlett, "Al-Qaida leaders say nuclear power stations were original targets," *Guardian* (UK), September 9, 2002, http://www.guardian.co.uk/world/2002/sep/09/september11. afghanistan.
24. *9/11 CR*, pp. 248 n165, 531.
25. *United States v. Zacarias Moussaoui*, "Chronology of Events for Hijackers, 8/16/01 - 9/11/01, Khalid Al-Mihdhar," http://www.vaed.uscourts.gov/notablecases/moussaoui/exhibits/prosecution/OG00020-11.pdf.
26. *9/11 CR*, p. 248.

intercepting his communications with KSM. It is therefore entirely possible that anyone monitoring the hijackers and bin al-Shibh learned the approximate date of the attacks around this time from such surveillance.

The way this looks is that the Alec Station group kept the information about Almihdhar and Alhazmi from the FBI for over a year and a half, until they learned that the attack was to occur within three weeks.

* * *

August 22 is significant for other reasons. First, it was the day John O'Neill, the FBI's top terrorism investigator who had accompanied Ali Soufan to Yemen, left the Bureau. His departure was forced by enemies he had made through his brash style, who had used errors he had committed, some minor, some less so, against him.[27] O'Neill went to work as director of security at the World Trade Center, where he died when the buildings collapsed. We cannot know what would have happened if O'Neill had remained at the FBI and had learned of the hunt for Almihdhar and Alhazmi. As we will see, an argument broke out at the Bureau over the search for the two men, and this led to very few resources being allocated to the search. Had O'Neill still been at the Bureau, he may have gotten involved and changed the outcome.

There is some support for the idea that Alec Station was keeping the information about Almihdhar secret specifically in order to keep John O'Neill away from the case. For example, an unnamed FBI agent told James Bamford:

> "They refused to tell us because they didn't want the FBI, they didn't want John O'Neill in particular, muddying up their operation. They didn't want the bureau meddling in their business—that's why they didn't tell the FBI. Alec Station worked for the CIA's CTC. They purposely hid from the FBI, purposely refused to tell the bureau that they were following a man in Malaysia who had a visa to come to America. The thing was, they didn't want John O'Neill and the FBI running over their case. And that's why September 11 happened. That is why it happened.... They have blood on their hands. They have three thousand deaths on their hands."[28]

---

27. Wright 2006, pp. 351-52.
28. Bamford 2005, p. 225.

Lawrence Wright claimed that a Malaysia photo of Khallad bin Attash was withheld from the FBI in order to keep O'Neill in the dark about Kuala Lumpur:

> That fourth photo would have prompted O'Neill to go to Mary Margaret Graham, who headed the New York office of the CIA, which was located in the World Trade Center, and demand that the agency turn over all information relating to Khallad [bin Attash] and his associates.[29]

However, we should bear in mind that personal animosity for O'Neill may not have been the only reason. After all, setting aside mere criminal insanity as "motive," if Richard Blee and Tom Wilshire wanted to keep O'Neill away from the case, they likely desired this for some purpose beyond allowing terrorists to operate in the US unchecked.

August 22 was also the day Ali Soufan, whose three requests about a meeting in Malaysia had received no response from the CIA, went back to Yemen with a group of other investigators. In fact, the very last thing John O'Neill did at the Bureau was to sign the order sending Soufan back to Yemen. Geographical distance was a barrier, and Soufan did not learn of the arguments in the Bureau's New York office until it was too late. Again, we cannot know what would have happened if Soufan had been present, but it is more than likely he would have gotten involved in the argument over the search for Almihdhar and Alhazmi and demanded extra resources.

In summary, there are four points that need to be made. First, there was no actual need for Margaret Gillespie's review of the Malaysia cables, as Tom Wilshire had all the relevant information in May, or, more realistically, at the start of the previous year. Second, Wilshire severely hampered the review by telling Gillespie to do it in her free time and by not giving her the relevant cables, which it allegedly took her three months to find. There are also indications of bad faith by Gillespie, as three months is more than enough time to find a few cables, and her apparent inability to recall key events cannot but raise suspicions of her conduct. Finally, the timing of the notification is suspicious.

---

29. Wright 2006, p. 342.

We must reject the explanation that this was a coincidence, that Gillespie did genuinely discover the information around the time Atta decided on the date of the attack and/or just before the two key figures at the Bureau who could have done something about the problems that ensued were taken out of the equation. Coincidence is discredited by the circumstances of the review itself, by the events that preceded it and by those that followed.

The alternative is that the sending of notification to the Bureau was orchestrated, timed to come at the earliest opportunity after the hijackers had decided to attack within a couple of weeks. The idea that the information was withheld specifically to spite O'Neill will not stand up because, as we have seen, Wilshire and Blee must have been linked to surveillance of the hijackers in the US. Even after O'Neill left, the FBI still retained investigators who could find Almihdhar and Alhazmi and then potentially discover their operation.

The reasoning for the claim that somebody in the Alec Station group must have wanted the attacks to succeed will be set out below. In this scenario, the explanation for sending notification at this time is as follows: having hid the information about Almihdhar and Alhazmi from the Bureau for over a year and a half, it was clear the CIA would take most of the blame following an attack. Therefore, it was both necessary to actually give the information to the Bureau and to ensure that the Bureau failed to do anything with it. Thus the blame after the attacks would be spread around.

If that was indeed the plan, then August 21-22 was the earliest time to implement it. Had notification been given before the Alec Station group learned the hijackers had determined the time of the attacks, it would have run the risk of having to stall the FBI for an undetermined period of time, a decidedly risky strategy. Stalling the Bureau for three weeks, however, would have seemed a much simpler task.

Had it been discovered after the attacks that the CIA had possessed the information about Almihdhar and not communicated it at all, the Agency would have been in a much worse position. By providing the FBI with visa information about Almihdhar just before the attacks, it did in fact get the blame shared around. Indeed, the apparent bureaucratic obstacles at the FBI during the search were the subject of much comment in the media, deflecting attention from the CIA. As we will see, Tom Wilshire and one of his associates at the FBI, Dina Corsi, were employed in the construction of these obstacles.

34

Someone saw something that wasn't there

arallel to the new review by Margaret Gillespie, Tom Wilshire initiated a series of events that led to the showing of photos of Alhazmi and Almihdhar taken at the Malaysia summit to investigators working on the FBI's *Cole* investigation. This was another opportunity to pass on information to the FBI that would have prevented 9/11. Had Wilshire and Clark Shannon, his colleague from the CIA, provided the FBI with all the information they had about the photos, the FBI would very probably have stopped the attacks, but the photos were handled in such a way that the *Cole* agents gleaned an absolute minimum of information about them. In addition, as in the case of the January 2001 identification of Khallad bin Attash, the photos that were passed and the way in which this was done indicates that there was a hidden purpose behind their passage.

The showing of the photos started with an e-mail exchange between Wilshire and Shannon, a terrorism analyst, about the cables Wilshire re-read in mid-May. Shannon had written a CIA report on the *Cole* bombing in which he found only circumstantial ties to al-Qaeda. It also omitted any mention of bin Attash's identification in the Malaysia photos by the source in Islamabad. Shannon sent Wilshire a timeline for the USS *Cole* bombing, and they discussed Fahad al-Quso and his connections to other *Cole* plotters, such as bin Attash and Almihdhar. The Justice Department inspector general's report says,

> In addition, [Wilshire] wrote that he was interested because Almihdhar was traveling with two "companions" who had left Malaysia and gone to Bangkok, Los Angeles, and Hong Kong and "also were couriers of a sort." [Wilshire] noted in the e-mail that "something bad was definitely up." [Shannon] replied in an e-mail dated May 18, "My head is spinning over this East Asia travel. Do

you know if anyone in [the CIA's Bin Laden Unit] or FBI mapped this?"[1]

Wilshire also spoke to Dina Corsi, an FBI headquarters agent assigned to its Osama bin Laden unit who was involved in the *Cole* bombing inquiry. At this point in the investigation, Corsi was interested in al-Quso and his interactions with bin Attash, thought to be one of the operation's masterminds. Wilshire obtained three photos taken at the Malaysia summit from the CIA, and these three photos would later be passed to Corsi. They became a bone of contention after the attacks.

Wilshire later claimed not to have read the cable that identified bin Attash as one of the people shown in the photographs (allegedly, he would not read this for another two months), but said that at this time he did know that bin Attash had been identified in one of these three photos.

However, he disagreed with the identification, saying none of the photos showed bin Attash. He wrote to Shannon saying he was "missing something" in the photographs or "someone saw something that wasn't there." As we now know, Wilshire was right and none of three photos he had at that time showed bin Attash, although one of them did show Alhazmi, who looked so similar to bin Attash that the al-Qaeda source who had made the identification in Islamabad thought it *was* bin Attash. This is remarkable: a CIA officer knew al-Qaeda's operatives better than did one of their own. The logical explanation for this is that Wilshire knew bin Attash, and he knew Alhazmi too. He could have, should have, seen them in the Malaysia photos. And he could also have seen Alhazmi if he was in the loop about the domestic surveillance of the hijackers and was getting photos from that. Unfortunately for Wilshire, this is a slip. He let on that he knew something he later claimed not to have known at this time.

In response to Wilshire's e-mail saying he had the three photos, Shannon suggested showing the photos to two FBI headquarters agents working on the *Cole* case, Corsi and another agent known only as "Kathy," at a meeting on May 29, 2001. Documentation indicates that the meeting took place, although Shannon, Corsi, Gil-

1. For the e-mail exchange, see Justice Department IG report, pp. 283-84; much of this chapter is based on these and subsequent pages in the Justice Department inspector general's report. See also *9/11 CR*, p. 537 n64.

lespie, and Kathy all later claimed to recall absolutely nothing about it, including whether they attended or not. On the other hand, Kathy did say Shannon's name sounded a little familiar to her when asked about it by investigators.

Whether at this meeting or some other time, Shannon mentioned the photographs in a discussion with Corsi,[2] and Corsi then obtained them from Wilshire. Neither Wilshire nor Shannon bothered to give her detailed information about who was actually in the photos, although Almihdhar's name was mentioned, and Corsi wrote it on the back of a photo that showed him. Corsi was allegedly not told bin Attash had been identified in one of the photos, as Wilshire apparently did not think the presence of the *Cole* bombing mastermind in photos passed to an agent investigating the *Cole* bombing was worth mentioning. However, as we will see later, some time that summer Corsi did learn that bin Attash had been at the Malaysia summit, but withheld this information for a time from the other FBI agents working with her on the investigation.

Naturally, Wilshire claimed his memory was a blank when asked by the Justice Department inspector general about his conversation with Corsi when the photos were passed. However, he did claim that he would not have mentioned bin Attash's presence in Malaysia at this time, because, even though he knew of (but had not read) reports saying bin Attash was present, he regarded them as "speculative."

Recall that the CIA later claimed that at this time it thought the FBI was aware of the apparent identification of bin Attash by the informant in Islamabad; the CIA's story is that they omitted to inform the FBI, convinced themselves they had done so, but a manager responsible for running the operation during which the photos were taken somehow remained unaware of this.

This is all fairly confusing, so let's recap. Wilshire and Shannon started e-mailing each other about the Malaysia summit, creating a paper trail. Wilshire mentioned the photos, and Shannon speculated that Fahad al-Quso might be one of the people shown in them. Shannon then mentioned the photos to Corsi, and Corsi got them from Wilshire. Neither Wilshire nor Shannon gave her the relevant information.

---

2. While according to Corsi, Shannon mentioned the photos to her, Shannon himself claimed to have no memory of doing so; see Justice Department IG report, p. 286.

Why Shannon and Wilshire thought these particular three photos—out of the dozens or even hundreds taken—would show al-Quso is unclear. After one FBI agent only made a tentative identification of al-Quso in the os, none of the other photos were shown to the FBI in an effort to have them identify al-Quso more certainly. Obviously, this makes one doubt the genuineness of Wilshire and Shannon: if they really wanted to know whether al-Quso had gone to Malaysia, why not show all the Malaysia photos to the FBI?

Commenting on one of the other photos not passed to the FBI at this time, Lawrence Wright wrote,

> There was a fourth photo of the Malaysia meeting, however, that [Shannon] did not produce. That was a picture of Khallad [bin Attash]. The *Cole* investigators certainly knew who he was. They had an active file on him and had already talked to a grand jury, preparing to indict him…. By withholding the picture of Khallad standing beside the future hijackers, however, the CIA blocked the bureau's investigation into the *Cole* attack and allowed the 9/11 plot to proceed.[3]

The content of the photos in which the FBI agents working on the *Cole* investigation were supposed to identify al-Quso is also remarkable. According to the Justice Department inspector general's report, one of them—the one on the back of which Almihdhar's name was written—showed Almihdhar.[4] Another was the photo of Alhazmi in which Omar thought he saw bin Attash. According to Wright, one was "shot from a low angle" and "showed Almihdhar and Alhazmi standing beside a tree."[5] Possibly there was one photo just showing Almihdhar and one showing Almihdhar, Alhazmi and the tree, possibly these are two references to the same photograph. How was the FBI supposed to identify al-Quso in a photograph showing Almihdhar, or Almihdhar, Alhazmi (who the CIA thought was bin Attash at this point, although Wilshire apparently doubted this) and a tree? Had the CIA genuinely wanted the FBI to identify al-Quso in the Malaysia photographs, it would have given them all the Malaysia photos, not just these three. In addition, it would not have given them photos in which the people shown had already <u>been identified</u> as persons other than al-Quso.

3. Wright 2006, p. 342.
4. For the photo in which Almihdhar had been identified, see Justice Department IG report, p. 284.
5. Wright 2006, p. 341.

The correct explanation seems to be that Wilshire did not want to know whether the FBI agents recognized al-Quso in the photos, but wanted to know whether they recognized Almihdhar and Alhazmi. The course of events here is remarkably similar to that which preceded the identification of bin Attash in the Malaysia photos in January. A paper trail was generated containing bizarre speculation (Almihdhar and bin Attash are the same person, a photo of Almihdhar is really of al-Quso), the photos are given to a person who might recognize Almihdhar and Alhazmi under this pretext, and the CIA then learns what it really wants to know—whether this person recognizes Almihdhar and Alhazmi—without having to openly ask that question.

A key question remains: why did Wilshire want to know whether the source handled out of Islamabad and the *Cole* agents at the FBI recognized Almihdhar and Alhazmi? The logical answer is that Almihdhar and Alhazmi were involved, either wittingly or unwittingly, in an operation Wilshire was helping to run or to keep secret, and Wilshire wanted to know if he and his associates could expect trouble from a certain direction.

35

Shouting match

T he centerpiece of this showing of the photographs was a meeting of intelligence officers and agents that also included crime investigators on June 11, 2001. Margaret Gillespie, Clark Shannon and Dina Corsi visited the FBI's New York field office, which was handling the *Cole* investigation, and met with Bureau agents Russell Fincher and Steve Bongardt. Bongardt later testified to the 9/11 Congressional Inquiry along with Tom Wilshire; he was an assistant to Ali Soufan, who was in Yemen at this point. Assistant US attorney David Kelley was also present. The meeting's exact duration is uncertain, but it lasted for something between two and four hours.[1]

The meeting had been arranged by Corsi, but she had not troubled herself to draft an agenda for it, so the New York agents started by briefing the others on how the FBI's investigation of the *Cole* bombing was going.

After they had talked for some time, Shannon told Corsi to take out the three photos Wilshire had given her and show them to Bongardt and Fincher. He asked the two agents whether they recognized anybody in the pictures and whether they saw al-Quso there. One of the agents made a tentative identification of al-Quso. Bongardt and Fincher did not recognize anybody else, but asked some straightforward questions like who was in the photos, why were they taken, and were there any other photos of the meeting. It was pretty clear that there was some connection between the men in the pictures and the *Cole* bombing—why else would they be shown to FBI agents investigating the bombing at a meeting specifically called to discuss the investigation?—but the nature of the connection was unclear.

---

1. The meeting is described, for example, in the Justice Department IG report, pp. 287-94.

Corsi eventually gave them Almihdhar's name, but it did not mean anything to them at this point, and Bongardt asked for a birth date or other details so he could start to investigate him:

> [Bongardt asked Shannon] to provide a date of birth or a passport number to go with Almihdhar's name. A name by itself was not sufficient to put a stop on his entry into the United States. Bongardt had just returned from Pakistan with a list of thirty names of suspected al-Qaeda associates and their dates of birth, which he had given to the State Department as a precaution to make sure they didn't get into the country. That was standard procedure, the very first thing most investigators would do. But [Shannon] declined to provide the additional information.[2]

Under pressure, Shannon admitted Almihdhar had been traveling on a Saudi passport when the pictures were taken, but then he and Gillespie left the meeting.

Bongardt and Fincher, who were not allowed to keep the photos, tried to get more out of Corsi, but Corsi refused to tell them anything. She had read some NSA reports of the intercepts before the Malaysia summit and knew that Almihdhar and Alhazmi had been to Malaysia and were linked to the al-Qaeda communications hub in Yemen, which was itself linked to the East African embassy and *Cole* bombings.

This is Barbara Grewe's version of why Corsi did not share this information with Bongardt and Fincher, from *The 9/11 Commission Report*:

> These reports, however, contained caveats that their contents could not be shared with criminal investigators without the permission of the Justice Department's Office of Intelligence Policy and Review (OIPR). Therefore "Jane" [Dina Corsi] concluded that she could not pass on information from those reports to the agents.[3]

This is the same event described in the Justice Department inspector general's report, presumably also written by Grewe:

> [Corsi] told us that she could not provide this information directly to the agents working the *Cole* criminal investigation due to the

---

2. Wright 2006, p. 341.
3. *9/11 CR*, p. 269.

caveat, which prevented all NSA counterterrorism-related intelligence information from being provided to FBI criminal agents without approval from the NSA.[4]

* * *

This explanation needs to be deconstructed at length.

First, there is a discrepancy between the Commission's report, which says that the passage of the information to criminal investigators had to be approved by the OIPR, and the Justice Department inspector general's report, which says that such passage had to be approved by the NSA. In fact, when the NSA reports were drafted, the caveat that was attached to them would have been one referencing the OIPR. However, this caveat was rescinded some time before the summer of 2001, and a new caveat, saying that the NSA's general counsel had to approve the dissemination, was in force, regardless of what was actually written in computer files or on a printout.[5]

Second, the caveat did not prevent dissemination, it merely required approval be obtained before being passed to criminal investigators. This is the exact wording:

> Except for information reflecting a direct threat to life, neither this product nor any information contained in this product may be disseminated to U.S. criminal investigators or prosecutors without prior approval of NSA. All subsequent product which contains information obtained or derived from this product must bear this caveat. Contact the Office of General Counsel of NSA for guidance concerning this caveat.[6]

The Justice Department inspector general falsely claimed that obtaining such approval involved "lengthy procedures,"[7] but nothing could be further from the truth. As we will see, the NSA general counsel did decide to approve passage of this information before 9/11, and it took no more than one day to reach this decision. If the caveat had been the real problem, Corsi could have filed a request that day, promptly received an affirmative reply from the NSA and then given it to Bongardt.

---

4. Justice Department IG report, pp. 292-93.

5. Ibid., p. 281.

6. Ibid., p. 38.

7. Ibid., p. 346.

In addition, both the caveats explicitly say that approval had to be obtained only before passage to FBI *criminal* investigators and prosecutors. Bongardt was a criminal agent, but there was at least one intelligence agent in the room. Bongardt commented to the Congressional Inquiry, "We had intelligence agents from the bureau that were in the room at the time and the rest of us criminal agents, even though we were frustrated, could have walked out of the room and then [the intelligence agents could have] received that information."[8] The 9/11 Commission's defense of Corsi is that she "apparently did not realize that one of the agents in attendance was a designated intelligence agent."[9] However, they had all been working the *Cole* bombing for months by this time, so this explanation is hard to believe.

The third point is that this caveat did not apply to the Kuala Lumpur photos. When Wilshire gave Corsi the photos, Corsi, according to a later claim she made to the Justice Department inspector general, somehow managed to convince herself that the photos were "not formally passed" to the FBI[10]—even though a CIA officer who functioned as Alec Station's liaison to the FBI's bin Laden unit had just given them to her. She also gave a second explanation, saying that the *Cole* agents could not have the photos because they were not authorized to show them to anyone *outside* the Bureau, although why Corsi thought this would prevent the *Cole* agents from having the photos themselves is unclear.

Wilshire agreed that passing the photos to Corsi did not entitle the FBI to show them to anybody else, such as Yemeni government officials—although the Yemenis had already seen the photos on January 3, 2001, when they presumably got them from the CIA—but said that since he had given them to an FBI agent, then the FBI could use them for internal purposes. These two explanations do not mesh, Wilshire and Corsi could not even get their stories straight on this point.

---

8. US Congress, The House Permanent Select Committee On Intelligence and the Senate Select Committee On Intelligence, The Intelligence Community's Knowledge of the September 11 Hijackers Prior to September 11, 2001: Hearing before the Joint Inquiry of the Senate Select Committee on Intelligence and the House Permanent Select Committee on Intelligence, September 20, 2002. The presence of an intelligence agent at the meeting was confirmed by the Justice Department IG report, p. 291.
9. *9/11 CR*, p. 537.
10. Justice Department IG report, p. 294.

To sum up, the caveat excuse does not work because (1) the caveat did not prevent dissemination of the NSA information, it merely said approval had to be obtained first, an easy process, (2) the caveat did not apply to the FBI intelligence agent(s) at the meeting, and (3) the caveat did not apply to the Kuala Lumpur photos.

As we will see, this was not the only occasion on which Dina Corsi made "mistakes." Indeed, the full list of Corsi's mistakes is almost as impressive as Wilshire's.

* * *

It is also worth taking a look at Clark Shannon's excuse for not sharing the information he had. He knew that Almihdhar had a US visa, that his visa application indicated he intended to travel to the US, that Alhazmi had traveled to the US, and that Almihdhar was an associate of bin Attash, one of the masterminds of the crime the officers and agents were all there to discuss.

Following the attacks, Shannon gave at least three interviews about his conduct at this meeting. One was to Director Tenet, the others to the Congressional Inquiry and the Justice Department inspector general. There is no record of his being interviewed by the 9/11 Commission. Presumably, this was because Barbara Grewe was handling this section of the Commission's report, and she was the official who had interviewed him for the Justice Department inspector general.

Shannon has given contradictory accounts of this meeting. One is referenced in George Tenet's October 2002 testimony to the Congressional Inquiry. Here is Tenet's exchange with Senator Carl Levin (emphasis added):

> MR. TENET: Almihdhar was not who they were talking about in this meeting. When I asked *our person at this meeting* as to whether he was specifically asked about Almihdhar and Alhazmi, he [Shannon] *has no recollection of the subject ever being directed to him or ever coming up.* So there's a factual issue here and I've only talked to two of the people involved. I haven't talked to everybody involved.
>
> SEN. LEVIN: Let me read you the staff report. The CIA analyst who attended the New York meeting [Shannon] acknowledged to the joint inquiry staff that he had seen the information regarding Almihdhar's U.S. visa and Alhazmi's travel to the United States

but he stated that he would not share information outside of the CIA unless he had authority to do so. That's what he told our staff. Do you disagree with that?

MR. TENET: Sir, I've talked to him as well.

SEN. LEVIN: Do you disagree that he said that to our staff?

MR. TENET: Well, no, I don't disagree he said it to your staff. I'm telling you what he told –

SEN. LEVIN: Did he tell you something differently?

MR. TENET: Yes, sir. He gave me a different perspective on the day.

SEN. LEVIN: So he told you and he told our staff something differently.[11]

A caveat should be applied here: Tenet's reputation for truthfulness is not the best. Perhaps Shannon did not tell Tenet that he had "no recollection ... of the subject ever coming up," and Tenet simply made this up.

According to a section of the Commission's report drafted by Barbara Grewe: "No one at the meeting asked him [Shannon] what he knew; he did not volunteer anything. He told investigators that as a CIA analyst, he was not authorized to answer FBI questions regarding CIA information."[12] However, according to the Justice Department inspector general's report, Shannon later admitted he was told that the meeting was an "information sharing and brainstorming session,"[13] which makes one wonder why he would have gone to information sharing session without authorization to share information. The claim that "no one at the meeting asked him what he knew" is demonstrably false. Not only is it contradicted by Lawrence Wright's account, but also by Dina Corsi's contemporaneous notes, which indicate that he responded to a question about Almihdhar by saying he was traveling on a Saudi passport at the time. The Commission sources the claim that nobody asked Shannon what he knew to his interview by the Justice Department inspector general.[14]

It is instructive to look at how the CIA's excuses developed. First Wilshire and "Michelle" blocked Miller's cable to the FBI saying that Almihdhar had a US visa. Then the CIA, in Michelle's cable,

---

11. Testimony From the Joint Intelligence Committee, October 17, 2002, http://www.nytimes.com/2002/10/17/politics/18ITEXT.html?pagewanted=1.

12. *9/11 CR* p. 269.

13. Justice Department IG report, p. 288.

14. *9/11 CR*, p. 538 n27.

allegedly somehow managed to convince itself that the FBI had been notified of Almihdhar's visa. After that, Shannon refused to share with the FBI information the CIA allegedly believed that it had already shared with the Bureau. Obviously, there could be no prohibition on referencing information that had already been shared. The simplest explanation here is that Shannon knew the Bureau did not have the information about Almihdhar's visa, he did not want them to have it, and the meeting was simply a fishing expedition to find out whether the *Cole* agents recognized Almihdhar and Alhazmi.

Last but not least, when the meeting was first reported in the press, it was described as a "shouting match."[15] The Justice Department inspector general sought to debunk this claim, and the relevant section of its report is full of language suggesting that the meeting was really not that heated. For example, Corsi, Gillespie, and Shannon asserted "that neither the display of the surveillance photographs nor the meeting overall was contentious," Shannon did "not recall the meeting becoming heated or contentious," and even Bongardt, in a second interview, "did not characterize the meeting as having the same level of combativeness" as he did in his first interview.

The way the inspector general managed to reach this conclusion is revealing. After the meeting had gone on for a few hours, Shannon and Gillespie departed, leaving Corsi alone with the *Cole* investigators, and that is when the real argument happened—the New York agents were pressing her for information about Almihdhar, and she was not providing it. This is the detail behind the inspector general's claim there was no argument at the meeting—the meeting formally ended when Gillespie and Shannon left, and the real argument was after they left, so there was no argument *at the meeting*. It's just that some of the people who attended the meeting happened to stay in the meeting room and have an argument about an issue that came up at the meeting.

Given the information that was withheld by Corsi and Shannon, as well as Shannon's later evasions, the June 11, 2001 meeting appears to be nothing more than an attempt orchestrated by Tom Wilshire to find out what the FBI knew. Essentially, could the *Cole*

---

15. "A Decade of Warnings," ABC, August 16, 2002, http://web.archive.org/web/20021017233132/ http://abcnews.go.com/sections/2020/DailyNews/wtc_yearTHECELL020816.html.

agents recognize Khalid Almihdhar and Nawaf Alhazmi? This indicates that, whatever operation the CIA was running that involved the two hijackers—as knowing participants or merely as surveillance targets—it was still ongoing at this time, despite the increasing number of threat warnings.

36

What's the story with the Almihdhar information, when is it going to get passed … when is it going to get passed

Following the June 11 meeting, Steve Bongardt kept asking Dina Corsi to get the relevant information about Almihdhar passed to him; as a headquarters agent it was Corsi's job to support the field office and get the information Bongardt wanted. The Justice Department inspector general found little documentation of this, but Bongardt said that he had "heated telephone conversations and e-mail exchanges" with Corsi.[1] He also told the Congressional Inquiry,

> I've had several conversations with the analyst [Corsi] after that, because we would talk on other matters, and almost every time I would ask her, "What's the story with the Almihdhar information, when is it going to get passed, do we have anything yet, when is it going to get passed," and each time I was told that the information had not been passed yet. And the sense I got from her, based on our conversations, was that she was trying as hard as she could to get the information passed or at least the ability to tell us about the information.[2]

The information in question was the NSA reporting that linked Almihdhar and Alhazmi to the Malaysia summit and the communications hub in Yemen, as well as the three photos, which the *Cole* investigators had not been allowed to keep, and information about the two al-Qaeda operatives.

---

1. Much of the material in this chapter is taken from the Justice Department IG report, pp. 291-97.
2. US Congress, The House Permanent Select Committee On Intelligence and the Senate Select Committee On Intelligence, The Intelligence Community's Knowledge of the September 11 Hijackers Prior to September 11, 2001: Hearing before the Joint Inquiry of the Senate Select Committee on Intelligence and the House Permanent Select Committee on Intelligence, September 20, 2002.

Despite these requests, there is no evidence of Corsi taking any action to get the information passed until over two months later.

As we saw in the previous chapter, Corsi did not let the *Cole* investigators keep the three photos because, she later claimed, she thought they were "not formally passed" to the Bureau by Wilshire. However, Wilshire later claimed that, as far as he was concerned, the *Cole* investigators could have the photos. Given its position in the middle of a pattern of conduct designed to withhold information from the Bureau, this appears to be a hastily-put-together cover story.

Even if we give Corsi and Wilshire the benefit of the very little doubt that can remain, and allow that it may have been a genuine misunderstanding at the time of the June 11 meeting, the continued failure to pass the photos over the summer of 2001 represents an even harder obstacle to cross. Corsi repeatedly spoke with Wilshire over the summer, and she later said she "probably" communicated with Wilshire, Shannon and Gillespie about getting the photographs passed so the *Cole* agents could use them. Gillespie even recalled such discussions. It is highly improbable, even if there was an original misunderstanding, that such a misunderstanding could survive three months of repeated interactions on the subject.

The situation with the NSA information is similar. Corsi's story is that she failed to give the *Cole* agents the NSA information because of a caveat that did not apply to intelligence agents. The problem here is that even in the unlikely event that Corsi had failed to realize that intelligence agents were present at the June 11 meeting, she must have known there were some intelligence agents on the *Cole* investigation. Indeed, as we will see later, she contacted one of them in August and was clearly aware he was on the intelligence side of the house. Had she been acting in good faith, she could have simply given him the NSA material soon after the June 11 meeting.

Although a caveat had prevented her from giving the information to Bongardt, a criminal agent, at the June 11 meeting, this caveat could be removed simply. All Corsi had to do was ask the NSA's general counsel, who surely would allow its passage. As we will see, Corsi waited until late August to ask for the caveat's removal, and even then continued to withhold the information from Bongardt and the other *Cole* agents.

The Justice Department inspector general dealt with this issue by claiming that Bongardt was mistaken and never spoke to Corsi about getting the photo information passed—Corsi said she did not speak to Bongardt at all about the photos after the meeting. However, in the absence of documentary evidence, it is a case of Bongardt's word against Corsi's, and, as we are beginning to see, there is ample reason to doubt much of what Corsi says.

The failure to pass on the Malaysia photos and the NSA information at the June 11 meeting is bad enough, but the fact that Corsi and Wilshire continued to sit on this information for months is even more damning. Indeed, the FBI's New York Field Office and the *Cole* investigators should have gotten this information in 2000.

37

The bad guys were in Yemen on this conversation

I n 2006, *New York Times* reporter Judy Miller, who had done jail time for contempt of court in the Valerie Plame Affair, revealed a previously little-known pre-9/11 warning. The warning may be connected to Khalid Almihdhar and the Yemen hub, although this is not certain.

In an interview about the warning, Miller said there were rumors of "intensified intercepts and tapping of telephones" before the July 4, 2001 weekend, when Miller went down to Washington. Some people in counterterrorism were very worried about the possibility of a "large, well-coordinated" al-Qaeda attack in the US or on US interests abroad, at least part of which was to take place that weekend. Others doubted this, and Miller formed the opinion she was being given information by her sources because officials wanted to get word to the president and his top aides through the press—the normal channels were blocked. However, as we know, there was no attack that weekend.

In the 2006 interview, Miller then dropped a bombshell (emphasis added):

> But I did manage to have a conversation with a source that weekend. The person told me that there was some concern about an intercept that had been picked up. *The incident that had gotten everyone's attention was a conversation between two members of al-Qaeda. And they had been talking to one another, supposedly expressing disappointment that the United States had not chosen to retaliate more seriously against what had happened to the Cole. And one al-Qaeda operative was overheard saying to the other, "Don't worry; we're planning something so big now that the U.S. will have to respond."*
>
> And I was obviously floored by that information. I thought it was a very good story: (1) the source was impeccable; (2) the information was specific, tying al-Qaeda operatives to, at least,

knowledge of the attack on the *Cole*; and (3) they were warning that something big was coming, to which the United States would have to respond. This struck me as a major page one-potential story.

I remember going back to work in New York the next day and meeting with my editor Stephen Engelberg. I was rather excited, as I usually get about information of this kind, and I said, "Steve, I think we have a great story. And the story is that two members of al-Qaeda overheard on an intercept (and I assumed that it was the National Security Agency, because that's who does these things) were heard complaining about the lack of American response to the *Cole*, but also … contemplating what would happen the next time, when there was, as they said, the impending major attack that was being planned. They said this was such a big attack that the U.S. would have to respond." Then I waited.

In the next section of the interview, Miller discussed why the story did not run in the *Times*. Essentially, she did not have enough details, and could not get more (emphases added):

I realized that this information was enormously sensitive, and that it was going to be difficult to get more information, but that my source undoubtedly knew more. So I promised to Steve [Engelberg] that I would go back and try to get more. And I did … try.

He knew who my source was. He knew that the source was impeccable. *I had also confirmed from a second source that such a conversation had taken place – that there was such an intercept* – though my second source did not seem to know as much about the content of the intercept as the first source did. But that was enough for me to know that there was a good story there.

But whoever knew about the "who" and the "where" was not willing tell me at that time. *After the fact I was told that, "The bad guys were in Yemen on this conversation."* I didn't know that at that time. I remember knowing that the person who'd told me seemed to know who had been overheard, but he was not about to share that information with me.[1]

Although questions were raised about the credibility of Miller's reporting following a series of articles she wrote about weapons of mass destruction and Iraq, this story was confirmed by her editor,

---

1. Rory O'Connor and William Scott Malone, "The 9/11 Story That Got Away," *Alternet*, May 18, 2006, http://www.alternet.org/story/36388/?page=entire. The anonymous counterterrorism official may have been counterterrorism "tsar" Richard Clarke or one of his staff.

Stephen Engelberg. In addition, it casts her in a very bad light. She dropped a scoop that might have prevented 9/11, had it had the effect her sources evidently wanted at the top of the national security apparatus. And if the story had not been enough to do that, remembering it may just have tipped the scales for those employees who saw the first plane hit the North Tower in the World Trade Center from its twin and went back to work at their desks; perhaps they would have decided to descend to safety, rather than ending up trapped and perishing.

There is no way to definitely determine who the operatives talking on the intercepted call were. However, if a short list were drawn up, Ahmed al-Hada, or at least someone using his phone, would be at the top of that list.

We know that at least one end of the call was in Yemen. This brings al-Hada to mind. People linked to al-Hada who made calls to and from his phone, for example Khalid Almihdhar and the Alhazmi brothers, certainly did know of a forthcoming al-Qaeda operation and could have said the things overheard by the NSA. On the other hand, we also know that at this time Western intelligence was intercepting other al-Qaeda targets in Yemen, primarily as a part of an Italian investigation, and that these targets knew of a forthcoming attack involving aircraft.

Nevertheless, it is clear the call was not just some anonymous chatter, because Judy Miller states, "I remember knowing that the person who'd told me seemed to know who had been overheard."

In addition, there seems to have been a reason to take this threat seriously—indeed, it seems to have been partially responsible for the alert on the July 4 weekend, although there was a lot of other worrying chatter at the time, and a holiday like July 4 is a natural time for terrorists to strike. Given his participation in the embassy bombings and the *Cole* operation, al-Hada certainly would have been a very credible maker of threats.

Almihdhar himself actually re-entered the US on July 4, the day on which the alert peaked. He immediately hooked up with Nawaf Alhazmi.[2] Almihdhar and Alhazmi must have communicated with each other while Almihdhar was outside the US, and one logical possibility is that this was through the switchboard of the Yemen

---

2. *9/11 CR*, pp. 239-40.

hub. One would certainly expect that the day Almihdhar, who spent about a month in Saudi Arabia before flying to New York, was to return to the US would have been communicated to Alhazmi and, quite possibly, overheard by the NSA. Indeed, the MSNBC report about the hub discussed earlier said, "The final call from Yemen to the hijackers came only weeks before 9/11," a timing that could certainly fit a call in early July.

As noted, information from the Yemen hub was reportedly exploited to foil an attack on the US embassy in Paris.[3] This plot was thwarted when an al-Qaeda operative named Djamel Beghal was arrested in Dubai, United Arab Emirates, in late July 2001.[4] Beghal's arrest and information extracted from him led to arrests of other al-Qaeda operatives across Europe,[5] including those involved in the Paris embassy plot. Just how calls between one or more of the Paris embassy bombers and the Yemen hub led to the thwarting of the plot is not known, although one possibility is that Beghal's calls were intercepted shortly before his arrest, possibly leading to it.[6] This at least indicates that the US was acting on information from the Yemen hub around the time of the warning mentioned by Judy Miller.

Finally, this heightened terrorist alert was mentioned by the 9/11 Commission in its final report, although its origins were not:

> Disruption operations against al-Qaeda affiliated cells were launched involving 20 countries. Several terrorist operatives were detained by foreign governments, possibly disrupting operations in the Gulf and Italy and perhaps averting attacks against two or three U.S. embassies. [Counterterrorism "tsar" Richard] Clarke and others told us of a particular concern about possible attacks on the Fourth of July. After it passed uneventfully, the [Counterterrorism Security Group] decided to maintain the alert.[7]

To sum up, Ahmed al-Hada, or one of his associates, would be a likely candidate as a party to this call, and there is some additional

3. David E. Kaplan and Kevin Whitelaw, "Pieces of the 9/11 Puzzle," *US News and World Report*, March 7, 2004, http://www.usnews.com/usnews/news/articles/040315/15nine11.htm.
4. Tenet 2007, p. 157.
5. Sean O'Neill and Daniel McGrory, *The Suicide Factory: Abu Hamza and the Finsbury Park Mosque* (London: Harper Perennial, 2006), pp. 93-94.
6. An alternative account of Beghal's arrest attributes it to blowing his cover at the airport. Stories of terrorist incompetence are sometimes peddled to cover up proper intelligence work and should not be taken at face value.
7. *9/11 CR*, p. 258.

evidence, such as Almihdhar's return to the US on the very day the alert peaked, to support this hypothesis.

If the Yemen hub was on one end of the call, it should have resulted in a huge red alert concerning the hub. It would be of prime importance to shake the tree, find out everything that could be found out, and prevent the attack. That should have included not just re-examining intelligence, which would have shone a spotlight on Almihdhar and the Malaysia summit, but also shutting the thing down, in an attempt to disrupt the plot. Shutting the hub down as a part of disruption attempts would have been a great idea anyway— al-Hada had already been involved in the embassy bombings and the *Cole* attack, and shutting down an organization's operations center is as good a way as any of disrupting its operations. Further, if the Yemen hub was one end of the call, this should have sparked interest in operatives known to be linked to it, such as Almihdhar.

* * *

There is no information about what happened to the Yemen hub in the period immediately after 9/11. Lawrence Wright gave an account of the FBI investigation in Yemen after the attacks, but his *New Yorker* article focused only on Ali Soufan's interrogations of two prisoners, and did not mention Ahmed al-Hada. Ahmed al-Hada's son Samir hit the world's headlines in mid-February 2002, when he was killed by a grenade after police tried to arrest him in Sana'a.[8]

According to a Yemeni organization calling itself "Sympathizers of the al-Qaeda Organization," in mid-May 2002 Ahmed al-Hada was among a group of militants' wives and elderly men being held by the Yemeni authorities.[9] An undated MSNBC article apparently written some time in 2005 listed al-Hada as being at large.[10] It is possible this was an error and that al-Hada was still in custody at the time. It is also possible that he had been released or had escaped, possibly aided by radical sympathizers in Yemen's security apparatus. In any case, Lawrence Wright's 2006 book said that al-Hada was "currently in Yemeni custody."[11]

8. See, for example, "Al-Qaeda suspect dies in Yemen blast," BBC, February 13, 2002, http://news.bbc.co.uk/2/hi/middle_east/1819380.stm.
9. "'Al-Qaeda Sympathizers' threaten suicide attacks on Yemen," Agence France-Presse, May 11, 2002.
10. Robert Windrem, "Al-Qaida leaders, associates," MSNBC, May 2005, http://www.msnbc.msn.com/id/4686491/.
11. Wright 2006, p. 378.

Where Ahmed al-Hada is now, whether the US has ever had access to him and, if so, what he said, remains a mystery.

— 38 —

How bad things look in Malaysia

Before proceeding, a summary is in order. At the start of this book we saw an argument between the NSA and Alec Station over access to al-Qaeda intercepts. This was a particularly nasty, pointless argument, but can be written off as nothing more sinister than a turf war. We then saw that some people at Alec Station deliberately withheld from the FBI information about Khalid Almihdhar's US visa. It appears that the immediate purpose of this was to allow Almihdhar to travel to the US, and to monitor him there, although the ultimate purpose of this cannot be determined based on the events of January and March 2000 alone.

When the events of early 2000 are examined in isolation, it seems that the most likely explanation is that Alec Station withheld information from the FBI simply so that it could itself monitor Almihdhar and Alhazmi in the US. This would have been illegal because of the prohibition on domestic CIA activities, but the Agency runs such operations from time to time, and nobody gets that excited. There are also ways to make such surveillance technically legal, at least from the CIA's viewpoint, such as by outsourcing it to a friendly foreign intelligence service. Perhaps the Agency wanted to gather information by monitoring Almihdhar and Alhazmi; perhaps it wanted to try to turn them into double agents.

Cracks begin to appear in this explanation in the run-up to the *Cole* bombing. A few months before the bombing, Almihdhar returned to the Yemen hub, which was then used to "put everything together" before the attack. Intercepts of calls to and from the hub had the potential to prevent the bombing, but this potential was not exploited. The CIA then deduced that Almihdhar may have been involved in the *Cole* operation, but did not tell the FBI. Indeed, the purpose of showing the photos of Almihdhar and Alhazmi to Omar, the informer who had previously identified Khallad bin Attash, seems to have been to ensure that the Bureau was not going to get this information from him. In addition, when Ali Soufan asked the CIA for information about the Malaysia summit, the Agency just shrugged its shoulders. At least one CIA officer in Yemen knew full well about Malaysia and the photos, but kept this from his FBI partners.

Withholding information about Almihdhar after *Cole* was much worse than withholding information about him beforehand, because of his involvement in the deaths of seventeen US sailors. As Lawrence Wright correctly commented, it hampered the pursuit of justice. In addition—as seen, for example, in the failure to pass on Omar's identification of bin Attash in the Malaysia photo—the withholding of information had now widened from Almihdhar and Alhazmi to Khallad bin Attash, who was then known to be a key player in the *Cole* bombing.

This, in itself, would be bad enough, but what follows is worse. By the late spring and early summer of 2001 there was a drumbeat of threat information indicating a major al-Qaeda attack was about to take place against US interests. As we will see over the next three chapters, Tom Wilshire, the key figure in the withholding of the information until now, realized that Almihdhar was linked to this threat reporting and was a likely participant in the forthcoming attack. He also learned that Almihdhar was in the US. Yet, Wilshire continued to shield him from the Bureau, enabling the attack to go forward.

* * *

Three of the most significant documents released in full or in part about 9/11 are e-mails sent by Wilshire to the CIA's Counterterrorist Center in the summer of 2001. Presumably, they were part of a larger group of e-mails and other communications and give us only a fragmentary picture of what was occurring. Nevertheless, they show that Wilshire and his associates knew Almihdhar was likely to be involved in a future attack.

There are three basic ways to view these e-mails. One explanation is that they are genuine and represent Wilshire's honest attempts to prevent the attacks. This option is probably incorrect, as what he wrote in the e-mails does not square with what he did at the FBI, from which he continued to withhold the information about Almihdhar and Alhazmi. Another view is that Wilshire had purposefully withheld information from the FBI, but now began to be concerned that the people about whom he was withholding information would carry out an attack, putting him in an extremely difficult position. Therefore, he generated documentation with a dual purpose: to warn others, in particular Richard Blee, of his fears, and to have documentation he could use to protect himself if anything did go wrong. A third view is that he knew an attack was coming, and the e-mails are simply an attempt by Wilshire to create a virtual reality with memos—they show him giving out prophetic warnings, painting him in a good light.

The first of the three e-mails, sent just one day after Almihdhar returned to the US, is described in the Justice Department inspector general's report (emphasis added):

> On July 5, 2001, John [Tom Wilshire] sent an e-mail to managers at the CTC's bin Laden Unit noting "how bad things look in Malaysia." *He wrote that there was a potential connection between the recent threat information and information developed about the Malaysia meetings in January 2000.* In addition, he noted that in January 2000 when Almihdhar was traveling to Malaysia, key figures in the failed attack against the U.S.S. *The Sullivans* and the subsequent successful attack against the U.S.S. *Cole* also were attempting to meet in Malaysia, and that one or more of these persons could have been in Malaysia at that time. Therefore, he recommended that the *Cole* and Malaysia meetings be reexamined for potential connections to the current threat information involving Malaysia. He wrote, "I know your resources are strained, but if we can prevent something in SE Asia, this would seem to be a productive place to start." He ended the e-mail by stating that "all the indicators are of a massively bad infrastructure being readily completed with just one purpose in mind."[1]

This e-mail raises a number of issues. It shows that Wilshire was aware of current reports that al-Qaeda was planning a major attack in the near future—that is what the "recent threat information" mentioned by the Justice Department inspector general was in reference to. Lawrence Wright agreed that Wilshire received this information, writing that "he was privy to the reports that al-Qaeda was planning a 'Hiroshima' inside America."[2] This is a key point that needs to be borne in mind when discussing Wilshire's actions.

---

1. Justice Department IG report, p. 298.
2. Wright 2006, p. 340.

It also shows that Wilshire associated Khalid Almihdhar and Nawaf Alhazmi with the current threat reporting. He had protected them before, and he would continue to protect them, even after he learned for certain that Almihdhar was in the US. Even if we provisionally accept an explanation where Wilshire did not desire a successful attack in the US, we have to appreciate that he knew what was at stake—letting these people operate could result in an attack. This is what makes this e-mail and the follow-up sent on July 23 so important, and what makes the omission of these two e-mails from the relevant section of *The 9/11 Commission Report* drafted by Barbara Grewe so serious.

The date of this e-mail may also be significant, as Almihdhar had returned to the US the previous day. This hints that Wilshire was not only aware Almihdhar was under surveillance, but was receiving reports on it. However, we cannot be sure of this.

Wilshire linked the current threat information in the summer of 2001 to the Malaysia summit. This was correct, although some people might regard it as a long shot, even in hindsight. On the other hand, al-Qaeda's core of operatives was very small, with operatives being reused for different operations, so the chances of one or more of the *Cole* bombers being used for the next operation were high.

As discussed earlier, we still do not have a complete list of the operatives who attended the Malaysia summit. The paraphrase used by the Justice Department inspector general's report is intriguing: "key figures in the failed attack against the U.S.S. *The Sullivans* and the subsequent successful attack against the U.S.S. *Cole* also were attempting to meet in Malaysia, and that one or more of these persons could have been in Malaysia at that time." Who were these "key figures" Wilshire was referring to? One was Fahad al-Quso, who was then in jail in Yemen; another was Ibrahim al-Thawar, who blew himself up during the *Cole* attack; a third was Khallad bin Attash. He had been involved in the 1998 embassy bombings and the 2000 attack on the *Cole*, so the odds of his being involved in the next attack were high. However, the report that bin Attash had been in Malaysia was based on the photo identification by Omar, and when Wilshire saw the photos, he said they did not show bin Attash. So to whom exactly Wilshire was referring here is unclear.

Tom Wilshire seems fixated on the idea that the upcoming attack was going to be in Malaysia, which is similar to both "Michelle's" excuse in January 2000 and the reason Wilshire gave for not telling the FBI about Almihdhar's visa and Alhazmi's travel to the US when he reviewed the cables discussing them in May 2001.

Even if we were to accept that the CIA was genuinely concerned in early January 2000 that there might be an al-Qaeda attack in Malaysia, this is no reason for Wilshire to make that country the sole, or even primary, focus of his concern in the summer of 2001. After all, Wilshire was aware that two of the operatives that had been in Malaysia for the summit had then traveled to Thailand and the US. If the pair's travel to Malaysia might have been in support of an attack, then it follows that their travel to Thailand and the US might also have been—and actually was—in support of a future attack. The 9/11 Commission itself described the links to the US in the cables Wilshire read about this travel as "evident."[3]

Wilshire's recommendation that, in the inspector general's words, "the *Cole* and Malaysia meetings be reexamined for potential connections to the current threat information involving Malaysia" makes no sense. There already was such a review being performed by Margaret Gillespie, as Wilshire well knew because he was the official who had initiated it about two months previously. Yet he had essentially sabotaged the re-examination by telling Gillespie to do it in her free time and not giving her the cables he already had, which it then allegedly took her three months to find.

Finally, the actual recipients of this e-mail, described only as Counterterrorist Center managers, are not known, although, as we will see below, it is likely that one of them was Richard Blee, Wilshire's former boss at Alec Station.

---

3. *9/11 CR*, p. 268.

Major-league killer

The second known e-mail in this series is also described in
the Justice Department inspector general's report:

> On July 13, John [Tom Wilshire] wrote another e-mail to CTC
> managers stating that he had discovered the CIA cable relating
> to the source's identification of "Khallad" [bin Attash] from the
> Kuala Lumpur surveillance photographs in early January 2001.
> John began the e-mail by announcing "OK. This is important."
> He then described Khallad as a "major league killer who orches-
> trated the *Cole* attack and possibly the Africa bombings." The e-
> mail recommended revisiting the Malaysia meetings, especially
> in relation to any potential information on Khallad. Significantly,
> John ended the e-mail asking, "can this [information] be sent via
> [official cable] to [the FBI]?"[1]

Again, this e-mail raises a number of issues. Tom Wilshire had
previously expressed skepticism about the identification of bin
Attash. When he obtained the photos in May 2001 for passage to
Dina Corsi, he wrote to Clark Shannon saying that he was "missing
something" and that "someone saw something that wasn't there."
Now, all these doubts seem to have evaporated, for which there
is no explanation, even though Wilshire had been right, and the
person identified by Omar was not actually bin Attash, but Nawaf
Alhazmi.

It is unclear why it took Wilshire until July 13 to find this cable,
which was drafted over six months earlier. It was clearly important,
as he acknowledged himself, and he had known of or suspected its
existence since at least the middle of May, when he got the photos
to which this cable related. One would have thought that Wilshire,
as a manager of the Malaysia surveillance operation during which
the photographs were taken and the deputy chief of the bin Laden
unit at the time the source in Islamabad made the identification,

---

1. Justice Department IG report, p. 298.

would have been informed of such an important piece of news and would not need months to locate the cable.

Wilshire again recommended the Malaysia summit be revisited. However, as we know, he had already initiated the review by Margaret Gillespie, but had hamstrung it by telling her to do it in her free time and by not giving her the relevant cables. If he truly desired a successful, rapid review, then what he should have done was to revoke the go-slow and give her the cables he had. However, he did neither. As noted above, the review Wilshire initiated did not come up with any information Wilshire did not already know. The only thing that was different from Wilshire's rereading of the cables in May—or his previous knowledge—was that Gillespie allegedly realized the evident US links.

The passage from the Justice Department inspector general's report appears to indicate that Wilshire needed to request permission to pass the information to the FBI, although there are a number of problems with this. As deputy chief of Alec Station, Wilshire had previously had the authority to permit the passage of such information to the Bureau—recall that it was Wilshire who had been asked to permit the passage to the FBI of the information about Almihdhar's visa in January 2000, but had instead blocked the cable. Possibly, Wilshire lost the ability to authorize the passage of such information when he was detailed to the FBI in May 2001. Possibly, Wilshire retained the authority to pass the information to the FBI, but declined to exercise it in this case, instead asking for permission from Alec Station, permission that he knew would not be forthcoming.

At this point, the CIA later alleged, they mistakenly believed that the FBI already had this information. It had, after all, come from a joint FBI-CIA source specially designated for use in criminal cases, and the reporting on the source can hardly have failed to make this clear. Why then was a CIA officer asking for permission to tell the FBI something the CIA allegedly thought the FBI already knew? Put another way, the fact that he asked for permission to pass the information to the FBI is evidence that the later claim by the CIA that they thought the FBI already had the information was a lie. In addition, as we will see below, this e-mail and at least the follow-up e-mail of July 23 were seen by at least two managers at the CIA, neither of whom claimed that the FBI already had this information. This indicates that these managers also thought that the FBI *did not* have the information.

In any case, because the source was a joint FBI-CIA source that was already being used by criminal agents in the *Cole* case, there was no reason for Wilshire to request permission from the CIA to discuss it with the Bureau. It was FBI information from an FBI source—how could Wilshire possibly think he needed such permission?

There is a tension between what the e-mail says—the Malaysia cables (which contained information that could have been used to prevent 9/11) should be reviewed and the FBI should be informed of the bin Attash identification—and Tom Wilshire's broader conduct. He had hamstrung the review, and if the CIA's later claims that it thought the FBI was informed of the bin Attash identification in January 2001 and Wilshire's protestations of good faith are to be believed, he should have thought the FBI was already aware of the identification. If he did not, which is more probable, he should have now ensured that the FBI was informed of it, as he was working with the FBI's *Cole* investigators, and the presence of the operation's mastermind at a summit of al-Qaeda leaders would certainly be of high interest to them.

* * *

In the case of this e-mail, we can deduce who one of the recipients was. The endnotes to *The 9/11 Commission Report* refer to a document called "CIA e-mail, Richard to Alan, identification of Khallad, July 13, 2001."[2] This e-mail is a source for a portion of the text that reads, "'John' [Tom Wilshire] was aware how dangerous Khallad was—at one point calling him a 'major league killer.' He concluded that 'something bad was definitely up.'"[3] Given that the date (July 13), topic (the identification of bin Attash by the source), and some sections of the text ("major league killer" and "something bad …" are identical, we can safely infer that "Richard" was one of the recipients of Wilshire's e-mail.

"Richard" was the name used by the 9/11 Commission to refer to Richard Blee. As Blee was the manager responsible for Alec Station

2. *9/11 CR*, p. 537 n64. While the text of *9/11 CR* uses quotation marks to indicate aliases, the endnotes do not.
3. *9/11 CR*, p. 268.

272

at the CIA and had been Wilshire's boss for around two years prior to the latter's departure on loan to the FBI, it is hardly surprising that Blee would be one of the recipients at the Agency.

If the July 13 e-mail was received by Blee, it is likely that the previously discussed e-mail dated July 5 and the one dated July 23 were also received by him, especially given the similarity of their subject matter and the fact that the third e-mail was clearly designated as a follow-up to the second one. The significance of Blee having received these three e-mails will be explained a bit further on.

The reply from the CIA to this e-mail from Wilshire made no mention of permission to pass the information. As pointed out above, neither did it claim that the FBI already had the information and there was therefore no need to give it to them again. It stated that Margaret Gillespie had been assigned to start a review of the Malaysia meeting cables, which Wilshire already knew, as the review had been his idea. It then stated that Doug Miller would be assigned to help Gillespie with the review, as detailed above.[4]

The reference to Miller in the reply is significant. Wilshire intentionally blocked Miller's cable to the FBI about Almihdhar's US visa in January 2000, and he cannot have failed to recall this upon receipt of the reply. Yet, Wilshire again made no move to inform the FBI of Khalid Almihdhar's US visa. It would be natural for Wilshire to respond to the suggestion about allocating Miller to help Gillespie in some way, but the response is not known. Neither do we know whether Miller did actually help Gillespie.

4. Justice Department IG report, p. 299.

40

Khalid Midhar should be very high interest anyway

The third e-mail in this series is described in Tom Wilshire's "substitution for testimony" at the Zacarias Moussaoui trial in 2006:

On July 23, 2001, having seen no action, John e-mailed a CTC manager inquiring as to the status of his request to pass information to the FBI. In the e-mail, John noted that, "When the next big op is carried out by UBL hardcore cadre, Khallad [bin Attash] will be at or near the top of the command food chain—and probably nowhere near either the attack site or Afghanistan. That makes people who are available and who have direct access to him of very high interest. Khalid Midhar [sic] should be [of] very high interest anyway, given his connection to the [redacted]."[1]

The redaction at the end is intriguing. Almihdhar is said to be "very high interest" in connection with the imminent major attack by bin Laden's "hardcore cadre" for two reasons. One is his link to bin Attash; the other could not be disclosed even in 2006. Although there is no way to definitively determine what the redacted phrase says, one leading contender would certainly be the al-Qaeda communications hub in Yemen run by Almihdhar's father-in-law, Ahmed al-Hada. It was not entirely unknown, but certainly not well-known in 2006. Given that the center had not been in use for some time by then, there would have been no real intelligence reason for the redaction.

Almihdhar was also connected to the *Cole* bombing, the Malaysia summit and perhaps the embassy bombings, but there would be no real reason to redact these three things in 2006. It is also possible that

1. *United States v. Zacarias Moussaoui*, "Substitution for the Testimony of 'John,'" July 31, 2006, http://www.vaed.uscourts.gov/notablecases/moussaoui/exhibits/defense/939.pdf, reproduced herein pp. 399-403. The quoted passage is on p. 401.

there was another connection between Almihdhar and al-Qaeda that we do not know, but that Wilshire knew in the summer of 2001.

This could be one of the most important, if not *the* most important, document ever discovered related to 9/11 and the US government's failure to prevent it: the e-mail clearly links Almihdhar, one of the eventual hijackers of the plane that hit the Pentagon, to the forthcoming attacks. It is similar to Wilshire's July 5 e-mail, in which he said the Malaysia summit, which Almihdhar attended, should be reexamined for links to the current threat reporting. However, this e-mail went even further, mentioning the "next big op," and saying Almihdhar was "very high interest" in connection with it.

This was actionable intelligence of the highest quality. As we have seen, one of the reasons the CIA withheld information about Almihdhar and Alhazmi from the FBI was likely the CIA's own desire to monitor them in the US, and Tom Wilshire would have been aware of this. Indeed, the fact that he wrote an e-mail linking Almihdhar to the current threat reporting the day after Almihdhar returned to the US would suggest he was closely involved in their surveillance and learned of Almihdhar's return to the US when it happened. Even if we suppose that Wilshire was cut off from the surveillance, and the timing of the July 5 e-mail is a mere coincidence, then that only entails a slight delay—Wilshire officially learned of Almihdhar's presence in the US on August 22 or 23, and there is documentary evidence confirming this. Therefore, by that time he knew that there was to be an attack against US interests, that Almihdhar was likely to be involved in some capacity and that Almihdhar was in the US. And al-Qaeda's history of attacking US interests and the presence of key operatives in the US indicated the location of the attack: the US itself.

The action that could have been taken was to find Almihdhar and Alhazmi, who were living openly in the US together with some of the other hijackers.[2] Even in late August, it was possible to find some or all of the hijackers, and to arrest at least some of them, either as material witnesses to the *Cole* bombing, or for immigration violations and other offenses. This would have been sufficient to disrupt the plot. Those hijackers who could not be arrested lawfully could have been monitored.

---

2. For an account saying Almihdhar left the US in the summer of 2000 and returned a year later see *9/11 CR* pp. 222, 237. Almihdhar may have actually visited the US during the year he is said to have been away, possibly using a false passport.

Yet, as we will see, Tom Wilshire, who was a senior manager involved in the hunt for Almihdhar in late August and early September, not only failed to tell anyone else involved in the hunt that Almihdhar would likely soon be a participant in a major al-Qaeda attack inside the US, but also supported a dubious procedure which meant that the FBI was only able to focus a fraction of the resources it had on the hunt. The scale of this "mistake" is hard to comprehend—why would anyone withhold information indicating a suspect was about to commit mass murder from other officials investigating the suspect?

But, you may ask, how do we know these e-mails are not a genuine attempt by Wilshire to do his job?

There are at least two things that make no sense. One is his suggestion in the July 5 and 13 e-mails that the Malaysia summit be re-examined for links to the current threat reporting. He already knew such a review was ongoing because he had started it, though he had hampered it severely. If he really wanted this review to succeed, he could simply have given Gillespie the cables he had and told her to get to work at once. The other problem is that he asked for permission to tell the FBI about the bin Attash identification. This identification was made by Omar, an FBI criminal asset run jointly with the CIA, and was therefore Bureau property. Unless he was a party to the scheme to withhold the bin Attash identification from the Bureau, there was no reason for him to assume the FBI did not already have this. And there was certainly no reason to ask the CIA's permission to remind the FBI of something one of its informers had told it six months ago.

We can also contrast the apparent concern shown in the three e-mails with Wilshire's wider conduct. For example, he blocked Miller's draft cable in January 2000, did not notify the Bureau of Almihdhar and Alhazmi's entry into the US when he re-read the cables in May 2001, only gave Dina Corsi three of the many Malaysia summit photographs, withholding at least one of *Cole* mastermind bin Attash, and, as we shall see, continued to withhold crucial information about Almihdhar after notification of his arrival in the US reached the FBI. These are not the actions of a man doing his best to keep the Bureau in the loop.

For the above reasons, we can discard the first of the three ways of viewing these three e-mails—that they were an honest attempt by Wilshire to do his job.

One purpose of the e-mails was surely to cast him in a good light for the investigators who would inevitably come calling following a successful attack. The investigators would naturally be suspicious of the blocking of Doug Miller's cable in January 2000 as well as Wilshire's other actions, but such suspicions could be allayed if Wilshire showed them it was he who had tried to warn the Bureau, but had been thwarted by inaction on the part of his superiors.

However, this motivation is consistent with both the second option and the third, that they were either an attempt to warn Richard Blee of impending trouble and cover Wilshire's ass if something went wrong, or that the e-mails were a pre-manufactured virtual reality to show investigators after an attack that he intended to facilitate. Confirming either of these scenarios may not be possible without further independent investigation employing the power of subpoena.

* * *

Given the key nature of this e-mail, it is worth examining how it was treated by the various investigations into the causes of 9/11. The short answer is clear: they ignored it. There is no mention of it in *The 9/11 Commission Report*, the redacted version of the 9/11 Congressional Inquiry's report, or the unclassified version of the Justice Department inspector general's report. Nor could I find any mention of it in supporting documentation related to these inquiries, such as transcripts of hearings held by the 9/11 Commission and the Congressional Inquiry.

On page 268 of its final report, the 9/11 Commission quoted from the July 13 e-mail that described bin Attash as a "major league killer," sourcing it to the follow-up e-mail from Blee to another CIA manager sent the same day. The Congressional Inquiry report also mentioned and quoted from the "major league killer" e-mail.[3] However, neither of them mentioned the July 5 e-mail in which Wilshire linked Almihdhar to the current surge in threat reporting.

The July 23 and, to a lesser extent, the July 5 e-mail are key dots that have to be connected to understand what really happened. If

---

3. The "major league killer" e-mail is quoted on page 152 of the redacted version of the Congressional Inquiry report.

you omit these two e-mails from the story, then you do not even have to ask why Wilshire withheld from his colleagues at the FBI the information that Almihdhar was "very high interest" in connection with the forthcoming attack, let alone provide an answer. And it is this withholding that indicates Wilshire's apparent bad faith continuing at the end of August and beginning of September 2001.

Since the Congressional Inquiry's report omitted all mention of Wilshire's role in the hunt for Almihdhar, even if it had pointed out that Wilshire was aware Almihdhar was probably going to be involved in the attacks, it would not have had to explain why he withheld this information from the FBI agents involved in the hunt.

The 9/11 Commission Report does mention Wilshire's role in the hunt for Almihdhar in passing, saying that Dina Corsi, who assigned the search for Almihdhar to the FBI's New York field office, discussed this with him before doing so.[4] However, it does not have to explain Wilshire's failure to notify his colleagues of Almihdhar's likely participation in the forthcoming attack, as it omitted the fact that Wilshire knew of this.

It is unclear why the Congressional Inquiry and 9/11 Commission omitted the July 23 e-mail from their reports, despite its significance. Both investigations spoke to Tom Wilshire, as well as other participants in the events, and the Congressional Inquiry even had him testify publicly.[5] Both the 9/11 Congressional Inquiry and the 9/11 Commission therefore had ample opportunity to learn of the July 23 e-mail: from a review of documents, from their interviews of Wilshire, and also probably from interviews of other people who read the e-mail at the time or knew of it. For example, the Commission interviewed Richard Blee, and, as discussed above, there is strong evidence to suggest he read the e-mail, as he had read the previous e-mail sent by Wilshire on July 13.[6]

---

4. *9/11 CR*, p. 270, "Before sending the lead, 'Jane' had discussed it with 'John,' the CIA official on detail to the FBI."

5. Wilshire testified publicly at the Congressional Inquiry hearing held on September 20, 2002; see US Congress, The House Permanent Select Committee On Intelligence and the Senate Select Committee On Intelligence, The Intelligence Community's Knowledge of the September 11 Hijackers Prior to September 11, 2001: Hearing before the Joint Inquiry of the Senate Select Committee on Intelligence and the House Permanent Select Committee on Intelligence, September 20, 2002. Wilshire was interviewed by the 9/11 Commission on April 2, 2004; see, for example, *9/11 CR*, p. 537 n63.

6. For the 9/11 Commission's interview of Blee, see, for example, *9/11 CR*, p. 479 n2. The interview took place on December 11, 2003.

There are no public records of all the documents provided to the 9/11 Congressional Inquiry and 9/11 Commission, so it is impossible to determine whether the CIA did provide them with the July 23 e-mail. If it did not, then the CIA failed to disclose a key document. If the inquiries received this document, but failed to include it in their final report, then they are culpable for this failure. Given that Barbara Grewe worked on the Justice Department inspector general's probe and, as explained below, the e-mail is probably mentioned in the classified version of this report, it is highly likely that she was aware of it.

The point about the omission of the July 23 e-mail also applies to the unclassified version of the Justice Department inspector general's report: it failed to mention this e-mail, despite mentioning the "major league killer" e-mail and the July 5 e-mail.[7] The report mentioned Wilshire in the context of the hunt for Almihdhar; it said that Corsi and Gillespie went to see him after Gillespie completed her review of the Malaysia summit cables, and it noted an e-mail Corsi sent him a day later about the investigation.[8] However, as it failed to point out that Wilshire was aware Almihdhar would probably be involved in the forthcoming attack on US interests, the inspector general's office apparently did not feel the need to explain why Wilshire kept this secret from the other agents with whom the investigation was discussed.

There is strong evidence that the July 23 e-mail was included in an earlier version of the inspector general's report, presumably the classified version that was completed on July 2, 2004,[9] but was deleted from the unclassified version that was released to the public.

One of the people who testified at the Zacarias Moussaoui trial was Erik Rigler, a former FBI agent who appeared as an expert summary witness for the defense. His role was to summarize the relevant chapter of the Inspector General's report for the jury, through testimony given with the aid of a PowerPoint presentation.[10] The

---

7. For the July 5 and July 13 e-mails, see Justice Department IG report, p. 298.
8. Justice Department IG report, pp. 301, 304.
9. The date of the classified version of the Justice Department IG report is taken from endnote 44 to chapter 6 of *The 9/11 Commission Report*.
10. The PowerPoint presentation can be found at http://www.vaed.uscourts.gov/notablecases/moussaoui/exhibits/defense/950.pdf. The trial testimony can be found in two parts: http://www.scribd.com/doc/20814106/Testimony-of-Summary-Witness-at-Moussaoui-Trial-about-9-11-Hijackers-Part-1-of-2 and http://www.scribd.com/doc/20814105/Testimony-of-Summary-Witness-

testimony was based mainly on the report, but Rigler also reviewed the supporting documentation for it.

The testimony and presentation essentially mirror the unclassified version of the report until it comes to the events of July 23, where the "very high interest" e-mail appears. There are two further departures from the unclassified version of the report, regarding August 23, when information embarrassing to Corsi's immediate superior Rodney Middleton appears, and September 5, when Corsi threw another monkey wrench in the works of the search for Almihdhar and Alhazmi. Both these incidents will be dealt with below.

Further, a comparison of Tom Wilshire's substitution for testimony at the Moussaoui trial, in which the existence of this e-mail was first disclosed, and the unclassified version of the Justice Department inspector general's report reveals some striking similarities. Entire passages of the substitution for testimony, which runs to only four pages, appear to have been lifted from a version of the report.[11] This makes it extremely likely that the passage in the

---

at-Moussaoui-Trial-about-9-11-Hijackers-Part-2-of-2.
11. The aliases used for Wilshire, Shannon and Gillespie have been replaced here; the other material in square brackets are redactions contained in the substitution for testimony and the Justice Department inspector general's report. On page 2 of the substitution we find:

> [Wilshire] and [Shannon] discussed the Malaysia meetings, and [Shannon] provided [Wilshire] with a copy of the timeline of events related to the *Cole* investigation that [Shannon] had compiled as part of his work on the *Cole* attack.

On page 283 of the unclassified version of the Justice Department inspector general's report:

> According to [Wilshire], he and [Shannon] discussed the Malaysia meetings, and [Shannon] provided him with a copy of the timeline of events related to the *Cole* investigation that [Shannon] had compiled as part of his work on the *Cole* attack.

On page 2 of the substitution:

> In an e-mail to [Shannon] in mid-May 2001, which was copied to [Gillespie] [Wilshire] noted that he [Wilshire] was interested because Almihdhar was traveling with two "companions" who had left Malaysia and gone to Bangkok, Los Angeles, and Hong Kong and "also were couriers of a sort." [Wilshire] noted in the e-mail that "something bad was definitely up." [Shannon] replied in an e-mail dated May 18, 2001, "My head is spinning over this East Asia travel. Do you know if anyone in [the CIA's Bin Laden Unit] or FBI mapped this?"

On page 283-284 of the unclassified version of the Justice Department inspector general's report:

> In an e-mail to [Shannon] in mid-May 2001, [Wilshire] noted that Almihdhar had arranged his travel to Malaysia and was associated with "[another terrorist organization] courier

substitution for testimony about the July 23 e-mail was also copied from a version of the report.

If this supposition is correct—that the section about the July 23 e-mail appeared in another version of the Justice Department inspector general's report, but was intentionally removed from the unclassified version—it would mean that the Justice Department inspector general was guilty of withholding relevant information from the public. It is this e-mail that shows Tom Wilshire knowing Khalid Almihdhar would probably be involved in the next major al-Qaeda attack. If this e-mail is omitted, then Wilshire's failure to inform his colleagues in the hunt that Almihdhar would probably be involved in a major terrorist attack against the US does not have to be explained. If one pretends Wilshire did not know this, one does not have to explain why he did nothing about it.

travel at the same time." [Wilshire] also noted in the e-mail that al-Quso, who was believed to be a courier since he had stated he had traveled to take money to Khallad, had traveled a few days earlier than Almihdhar.[222] In addition, [Wilshire] wrote that he was interested because Almihdhar was traveling with two "companions" who had left Malaysia and gone to Bangkok, Los Angeles, and Hong Kong and "also were couriers of a sort." [Wilshire] noted in the e-mail that "something bad was definitely up." [Shannon] replied in an e-mail dated May 18, "My head is spinning over this East Asia travel. Do you know if anyone in [the CIA's Bin Laden Unit] or FBI mapped this?"

On page 2 of the substitution:

On July 13, 2001, [Wilshire] wrote another e-mail to CTC managers stating that he had discovered a CIA cable stating that a joint CIA-FBI source had, in early January 2001, identified Khallad in the Kuala Lumpur surveillance photographs with a high degree of certainty. [Wilshire] began the e-mail by announcing "OK. This is important." He then described Khallad as a "major league killer who orchestrated the *Cole* attack and possibly the Africa bombings." The e-mail recommended revisiting the Malaysia meetings, especially in relation to any potential information on Khallad. [Wilshire] ended the e-mail asking, "can this [information] be sent by [Central Intelligence Report] to [the FBI]?"

On page 298 of the unclassified version of the Justice Department inspector general's report:

On July 13, [Wilshire] wrote another e-mail to CTC managers stating that he had discovered the CIA cable relating to the source's identification of "Khallad" from the Kuala Lumpur surveillance photographs in early January 2001. [Wilshire] began the e-mail by announcing "OK. This is important." He then described Khallad as a "major league killer who orchestrated the *Cole* attack and possibly the Africa bombings." The e-mail recommended revisiting the Malaysia meetings, especially in relation to any potential information on Khallad. Significantly, [Wilshire] ended the e-mail asking, "can this [information] be sent via CIR to [the FBI]?"

There are other passages that are parallel, but these three sections are sufficient to indicate that, at the very least, much of Wilshire's substitution for testimony was surely copied from the Justice Department inspector general's report.

This appears to be the situation regarding the Justice Department inspector general: it uncovered evidence that the FBI's failure to prevent 9/11 was not a mere string of bizarre mishaps, but the work of a CIA officer, possibly acting with others, who sabotaged the FBI's efforts by, for example, blocking the original cable about Almihdhar's visa in January 2000, failing to pass on information to the FBI about Almihdhar and Alhazmi throughout the spring and summer of 2001, failing to inform his colleagues in the hunt for Almihdhar that he was probably going to be involved in a major al-Qaeda attack inside the US, and even supporting restrictions on the hunt that made it less effective. In addition, as we will see, Wilshire was also involved in the failure to obtain a warrant to search Zacarias Moussaoui's belongings and the failure to inform the FBI's management of the Moussaoui case. Upon learning this, the Justice Department inspector general apparently covered it up.

Why?

— 41 —

They're coming here

Throughout the heightened period of threat reporting in the summer of 2001, the main government briefer on the reports was Richard Blee, head of the Sunni Extremist Group that included Alec Station. Two aspects of these briefings are of interest: what was said in them, and, perhaps more importantly, what was not said.

There is evidence that Richard Blee had conspired with Tom Wilshire and others to hide information about Nawaf Alhazmi and Khalid Almihdhar. During the Malaysia summit, Blee had misinformed his superiors, claiming that surveillance of Almihdhar and Alhazmi was continuing, although they were allegedly lost at that time. He then received at least one, probably more, of Wilshire's three summer 2001 e-mails, but failed to approve Wilshire's request to pass the information about the bin Attash identification to the FBI, or to point out that he thought the FBI already had it and that it was FBI information anyway. He was aware of the likelihood of an attack; Wilshire's July 23 e-mail told him Almihdhar was "high interest" in connection with it, and he later must have learned that Almihdhar was in the US, but took no action on this.

One of the first briefings by Blee during the heightened threat alert occurred on May 30, when he briefed National Security Adviser Condoleezza Rice, counterterrorism "tsar" Richard Clarke, National Security Council staffer Mary McCarthy, CIA Director George Tenet, his deputy John McLaughlin, and Counterterrorist Center chief Cofer Black. The meeting is described in Tenet's book:

> Rich ran through the mounting warning signs of a coming attack. They were truly frightening. Among other things, we told Condi that a notorious al-Qaeda operative named Abu Zubaydah was working on attack plans.

Some intelligence suggested that those plans were ready to be executed; others suggested they would not be ready for six months. The primary target appeared to be in Israel, but other US assets around the world were at risk.[1]

Tenet also added, "We were asked to brief other Cabinet members" about the information, although he did not say whom.

Contrast this with Wilshire's "focused on Malaysia" comment the same month. Wilshire had been one of Blee's top subordinates until the first half of the month and evidently continued to communicate with him after he went to the FBI. It is certainly noteworthy that one was saying that Israel was the likeliest location of the attack, while the other later claimed he thought it was Malaysia.

The next briefing by Blee that Tenet described occurred in late June:

On June 28, 2001—I remember the date exactly and the event vividly—Cofer Black and I sat down for a briefing on the state of the global terrorism threat. Cofer had again brought along Rich B. It was Rich who did most of the talking. We now had more than ten specific pieces of intelligence about impending attacks, he said. The NSA and CTC analysts who had been watching bin Laden and al-Qaeda over the years believed that the intelligence was both unprecedented and virtually 100 percent reliable. Over the last three to five months we had been witness to never-before-seen efforts by Ayman al-Zawahiri to prepare terrorist operations. Abd al-Rahim al-Nashiri, the mastermind of the *Cole* attack, had disappeared. A key Afghan camp commander was reportedly weeping with joy because his he believed he could see his trainees in heaven. All around the Muslim world, important operatives were disappearing while others were preparing for martyrdom. Rich's June 28 briefing concluded with a PowerPoint slide saying, "Based on a review of all source reporting, we believe that Osama bin Laden will launch a significant terrorist attack against the US and/or Israeli interests in the coming weeks."[2]

The statement that al-Nashiri had "disappeared" is intriguing, as it suggests the CIA had him under surveillance beforehand. If they did, how were they monitoring him? And why didn't they grab him?

The second briefing Blee gave Rice, on July 10, is much better known, as it caused controversy when it was highlighted by Bob

1. Tenet 2007, pp. 145-46.
2. Ibid., p. 149.

Woodward in his book *State of Denial* in 2006.[3] The meeting had been mentioned in passing in a 2002 *Time* magazine article,[4] but had been wholly omitted from *The 9/11 Commission Report*. A media storm followed Woodward's description of it. Rice claimed there had been no such meeting, but it was later proved to have taken place and that she had attended it.[5] Several 9/11 Commissioners and the Commission's Executive Director Philip Zelikow expressed alarm at not being told of the meeting and insisted they would have noted it in the report if they had been told. It was then discovered that George Tenet had discussed the meeting in his January 28, 2004 testimony before Zelikow and other Commission staff.[6] This is certainly amusing, scandalous even, but not our primary concern here.

In the event, Cofer Black, Blee and their subordinates worked the current threat reporting into a strategic assessment, and Black took it to Tenet, who said the briefing "literally made my hair stand on end." Tenet immediately called Rice, telling her he had to see her at once, the only time he ever made such a request during his seven years at the CIA. Rice agreed to meet him, and he took Black and Blee to the White House, where Rice, her deputy Stephen Hadley, and counterterrorism "tsar" Richard Clarke were waiting.[7]

The briefing was delivered not by Tenet or Black, but by Richard Blee, who apparently opened by saying, "There will be a significant terrorist attack in the coming weeks or months!" Blee then set out several specific bits of intelligence showing why he had come to this conclusion.

---

3. Bob Woodward, *State of Denial* (London: Pocket Books, 2006); Bob Woodward, "Two Months Before 9/11, an Urgent Warning to Rice," *Washington Post*, October 1, 2006, http://www.washingtonpost.com/wp-dyn/content/article/2006/09/30/AR2006093000282_pf.html.
4. Michael Elliott, "Could 9/11 Have Been Prevented?" *Time*, August 4, 2002, http://www.time.com/time/covers/1101020812/story.html.
5. Anna Gearan, "Rice: No Memory of CIA Warning of Attack," Associated Press, October 2, 2006, http://www.wthr.com/Global/story.asp?S=5485187; Dan Eggen and Robin Wright, "Tenet Recalled Warning Rice," *Washington Post*, October 3, 2006, http://www.washingtonpost.com/wp-dyn/content/article/2006/10/02/AR2006100200187_pf.html.
6. Peter Baker, "New Book Fuels Election Year Debate Over Bush, Rumsfeld," *Washington Post*, September 30, 2006, http://www.washingtonpost.com/wp-dyn/content/article/2006/09/29/AR2006092901593.html; Philip Shenon, "Sept. 11 Panel Wasn't Told of Meeting, Members Say," *New York Times*, October 2, 2006, http://www.nytimes.com/2006/10/02/washington/02woodward.html; Dan Eggen and Robin Wright, see note 5.
7. This section is based on Tenet 2007, pp. 150-54; see also Bob Woodward, *State of Denial* (London: Pocket Books, 2006), pp. 49-52.

One of these pieces of intelligence was, according to Tenet, "Two separate bits of information collected only a few days before our meeting in which people were predicting a stunning turn of events in the weeks ahead." Compare this with the information, emphasized earlier, that Judy Miller had hoped to report:

> The incident that had gotten everyone's attention was a conversation between two members of al-Qaeda. And they had been talking to one another, supposedly expressing disappointment that the United States had not chosen to retaliate more seriously against what had happened to the *Cole*. And one al-Qaeda operative was overheard saying to the other, "Don't worry; we're planning something so big now that the U.S. will have to respond."

It is not certain that the "Judy Miller call" was mentioned at this meeting, although it would certainly have been appropriate to mention it. As we saw, the call may have been related to the Yemen hub, and one of the hijackers may even have been a party to it. It would certainly be noteworthy if Condoleezza Rice had been given information about the Yemen hub call just two months before 9/11, but failed to follow it up. However, even if the call did involve the Yemen hub—which is not certain—there is no indication in either Tenet's or Woodward's account of the meeting that Blee identified it as such to Rice and the others.

Blee also apparently said that the attack would be "spectacular," designed to inflict mass casualties against US interests and facilities, and that there was a possibility it would be inside the US, adding, "Attack preparations have been made. Multiple and simultaneous attacks are possible, and they will occur with little or no warning."[8] The attendees at the meeting then discussed what to do about the threat.

There was no mention of Malaysia, or Southeast Asia. If Blee was party to some secret intelligence indicating the next major al-Qaeda attack would be in Southeast Asia, he did not tell the national security adviser, at least according to Tenet and Woodward. Of course, there is ample reason to be skeptical about the existence of such intelligence.

There was an effort by some officers in Alec Station to conceal information about Almihdhar and Alhazmi from the FBI. It is likely

---

8. Tenet does not mention the location for an attack in his book. That detail was reported by Michael Elliott (see note 4) and by Dan Eggen and Robin Wright (see note 5).

they did this because of a separate operation that involved monitoring the hijackers, and which perhaps had other aspects, by people linked to these officers. Blee's misleading reports to his superiors in January 2000, his correspondence with Wilshire in the summer of 2001 and his inaction after Alec Station learned Almihdhar was in the US in late August 2001 indicate that he was part of these efforts. In addition, it is unlikely that such withholding of information could have been initiated by an officer as junior as Tom Wilshire.

At the time of this briefing, Blee should have been aware that Almihdhar was a possible participant in the forthcoming attack. Almihdhar had returned to the US six days before this meeting, and surveillance of the hijackers in the US could hardly have failed to register this. One day after Almihdhar returned to the US and five days before this meeting, CTC officers, apparently including Blee, received the "how bad things look in Malaysia" e-mail from Wilshire. Again, the Justice Department inspector general's report described the e-mail:

> In addition, [Wilshire] noted that in January 2000 when Almihdhar was traveling to Malaysia, key figures in the failed attack against the U.S.S. *The Sullivans* and the subsequent successful attack against the U.S.S. *Cole* also were attempting to meet in Malaysia, and that one or more of these persons could have been in Malaysia at that time. Therefore, he recommended that the *Cole* and Malaysia meetings be reexamined for potential connections to the current threat information involving Malaysia.

Yet none of the accounts of the July 10 meeting with Rice have Blee mentioning Almihdhar or Malaysia at all. The national security adviser would certainly have been interested to learn that one of the likely attackers had just arrived in the US and met with another leading al-Qaeda operative, Nawaf Alhazmi, and several other associates, and that he was being monitored by associates of Blee or by an allied intelligence agency. However, there is no record of Rice being told this.

Much criticism was leveled at Condoleezza Rice after 9/11, and a good portion of it may well have been justified—she certainly could have done more in response to this meeting, such as paying more attention to the topic and trying to learn more. However, she could not have acted on information Blee withheld from her.

George Tenet also described an odd episode later the same month:

> Imagine how we felt at the time living through it [the period of high threat reporting in the summer of 2001]. And imagine how I and everyone else in the room reacted during one of my updates in late July when, as we speculated about the kind of attacks we could face, Rich B. suddenly said, with complete conviction, "They're coming here." I'll never forget the silence that followed.[9]

Tenet was apparently so affected by this episode that it provided the title of the chapter of his 2007 book that dealt with the pre-9/11 warnings: "They're Coming Here."

As set out above, it appears that Richard Blee must have been party to the surveillance of Almihdhar and Alhazmi in the US and had likely received a series of e-mails from Wilshire about Almihdhar, culminating in one, dated July 23, that stated he was "very high interest" in connection with the forthcoming attacks. Blee therefore had very good reason to say, "They're coming here." They were *already* here.

---

9. Tenet 2007, p. 158.

42

The Minneapolis Airplane IV crowd

In the middle of August, a week before the Bureau was informed of Almihdhar's entry to the US, the FBI's Minneapolis field office began an investigation of Zacarias Moussaoui, another man sometimes referred to as "the 20th hijacker." The Moussaoui investigation could have and should have been enough to prevent 9/11, but the FBI failed in two ways.

First it failed to obtain a warrant to search Moussaoui's belongings, which contained evidence linking him to eleven of the other hijackers. Second, headquarters staff failed to pass on notification of the case to the Bureau's acting director and his senior assistants. Had such notification been made, the director could have broken the logjam over the warrant through personal intervention.

Tom Wilshire played a key role in both these failures, but, to understand why what Wilshire did in the investigation was so important, it is first necessary to briefly summarize who Moussaoui was and why the FBI started to investigate him.

Moussaoui was clearly a radical Islamist, and, as he was mostly based in Britain, he had been under surveillance by the British authorities. For example, Reda Hassaine, an Algerian informer who worked for French and British intelligence, had helped MI5 keep tabs on him in London,[1] French authorities had investigated him over the assassination of three French consular officials in Algeria,[2]

---

1. Keith Dovkants, "I Spied on Abu Qatada for MI5," *London Evening Standard*, January 28, 2005; also Sean O'Neill and Daniel McGrory, *The Suicide Factory: Abu Hamza and the Finsbury Park Mosque* (London: Harper Perennial, 2006), p. 133.
2. Jim Boulden, "France Opened Moussaoui File in '94," CNN, December 11, 2001, http://archives. cnn.com/2001/WORLD/europe/12/06/gen.moussaoui.background/; David Zucchino, "Pain, Disbelief for Suspect's Mother," *Los Angeles Times*, December 13, 2001, http://articles.latimes. com/2001/dec/13/news/mn-14499; Ian Burrell, Andrew Gumbell and Kim Sengupta, "The '20th Hijacker' Had Been a Suspect for Years – But He Was Ignored by Intelligence Agencies," *Independent* (UK), December 11, 2001, http://www.independent.co.uk/news/world/americas/the-20th-hijacker-had-been-a-suspect-for-years--but-he-was-ignored-by-intelligence-agencies-619827. html.

and MI5 had monitored calls between him and future shoe-bomber Richard Reid.[3]

The French also built up a "thick file" about Moussaoui's activities[4] and put him on their anti-terrorist watch list in 1999.[5] A CIA asset had met Moussaoui in Azerbaijan in 1997 and later reported on him to the CIA, but allegedly only under one of Moussaoui's aliases.[6] Moussaoui also stayed at the same apartment that had hosted the Malaysia summit in Kuala Lumpur in the fall of 2000, but by then the Malaysians had stopped monitoring the apartment, at the CIA's request.[7] The French were aware that Moussaoui had recruited a fighter who had died in combat in Chechnya, where he had been associated with Ibn Khattab, an associate of Osama bin Laden's from the anti-Soviet jihad. They also knew he had been to Afghanistan.[8]

Moussaoui became involved in an airplanes-as-missiles plot sometime in mid-2000, at the latest. At this time Khalid Shaikh Mohammed had not only one airplanes-as-missiles plot, but several. It appears that KSM initially saw Moussaoui as a pilot to be involved in a second wave to follow 9/11. The reasoning behind this was that while the hijackers in the first wave could be Middle Eastern, greater scrutiny of Middle Easterners in the US after the first attacks meant that the second wave would have to utilize operatives with Western passports, such as Moussaoui's French one. Although KSM may have briefly considered Moussaoui as a pilot of a fifth jet on 9/11, events overtook such considerations. One of the alleged hijacker pilots, Ziad Jarrah, began to waver over participation in the plot, meaning that Moussaoui would be needed for the first wave. However, Jarrah then decided to go through with it, and Moussaoui was arrested, removing the decision from KSM's hands.

Moussaoui arrived in the US in February 2001 and went into flight training in Norman, Oklahoma. However, he experienced

3. Nick Paton Walsh, Kamal Ahmed and Paul Harris, "MI5 Blunders over Bomber," *Observer* (UK), December 30, 2001, http://www.guardian.co.uk/world/2001/dec/30/terrorism.september11.
4. "Could It Have Been Stopped?" CBS News, May 8, 2002, http://www.cbsnews.com/stories/2002/05/08/60II/main508362.shtml.
5. Ian Burrell, Andrew Gumbell and Kim Sengupta, see note 2.
6. Tenet 2007, p. 201.
7. Michael Isikoff and Daniel Klaidman, "The Hijackers We Let Escape," *Newsweek*, June 2, 2002, http://holtz.org/Library/ToFile/The%20Hijackers%20We%20Let%20Escape.htm.
8. Justice Department IG report, pp. 140-41,

difficulty in his classes and proved an inept student. Unable to obtain even a private pilot's license there, he dropped out of the course and, in early August, arrived in Minnesota to attend flight school there. He was to receive instruction in how to fly a Boeing 747, including sessions on a simulator. However, he immediately raised suspicions at flight school due to his lack of experience and odd conduct, and some staff at the school contacted the FBI on August 15, 2001. The FBI arrested Moussaoui and an associate he was staying with, Hussein al-Attas, the next day, with Moussaoui held on an immigration violation.[9]

During interviews over the next couple of days, Moussaoui and al-Attas made a number of statements that confirmed the arresting agents' suspicions. For example, when al-Attas was asked whether he had ever heard Moussaoui "make a plan to kill those who harm Muslims and in so doing become a martyr," al-Attas replied that he "may have heard him do so, but that because it is not in his [al-Attas'] own heart to carry out acts of this nature, he claimed that he kept himself from actually hearing and understanding."[10] Moussaoui also had difficulty remembering his cover story. He claimed to work for a British company called "NOP," but failed to recall what the initials stood for, his salary, his job description, or any other details of the business.[11]

The FBI's Minneapolis field office therefore formed the impression that Moussaoui was a radical, violent Islamist who was learning to fly to commit a terrorist act. They also correctly surmised that Moussaoui and al-Attas would not be alone in this and that they surely had accomplices, who we now know included the nineteen hijackers. Understandably, the agents wished to discover who these accomplices were, and thought that Moussaoui's belongings might contain clues that would allow them to learn this.[12]

It is uncertain whether Moussaoui ever physically met any of the nineteen hijackers.[13] However, he certainly did meet and talk to

9. For a summary of the start of the Moussaoui case see Justice Department IG report, pp. 103-12.
10. Justice Department IG report, p. 113.
11. *United States v. Zacarias Moussaoui*, trial transcript for March 9, 2006, http://www.law.umkc.edu/faculty/projects/ftrials/moussaoui/zmsamit.html.
12. Rick Linsk, "Once Secret Documents Reveal Alarming Profile," *Pioneer Press*, April 4, 2006, http://www.highbeam.com/doc/1G1-144034081.html; Justice Department IG report, pp. 114-15, 120-22.
13. There are reports that Moussaoui met Atta and Alshehhi in Oklahoma in early August 2001; see Jim Crogan, "The Terrorist Motel," *LA Weekly*, August 1, 2002, http://www.laweekly.com/2002-

some of their close associates. For example, when he was arrested he had in his possession a letter signed by Yazid Sufaat, who had hosted both al-Qaeda's Malaysia summit and Moussaoui himself while he was in Kuala Lumpur. The CIA was aware of Sufaat's links to Khalid Almihdhar and Nawaf Alhazmi, having monitored the three of them together in January 2000.[14]

Moussaoui was also linked to Ramzi bin al-Shibh, who had closely associated with three of the alleged suicide pilots, Mohamed Atta, Ziad Jarrah and Marwan Alshehhi, in Germany, and played a major role supporting the operation. For example, bin al-Shibh had wired money from Germany to both the hijackers and Moussaoui in the US, and Moussaoui's belongings contained documentation related to the transfers he received. Any investigation of bin al-Shibh would have revealed links to his associate Mustafa al-Hawsawi, a facilitator of the attacks based in the United Arab Emirates who had come into contact with several of the hijackers.[15]

Altogether, these links would have led investigators to eleven of the hijackers: Mohamed Atta, Ziad Jarrah, Marwan Alshehhi, Hani Hanjour, Khalid Almihdhar, Nawaf Alhazmi, Fayez Banihammad, Ahmed Alhaznawi, Hamza Alghamdi, Satam al Suqami and Waleed Alshehri. As we have seen, there were numerous links among the hijackers, and the discovery of these eleven would have led to the discovery of some or all of the other eight.

The Minneapolis field office's nemesis in the Moussaoui investigation was FBI headquarters. In order to search Moussaoui's belongings, Minneapolis needed a warrant, either a criminal warrant or an intelligence warrant issued under the Foreign Intelligence Surveillance Act (FISA). A criminal warrant could be obtained from a local judge, but, because Minneapolis had opened its investigation of Moussaoui as an intelligence investigation, according to FBI regulations, headquarters had a veto over whether they would be allowed to make such an application. Furthermore, any application for an intelligence warrant would be submitted to the special

08-01/news/the-terrorist-motel. However, no mention of any such meeting was made at his trial, and it is unclear if the meeting ever took place.
14. *United States v. Zacarias Moussaoui*, presentation for Aaron Zebley, http://www.vaed.uscourts. gov/notablecases/moussaoui/exhibits/prosecution/OG00011.html. An image of the letter can be found at the relevant entry in the 9/11 Timeline: http://www.historycommons.org/context.jsp?ite m=a081601moussaouiinformation&scale=0#a081601moussaouiinformation; Tenet 2007, p. 204.
15. *United States v. Zacarias Moussaoui*, presentation for Aaron Zebley, see note 14.

FISA court by headquarters. This of course also gave headquarters a veto over all FISA applications.

The dynamic in the Moussaoui case was one of Minneapolis officials battling for a warrant application to be submitted, and headquarters blocking them at every turn. The headquarters unit that dealt with the case was called the Radical Fundamentalist Unit (RFU), which handled cases related to Sunni Islamist extremists who were thought not to be directly related to Osama bin Laden. The three headquarters employees who were involved in the discussions there were Rita Flack, an intelligence operations specialist, Michael Maltbie, a supervisory special agent, and Dave Frasca, chief of the RFU. Two managerial-level officers, Michael Rolince, head of the International Terrorism Operations Section, of which the RFU was a component, *and Tom Wilshire himself*, were also involved in the case, as were four FBI attorneys.[16]

Initially, Minneapolis wanted to obtain a criminal warrant. This meant setting up a criminal investigation parallel to the intelligence investigation that had begun before Moussaoui was arrested. After this was done, an intelligence agent in Minneapolis would then give some of the information from the intelligence investigation to a criminal agent by passing it over the "wall"—the name for the set of procedures that regulated the passage of information between intelligence and criminal agents. An agent on the criminal side would then take the information to a judge and get a warrant.

However, when one of the Minneapolis agents, Harry Samit, asked Frasca for permission to apply for a criminal warrant, Frasca refused, saying, "You will not open it. You will not open a criminal case." Frasca stated that the argument for probable cause for a criminal warrant was "shaky," saying that, due to the way the wall was interpreted by the FISA court, if a judge rejected a criminal warrant, the FISA court might later reject an application for a FISA warrant because of the prior rejection of the criminal warrant application. Samit actually wrote on the documentation he had prepared for the criminal investigation, "Not opened per instructions of Dave Frasca."[17]

---

16. Much of the material for the section about Moussaoui is taken from the Justice Department inspector general's report. Frasca is referred to by the alias "Don" in the report, Maltbie is "Martin," and Flack is "Robin."

17. Justice Department IG report, pp. 128-32.

Therefore, the Minneapolis agents' only chance was to make an application for a FISA warrant through the RFU. Unfortunately, they were unable to convince the RFU, and the FISA warrant application never even reached the Justice Department component that would have actually submitted it. This was largely due to a series of roadblocks thrown up by the RFU, for example:

- When French authorities were contacted and stated that they were aware of Moussaoui and had evidence linking him to the Chechen mujaheddin, Michael Maltbie claimed that the French might be referring to a different Zacarias Moussaoui, and he insisted that the FBI's representative in Paris go through all the telephone directories in France to determine how many people named Zacarias Moussaoui lived there.[18]

- Maltbie blocked notification to the Criminal Division at the Justice Department about the case.[19]

- Minneapolis drafted documentation about the case, and this documentation should have been given to attorneys who assessed the FISA warrant applications. However, Rita Flack and Maltbie repeatedly withheld this documentation from the attorneys.[20]

- Flack read a document that became known as the Phoenix memo, but also failed to pass this on to the attorneys, or apparently mention it to anyone else involved in the investigation. The memo recounted evidence that Osama bin Laden was sending operatives to the US to learn to fly, making it highly relevant to the Moussaoui investigation. Naturally, when asked about this by investigators, Flack had no recollection.[21]

- When Minneapolis learned, via al-Attas' imam, that Moussaoui wanted to go on "jihad," Dave Frasca claimed that the word jihad had a lot of meanings beyond "holy war."[22]

- When Minneapolis sent the RFU a draft warrant application for submission, Maltbie made alterations to it that weakened

18. Ibid., pp. 140-44.
19. Ibid., pp. 127-28, 143-44.
20. Ibid., pp. 146-47, 158-60, 164-66.
21. Ibid., pp. 139-60, 208, 217-18.
22. Ibid., pp. 134, 167-68, 201.

the application.[23]

- Maltbie and Flack told an attorney who was to assess the application to say that it should not be submitted.[24]

- Frasca opposed a plan to put an undercover agent in Moussaoui's cell to glean more information from him.[25]

When the interactions between the Minneapolis field office and FBI headquarters are examined, two things, in particular, stand out: the field agents were alarmed by the case; headquarters personnel generally were not. For example, one of the Minneapolis agents, Greg Jones, called Maltbie on August 27 to discuss the application for the FISA warrant. The Justice Department inspector general's report says,

> According to [Jones'] notes of the conversation, [Maltbie] told them that "what you have done is couched it in such a way that people get spun up." [Jones] told the OIG that after [Maltbie] made this statement, [Jones] said "good" and then stated that Minneapolis was trying to keep Moussaoui from crashing an airplane into the World Trade Center. [Jones'] notes of the conversation indicate that [Jones] stated, "We want to make sure he doesn't get control of an airplane and crash it into the [World Trade Center] or something like that." According to [Jones'] notes, [Maltbie] responded by stating that Minneapolis did not have the evidence to support that Moussaoui was a terrorist. [Jones'] notes indicate that [Maltbie] also stated, "You have a guy interested in this type of aircraft. That is it."[26]

Michael Maltbie later said he did not recall using the words "spun up," but could have accused Minneapolis of overreacting to the evidence.

Rita Flack later shared her thoughts about Maltbie's edits to the FISA warrant application with the inspector general (emphases added):

> She said that [Maltbie's] edits were normal and that *the changes were designed* to create "a logical, intelligent package that we

---

23. Ibid., pp. 161-64.
24. Ibid., pp. 164-166.
25. Ibid., pp. 166-67.
26. Ibid., p. 153.

thought would get to court" and *to make the [Minneapolis memo] less "inflammatory."* She explained that by "inflammatory" she meant that the Minneapolis [memo] was not focused, but rather used terms that were geared toward getting someone's attention without providing any evidential support. [Flack] asserted that [Maltbie] was streamlining the document and adding the "buzz-words" that he knew from experience OIPR [the Office of Intelligence Policy and Review, a Justice Department unit to which the memo was never forwarded] would require in order to get the package to the FISA Court. [Flack] stated that the RFU wanted FISA requests to get OIPR's attention but *did not want the RFU to seem like "maniacs."*[27]

So, Flack considered the Minneapolis memo to be "inflammatory" and the people who wrote it—the Minneapolis field agents—to be "maniacs." However, the agents' fears turned out to be mild in comparison to what happened and, given the facts of the case—a radical Islamist linked to the Chechen mujaheddin who wanted to go on jihad learning to fly a large airliner for no ostensible reason—seem to have been entirely reasonable at the time. This involved not just one FBI agent in Minneapolis, but *all of them*, in addition to agents from other organizations working with them.

Their fears were shared by an anonymous CIA officer stationed at FBI headquarters, who wrote in an e-mail dated August 30, 2001 (emphasis added):

> Please excuse my obvious frustration in this case. I am highly concerned that this is not paid the amount of attention it deserves. I do not want to be responsible when [Moussaoui and his associate Hussein al-Attas] surface again as members of a suicide terrorist op ... I want an answer from a named FBI group chief [presumably Frasca] for the record on these questions ... several of which I have been asking since a week and a half ago. It is critical that the paper trail is established and clear. If this guy is let go, two years from now *he will be talking to a control tower while aiming a 747 at the White House.*[28]

One of the key questions about the Moussaoui case is clear: where did FBI headquarters' obstructionist attitude come from? It was the main reason the information from Minneapolis was not handled the way it should have been, meaning that understanding

---

27. Ibid., pp. 163-64.
28. Tenet 2007, p. 203.

it is extremely important to any analysis of why the FBI failed to obtain a warrant. The attitude was shared by Dave Frasca, Michael Maltbie, and Rita Flack. How did they come to share it? Did one of them decide the Minneapolis agents were alarmist and then convince the others of the rightness of this position, or did they all arrive at this attitude spontaneously and independently?

This is where Tom Wilshire comes in. On August 24, he wrote to Frasca, Maltbie, and Flack:

> Dave, please advise when you get a chance this AM where we are re the Minneapolis Airplane IV crowd. Has the tasking gone out to try to obtain more bio info on the guys [redacted]. Do we have photos yet? Can the agency get the photos so they can get them on the wire to assets? Thanks.

Maltbie replied to Wilshire's questions at the end of the day, adding (emphasis in original), "Please bear in mind that there is *no* indication that either of these two had plans for nefarious activity, as was indicated in an earlier communication."[29]

This is the only confirmed link between Wilshire and the Moussaoui case, but there must be other links, other documents he wrote and received. For example, if he is asking, "Do we have photos yet?" then he must previously have discussed obtaining photos with the agents in the RFU. Further, it is highly likely that this was not his last communication on the matter and that he later discussed other aspects of the case. However, such details are not publicly available.

The August 24 e-mail shows he was not only aware of the general outline of the case, but was checking up on specifics, such as whether the RFU agents had asked for biographical information about Moussaoui and al-Attas and whether they had photos of the two men. This indicates a high degree of involvement in the case.

The phrase "Minneapolis Airplane IV crowd" is also telling. It is apparently a reference to the films *Airplane* and *Airplane II*, disaster-movie parodies in which the crew of an airliner become unable to fly the plane, and a pilot who just happens to be traveling as a passenger has to land the stricken airliner, or space ship in the sequel. There never was any *Airplane III*, let alone *Airplane IV*.

---

29. *United States v. Zacarias Moussaoui*, "Substitution for the Testimony of 'John,'" July 31, 2006, http://www.vaed.uscourts.gov/notablecases/moussaoui/exhibits/defense/939.pdf, reproduced herein pp. 399–403. The e-mails are shown on p. 403.

It is unclear whether the phrase "Minneapolis Airplane IV crowd" referred to the FBI field office or to Moussaoui and al-Attas. If Tom Wilshire was equating the field office with a disaster movie parody, this cannot be understood as a compliment to the field office—no matter how humorous the film. If he was referring to Moussaoui and al-Attas, then he was making light of a serious threat. By this phrase Wilshire indicated that he shared the obstructionist attitude of the three RFU agents. Obviously, this does not prove that the attitude originated with Wilshire, although this may well have been the case.

Here, we should recall Wilshire's specific position at the FBI. Although he said he was not the line manager of any of the three RFU agents, he was either consultant to the boss of the most senior of them, or this boss's deputy, placing him higher up the FBI hierarchy than Rita Flack, Michael Maltbie, and, arguably, Dave Frasca. In addition, Wilshire's employment with the CIA, sometimes perceived as a more glamorous and exciting agency, might have given him increased status with his FBI colleagues.

The most senior FBI agent to whom the Moussaoui case was mentioned was Wilshire's counterpart Michael Rolince. There is no documented involvement of Rolince in the case until late on in the investigation. However, Rolince did later admit that around August 27 he had two brief conversations with Dave Frasca in which Frasca informed him that the Minneapolis agents might contact him to complain about the way the RFU was handling the case, although they never did. As the final decision not to proceed with the FISA warrant application was taken the next day, Rolince had very little information about the case and very little time to act on it. However, he was later involved in discussions about Moussaoui's deportation to France.[30]

Four people whose resistance blighted the Moussaoui case—Frasca, Maltbie, Flack, and Wilshire—are known. However, not enough is known about the internal dynamics of this group to be able to apportion blame within it. Possibly Maltbie convinced all the others that the Minneapolis field office was nuts, and they just went along with him, even though Frasca and Wilshire were more

30. 9/11 CR, p. 275; Michael J. Sniffen, "Supervisor: I Never Read Moussaoui Memo," Associated Press, March 21, 2006, http://www.yourbbsucks.com/forum/showpost.php?p=55227&postcount=36; Justice Department IG report, pp. 158, 171.

senior than he. Possibly the mulish attitude originated with Flack, and she influenced the others. We do not know. It would be necessary to investigate how the information circulated at FBI headquarters, and who said what to whom.

What we can say is that Tom Wilshire was part of the group of staff at FBI headquarters who shackled the case, that he was a senior member of this group, and that he was either the originator of the obstructionism or endorsed and strengthened it, undermining the FBI's investigation. We can also say that this obstructionism was objectively wrongheaded—Moussaoui was demonstrably part of a wider conspiracy to hijack airliners and crash them into buildings—and, given the number of other people who realized the significance of the facts uncovered in the investigation before 9/11, at both the FBI's Minneapolis field office and elsewhere, it must have seemed wrongheaded at the time.

43

I had no idea that the Bureau wasn't aware of what its own people were doing

Tom Wilshire, however, must shoulder an even greater amount of blame for the second failure committed by the FBI regarding the case—the failure to pass information on Moussaoui up the chain of command, all the way to the acting director if need be. Logically, this blame should be placed on the last official to "sit" on the information and not pass it on in the appropriate direction.

Neither Michael Maltbie nor Rita Flack can be blamed for this, as their superior, Dave Frasca, was aware of the case. It is also hard to blame Michael Rolince because he only received a small amount of information rather late in the case. The blame should therefore be apportioned between Frasca and Wilshire. Given that Frasca knew that Wilshire knew about the case, and that Wilshire was either a consultant to Rolince or his deputy, it may be correct to assume that Frasca figured Wilshire had already told Rolince or would do so if he thought it were important.

There is no record of Wilshire ever explaining his failure to inform Michael Rolince, or even of his being asked to do so.

This failing at the FBI is highlighted by the CIA's very different treatment of the case. To quote 9/11 Commissioner Tim Roemer: "The report about Moussaoui [shot] up the chain of command at the CIA like the lit fuse on a bomb."[1] As CIA Director Tenet was away when the news reached the top of the Agency, his deputy John McLaughlin was briefed on the case, probably around August 21 or 22.[2] Tenet was then briefed on the case on August 23 after he

---

1. Philip Shenon, *The Commission: The Uncensored History of the 9/11 Investigation* (New York: Twelve, 2008), p. 261.
2. *9/11 CR*, p. 541 n103.

returned, in a document entitled "Islamic Extremist Learns to Fly."[3] Senior officials at the CIA then received at least another five briefings about the case.[4] Senior FBI officials were *never* briefed about it before 9/11.

What treatment did this failure receive in the three reports about 9/11—by the 9/11 Commission, the 9/11 Congressional Inquiry, and the Justice Department's inspector general?

This is the relevant passage from *The 9/11 Commission Report*:

> There is no evidence that either FBI Acting Director [Thomas] Pickard or Assistant Director for Counterterrorism Dale Watson was briefed on the Moussaoui case prior to 9/11. Michael Rolince, the FBI assistant director heading the Bureau's International Terrorism Operations Section (ITOS), recalled being told about Moussaoui in two passing hallway conversations but only in the context that he might be receiving telephone calls from Minneapolis complaining about how headquarters was handling the matter. He never received such a call. Although the acting special agent in charge of Minneapolis called the ITOS supervisors to discuss the Moussaoui case on August 27, he declined to go up the chain of command at FBI headquarters and call Rolince.[5]

No blame for this is allocated to any specific official, although it clearly appears to be the fault of Wilshire or Frasca, or both of them. Not only that, although Wilshire is mentioned several times by his alias "John" in *The 9/11 Commission Report*, he is not mentioned at all in the section dealing with Moussaoui. This gives the reader the false impression he had no role in the case. As we have seen, the Commission also omitted his role in the blocking of Doug Miller's cable in January 2000, as well as the July 5 and July 23, 2001 e-mails.

---

3. Central Intelligence Agency, "DCI Update Terrorist Threat Review," August 23, 2001, http://www.vaed.uscourts.gov/notablecases/moussaoui/exhibits/defense/660.pdf. See page 226.
4. Central Intelligence Agency, "DDO Update Terrorist Threat Review," August 27, 2001, http://www.vaed.uscourts.gov/notablecases/moussaoui/exhibits/defense/670.pdf; CIA, "EXDIR Update Terrorist Threat Review," August 28, 2001, http://www.vaed.uscourts.gov/notablecases/moussaoui/exhibits/defense/671.pdf; CIA, "DCI Update Terrorist Threat Review," August 30, 2001, http://www.vaed.uscourts.gov/notablecases/moussaoui/exhibits/defense/672.pdf; CIA, "EXDIR Update Terrorist Threat Review," September 4, 2001, http://www.vaed.uscourts.gov/notablecases/moussaoui/exhibits/defense/673.pdf; CIA, "DDO Update Terrorist Threat Review," September 10, 2001, http://www.vaed.uscourts.gov/notablecases/moussaoui/exhibits/defense/674.pdf.
5. 9/11 CR, p. 275.

Neither does *The 9/11 Commission Report*'s treatment of the Moussaoui case mention, for example, Michael Maltbie's insistence on checking phone books in France, his edits that weakened the warrant application, the "wants to go on jihad" comment by al-Attas' imam that Dave Frasca dismissed, or the fact that the RFU thought the Minneapolis agents were "maniacs."

The redacted, unclassified version of the 9/11 Congressional Inquiry report did not specifically mention the failure to inform the Bureau's director, and did not apportion blame for this failure.[6] It merely commented that the three key investigations in the summer of 2001—involving the Phoenix memo, the Moussaoui case and the hunt for Almihdhar and Alhazmi—were not linked at the FBI:

> The FBI field office agents in Minneapolis who were investigating Moussaoui knew nothing about the Phoenix communication or Alhazmi and Almihdhar. The Phoenix field office agent had never heard about Moussaoui or the two future hijackers. The FBI agents in New York who were informed on August 23, 2001 that Alhazmi and Almihdhar had entered the United States knew nothing about the other events of that summer.[7]

At best, this is highly misleading. It failed to mention that Tom Wilshire worked on both the Moussaoui and Almihdhar cases, that Rita Flack worked on the Moussaoui case and read the Phoenix memo, and that New York agent Jack Cloonan read the Phoenix memo and was involved in the Almihdhar case.

There is one passage in the Congressional Inquiry report that may refer to Wilshire in the context of the Moussaoui investigation, although this is not certain because the "CIA officer" is unnamed.[8]

---

6. The main discussion of the Moussaoui case in the 9/11 Congressional Inquiry report is on pp. 315-25.
7. 9/11 Congressional Inquiry report, p. 25.
8. Ibid., p. 320. The entire passage is instructive: "A CIA officer detailed to FBI Headquarters learned of the Moussaoui investigation from CTC personnel in the third week of August. The officer was alarmed about Moussaoui for several reasons. First, Moussaoui had denied being a Muslim to the flight instructor, while al-Attas, Moussaoui's companion at the flight school, informed the FBI that Moussaoui was a fundamentalist. Further, the fact that Moussaoui was interested in using the Minneapolis flight school simulator to learn to fly from Heathrow to Kennedy Airport made the CIA officer suspect that Moussaoui was a potential hijacker. As a result of these concerns, CIA Stations were advised by cable of the facts known about Moussaoui and al-Attas and were asked to provide information they had. Based on information received from the FBI, CIA described the two in the cable as 'suspect 747 airline attackers' and 'suspect airline suicide attacker[s],' who might be 'involved in a larger plot to target airlines traveling from Europe to the U.S.'"

The Justice Department inspector general's report is even worse in this regard. Its title is "A Review of the FBI's Handling of Intelligence Information Related to the September 11 Attacks," and it devotes over 120 pages to the Moussaoui case, but omits explicit mention of the fact that the FBI failed to inform its own director about it.

The only section that relates even tangentially to this failure is a mere two paragraphs on page 158, about the case being mentioned by Dave Frasca to Michael Rolince:

> Rolince told the OIG [office of inspector general] that some time in August 2001, [Frasca] stopped briefly at his office to give him a "heads up" on a case in the Minneapolis Field Office. Rolince said that the conversation lasted approximately 20 seconds. Rolince said he did not recall if [Frasca] mentioned the name Moussaoui or not. According to Rolince, [Frasca] indicated there was an issue with a FISA and Rolince might receive a call from FBI management in Minneapolis. Rolince said [Frasca] told him the subject of the investigation was in jail on an immigration charge and the logical leads had been sent out. Rolince told the OIG he did not receive any further details from [Frasca] about the issue in Minneapolis, but this type of heads up was not atypical. Rolince stated that he received this type of brief notification as often as 10-15 times a week from his subordinates about potential contacts from the field.
>
> Rolince told the OIG that he never received a telephone call or other contact from the Minneapolis FBI about the Moussaoui matter. He said that he did not raise the limited information he received from [Frasca].[9]

If, knowing nothing about the case, one were to read the Justice Department inspector general's report, one would not even realize that the Bureau's failure to inform its own acting director and senior management about the case was a serious error, or even an error of any description.

On the contrary, it is this error, perhaps more than any other, that made the Bureau a laughing stock after the attacks. For example, in his 2007 book former CIA Director Tenet could not help but comment on a claim by then-acting FBI Director Thomas Pickard,

---

9. After it was decided that a warrant would not be sought, Rolince became involved in discussions about Moussaoui's deportation to France; see Justice Department IG report, p. 171.

who said Tenet should have told him about the case (emphases in original):

> I was stunned to hear [Pickard's comments] suggesting that *I* had somehow failed to notify *him* about Moussaoui. Failed to tell him? Hell, it was the FBI's case, their arrest. I had no idea that the Bureau wasn't aware of what its own people were doing.[10]

Even more amazing is the inspector general's failure to mention Tom Wilshire by his alias ("John") in its 120-plus-page discussion of the Moussaoui case, although Wilshire is mentioned dozens of times in the report in connection with the failures related to Almihdhar and Alhazmi. Here is the only section of the report that deals with Wilshire's actions regarding the Moussaoui case:

> A CIA manager who was working in ITOS at FBI Headquarters as a "consultant" on intelligence issues e-mailed [Frasca] about the Moussaoui case. The CIA manager asked whether leads had been sent out to obtain additional biographical information, including any overseas numbers, and whether the FBI had obtained photographs and could provide them to the CIA.[11]

This is a reference to the e-mail disclosed at the Moussaoui trial that was discussed above. However, a person reading the report would have no way of realizing that the "CIA manager" discussed here was in fact Tom Wilshire and would come away from the inspector general's report thinking that Wilshire had no role whatsoever in the Moussaoui case.

We now have several failures by the Justice Department inspector general, for example the failures to interview Doug Miller and Mark Rossini separately and without minders, to mention Wilshire's e-mail of July 23, to address the failure to pass notification of the Moussaoui case up the chain of command at the FBI, and to include Wilshire in the section about the Moussaoui case. These failures all tend to reduce the degree of blame that might be attributed by readers to Wilshire. As we will see, these are not the only failings in the Justice Department inspector general's report.

* * *

10. Tenet 2007, pp. 200-01.
11. Justice Department IG report, p. 151.

The final matter that needs to be addressed here is a serious misstatement George Tenet made during sworn testimony to the 9/11 Commission. Tenet was questioned about his interactions with President Bush by 9/11 Commissioner Tim Roemer at a public hearing of the Commission on April 14, 2004. Roemer was trying to determine when Tenet had communicated with Bush in August 2001.

Though Tenet had spent many days preparing himself for the interview with the Commission, he failed to recall two key meetings:

> MR. TENET: I didn't see the President. I was not in briefings with him during this time. He was on vacation. I was here.
>
> MR. ROEMER: You didn't see the President between August 6th, 2001, and September 10th?
>
> MR. TENET: Well, no, but before – saw him after Labor Day, to be sure.
>
> MR. ROEMER: So you saw him September 4th, at the principals' meeting.
>
> MR. TENET: He was not at the principals' meeting.
>
> MR. ROEMER: Well, you don't see him –
>
> MR. TENET: Condoleezza Rice – I saw him in this time frame, to be sure.
>
> MR. ROEMER: Okay. I'm just confused. You see him on August 6th with the PDB [Presidential Daily Brief].
>
> MR. TENET: No, I do not, sir. I'm not there.
>
> MR. ROEMER: Okay. You're not the – when do you see him in August?
>
> MR. TENET: I don't believe I do.
>
> MR. ROEMER: You don't see the President of the United States once in the month of August?
>
> MR. TENET: He's in Texas, and I'm either here or on leave for some of that time. So I'm not here.
>
> MR. ROEMER: So who's briefing him on the PDBs?
>
> MR. TENET: The briefer himself. We have a presidential briefer.
>
> MR. ROEMER: So – but you never get on the phone or in any kind of conference with him to talk, at this level of high chatter and huge warnings during the spring and summer, to talk to him, through the whole month of August?
>
> MR. TENET: Talked to – we talked to him directly throughout the spring and early summer, almost every day –
>
> MR. ROEMER: But not in August?
>
> MR. TENET: In this time period, I'm not talking to him, no.[12]

---

12. National Commission on Terrorist Attacks upon the United States, Tenth Public Hearing,

Clearly, this is high-stepping worthy of the Rockettes. The testimony was also untrue, as, in addition to whatever phone conversations they likely had, Tenet had met Bush twice that month: on August 17 and 31.

Remarkably, on the evening of the day Tenet testified, the CIA's press office called reporters around Washington and told them that Tenet had "momentarily forgot" about the meetings. Roemer was understandably furious, as he had but one chance to ask Tenet about the meetings under oath: at the Commission's public hearing. Tenet's "misstatement" had prevented him from doing so, and Roemer would never get a chance to ask Tenet again, at least not publicly and under oath.

Roemer felt that he was entitled to "assume the worst about Tenet's veracity—and the worst about what had happened in August between him and the president." He was especially skeptical of Tenet's claim that he could not recall visiting Bush on his Texas ranch in the middle of August: "It's probably 110 degrees down there, hotter than Hades ... You make one trip down there the whole month and you can't remember what motivates you to go down there to talk to the president?"[13]

The topic of the conversations between Bush and Tenet is not known, and it is unlikely that Moussaoui would have been mentioned on August 17, as the CIA had only just become aware of the case, and written reports of it did not reach Tenet until August 23. However, in his 2007 book, Tenet indicated that the meeting on August 17 was related to the surge in threat reporting, writing, "A few weeks after the Aug. 6 PDB [the Presidential Daily Brief entitled 'Bin laden Determined to Strike in US'] was delivered, I followed it to Crawford to make sure the president stayed current on events." Tenet also recalled being driven around the ranch by Bush and discussing the plants and animals on it with him. One might ask how Tenet managed to recall so much more when writing a book years later.

One might also ask what he was trying to hide from the 9/11 Commission.

April 14, 2004, http://govinfo.library.unt.edu/911/archive/hearing10/9-11Commission_Hearing_2004-04-14.htm.
13. For this section see Dana Priest, "Forgotten Briefings of August 2001," *Washington Post*, April 15, 2004, http://www.washingtonpost.com/wp-dyn/articles/A12951-2004Apr14.html; also Philip Shenon, see note 2, pp. 361-62.

44

Donna was unable to recall how she first discovered the information on the Khallad identification

On August 21, Margaret Gillespie's review of the Malaysia summit cables, which had started in May, finally turned up something. She located the cable from the CIA station in Thailand saying that Nawaf Alhazmi had entered the US in early 2000 with a companion. She then checked with the INS for records of Alhazmi and his associate Khalid Almihdhar, and the INS found not only records of their entry in January 2000, but also a record of Almihdhar's entry on July 4, 2001. Finally, Gillespie notified Dina Corsi at the FBI.[1]

The information was obviously important in its own right, but Corsi's attention was attracted even more because one of the men was called "Khalid." At that time, there was threat information that led the CIA to look closely at everybody who used that first name.[2] This was because in mid-June the CIA had learned that a man named Khalid was actively recruiting people to go to the US to stage a terrorist attack there, although by late August the Agency had already figured out that this "Khalid" was actually Khalid Shaikh Mohammed.[3]

This notification started a complex chain of events that ended with the FBI failing to find the hijackers before the attacks, even though they lived openly in the US. But before the details of this failure are examined, there is another problem with Dina Corsi's actions that needs to be examined.

As we saw above, Corsi had failed to provide Steve Bongardt with the information he requested at the June 11 "shouting match"

---

1. Justice Department IG report, pp. 300-01, 313; *United States v. Zacarias Moussaoui*, "Substitution for Testimony – Mary with EX. 468 attached," July 31, 2006, http://www.vaed.uscourts.gov/notablecases/moussaoui/exhibits/defense/940.pdf.
2. Justice Department IG report, p. 295.
3. *9/11 CR*, p. 277.

meeting concerning the two hijackers. However, by the time Gillespie told her of Almihdhar's presence in the US, Corsi had also learned that Khallad bin Attash had attended al-Qaeda's Malaysia summit. We know this because on August 22 she e-mailed an FBI agent in New York about the information Gillespie had given her, writing that Omar, the joint FBI-CIA source handled out of Islamabad, had identified bin Attash in the Kuala Lumpur photographs.[4]

The Justice Department inspector general commented that this was "the first reference in any FBI document to the identification of Khallad [bin Attash] in the Kuala Lumpur photographs."[5] Corsi presumably had this information for some time before August 22 and failed to communicate it to her colleagues in the investigation. After this date, she continued to withhold it from them, and there is no record of anyone on the *Cole* investigation being told of bin Attash's presence in Malaysia until after 9/11.

The Justice Department inspector general stated, "Donna [Corsi] was unable to recall how she first discovered the information on the Khallad identification. We were unable to find any documents or other evidence clarifying this issue."[6] However, we do know that Corsi discussed related matters with two people who knew of the identification, Tom Wilshire and Clark Shannon, and one of Shannon's e-mails indicated that he planned to discuss the identification at the May 29 meeting with Corsi and "Kathy," although nobody could later remember whether it was held or not.[7] It is therefore likely that she learned of the identification from either Wilshire or Shannon.

The importance of this information to the *Cole* bombing investigation cannot be overstated. Bin Attash was suspected of being a mastermind of the bombing, and the identification by Omar placed him at a summit meeting of al-Qaeda leaders two days after the failed attack on *The Sullivans*. Any information about him was crucial to the investigation, yet Corsi withheld this information from her colleagues at the Bureau.

Corsi was clearly aware of bin Attash's importance to the investigation. According to the Justice Department inspector general's

---

4. As pointed out above, the photograph in which the source saw bin Attash was not a photograph of bin Attash, but of Alhazmi. Nevertheless, bin Attash was actually at the Malaysia summit and the CIA had photographs of him there; they just did not show them to the source.
5. Justice Department IG report, p. 302.
6. Ibid., p. 296. Corsi is "Donna" in the Justice Department IG report, becoming "Jane" in *9/11 CR*.
7. Justice Department IG report, p. 302.

report: "She said that she was focused on the identity and where-abouts of [bin Attash], since he was the purported mastermind of the *Cole* attack." She also said that she was "interested in identifying [bin Attash]" and that his presence in Malaysia would link the photos shown at the June 11 meeting to the *Cole* investigation. In addition, she told the Justice Department inspector general that she was "aware of the significance of [bin Attash] to the *Cole* investigation."[8]

The information came from a joint FBI-CIA source, so there cannot have been any need to request, and wait for, the CIA's permission to share it with others at the FBI. Yet, as we will see, this is precisely what she did. The CIA then sat on this request for about a week and, when it was approved, Corsi still failed to communicate it to the other FBI investigators.

To sum up, Dina Corsi knew bin Attash was present at the Malaysia summit and knew this information was important, but she failed to pass it on to her colleagues, although there was no legal barrier to her doing so.

If she offered any explanation for her conduct—why she did not pass this information on to the other *Cole* investigators—we do not know what it was, because it is absent from *The 9/11 Commission Report*, the 9/11 Congressional Inquiry report and the Justice Department inspector general's report. The Justice Department inspector general's report spends pages discussing Corsi, and its authors cannot have failed to appreciate the importance of this information or the seriousness of its being withheld. Yet the office of inspector general either failed to ask Dina Corsi about it, or did not trouble to include her explanation in its final report.

8. Ibid., pp. 284, 286, 293.

45

If this guy is in the country, it's not because he's going to fucking Disneyland

T he key to understanding the purpose of withholding the information about Khalid Almihdhar can be found in the events of late August 2001. There is no argument that Alec Station had information that should have been sent to the FBI, but was not. There is no argument that this information would have had the potential to prevent 9/11. Given the facts outlined to this point, it is clear that this information was not withheld through a series of bizarre accidents, but intentionally. Nevertheless, until we come to the summer of 2001, we cannot deduce the purpose of withholding the information.

The chapters on the July 5 and 23 e-mails showed that Tom Wilshire was aware that Almihdhar was "very high interest" in connection with the next al-Qaeda attack. After Margaret Gillespie sent notification of Almihdhar's and Nawaf Alhazmi's entry into the US to the FBI, Wilshire became involved in the hunt for Almihdhar, but failed to tell anybody at the FBI—even Dina Corsi—that Almihdhar was "very high interest," meaning that the case was handled as routine. This looks like bad faith by Wilshire and is a good foundation for a case that he knew what was coming, and let it happen intentionally. However, it may be that Richard Blee or another superior told Wilshire that Almihdhar was under tight surveillance and would not be allowed to do anything harmful.

The events of late August suggest bad faith not only by Wilshire, but also by Corsi. This happened because the Alec Station group suffered yet another mishap. One mishap had occurred in January 2000, when Doug Miller read the cables about Almihdhar's US visa and started drafting notification to the Bureau about it. This was dealt with, but a potentially embarrassing paper trail was created linking both "Michelle" and Wilshire, as well as "James," Mark Rossini and Margaret Gillespie, to knowledge of Almihdhar. A second mishap occurred in January 2001, when Omar looked at a photo of Alhazmi and declared it to be bin Attash. Alec Station now officially thought bin Attash had been at the Malaysia summit, and had to conceal this from the Bureau, causing a whole number of problems. By this point, the protective screening had become so complicated that even Wilshire himself was losing track of it. In May he foolishly put in writing that he did not think the photo of Alhazmi was bin Attash; in July he asked for permission to pass on to the FBI information that the CIA would later claim it thought the Bureau already had.

The August 2001 mishap, described in detail below, stemmed from the fact that notification of Almihdhar and Alhazmi's January 2000 entry had to be sent from Alec Station to the Bureau before the attacks. If the events are viewed from the perspective that the attacks were abetted, then the motivation for notification at this time is that the attacks would naturally lead to an investigation. If the investigation found that Alec Station had information about the attackers, but had withheld it from the Bureau for over a year and a half, then that would be very bad for a number of individuals. This would be particularly true for Wilshire and Michelle, who had to worry about the paper trail linking them to Doug Miller's blocked cable. On the other hand, if notification of Almihdhar and Alhazmi's entry were passed to the FBI a couple of weeks before the attacks, and the Bureau did not do much with it, then that would make the CIA look less bad, and would have the added bonus of disgracing the FBI. Wilshire, now detailed to the FBI, was in a position to make sure any investigation by the Bureau went nowhere.

The plan to pass the information to the Bureau might have seemed like a good idea when conceived, but somebody at the Bureau's New York field office inadvertently forwarded the notification to Steve Bongardt, one of the agents Dina Corsi had withheld information from at the June 11 meeting. Bongardt recognized Almihdhar's name and demanded in on the hunt for him. To keep Bongardt away from Almihdhar, Corsi had to tie herself up in knots from which there could be no escape. But to understand exactly what Wilshire and Corsi did wrong, and why she must have known she was acting in bad faith, we have to take the events in order, picking them up after Margaret Gillespie's notification of August 21.

After Gillespie had informed Corsi of the two hijackers' January 2000 entry into the US and Almihdhar's July 2001 re-entry, Gillespie sent their names to the State Department for inclusion on the TIPOFF watch list, along with bin Attash's "Saleh Saeed" alias and the name of the Iraqi whom Almihdhar had met at the airport in Kuala Lumpur: Ahmad Hikmat Shakir. The notification was sent on August 23, the day after John O'Neill had retired and Ali Soufan and his team had departed for Yemen. The State Department placed them on the watch list on August 24, meaning that Almihdhar and Alhazmi would have trouble boarding a plane to or from the US.[1] However, the State Department watch list was not used for domestic flights, and they were not placed on the domestic no-fly list.[2]

This is the only known watchlisting of Khallad bin Attash, a known al-Qaeda leader, under any name before 9/11. No information made public before or after 9/11 has indicated he was watchlisted by the US under his real name or any name other than this alias. Possibly, no such watchlisting occurred, possibly it occurred and has not been made public.

However, although they were placed on the main TIPOFF watch list, a lot of things were not done. In what the *Washington Post* called a "critical omission," neither the Federal Aviation Administration, nor the Treasury Department's Financial Crimes Enforcement Network, nor the FBI's Financial Review Group were notified of Almihdhar. The two latter organizations had the power to tap into private credit card and bank data, and later said they could have readily found Alhazmi and Almihdhar, given the frequency with which the two used credit cards.[3] Other people and organizations not notified included Richard Clarke's White House Counterterrorism Security Group, and management at both the CIA and FBI.[4]

---

1. Justice Department IG report, pp. 302-03; *9/11 CR*, p. 538 n76.

2. 9/11 Commission, public hearing on January 26, 2004, http://www.9-11commission.gov/archive/hearing7/9-11Commission_Hearing_2004-01-26.htm.

3. R. Jeffrey Smith, "A History of Missed Connections," *Washington Post*, July 25, 2003, http://www.washingtonpost.com/ac2/wp-dyn?pagename=article&node=&contentId=A43165-2003Jul24&notFound=true.

4. *9/11 CR*, pp. 270-271; Michael Isikoff and Mark Hosenball, "Your Government Failed You," *Newsweek*, March 24, 2004, http://www.newsweek.com/id/53257.

Although Gillespie, at the CIA, had informed Corsi, at FBI head-quarters, of Almihdhar's presence in the US, Corsi would not per-form the search for Almihdhar and Alhazmi herself, but would delegate it to a field office. This was the way things worked at the FBI. Field offices did investigations, while headquarters supported them by coordinating, for example, liaisons with foreign services. The logical choice for the investigation was the FBI's New York field office, which handled many terrorism cases for the Bureau, includ-ing the *Cole* bombing. Additionally, Almihdhar had flown into New York in July, saying he would stay there on the immigration docu-mentation that had by now been discovered.

Corsi informed her boss Rodney Middleton about Almihd-har's travel to the US on August 23. The unclassified Justice De-partment inspector general's report mentions this and says that Middleton approved the way that Corsi intended to handle the case.[5] However, it does not record Middleton's reaction to the information. This is one of the three points, alongside Wilshire's July 23 e-mail and one other matter, that appeared in the testi-mony of the summary witness, Erik Rigler, at the Moussaoui trial based on a version of the same report, presumably the classified one. According to Rigler, Middleton later recalled his reaction as an "'Oh, shit' moment."[6]

Middleton's reaction was clearly relevant to the events, as he was acting head of the FBI's bin Laden unit. Its omission from the unclassified version was unjustifiable on national security or any other grounds. On the other hand, Middleton was not heavily in-volved with the events described in this book, and compared to other major omissions in the reports, the omission of Middleton's reaction is rather trivial.

The Bureau had a choice: the investigation could be handled either as an intelligence investigation or a criminal investigation. The distinction was significant because of the "wall," the set of pro-cedures that regulated the sharing of information between intelli-gence and criminal agents at the FBI. If it were handled as an intel-

5. Justice Department IG report, p. 303.
6. Rigler's PowerPoint presentation can be found at http://www.vaed.uscourts.gov/notablecases/moussaoui/exhibits/defense/950.pdf. His trial testimony can be found in two parts: http://www.scribd.com/doc/20814106/Testimony-of-Summary-Witness-at-Moussaoui-Trial-about-9-11-Hi-jackers-Part-1-of-2 and http://www.scribd.com/doc/20814105/Testimony-of-Summary-Witness-at-Moussaoui-Trial-about-9-11-Hijackers-Part-2-of-2.

ligence investigation, it might be tricky—but not impossible—for criminal agents to get access to the information.

Another important distinction was the different tools available to criminal and intelligence investigators. During the debate between Corsi and the New York field office, Steve Bongardt emphasized that the investigation should be a criminal investigation, because it would be easier for criminal investigators to find Almihdhar.

Events proved Bongardt right. As we will see, Corsi got her way, and an intelligence investigation was started. The investigation failed to turn up anything before 9/11. Bongardt was allowed to join the search shortly after the attacks, and, using his criminal-investigation tools, turned up leads within a matter of hours.

Had Bongardt been allowed to search for Almihdhar and Alhazmi under a criminal investigation from August, it is more than likely he would have found them. If Corsi had provided criminal investigators with all the information, Almihdhar could even have been arrested as a material witness to the *Cole* bombing—for having met one of the attack's alleged masterminds in Malaysia—as could Alhazmi. Almihdhar could also have been arrested on an immigration violation, having lied on his second visa application, in which he falsely claimed he had never before applied for a US visa.

Cursory surveillance and investigation of Alhazmi and Almihdhar could hardly have failed to uncover their links to some, perhaps many, of the other hijackers, because, as noted, they lived together,[7] banked together,[8] obtained ID cards together[9] and telephoned each other repeatedly.[10] Some of the other hijackers could also have been arrested; for example Satam al Suqami had been an illegal overstay for some time,[11] and there was a warrant for the arrest of Mohamed

---

7. For example, as pointed out above, in the summer of 2001 Almihdhar lived in an apartment in Paterson, New Jersey, together with fellow Flight 77 hijackers Nawaf Alhazmi, Hani Hanjour, Majed Moqed and Salem Alhazmi, as well as Flight 175 hijacker Ahmed Alghamdi and Flight 11 hijacker Abdulaziz Alomari; see *9/11 CR*, p. 230.

8. National Commission on Terrorist Attacks upon the United States, Monograph on Terrorist Financing, Staff Report to the Commission, pp. 58-59, 141, http://govinfo.library.unt.edu/911/staff_statements/911_TerrFin_Monograph.pdf.

9. Chapter 2 of the 9/11 Commission's Terrorist Travel report outlines numerous instances of the hijackers obtaining identification documents together.

10. *United States v. Zacarias Moussaoui*, presentation for Aaron Zebley, http://www.vaed.uscourts.gov/notablecases/moussaoui/exhibits/prosecution/OG00011.html,

11. Terrorist Travel report, pp. 8, 21, 23.

Atta for driving without a valid license.[12] Any such disruption would clearly have foiled the plot.

The decision that the search for Almihdhar had to be an intelligence investigation was in error. It could have been a criminal investigation. In a passage presumably drafted by Barbara Grewe, the 9/11 Commission commented,

> Because Almihdhar was being sought for his possible connection to or knowledge of the *Cole* bombing, he could be investigated or tracked under the existing *Cole* criminal case. No new criminal case was needed for the criminal agent to begin searching for Almihdhar.... As a result of this confusion, the criminal agents who were knowledgeable about al-Qaeda and experienced with criminal investigative techniques, including finding suspects and possible criminal charges, were thus excluded from the search.[13]

Especially when viewed in the context of Dina Corsi's previous failings—the failure to obtain the photos and information Bongardt requested at the June 11 meeting, and the failure to tell any of the other *Cole* investigators that bin Attash had attended al-Qaeda's Malaysia summit—the way in which Corsi insisted the search be an intelligence investigation indicates that she was deliberately hampering the hunt for Almihdhar.

When Corsi finally had the transmission of the NSA information about Almihdhar to the *Cole* investigators approved by the NSA, she then continued to withhold it from them. As we will see, had she not withheld the information, it is likely that Steve Bongardt would have successfully insisted that the search for Almihdhar be conducted as a criminal investigation, and would probably have found him and disrupted the attacks. In addition, Corsi has been accused of fabricating a portion of a key legal opinion on the search that was unfavorable to Bongardt.

Corsi encountered severe opposition when she insisted the search be conducted as an intelligence investigation. This opposition came from three agents in New York. The first was Craig Donnachie, an intelligence agent. Donnachie said that the attempt to locate Almihdhar seemed to relate to the criminal investigation of the *Cole*

---

12. "A Mission to Die For: Timeline," Australian Broadcasting Company, November 12, 2001, http://www.abc.net.au/4corners/atta/maps/timeline.htm.
13. *9/11 CR*, p. 271.

attack, and that efforts to locate such an individual normally would be handled through a sub-file to the main investigation and not as a separate full field investigation. Nevertheless, Donnachie agreed that Corsi's instructions could be followed, and that the investigation would be an intelligence investigation.[14]

Jack Cloonan, the experienced FBI agent who had read the Phoenix memo, also opposed an intelligence investigation, saying that the search should be conducted by criminal agents, as they would have more freedom and resources due to the existing indictment of Osama bin Laden and many of his associates.[15]

The agent who objected most strongly was Steve Bongardt, who received a copy of a draft lead sent by Corsi to the New York field office on August 28. The lead was forwarded to Bongardt by one of his supervisors in error, and was not intended for him. Bongardt immediately realized the significance and called Corsi to discuss it: "Dina, you got to be kidding me! Almihdhar is in the country?"[16] Bongardt argued strongly that the search for Almihdhar should be a criminal investigation, not an intelligence investigation. Corsi not only continued to insist that the search be an intelligence investigation, but even told Bongardt that he could not keep a copy of the memo on his computer, and ordered him to delete it.[17]

This incident was followed by a conference call between Bongardt, Corsi, and Rodney Middleton, Corsi's acting boss, specifically to discuss whether the search should be a criminal or intelligence investigation. Bongardt told Corsi and Middleton that it should be a criminal investigation, giving his reasons as the obvious link to the *Cole* investigation and the greater investigative resources that could be brought to bear in a criminal investigation. He told them that more agents could be assigned to a criminal investigation due to the squad designations at the New York field office. He also said that criminal investigation tools, such as grand jury subpoenas, were far quicker and easier to obtain than the tools available in an intelligence investigation, such as a national security letter.

---

14. Justice Department IG report, p. 304.
15. Wright 2008, p. 353.
16. Lawrence Wright, "The Agent: Did the C.I.A. stop an F.B.I. Detective from Preventing 9/11?" *New Yorker*, July 10 and 17, 2006, http://www.lawrencewright.com/WrightSoufan.pdf.
17. Justice Department IG report, p. 306.

Corsi replied that the information on Almihdhar was received through intelligence channels and, because of restrictions on using intelligence information, could not be provided directly to the criminal agents working the *Cole* investigation. She added that without the intelligence information on Almihdhar, there would have been no potential link to the *Cole* investigation and therefore no basis for a criminal investigation. Middleton agreed with Corsi that it should be an intelligence investigation, but Bongardt disagreed and asked for a legal opinion.[18]

* * *

To understand exactly why Corsi's argument was wrong, we need to know a little more about the "wall." During the fallout from Watergate in the 1970s, Congress investigated domestic spying by the Nixon administration (and others before it) and, worried by what it found, passed the 1978 Foreign Intelligence Surveillance Act (FISA). The new act covered cases in which a government agency wanted to monitor a person not because it thought there was a reasonable suspicion of a crime, but because it thought the person was an agent of a foreign power.[19]

Sometimes while monitoring a person pursuant to an intelligence warrant issued under FISA, the FBI came across evidence of criminal wrongdoing and gathered evidence that was later used in a criminal prosecution. In court, the defense attorney invariably tried to have evidence gathered under FISA thrown out, because the standards for obtaining the warrants were different. A criminal warrant required "probable cause" to believe evidence of criminal activity would be found, whereas an application for a warrant under FISA did not have to allege that any crime had been committed, merely that the warrant's target was an agent of a foreign power. These claims by defense attorneys never succeeded, but they did cause the FBI to gradually introduce procedures regulating the passage of information from intelligence investigations to criminal investigations. These procedures were codified in mid-1995 by Attorney General Janet Reno.

However, the wall did not apply to all intelligence information regardless of source. It primarily applied to information gathered

18. Ibid.
19. For the history of the "wall," see the Justice Department IG report, pp. 21 et seq.

by the FBI under a FISA warrant. Precisely *none* of the information Corsi and Wilshire had about Almihdhar was generated under FISA. It came from the NSA monitoring the communications hub in Yemen, from the CIA breaking into his hotel room in Dubai, from his being followed around Kuala Lumpur by the Malaysians, from INS records and from State Department records. The wall, as codified by Reno in 1995, also applied to any information gathered by an FBI intelligence investigation. At this point there was no FBI intelligence investigation—the lead would not officially be sent until the next day—so this restriction also did not apply. Apparently, Corsi was trying to pull a fast one, the restrictions on sharing intelligence information with criminal agents did not apply in this case, because of both the non-FISA origin of the intelligence information and the absence of any established intelligence investigation.

The 9/11 Commission commented on one of the communications Corsi sent containing these arguments:

> The analyst's email, however, reflects that she was confusing a broad array of caveats and legal barriers to information sharing and rules governing criminal agents' use of information gathered through intelligence channels. There was no broad prohibition against sharing information gathered through intelligence channels with criminal agents. This type of sharing occurred on a regular basis in the field. The [FISA] court's procedures did not apply to all intelligence gathered regardless of collection method or source. Moreover, once information was properly shared, the criminal agent could use it for further investigation.[20]

Unfortunately, however, like so much of what is most interesting in *The 9/11 Commission Report*, this was relegated to the small-type endnotes.

Further, the "wall" procedures did not strictly prevent the sharing of information, but regulated it. This meant that sometimes if an intelligence agent wanted to share certain information with a criminal agent, he had to get approval before doing so, and approval could be granted or denied. However, if the FBI discovered evidence of a significant federal crime during an intelligence investigation, it did not have a choice about whether the information could be passed to criminal agents. Passing it to

---

20. *9/11 CR*, p. 538 n80.

them was *mandatory*. Section B(1) of Janet Reno's 1995 procedures states (emphasis added),

> If, in the course of an FI [foreign intelligence] or FCI [foreign counterintelligence] investigation in which FISA electronic surveillance or physical searches are not being conducted, facts or circumstances are developed that reasonably indicate that a significant federal crime has been, is being, or may be committed, *the FBI shall notify the Criminal Division*. Notice to the Criminal Division shall include the facts and circumstances developed during the investigation that support the indication of significant federal criminal activity. The Criminal Division may, in appropriate circumstances, contact the pertinent U.S. Attorney's Office for the purpose of evaluating the information.[21]

This provision had, however, been amended by 2001. In cases involving the FBI's New York field office, instead of notification to the Criminal Division at the Justice Department, the local US attorney was to be notified.

Not only did the wall procedures not say what Corsi was representing them to say—that a criminal agent like Bongardt could not have the information about Almihdhar—but they arguably said the exact opposite, that the information about Almihdhar *was required* to be passed to a US attorney (who would then provide it to criminal investigators like Bongardt).

In addition, it could be argued that the presence of Almihdhar, an operative of an anti-American terrorist organization, in the US during a high-threat period was sufficient indication of an impending crime in itself. Bongardt put it succinctly during one of his discussions with Corsi about Almihdhar: "If this guy is in the country, it's not because he's going to fucking Disneyland!"[22]

Even more damaging to Corsi than her contorted legal arguments is how she handled the NSA portion of the information. As we have seen, the NSA information was not covered by the "wall" as defined in the 1995 procedures, and passing it to Bongardt and the other *Cole* investigators did not need to be approved by anybody at the Justice Department. However, before NSA information

21. Department of Justice, Office of the Attorney General, Procedures for Contacts Between the FBI and the Criminal Division Concerning Foreign Intelligence and Foreign Counterintelligence Investigations, July 19, 1995, http://www.fas.org/irp/agency/doj/fisa/1995procs.html.
22. Wright 2006, p. 354.

could be passed to criminal investigators at the FBI, this had to be approved by the NSA's general counsel.

For some reason that has never been explained, at the June 11 meeting and after, Corsi failed to provide this information to *intelligence* agents working on the *Cole* investigation, which could have been done without the NSA's permission, and did not ask the NSA's general counsel to approve its passage to the criminal agents. Given Corsi's role as a headquarters agent supporting the *Cole* inquiry, it was her job to submit such requests.

All this changed on August 27, the day before the argument with Bongardt started, when Corsi asked the NSA's representative to the FBI to clear the passage of the information to the *Cole* criminal agents with the NSA's general counsel. Approving such requests was usually a formality, as the general counsel simply had to check whether the information concerned a small group of individuals.[23] If the information did not concern them, he approved its passage within a day or so. In this case, it took one day, as the NSA general counsel wrote back to the NSA's representative to the FBI on August 28 saying that the information could be passed to criminal investigators working on the *Cole* case.

It is unclear whether Corsi had been informed of the request's approval by the general counsel by the time of the two conversations with Bongardt on August 28, as we do not know the timing of the call between the two of them or the timing of the conference call. We do know that Bongardt received the draft lead at around 2:00 p.m. and that the e-mail from the NSA's general counsel to the NSA's representative at the FBI was sent at 3:48 p.m.[24]

It is entirely possible that Corsi was telling Bongardt he could not have the NSA information while holding in her hand approval from the NSA to share that very information with criminal investiga-

---

23. Although this group of individuals had been monitored outside the US without a FISA warrant around the time of the Millennium alert, they were US persons; thus criminal agents could not have unrestricted access to the information gathered.

24. For the time Bongardt received the e-mail, see Justice Department IG report, p. 305. For the time of the e-mail to the NSA's representative to the FBI, see "NSA E-mail re: sharing of information with FBI," dated 8/28/01, http://www.vaed.uscourts.gov/notablecases/moussaoui/exhibits/defense/448.pdf. The e-mail was used as evidence at the Zacarias Moussaoui trial. The e-mail documentation states that the information is for both intelligence and criminal investigators. However, there was no need to obtain the NSA's approval to share the information with intelligence investigators, and both the Justice Department inspector general's report (p. 304) and *9/11 CR* (p. 271) say that the NSA approved the passage of the information to criminal agents.

tors like Bongardt. It is also possible she received such notification from the NSA shortly after putting the phone down. In the latter case, she should certainly have picked the phone up again, calling Bongardt and telling him he had been cleared to get the NSA information and could start a criminal investigation. However, there is no record of her telling Bongardt she had submitted the request, and there is no record of her telling Bongardt it had been approved, even when the discussions continued the next day.

After her failure to provide the information about the Malaysia photographs, and her failure to tell the other *Cole* investigators about bin Attash's presence in Malaysia, this was her third incomprehensible error on the case. As we will see, it was not her last.

The 9/11 Commission and Justice Department inspector general's reports mentioned the issue of the NSA information. The Commission noted (emphasis added), "As NSA had approved the passage of its information to the criminal agent [Bongardt], *he could have conducted a search using all available information.*"[25] It did not point out that Corsi must have known that the NSA had approved the passage of this information to Bongardt, and so it did not have to explain why she insisted that the search for Almihdhar must be an intelligence investigation despite this. It merely attributed her errors to being "confused."

The Justice Department inspector general's report is equally bad in this regard. It merely states,

> On August 27, Donna requested permission through the NSA representative to the FBI to pass to the FBI agents working on the *Cole* investigation the information associating Almihdhar with a suspected terrorist facility in the Middle East linked to al-Qaeda activities. Donna told the OIG that she thought that the NSA information on Almihdhar could be useful to the *Cole* criminal investigators, even if the Almihdhar search remained an intelligence investigation.[26]

A footnote adds, "According to the NSA, the request was approved later that same day." The same problem occurs here as in *The 9/11 Commission Report*: no explanation is offered for why Corsi would have told Bongardt that he could not have informa-

25. *9/11 CR*, p. 271.
26. Justice Department IG report, p. 304.

tion she knew he could have. Given the circumstances, it is hard to provide any reason but that Dina Corsi intended to hamper the search for Almihdhar.

This footnote is artfully constructed—sourcing the date of the request's approval to the NSA—to give the reader the impression that the Justice Department inspector general had to contact the NSA to find out when the request was approved. This suggests that Corsi remained unaware of the approval during the crucial period, whereas in fact the FBI had documentation indicating it did receive the information and the time of receipt. Corsi must have been aware of the approval, and the Justice Department inspector general must have known this. Are we really to believe that the Justice Department inspector general did not investigate what happened to the response after it was approved by the NSA, or simply forgot to mention it, especially when it troubled itself to inquire of the NSA's general counsel what he had done with the request?

What is deeply troubling here is the artfulness of the passage and footnote. A lawyer could certainly argue that this section of the Justice Department inspector general's report did not contain any untruths, but it *is* misleading, and the subtlety of its wording indicates that it was designed to be so.

46

Someday someone will die

Throughout this period, Dina Corsi was working closely with Tom Wilshire. For example, both Margaret Gillespie, who had e-mailed Wilshire about the case on August 21,[1] and Corsi went to see Wilshire in his office at FBI headquarters to discuss the matter on August 22. Once again, none of them could remember much about what was said when interviewed by the Justice Department inspector general, but initiating an investigation to find Almihdhar was apparently discussed.[2] James Bamford commented that Wilshire "apparently made no mention of the fact that he had known most of the details for a year and a half or more and actively kept the information secret from the bureau."[3]

Corsi also e-mailed Wilshire about the case the next day, describing a conversation she had with Craig Donnachie, the intelligence agent in New York, as well as saying that New York would open an intelligence case, that Almihdhar's connection to the *Cole* bombing was more definitive than she had previously thought, and that the official document New York needed to open the case would probably not be ready that day.[4] In fact, it would be another six days before she formally sent the document to New York. According to the 9/11 Commission, Corsi also discussed the lead with Wilshire before sending it.[5] Finally, Wilshire may have participated in a conference call with Bongardt and Corsi on August 29.

---

1. *9/11 CR*, p. 541 n106.
2. Justice Department IG report, pp. 301-02. According to the report: "[Gillespie] and [Corsi] met with [Wilshire] on August 22 in his office at FBI Headquarters to discuss their discovery that Almihdhar recently had entered the United States and there was no record of his departure. All of them said they could not recall the specifics of the conversation, but all agreed that they realized it was important to initiate an investigation to determine whether Almihdhar was still in the United States and locate him if he was."
3. Bamford 2008, p. 74.
4. Justice Department IG report, p. 304.
5. *9/11 CR*, p. 270.

Gillespie's e-mail of August 21 is interesting in its own right. She suggested to Wilshire that the FBI contact Ahmed Ressam, an al-Qaeda operative in US custody following the failed Millennium plot against Los Angeles Airport, to see if he recognized Almihdhar. Ressam was never asked—it seems Wilshire sat on the idea. However, it would not have made much difference, as Ressam did not recognize Almihdhar when shown his picture after 9/11.

After 9/11, however, Ressam did recognize Zacarias Moussaoui. Had he been shown and identified a picture of Moussaoui before 9/11, a warrant would have been granted to search Moussaoui's belongings.[6] It is not known whether anybody related to the Moussaoui investigation suggested this before the attacks or whether Tom Wilshire may have been aware of any such suggestion.

Wilshire supported the argument that the search for Almihdhar should be an intelligence case. He was clearly informed of this approach by Corsi, and there is no record of his protesting. He also discussed the matter in his public testimony before the 9/11 Congressional Inquiry, saying,

> If I may, sir, one point on that, because I was part of the conversation that took place with regards to opening a criminal or intelligence matter, not only do these things restrict us in what we can do today, but the possibility of what might happen in the future are also restricted. So the example that was given to me that day on the telephone was if we try to go criminally and we do not find this individual, if in the future we try to go intel a FISA court judge will say, "Hey, you struck out criminally; that's why you're coming to me intel-wise." So not only do we have to take a snapshot of what we look now where we make these decisions, but management is trying to project ahead.
>
> Let's say we subpoena everything and nothing is in there, we can't find this individual. But we find him one day and we want to then open an intel investigation. We're prevented from doing it because then the judge is going to say, "Oh, you struck out criminally; that's why you're coming back intel-wise." So that's just another thing that was used.[7]

---

6. Ibid., pp. 275–76, 541 n106.

7. US Congress, The House Permanent Select Committee On Intelligence and the Senate Select Committee On Intelligence, The Intelligence Community's Knowledge of the September 11 Hijackers Prior to September 11, 2001: Hearing before the Joint Inquiry of the Senate Select Committee on Intelligence and the House Permanent Select Committee on Intelligence, September 20, 2002.

This is nonsense. When the FBI was worried that a judge might deny an application for an intelligence warrant because the FBI had "struck out" criminally, this did not mean that the criminal warrant had been granted and that searches had turned up nothing. It meant that the application for a criminal warrant *had not been granted because the judge perceived a lack of probable cause*, and no searches had been performed. Therefore, a FISA court judge might later think that the FBI did not really want a warrant for intelligence purposes, would consider the application for an intelligence warrant a mere device to assist a criminal investigation, and would therefore reject it. Wilshire evidently did not properly understand the excuse he was giving Congress. And a criminal investigation would have turned up plenty of information on Almihdhar.

Tom Wilshire also appears to have been the most senior official at FBI headquarters involved in the hunt for Almihdhar and Alhazmi. There is no record of anyone above him, such as Michael Rolince, being informed of this matter—a curious parallel to the Moussaoui case.[8]

By this time Wilshire knew three things: that a big al-Qaeda attack was coming; that Almihdhar was a likely participant in such attack, which is laid out in the three July e-mails; and that Almihdhar was in the US. When these three facts are put together, the logical inference is that the attack itself would be in the US. Yet there is no record of his telling anyone else who worked on the investigation of this. It seems he did not even share this information with Corsi. According to the Justice Department inspector general's report, "[Corsi] told us, however, that Almihdhar's significance continued to be his potential connection to [bin Attash] and the *Cole* attack – not that he was operational in the US."[9]

What motivation could Wilshire have had for concealing Almihdhar's likely participation in a forthcoming major al-Qaeda attack from the other agents involved in the search for him? His probable link to the next major attack was a key piece of information and should have led to a huge manhunt, yet instead, as we shall see below, a single inexperienced agent who was already busy was assigned to the search.

8. There is an allegation that Rolince was informed of the case, but Rolince denies it. It is unclear who made the allegation, possibly Wilshire himself. See *9/11 CR*, pp. 270, 538.
9. For Corsi's understanding of Almihdhar's significance, see Justice Department IG report, p. 303.

It seems that Wilshire did not want the FBI to find Almihdhar even in August 2001. In these circumstances, one explanation is that he wanted the attacks to succeed. An alternative explanation, however, might be that he was willing to be part of an unlawful off-the-books operation in the US and happy to keep the FBI out of the loop, but was misled as to the true scope of what was happening.

What is additionally alarming here is that there is no record of Alec Station doing anything after Margaret Gillespie found that the two al-Qaeda operatives had entered the US in January 2000 and that Almihdhar had re-entered in July 2001. By this time Richard Blee must have known the same three things as Wilshire. He knew a major al-Qaeda attack was coming and had even briefed George Tenet and Condoleezza Rice on this. He had even told Tenet point blank: "They're coming here." He knew of Almihdhar's likely connection to the attacks because he had received the July e-mails from Wilshire. And he can hardly have failed to have been informed of Gillespie's major discovery. After all, he was the manager of the group she worked in. Yet there is no record of Blee, or anyone else, briefing Tenet, Rice or Cofer Black about this.

It was actionable intelligence of the highest quality, and he did nothing with it.

* * *

Another of Dina Corsi's errors concerns a legal opinion requested by Steve Bongardt in the conference call with Corsi and Rodney Middleton. Bongardt asked for the legal opinion because he was not happy with Corsi's definition of the "wall," and he thought a lawyer might disagree with her and back him up. There are several disputed points concerning this legal opinion, but it is agreed that there were two questions that needed to be answered: should the search for Almihdhar be a criminal or intelligence investigation, and, if it was to be an intelligence investigation and Almihdhar was interviewed by an intelligence agent, could a criminal agent be present at the interview?

There are two sources for what happened during this legal consultation. First, the Justice Department inspector general's version (emphasis added):

According to Donna [Dina Corsi], she subsequently contacted the NSLU [National Security Law Unit] attorney Susan [Sherry Sabol] on August 28, and she and Rob [Rodney Middleton] discussed the issue with Susan. It is unclear how she presented the matter to Susan because there were no documents about the conversation and she and Susan had little or no recollection of the specific conversation. Donna told the OIG that she provided the EC [electronic communication about the case] to Susan. According to Donna, Susan agreed with her that the matter should be opened as an intelligence investigation. Donna said Susan also advised that a criminal agent should not be present for an interview of Almihdhar if he was located. During an OIG interview, *Susan said she could not specifically recall this matter or the advice she gave.* Rob told the OIG that he did not recall the specifics of this consultation, but he stated that the NSLU opinion was supportive of FBI Headquarters' determination that the case should be opened as an intelligence investigation.[10]

Later on in the same report: "Donna consulted with an NSLU attorney, Susan. According to Donna, Susan concurred that the matter should be handled as an intelligence investigation and that because of the wall, a criminal agent could not participate in the search for or any interview of Almihdhar." This is followed by a footnote (emphasis added): "As discussed above, *Susan told the OIG that she did not recall this discussion with Donna.*"[11]

The 9/11 Commission's take on this meeting was radically different. Here is the relevant part of the main text of the report:

"Jane" [Corsi] sent an e-mail to the Cole case agent [Bongardt] explaining that according to the NSLU, the case could be opened only as an intelligence matter, and that if Almihdhar was found, only designated intelligence agents could conduct or even be present at any interview. She appears to have misunderstood the complex rules that could apply to this situation.[12]

However, when we get to the endnotes, a different picture emerges (emphasis added):

"Jane" says she only asked whether there was sufficient probable cause to open the matter as a criminal case and whether the criminal agent could attend any interview if Almihdhar was found.

10. Ibid., p. 307.
11. Ibid., pp. 350-51.
12. *9/11 CR*, p. 271.

She said the answer she received to both questions was no. She did not ask whether the underlying information could have been shared. Jane interview (July 13, 2004). *The NSLU attorney [Sabol] denies advising that the agent could not participate in an interview and notes that she would not have given such inaccurate advice.* The attorney told investigators that the NSA caveats would not have precluded criminal agents from joining in any search for Almihdhar or from participating in any interview. Moreover, she said that she could have gone to the NSA and obtained a waiver of any such caveat because there was no FISA information involved in this case. There are no records of the conversation between "Jane" and the attorney. "Jane" did not copy the attorney on her e-mail to the agent, so the attorney did not have an opportunity to confirm or reject the advice "Jane" was giving to the agent. DOJ Inspector General interview of Sherry S, Nov. 7, 2002.[13]

There is no record of the 9/11 Commission re-interviewing Sabol for its report. As we can see from the sourcing for the endnote, its take on the matter was based on an interview conducted by the Justice Department inspector general in November 2002. Yet these two interpretations of what Sabol said in the interview are contradictory. In the Justice Department inspector general's version of the interview, Sabol "said she could not specifically recall this matter or the advice she gave." In the 9/11 Commission version, Sabol "denies advising that the agent could not participate in an interview and notes that she would not have given such inaccurate advice." Which of these accounts is accurate?

This is even more bizarre because Sabol was presumably interviewed by Barbara Grewe, who then went on to write the relevant sections of the reports by both the Commission and the Justice Department inspector general. Having said this, the version of the inspector general's report we have is the unclassified one, not the still-secret classified version Grewe contributed to directly. It is hard to imagine that a 9/11 Commission staffer, especially Grewe, would read a summary of the November 2002 interview with Sabol in which Sabol claimed not to remember anything about the meeting and then begin attributing wholly fabricated opinions to her. Given the numerous other omissions and distortions in the Justice Department inspector general's report, it is not hard to imagine the Justice Department inspector general, or someone rewriting the

13. Ibid., p. 538 n81.

report for publication of the unclassified version, taking a statement by Sabol to the effect that she did not recall the meeting with absolute clarity, that she would not have given the second opinion attributed to her by Corsi, and, no, she is reasonably sure she did not tell Corsi that, and turning it into "she could not specifically recall this matter or the advice she gave."

In addition, later on in its report, the Justice Department inspector general says, "While [Bongardt] was correct that the wall had been created to deal with the handling of only FISA information and that there was no legal barrier to a criminal agent being present for an interview with Almihdhar if it occurred in the intelligence investigation, FBI Headquarters and [the National Security Law Unit (NSLU), for which Sabol worked] believed that the original wall had been extended by the FISA Court and [the Office of Intelligence Policy and Review] to cover such an interview."[14] According to the 9/11 Commission's account of the Justice Department inspector general's interview, the Justice Department inspector general specifically discussed this question with Sabol and she told them the exact opposite of what they wrote in their final report, saying she believed there was no bar on a criminal agent being present for an interview. At the very least, the Justice Department inspector general should have pointed out that Sabol disagreed with the opinion it was attributing to the NSLU.

When asked by Barbara Grewe in 2004, former FBI General Counsel Larry Parkinson told the 9/11 Commission that there was no bar to an intelligence agent being present for an interview of Almihdhar. Grewe summarized this in a memo:

> When told that Dina Corsi alleged that NSLU had told her that no criminal agents could be involved in the search for the two men and none could participate in any interview if they were found, Parkinson said he would be shocked if anyone in NSLU gave such advice. He said there would have been no problem with a criminal agent hopping in on the search or participating in the interview. There was no FISA on these individuals so no internal walls would have been applicable.[15]

---

14. Justice Department IG report, p. 351.
15. 9/11 Commission, Barbara Grewe, "Memorandum for the Record: Interview of Larry R. Parkinson," February 24, 2004, http://www.scribd.com/doc/20930477/9-11-Commission-Memo-on-Interview-of-Former-FBI-General-Counsel.

There is also an internal contradiction in the Justice Department inspector general's treatment of Rodney Middleton. In the key paragraph quoted in full above: "Rob told the OIG that he did not recall the specifics of this consultation, but he stated that the NSLU opinion was supportive of FBI Headquarters' determination that the case should be opened as an intelligence investigation." However, later in the report, a footnote tells us: "Rob told the OIG that he could not recall whether he had talked to anyone from the NSLU about this issue."[16] These two statements are contradictory, saying that he could not recall the *specifics* of the conversation implies he could actually recall the conversation, but on the next page the report says the opposite. Which is it?

The 9/11 Commission's account of the Justice Department inspector general's interview of Sabol seems to be the accurate one, but which account of the consultation on August 28 is correct: Dina Corsi's or Sherry Sabol's? Both agree that Sabol inappropriately advised that the search for Almihdhar should be an intelligence investigation. But, did Sabol tell Corsi a criminal agent could not be present at an interview or did she not say this?

Essentially, it is Corsi's word against Sabol's. However, Sabol is a lawyer of unblemished reputation, Corsi had already hampered the investigation of Almihdhar in three ways at this point: by failing to get the information from the June 11 meeting passed to Steve Bongardt, by failing to pass on the fact that bin Attash had attended al-Qaeda's Malaysia summit to other members of the investigatory team, and by withholding the NSA information from Bongardt even after the NSA had approved its passage to criminal agents. She was also working closely with Tom Wilshire, who, together with "Michelle" and others, had been shielding Almihdhar and Alhazmi from the Bureau for over a year and a half. Whom are we to believe?

There is another small point in favor of Sherry Sabol. As the 9/11 Commission pointed out, "'Jane' did not copy the attorney on her e-mail to the agent, so the attorney did not have an opportunity to confirm or reject the advice 'Jane' was giving to the agent." When that statement is read in the context of the longer passage quoted above, it gives the impression that the Commission staffer who researched the matter and wrote the endnote favored Sabol's account.

16. Justice Department IG report, p. 308.

Put bluntly, what appears to have happened here is that Corsi simply fabricated the legal opinion that a criminal agent could not be present at the interview of Almihdhar. There can be no excuses for this; it is not a matter of crossed wires, misunderstanding complex regulations or incompetence. How can it be anything but clear-cut malfeasance? Wrongdoing that the 9/11 Commission and, in particular, the Justice Department inspector general failed to point out?

* * *

Armed with the legal opinion Sabol said she never issued, Corsi wrote to John Liguori, an FBI supervisor in New York, at 7:30 a.m. the next morning, August 29:

> I think I might have caused some unnecessary confusion. I sent the EC [electronic communication, the draft lead] on Almihdhar to Craig [Donnachie] via e-mail marking it as DRAFT so he could read it before he went on vacation. There is material in the EC … which is not cleared for criminal investigators. Steve [Bongardt] called and Rod [Middleton] and I spoke with him and tried to explain why this case had to stay on the intel. side of the house … In order to be confident … for this case to be a 199 [intelligence case], and to answer some questions that Steve had, Rod and I spoke with the NSLU yesterday afternoon … The opinion is as follows: Almihdhar can be opened directly as a FFI [Full Field Investigation] … The EC is still not cleared for criminal investigators … Per NSLU, if Almihdhar is located the interview must be conducted by an intel agent. A criminal agent CAN NOT be present at the interview. This case, in its entirety, is based on intel. If … information is developed indicating the existence of a substantial federal crime, that information will be passed over the wall according to the proper procedures and turned over for follow-up criminal investigation.[17]

This e-mail contains inaccuracies so evident that I find it impossible to imagine Corsi herself did not know they were lies. Primarily, the NSA material about Almihdhar had been cleared for Bongardt and, as we have just seen, there is strong evidence to suggest Sherry Sabol did not give the opinion Corsi attributed to her. The use of capital letters for the words in the phrase "a criminal agent CAN

---

17. Ibid., pp. 307–08. The e-mail is reproduced on p. 398 herein.

NOT be present at the interview" is supremely ironic, because that is the biggest "misstatement" in the whole e-mail.

She then sent more or less the same e-mail to Steve Bongardt about fifteen minutes later. This was used, along with his frustrated response and her "sympathetic" reply to that, as a defense exhibit at the Zacarias Moussaoui trial. The exhibit is reproduced at the end of this chapter.

Corsi's statement that any information related to "a substantial federal crime" would be "passed over the wall" also suggests consummate gall. Khalid Almihdhar had been involved in the bombing of the USS *Cole*, a substantial federal crime by any definition. Not only was Corsi aware of his link to the bombing, but on August 23, six days before she wrote this e-mail, she had looked at the material linking him to the bombing and concluded that "we have more of a definitive connection to the *Cole* here than we thought."[18] Under the wall procedures, as we saw above, FBI intelligence investigators at the Bureau were under a *duty* to pass on information to prosecutors about a significant federal crime, arguably even if the prosecutors already knew of the crime. The information developed by the intelligence investigation here would certainly have been new to them.

In addition, this provision applied to significant federal crimes that might be committed in the future. It is obvious that the presence of a significant al-Qaeda operative in the US during a period of high threat reporting concerning an attack by al-Qaeda against US interests indicated that a significant federal crime might be impending. This was doubly true in the case of Almihdhar, whom Corsi knew to be linked to the *Cole* bombing, the previous al-Qaeda attack against US interests ten months prior. This is not only obvious in hindsight. It was appreciated at the time, especially by Steve Bongardt.

Bongardt replied to Corsi's e-mail the same morning:

> Where is the wall defined? Isn't it dealing with FISA information? I think everyone is still confusing this issue ... someday someone will die – and wall or not – the public will not understand why we were not more effective and throwing every resource we had at certain "problems." Let's hope the National Security Law Unit will stand by

---

18. Ibid, p. 304.

their decisions then, especially since the biggest threat to us now, UBL [Osama bin Laden], is getting the most "protection."[19]

Corsi wrote back:

I don't think you understand that we (FBIHQ) are all frustrated with this issue. I don't know what to tell you. I don't know how many other ways I can tell this to you. These are the rules. NSLU does not make them up and neither does UBLU [Osama bin Laden Unit]. They are in the MIOG251 [Manual of Investigative Operations and Guidelines] and ordered by the [FISA] Court and every office of the FBI is required to follow them including FBINY [FBI New York].[20]

Bongardt was right, and Corsi was wrong. The rules did not say what she said they said. The sheer scope of Corsi's "mistakes"—not getting the Kuala Lumpur photos passed, withholding the information that bin Attash was in Malaysia, withholding the NSA information even after its passage was approved, and apparently fabricating a portion of Sabol's opinion—discredits their attribution to mere ignorance, incompetence, or any other "innocent" cause. It is likely that Steve Bongardt could not win this argument because he did not know what and/or whom he was up against.

* * *

Lawrence Wright stated that there was an additional teleconference about the search, during which Bongardt made his acerbic dismissal of Almihdhar's tourist status:

Corsi called over the secure phone. A CIA supervisor at Alec Station was also on the line. They told Bongardt he would have to "stand down" in the effort to find Almihdhar. They explained how the wall prevented them from sharing any further information. Bongardt repeated his complaints that the wall was a bureaucratic fiction, and that it was preventing the agents from doing their work. "If this guy is in the country, it's not because he's going to fucking Disneyland!" he said. But he was told once again, not only by Corsi but also by his supervisor at the bureau, to stand down.[21]

19. Ibid., p. 308.
20. Ibid., pp. 308-09.
21. Wright 2006, pp. 353-54.

This incident, a conference call with a "CIA supervisor at Alec Station," is not mentioned in *The 9/11 Commission Report*, the unclassified version of the Justice Department inspector general's report, the 9/11 Congressional Inquiry report or anywhere else, although the Justice Department inspector general's report does mention a conference call involving Corsi, Middleton, and Bongardt, as detailed above.[22]

The alleged presence of the CIA supervisor at Alec Station in the call is baffling. This was an internal FBI matter about a legal issue foreign to CIA officers, so what was the officer doing on the call? One explanation is that the officer was Tom Wilshire, who was a CIA supervisor and was involved in the discussions about how to conduct the search for Almihdhar due to his assignment to the FBI. However, Wilshire is repeatedly named throughout Wright's book, so why would he refer to him here as simply a CIA supervisor? Wright does not source this passage, but it may be based on an interview with Steve Bongardt. Although Bongardt had met Wilshire at least once by the time Wright's book was published,[23] he may not have realized that Wilshire was the CIA supervisor on this call.

If indeed it was Wilshire, then this would be further evidence of his involvement in the hunt for Almihdhar. It would also have been another chance for him to tell Bongardt and the others that Almihdhar was shortly to be involved in a major al-Qaeda attack against the US.

* * *

When the pre-9/11 failings began to emerge after the attacks, this incident—the failure to allow criminal agents to search for Almihdhar—appeared to be just another example of the dysfunctional FBI. However, a different picture has appeared after closer examination.

Dina Corsi's major failings seem far too many to be regarded as coincidence, especially when their nature is taken into consideration. However, no matter how poor our opinion may be of Corsi

22. According to Wright 2006, this call took place the day after Corsi forced Bongardt to delete the e-mail, which happened on August 28, and the day before Bongardt sent Corsi the "someday somebody will die" e-mail, which happened on August 29. Wright is clearly confused about the timing, but the conference call presumably happened on either August 28 or 29.

23. Bongardt and Wilshire testified together for the 9/11 Congressional Inquiry on September 20, 2002.

and her conduct, we should not forget that there is no evidence to show she knew that Almihdhar was of "very high interest" in connection with a forthcoming attack against the US. Presumably, she was acting at Wilshire's direction, assumed he knew what he was doing and had no idea of what was to follow.[24]

In contrast, Tom Wilshire, the CIA officer who initially blocked the passage of the information about Almihdhar's US visa, was the most senior figure involved in the discussions about the search for Almihdhar. He had been alerted about an impending attack and knew Almihdhar was of "very high interest" in connection with it, but failed to communicate this to his FBI colleagues. We seem forced to conclude that Wilshire initially acted in bad faith and then also deliberately hampered the investigation. But we may not have the whole picture.

If there was a surveillance team linked to the Alec Station group monitoring the hijackers, they took no action against Almihdhar and Alhazmi either. Richard Blee likely had the same information at Alec Station that Wilshire had at FBI headquarters, but he also did nothing.

Seen in this light, it is hard to come to any conclusion except this: whoever was running the surveillance and concealment operation wanted the attacks to succeed. This may have been Wilshire and/or Blee. However, they may have been acting on instructions from someone superior, and the purpose of what they were doing may have remained obscure to them until it was too late.

24. Corsi was later promoted, becoming a supervisory intelligence analyst; see *CNN Newsnight with Aaron Brown*, July 22, 2005, http://transcripts.cnn.com/TRANSCRIPTS/0507/22/asb.01.html.

682

From: DINA CORSI
To: BONGARDT, STEVE A
Date: Wed, Aug 29, 2001 9:27 AM
Subject: Re: Steve,

Steve, I do know how you feel. I don't think you understand that we (FBIHQ) are all frustrated with this
issue. I don't know what to tell you. I don't know how many other ways I can explain this to you. These
are the rules. NSLU does not make them up and neither does UBLU. They are in the MIOG and ordered
by the Court and every office of the FBI is required to follow them
including FBINY. You are preaching to the choir and I just want to move on to another tune!   Dina

>>> STEVE A BONGARDT 08/29 8:38 AM >>>
OK ....

I know you know how I feel about this.

Dina - where is "the wall" defined? Isn't it dealing with FISA information? I think everyone is still confusing
this issue. I know we have discussed this ad nauseum but "the wall" concept grew out of the fear that a
FISA would be obtained as opposed to a Title III. Whatever has happened to this - someday someone
will die - and wall or not - the public will not understand why we were not more effective and throwing
every resource we had at certain 'problems'.

Let's hope the National Security Law Unit will stand behind their decisions then, especially since the
biggest threat to us now, UBL, is getting the most 'protection'.

- Steve

>>> DINA CORSI 08/29 7:44 AM >>>
Steve,
   Rod and I spoke with National Security Law Unit (NSLU) in order to confirm that our recommendations
were accurate and to get answers to the questions you posed. They responded as follows:
   Al-Midhar should be opened directly as a FFI. If Al-Midhar is located, the interview must be conducted
by an intel agent. A criminal agent CAN NOT be present at the interview. This case, in its entirety, is
based on intel. If at such time as information is developed indicating the existence of a substantial federal
crime, that information will be passed over the wall according to the proper procedures and turned over for
follow-up criminal investigation. We can discuss what constitutes moving that information over the wall if
and when Al-Midhar is located and interviewed.   I hope this answers your questions. Dina

DEFENDANT'S
EXHIBIT
692
U.S. v. Moussaoui
Cr. No. 01-455-A

M-HQI-78000026

NA-1666

Exhibit at Zacarias Moussaoui trial: e-mail exchange between FBI agents
Dina Corsi and Steve Bongardt on the morning of August 29, 2001.

47

He ran into the bathroom and retched

T he CIA had notified the FBI of Khalid Almihdhar's entry into the US on August 21/22. Over a week later, on August 30, it passed on formal notification of Omar's apparent identification of Khallad bin Attash in a Malaysia summit photograph. The notification was sent as a result of a request from Dina Corsi and was passed through "a CTC representative to the FBI," presumably Tom Wilshire.[1] As outlined above, Corsi had known this information for a period of time before she requested its formal passage, but had failed to communicate it to other FBI agents.

The CIA later alleged that it thought the FBI knew of this identification from the time it had been made, early January 2001. However, the notification sent on August 30 stated, "We wish to advise you that, during a previously scheduled meeting with our joint source," bin Attash was identified in a surveillance photo.[2] If the CIA already thought the FBI knew of the identification—which the notification explicitly acknowledges was made by a joint FBI-CIA source—why did it "wish to advise" them of it?

The other issues related to this notification are best dealt with in an analysis of the Justice Department inspector general's report. This is the relevant paragraph:

> On August 30, 2001, the CIA sent a CIR [Central Intelligence Report] to the FBI outlining the identification of "Khallad" [bin Attash] from one of the Kuala Lumpur surveillance photographs in January 2001 by the source. The first line of the text stated the information should be passed to [Middleton]. The CIA cable stated the FBI should advise the CIA if the FBI did not have the Kuala Lumpur photographs so they may be provided. This is the first record documenting that the source's identification of Khallad in the Kuala Lumpur photographs was provided by the CIA to the FBI.[3]

1. Justice Department IG report, p. 305.
2. 9/11 Congressional Inquiry report, p. 150.
3. Justice Department IG report, p. 310.

This passage is bizarre in what it does not say. It makes no mention of the people involved in this passage: Corsi, who requested it, and the "CTC representative to the FBI," presumably Wilshire. The reference to their role in this is found five pages before this paragraph.

It states that "The first line of the text stated the information should be passed to Rob." This allows the reader to assume that the acting chief of the FBI's bin Laden unit actually received the message, although this may not be the case, and the Justice Department inspector general report does not specifically say he did. Did Rodney Middleton receive the information? If not, why not?

It was Corsi who requested the information, so it was presumably Corsi who received it, but what she did with it then is a mystery. It should have gone not only to Middleton, but also to the rookie agent conducting the search for Almihdhar and to the *Cole* investigators. However, there is no evidence of Corsi doing anything with this information at all. Neither is there any record of her asking for the other Kuala Lumpur photographs, although they were of great interest to the FBI.

Regarding the agent searching for Almihdhar, Corsi had initially omitted this information from the lead she sent to New York, later saying that this was because it had not been officially passed to the FBI.[4] The fact that she did not need CIA approval to pass on information from an FBI source to FBI agents apparently did not occur to her. The section of the Justice Department inspector general's report about the agent's hunt for Almihdhar contains no mention of Corsi informing the agent about the source's apparent identification of bin Attash in the Kuala Lumpur photos, although it is possible that she did, and that the Justice Department inspector general simply omitted this in the report.

There is no mention—anywhere—of this information being forwarded to the *Cole* investigators before 9/11. It was clearly relevant to the *Cole* investigation, as it concerned one of the operation's masterminds. Corsi, who had been working on the *Cole* investigation for some time, must have been aware of this. She must also have known that this clearly linked bin Attash to Almihdhar, as they were both in Malaysia at the same time.

---

4. Ibid., p. 305.

The absence of evidence that Corsi gave the CIA notification to Middleton is not proof that she did not provide the notification to him, as Middleton may have glanced at the notification and not paid it any significant mind, and the Justice Department inspector general may have omitted this because it was of no great importance. However, the absence of evidence that Corsi gave the CIA notification to the *Cole* criminal investigators essentially proves that she did not do so, because *they* would have been swarming over it.

Imagine that, on August 30, one day after the end of the argument about the search for Almihdhar, Steve Bongardt had received notification from Corsi that bin Attash had been identified in one of the Kuala Lumpur photos. The notification was proof of the Malaysia summit, something the *Cole* investigators has suspected since the previous year, but the CIA had repeatedly denied. If he obtained the photos shown to Omar, he would have realized that they were two of the three he was shown at the June 11 meeting. He would have immediately linked it to Almihdhar, whose photo he was also shown as a part of the same series at that meeting.

This in turn would show a much closer connection between Almihdhar and bin Attash than that contained in the draft lead sent by Corsi to New York, which simply indicated that they both visited Bangkok around the same time. It is highly likely that Bongardt would have insisted in the strongest possible terms that the decision to search for Almihdhar under an intelligence investigation be revisited, and that he be allowed to join the search as a criminal agent. We should have learned of events such as this through the Justice Department inspector general's report, *The 9/11 Commission Report*, and the report of the Congressional Inquiry, to which he gave public testimony. However, there is no mention of any such discussion in any of the reports.

In addition, Lawrence Wright describes Ali Soufan's day on September 12, 2001. It is clear that Soufan had not seen the photos previously:

> When they returned to the embassy [in Yemen], a fax came over a secure line with photos of suspects. Then the CIA chief drew Soufan aside and handed him a manila envelope. Inside were three surveillance photos and a complete report about the Ma-

laysia meeting—the very material Soufan had been asking for, which the CIA had denied him until now. The wall had come down. When Soufan realized that the agency and some people in the bureau had known for more than a year and a half that two of the hijackers were in the country, he ran into the bathroom and retched.[5]

There are things we do not know about the passage of the CIA notification on August 30, such as whether it really was Dina Corsi who received the notification, whether she passed it on to Rodney Middleton, and what excuse she might offer for not forwarding it to the *Cole* investigators in New York. These gaps in our knowledge prevent us from citing this as evidence of Corsi's bad faith. Nevertheless, we know that Corsi was aware Khallad bin Attash had been in Malaysia and requested that the information be passed to the FBI, so there is certainly reason to suspect she deliberately withheld information she knew to be relevant.

5. Wright 2006, p. 362.

48

Searches of readily available databases could have unearthed the driver's licenses, the car registration, and the telephone listing

The search for Khalid Almihdhar and Nawaf Alhazmi in the US, when it finally got underway, raises even more questions. Given the openness with which the hijackers lived in the US, even a rookie agent with a full case load and a limited array of tools should have turned up some information about them. However, even though that agent, Robert Fuller, did search some databases, he appears not to have searched all of them. Some of the databases he says he searched did contain information about Alhazmi and Almihdhar, but he says he did not find it. Fuller's work had only one specific result: on the last day in August, Almihdhar had been listed in a government database as "armed and dangerous," but at the beginning of September, Fuller, working with another agent, took actions which caused this warning to be supplanted.

The same day as the final e-mail exchange with Steve Bongardt, August 29, Dina Corsi sent the formal lead to the New York Field Office, which opened a full field investigation. Corsi had learned of Almihdhar's presence in the US on August 22, but it had taken her seven days to send the lead, which consisted of three pages of text.[1] In addition to the delay, Corsi assigned the lead the lowest possible priority: routine.

Here is what the Justice Department inspector general's report had to say on this aspect of the case:

> While [Corsi] had relayed urgency to opening the investigation in her telephone conversation with [Craig Donnachie] and in her cover e-mail, she designated the EC precedence as "routine," the

---

1. A draft lead dated August 28 was introduced as evidence at the Moussaoui trial: http://www. vaed.uscourts.gov/notablecases/moussaoui/exhibits/defense/469.pdf.

lowest precedence level. She explained this by saying this case was "no bigger" than any other intelligence case. She also told us, however, that there was a time consideration because Almihdhar could be leaving the United States at any time and that is why she had personally contacted [Donnachie].[2]

This passage is another good example of the failings of the Justice Department inspector general's report. Corsi's explanation for first indicating that the search had high priority, but then only marking it "routine" makes no sense. Routine precedence meant that an agent had 30 days to open an inquiry. If Almihdhar, a known al-Qaeda operative who Corsi knew was connected to the then-unsolved *Cole* bombing, could be leaving the US, this was a very good reason to start searching for him right away and to throw everything at the search. However, the Justice Department inspector general's report does not highlight this, and no assessment, whether positive or negative, of Corsi's excuses is offered. At best, the reader is left to read between the lines and deduce that Corsi is talking nonsense. At worst, the reader assumes that the Justice Department inspector general did not say her excuse was nonsense because the inspector general thought it *did* make sense.

In any event, the search had been assigned to Robert Fuller, who was inexperienced and had only recently transferred to the bin Laden unit. In fact, this was to be Fuller's very first intelligence investigation.[3] By the time it reached Fuller, however, two chances of finding the two men had already been blown. As one of the Congressional Inquiry's staff statements points out:

> The Bureau of Diplomatic Security at the State Department was contacted on August 28, 2001 and asked to supply the FBI with visa information but was not asked to assist in locating the individuals, nor was any other information provided to it that would have indicated either a high priority or imminent danger. The same is true of INS, since the notice regarding these two individuals was considered to be routine. Thus, INS provided FBI only with the address listed on Almihdhar's I-94 immigration form and did not query its database for other locator information.
>
> INS indicates that, if it had been asked to locate the two suspected terrorists, Nawaf Alhazmi and Khalid Almihdhar, in late

2. Justice Department IG report, p. 305.
3. The search for Almihdhar is described in the Justice Department IG report, pp. 309-12.
342

August on an urgent, emergency basis, it would have been able to run those names through its extensive database system and might have been able to locate them. Absent a sense of highest priority, however, INS states that it equated the search for these two individuals with other, more routine name searches, sometimes 50 or more per day, that it was running at the time. The Bureau of Diplomatic Security at the State Department also has told the Joint Inquiry Staff that it has extensive means of locating individuals who are involved in visa fraud or visa violations and also contends that it might have been able to locate the two suspected terrorists if it had been asked to do so.[4]

Dina Corsi e-mailed Robert Fuller on August 30, attaching a copy of the visa application Almihdhar submitted in June, and also phoned him. According to Fuller, Corsi told him the goal of the intelligence investigation was to locate and identify Almihdhar for a potential interview. She did not indicate the situation was an emergency.

After this, nothing happened at the New York Field Office for five days. Fuller worked that weekend (September 1 and 2), but on another matter, coincidentally involving a hijacking.

Meanwhile, Almihdhar was listed on August 31 in the INS and Customs database as someone who was "armed and dangerous" and who should be referred to secondary inspection. On September 4, the State Department revoked his visa due to what the 9/11 Commission described as "participation in terrorist activities." The revocation was entered into the INS lookout system the next day, but the State Department then identified him as a potential witness in an FBI investigation, and *inspectors were told not to detain him*. The text of the lookout explaining what inspectors *should* do was later apparently lost; it could not be found by the 9/11 Commission.[5]

Supplanting the "armed and dangerous" designation with a notice telling inspectors not to detain Almihdhar was obviously a step backwards in the investigation, which had barely begun by this point. It was the result of something Fuller did on September 4, when he completed a lookout request form for the INS. This was the first day Fuller spent working on the case, and in the Justice Department inspector general's report it is listed as the first of his

4. 9/11 Congressional Inquiry, "The Intelligence Community's Knowledge of the September 11 Hijackers Prior to September 11, 2001," September 20, 2002, http://www.fas.org/irp/congress/2002_hr/092002hill.html.
5. Terrorist Travel report, pp. 31-32, 43.

actions taken on this day. It therefore appears that Fuller's very first action on the case was to have the "armed and dangerous" designation supplanted by another, less alarming one.

How did this happen?

Fuller later told the inspector general that because he was new, he was unfamiliar with the lookout request form, so he asked a more experienced agent, Peter Robustelli, for help. The form had a box indicating whether an individual was wanted for "security/terrorism" reasons, which was not ticked. Fuller later said it was not ticked because Robustelli told him not to tick it, and that Robustelli told him not to tick it to prevent overzealous immigration officials from overreacting. Robustelli denied saying this, claiming he always checked this box on the form when dealing with a potential witness in a terrorism investigation.[6] However, Robustelli did say that Fuller asked him to review the form and he did so, apparently leaving the "security/terrorism" box unchecked. Fuller also initially claimed that he showed the documentation on Almihdhar to Robustelli, but, in a second interview, said he could not definitely recall this. Robustelli said he had not seen the underlying documentation and, even if he had, any review of it would be cursory.

This account makes no sense. Fuller changed his story, Fuller and Robustelli contradicted each other, and the lookout documentation went missing. And the upshot in the event is that inspectors were told not to detain Almihdhar on his way to a plane. While Fuller's search for Almihdhar produced no useful results, the supplanting of the "armed and dangerous" notification actually made it easier for Almihdhar to operate, not harder.

There is much dispute over the database checks Fuller may or may not have performed as a part of his search, and there is contradictory information about whether some of them were performed at all. If they were performed, it is certainly odd that Fuller was unable to find records of the hijackers' activities in databases that contained them.

First, we should clarify the importance of the search for Almihdhar by Fuller. The 9/11 Commission commented,

> We believe that if more resources had been applied and a significantly different approach taken, Almihdhar and Alhazmi

6. Justice Department IG report, pp. 310-11.

might have been found. They had used their true names in the United States. Still, the investigators would have needed luck as well as skill to find them prior to September 11 even if such searches had begun as early as August 23, when the lead was first drafted.

Many FBI witnesses have suggested that even if Almihdhar had been found, there was nothing the agents could have done except follow him onto the planes. We believe this is incorrect. Both Alhazmi and Almihdhar could have been held for immigration violations or as material witnesses in the *Cole* bombing case. Investigation or interrogation of them, and investigation of their travel and financial activities, could have yielded evidence of connections to other participants in the 9/11 plot. The simple fact of their detention could have derailed the plan. In any case, the opportunity did not arise.[7]

Now let's look at what Fuller did—or did not do—by comparing two accounts. First the Justice Department inspector general's report:

> On September 5, Richard [Robert Fuller] requested an NCIC [National Crime Information Center] criminal history check, credit checks, and motor vehicle records be searched in reference to Almihdhar and Alhazmi....
>
> Richard stated he also conducted Choicepoint™ searches on Alhazmi and Almihdhar. Richard said he recalled he had another JTTF [Joint Terrorism Task Force] officer assist him with the searches because he was not familiar with the system. Richard did not locate any records on either Alhazmi or Almihdhar in Choicepoint™. Richard told the OIG that it was not uncommon not to find a record because of variations in spelling of names or other identifying information.[8]

The Justice Department inspector general also described the ChoicePoint database:

> Choicepoint™ is a commercial service that mines information such as names, addresses, phone numbers, and other identifying information from public sources (such as telephone directories, local taxing authorities, and court records), as well as purchase information from merchants or other companies. The informa-

---

7. *9/11 CR*, p. 272.
8. Justice Department IG report, p. 312.

tion is then consolidated into a large database and is accessible to law enforcement and other subscribers for a fee.

Fuller requested a local criminal history check on Almihdhar and Alhazmi through the New York City Police Department on September 4. He also checked with the six Marriot hotels in New York, which Almihdhar had listed as his destination on his visa application in June, but found he had not stayed at any of them.

So the Justice Department inspector general said Fuller did an NCIC criminal history check, credit checks, and a motor vehicle records search. It also reported Fuller's claim that he did a Choice-Point check, saying that he was not familiar with the system and that another agent had helped him.

Contrast this with the 9/11 Commission's account (emphasis added):

> Alhazmi and Almihdhar used their true names to obtain California driver's licenses and open New Jersey bank accounts. Alhazmi also had a car registered and had been listed in the San Diego telephone book. *Searches of readily available databases could have unearthed the driver's licenses, the car registration, and the telephone listing.* A search on the car registration would have unearthed a license check by the South Hackensack Police Department that would have led to information placing Alhazmi in the area and placing Almihdhar at a local hotel for a week in early July 2001.

The Justice Department inspector general's report says that three of the searches were done, and Fuller claims the fourth search was done as well. The Commission is clearly implying that at least some of the searches were not done. These claims are contradictory. Who is right? Did Fuller search ChoicePoint?

In late 2004, the *New York Observer* added some important details:

> "There was information about the people who turned out to be hijackers in the ChoicePoint databases prior to 9/11, that's a true statement," ChoicePoint chairman and chief executive Derek Smith confirmed.
> How does he know? The F.B.I. got a court subpoena for Choice-Point to go through its records and pull out what it had on Alhazmi and Almihdhar after the Twin Towers fell. Why the F.B.I.

didn't do this before 9/11, Mr. Smith can't say, but he confirmed that the F.B.I. didn't seek this information before 9/11.[9]

According to author Bob Woodward, CIA Director Tenet claimed that the FBI had not performed a credit card check:

> Tenet thought the CIA had been working flat out, and that comparatively the FBI got a free pass. If the FBI had done a simple credit card check on the two 9/11 hijackers who had been identified in the United States before 9/11, Nawaf Alhazmi and Khalid Almihdhar, they would have found that the two men had bought 10 tickets for early morning flights for groups of other Middle Eastern men for September 11, 2001. That was knowledge that might conceivably have stopped the attacks.[10]

The claim that they bought ten tickets for the 9/11 flights may be an exaggeration, as Alhazmi bought a ticket for himself and his brother, whereas Majed Moqed initially attempted to purchase tickets with his debit card for himself and Almihdhar, but ended up paying cash because of a problem with the billing address.[11] However, the hijackers bought numerous tickets for flights after the attacks.[12] Possibly Almihdhar and Alhazmi bought tickets for afternoon flights, with Tenet simply confusing morning and afternoon travel.

Robert Fuller claimed he searched ChoicePoint and failed to find information it contained about the two hijackers, and he even recalled asking for assistance with it. But ChoicePoint's CEO said that neither he nor anyone at the FBI had checked the database for information regarding Almihdhar or Alhazmi. The 9/11 Commission strongly implied that Fuller did no search. It is hard to believe that Fuller could have failed to search ChoicePoint, but then somehow

9. Gwen Kinkead, "Amid C.I.A. Shake-up, Questions about F.B.I.," *New York Observer*, November 28, 2004, http://www.breakfornews.com/articles/QuestionsAboutFBI.htm.
10. Bob Woodward, *State of Denial* (London: Simon & Schuster, 2006), pp. 79-80.
11. *United States v. Zacarias Moussaoui*, "Stipulation [Regarding flights hijacked on September 11, 2001; September 11, 2001 deaths; al Qaeda; chronology of hijackers' activities; Zacarias Moussaoui; and the Computer Assisted Passenger Pre-screening System (CAPPS)]," Part A, pp. 72, 74, http://www.vaed.uscourts.gov/notablecases/moussaoui/exhibits/prosecution/ST00001.html; *United States v. Zacarias Moussaoui*, "Chronology of Events for Hijackers, 8/16/01 - 9/11/01, Khalid Al-Mihdhar," http://www.vaed.uscourts.gov/notablecases/moussaoui/exhibits/prosecution/OG00020-11.pdf.
12. Federal Bureau of Investigation, "Working Draft Chronology of Events for Hijackers," October 2001, pp. 233, 238, 242, 246, 288, http://www.historycommons.org/sourcedocuments/2001/pdfs/fbi911timeline210-297.pdf.

acquired a false memory of doing so and of being assisted by another agent. The conclusion that Fuller lied about this to the Justice Department inspector general seems very hard to avoid.

The "variations on spelling" excuse is hard to accept. An FBI timeline I obtained by FOIA request stated that "according to ChoicePoint" the phone number Almihdhar gave in April 2000 when he obtained a photo ID from the California motor vehicle administration was "subscribed to by NAWAF M. AL HAZMI,"[13] which shows that Alhazmi was certainly in the database. In the draft lead on which Fuller allegedly based his search, Alhazmi's name was given as "Nawaf Al-Hazmi," hardly a great difference. One of the other databases Fuller should have searched, the NCIC, which will be discussed below, had the sophistication to return close matches, so it is certainly possible ChoicePoint had a similar feature.

In addition, then-acting FBI Director Thomas Pickard was also less than honest about this issue. At a public hearing of the 9/11 Commission, Commissioner John Lehman asked Pickard:

> As you know, very shortly after the September 11th attack, some of the commercial databases, like Axion, ISO, ChoicePoint, so forth, were queried, and nearly all of the 19 hijackers were very prominently covered with addresses, credit cards, locations, et cetera. Why did not the FBI make use of those commercial databases before 9/11?

Pickard responded:

> We were prohibited from utilizing a lot of those commercial databases by statutes and things like that. That was one of benefits of the PATRIOT Act, as I understand it. I have not read the act and I'm not an attorney and don't want to start practicing.[14]

Here again we have obfuscation disguised as an answer. The FBI certainly was *not* prohibited from using ChoicePoint by any act before 9/11. In fact, it had a formal subscription to ChoicePoint[15] and had made extensive use of it, so why not during the search for

---

13. Ibid.
14. National Commission on Terrorist Attacks Upon the United States, Tenth Public Hearing, April 13, 2004, http://govinfo.library.unt.edu/911/archive/hearing10/9-11Commission_Hearing_2004-04-13.htm.
15. Justice Department IG report, p. 312; Gwen Kinkead, see note 9.

Almihdhar? And why did the acting FBI director tap dance around this under oath to the 9/11 Commission?

Both the Justice Department inspector general and the 9/11 Commission should be criticized for their reporting concerning ChoicePoint. The Justice Department inspector general's report simply repeats Fuller's claim that he searched that database, without pointing out that he apparently did not. By allowing the claim to stand unchallenged, it implicitly endorses the claim, especially as it also passes on Fuller's excuse for not finding the records there that he should have found—that it must have been because of the varying spellings of Arabic names. The Justice Department inspector general certainly should have checked whether Fuller did make the search and should have then taken the appropriate investigative action, asking Fuller why he apparently lied about it. However, the Justice Department inspector general appears to have been disinclined to do so.

There is no record of the 9/11 Commission interviewing Robert Fuller, although the relevant section of the Commission's report was drafted by Barbara Grewe, and she was probably the official who interviewed Fuller for the Justice Department inspector general. Whatever the case, the Commission must have been aware of the problem, as it cites a transcript of Fuller's interview with the inspector general as a source for the statement that Fuller "checked local New York databases for criminal record and driver's license information."[16] Presumably, Fuller also claimed that he searched ChoicePoint in the same interview, with the Commission letting this apparently false claim pass without comment or investigation.

The same applies to the check of the National Crime Information Center's database which the Justice Department inspector general's report says Fuller requested on September 4. To the contrary, the *Bergen (NJ) Record*, a newspaper that produced a lot of 9/11 stories because several of the hijackers had lived in the area it covered, wrote, "[Fuller] never performed one of the most basic tasks of a police manhunt. He never ran Almihdhar or Alhazmi through the NCIC computer. That simple act would have alerted local cops to look for the suspected terrorists."[17]

---

16. *9/11 CR*, pp. 271-72, 539 n84.
17. Peter Pochna, "Where Crime Pays: Where Route 46 Fills Police Coffers in S. Hackensack," *Bergen (NJ) Record*, July 11, 2002; Mike Kelly, "A Tragic Tale of Ones that Got Away," *Bergen (NJ) Record*, May

If Fuller had searched the NCIC database, he certainly should have turned up some hits. The FBI timeline I obtained showed the following events were entered in the database:

- April 1, 2001. Nawaf Alhazmi received a speeding ticket from the Oklahoma State Highway Patrol. Both the car and Alhazmi were queried in the NCIC database (p. 131).

- July 7, 2001. Alhazmi's car was queried by police in South Hackensack, New Jersey, and this was added to the NCIC database (p. 179).

- August 26, 2001. A car rented by Alhazmi was queried by police in Totowa, New Jersey (p. 236).

Fuller's excuse that he found nothing because the spelling must have been different would not have applied here, as an archived version of the NCIC website, dated May 5, 2001, stated that the database had "enhanced name search" and that it returned "phonetically similar names (e.g. Marko, Marco or Knowles, Nowles or derivatives such as William, Willie, Bill)."[18]

The problem presented by the NCIC database is similar to what we found with ChoicePoint. Robert Fuller certainly should have searched it, and would have found information about Almihdhar and Alhazmi if he had done so, but it appears he did not, even though the Justice Department inspector general claims Fuller requested a search a full week before 9/11.

Dina Corsi again became involved in the search around September 5, when Fuller contacted her about the request to locate Almihdhar. They discussed ways of getting additional information about him, such as approaching Saudi Arabian Airlines, on which he had flown to the US in July, for a credit card number. However, Fuller never contacted the airline, and later told investigators that this was because Corsi told him it would not be prudent to do so.[19]

This is the third piece of information absent from the unclassified version of the Justice Department inspector general's report, but present in the Moussaoui trial testimony of summary witness Erik Rigler based on another version of the report. Compared to the other two items, it is not as damning as Wilshire's "very high interest" e-mail of July 23, but more significant than Middleton's "Oh, shit" moment. Given the seriousness of the derogatory information included elsewhere in the unclassified version about Dina Corsi, it is puzzling that this would be omitted from that version. Her failure, for example, to pass on the NSA information to Steve Bongardt after it had been cleared for him at her request seems much worse. Nevertheless, it is another point against Corsi's good faith, as it is hard to imagine why she would block a request to the Saudi airline for credit card information.

After the activity on September 4 and 5, Fuller then did nothing with the search for the next four days. No explanation has ever been offered for this inaction.

Timeline: Opportunity FIVE

On or About September 5, 2001

- Fuller contacts Corsi concerning her request to have him locate Khalid al-Mihdhar.

- Fuller & Corsi discuss potential for obtaining additional data on Mihdhar such as credit card number from Saudi Arabian Airlines.

- According to Fuller, Corsi tells him that it would not be prudent to do so.

Slide from former FBI agent Eric Rigler's PowerPoint presentation at the Zacarias Moussaoui trial in March 2006. [65]

On September 10, Fuller drafted an investigative lead for the FBI's Los Angeles Field Office, as that was where Alhazmi and Almihdhar had arrived when they came to the US in January 2000.

351

The lead asked that the field office search the Sheraton hotel records for stays by the two men in early 2000, as their immigration documentation mentioned this hotel. It also asked them to check records of United Airlines, on which the two men had flown to the US in January 2000, and Lufthansa, on which Almihdhar had flown from Los Angeles to Germany in June 2000, for other information concerning them. However, this lead was not transmitted to Los Angeles until the next, fateful day.[20]

Despite all the failures, whether deliberate or not, over the prior twenty months, Fuller's search was an opportunity to overcome what had gone before, to make it right at the last possible moment. All he needed was one hit. Almihdhar and Alhazmi had lived openly in the US for over a year and a half with credit cards, phones, bank accounts, a police report, apartments, hotel stays, everything in their own names. If the FBI had found Almihdhar and Alhazmi, it would have found the other Flight 77 hijackers, who had been living with Alhazmi for months. Given the frequent interactions between the teams of hijackers, it would not have been difficult to discover the other fourteen, especially given the parallel ticket purchases for 9/11. Yet, we are told, Fuller could not find a thing, even though he alleged that he searched databases that demonstrably did contain references to them.

All this is doubly incredible if we consider the priority that the search should have had. The Bureau was looking for a witness who had met some of the *Cole* bombers just after the attack on *The Sullivans* had failed. The *Cole* inquiry was one of the biggest cases the FBI had at this time, perhaps one of the biggest it had had in the prior decade, involving the murder of seventeen US sailors. The presence of an associate of the bombers in the US was a huge potential break. Nevertheless, one rookie agent who already had other urgent tasks was assigned to do it.

It is hard to resolve the question of whether Fuller was acting in good or bad faith. His investigation was poor, and there is strong evidence to suggest that Fuller did not take all the steps he should have. In particular, he carried out some local searches for Almihdhar and Alhazmi, but seems not to have searched the ChoicePoint and NCIC national databases. Nevertheless, we must bear in mind

20. Justice Department IG report, pp. 311-12.

that he was a rookie, and rookies do sometimes make mistakes. He then apparently lied about the extent of the searches, with the Justice Department inspector general endorsing these lies. This is certainly worthy of further investigation, although Fuller may have made false statements about performing searches that were not performed simply in an attempt to hide what he perceived as his own poor performance.

On the other hand, Robert Fuller was working at Dina Corsi's direction, and Corsi worked for Tom Wilshire. It appears that Corsi acted in bad faith: preventing Fuller from contacting Saudi Arabian Airlines for a credit card number would be another major error, following the failure to share information at and after the June 11 meeting, the failure to pass on the information about bin Attash in Kuala Lumpur, the apparent misrepresentation of Sherry Sabol's legal advice, and the non-forwarding of the NSA information to Steve Bongardt even after the NSA had cleared it. The poor quality of Fuller's work, such as his actions causing the "armed and dangerous" notice to be supplanted in the INS database, and his association with Corsi give rise to suspicion and, at the very least, his conduct requires further investigation.

We can also ask why the Justice Department inspector general did not point out these discrepancies in its report. Time and time again the inspector general missed things, erring in favor of Tom Wilshire and his associates to the point where it becomes hard to believe this is a coincidence and not a cover-up.

* * *

Robert Fuller continued with the Bureau after 9/11 and became involved in at least four high-profile cases: those of Salim Hamdan, Mohamed Alanssi, Omar Khadr and the Newburgh Four.

Hamdan later became famous for the case of *Hamdan v. Rumsfeld*, in which the US Supreme Court held that the version of military commissions in use at Guantanamo at that time was in conflict with various legal standards. In the end Hamdan was sentenced to a few years in jail and sent back to Yemen. Fuller questioned Hamdan in Afghanistan in 2000, but neither Fuller nor any of the other agents with him read Hamdan his rights. Despite this, Hamdan took them on a tour of al-Qaeda facilities in the area, and Fuller later testified at a hearing about Hamdan in Guantanamo.[21]

Alanssi was a Yemeni walk-in who, shortly after 9/11, offered to provide information to help the Bureau against terrorist financiers. Alanssi, handled by Fuller, helped draw a significant player, Mohammed Ali Hassan al-Moayad, outside Yemen. The FBI grabbed al-Moayad in Germany and had him extradited to New York to stand trial. However, Alanssi's name found its way into the press, and Fuller prevented him from returning to Yemen to visit his wife, who was dying of stomach cancer. As a result, Alanssi went to the White House, and tried to immolate himself in protest of Fuller's treatment of him.[22]

Omar Khadr was a Canadian teenager interrogated by Fuller at Bagram Air Base in Afghanistan for several days starting on October 7, 2002. Khadr was accused of throwing a hand grenade that killed a US soldier in a firefight. On the first day, Fuller showed Khadr a photo of Maher Arar, a dual Canadian-Syrian citizen in custody in the US, and Khadr said he had seen him in an al-Qaeda safe house in Afghanistan. This identification appears to have been false, as Khadr's lawyer later said that Khadr lied repeatedly to investigators and that Arar was demonstrably in the US and Canada at the time Khadr said he saw him in Afghanistan. Fuller later claimed that Khadr made the identification immediately, but the agent was forced to backtrack under cross-examination at a Guantanamo hearing. The day after Khadr had claimed he had seen Arar in Afghanistan, possibly influenced by the false identification Fuller had obtained, Arar was deported first to Jordan and then to Syria, where he was tortured for ten months.[23]

Not reading Salim Hamdan his rights was arguably the correct thing to do in the circumstances, and his lack of compassion for

21. Alan Gomez, "Hamdan Apologizes during War Crimes Trial," *USA Today*, July 24, 2008, http://www.usatoday.com/news/world/2008-07-24-Hamdan_N.htm; Randall Mikkelsen, "Bin Laden Driver Was Not Read Rights, Court Told," Reuters, July 24, 2008, http://www.alertnet.org/thenews/newsdesk/N24343055.htm.

22. Caryle Murphy and Del Quentin Wilber, "Terror Informant Ignites Himself Near White House," *Washington Post*, November 16, 2004, http://www.washingtonpost.com/wp-dyn/articles/A51575-2004Nov15.html.

23. "Khadr Couldn't Pick Out Arar Immediately, FBI Agent Admits," CBC News, January 20, 2009, http://www.cbc.ca/world/story/2009/01/20/khadr-hearing.html; Steven Edwards, "Khadr Identified Arar as Visitor," Canwest News Service, January 20, 2009, http://www.montrealgazette.com/news/Khadr+identified+Arar+visitor+Witness/1195141/story.html.

Mohamed Alanssi may be written off to investigatory zeal. Fuller's involvement in the Khadr case, however, is far more serious. It appears that Fuller pressured Khadr into making a false identification, based upon which an Ottawa software engineer was shipped to Syria for almost a year of torture. In 2006, a Canadian public inquiry cleared Maher Arar of any links to terrorism.

In October 2010, Omar Khadr, the last Western detainee held at Guantanamo, pleaded guilty to five "war crimes" counts, including murder, as a part of a plea bargain. He received an additional eight years in prison, only one of which was to be served in the US, the remainder in Canada. The assumption is that Khadr will be released as soon as he is repatriated.

The Newburgh Four were involved in one of several high-profile terrorist plots in the decade after 9/11 that were foiled with the help of an FBI informer. In this case the mole was Shahed Hussain, who was handled by Robert Fuller. The four claimed that they had been entrapped, but were found guilty at trial. The first weapon the plotters purchased was a pistol, bought by one of them accompanied by Hussain for $700 from a New York gang leader on April 30, 2009.[24] At the trial, the defense produced a note apparently from Fuller to another FBI agent, written shortly before the purchase, saying that Hussain should get them to buy a weapon, so they could at least be charged with something if "things go south."[25] Naturally, the stinger missiles and explosives the plotters were caught with were provided by the FBI.

Fuller's involvement in the Newburgh Four case shows how the fruits of 9/11 have gone on to poison the US with a string of terror alerts hyped up beyond all proportion. The four guilty plotters certainly harbored evil intentions and were willing to go along with the attacks. However, the informer was the driving force in the group, and he was working at Fuller's direction.

---

24. Rebecca Rosenberg, Murray Weiss and Dan Mangan, "'Terror' Thugs' Sick Bloodlust," *New York Post*, May 22, 2009, http://www.nypost.com/p/news/regional/item_UzMlWvVLqOtSazhC5fC4IL;j sessionid=6AE334CD65FF10034653643CF13BF728.
25. Doyle Murphy, "Defense takes on FBI agent in trial of Newburgh 4," *Times Herald-Record*, August 27, 2010, http://www.recordonline.com/apps/pbcs.dll/article?AID=/20100827/NEWS/8270361/-1/SITEMAP.

49

Find and kill ... Khalid Shaikh Mohammed

As well as failing to pass on information about Alhazmi and Almihdhar before the attacks, the CIA had also failed to pass on information about Khalid Shaikh Mohammed. This situation changed after 9/11, with the Agency providing some information about the plot, and about Alhazmi and Almihdhar, to the FBI. For example, a report on al-Qaeda's Malaysia summit was provided to Ali Soufan. However, the CIA had evidence linking KSM to the plot and indicating that he was a senior person in it, but it did not disseminate this. The Agency's story is that it failed to realize what it had, again failing to connect the dots. KSM's involvement was allegedly first discovered by the US government when Soufan reached militant-training-camp facilitator Abu Zubaida in April 2002, shortly after his capture in Pakistan.

Given the amount of intelligence linking KSM to al-Qaeda and the hijacking operation before 9/11, the CIA's excuse for the lead-up period is hard to believe. It is even less credible after the attacks, due to the increased level of resources devoted to counterterrorism and the extremely high level of interest in understanding 9/11. In addition, although the CIA claims it did not recognize a link between KSM and al-Qaeda until early 2002, KSM was the fourth target on the Agency's hit list in Afghanistan in November 2001, after bin Laden, his deputy Ayman al-Zawahiri and al-Qaeda military commander Mohammed Atef.

The links between KSM and Osama bin Laden had been indirect at first. Both of them helped fund the terror cell in New York that carried out the World Trade Center bombing in 1993. Bin Laden provided some money for the defense of one of the cell's members, El Sayyid Nosair, after he assassinated Jewish leader Meir Kahane,[1]

1. Greg B. Smith, "Bin Laden bankrolled Kahane killer defense," *New York Daily News*, October 9, 2002, http://www.nydailynews.com/archives/news/2002/10/09/2002-10-09_bin_laden_bankrolled_kahane_.html.

whereas KSM sent $660 to one of the WTC bombers to fund the operation.

Bin Laden then racked up multiple links to the failed Bojinka operation, of which KSM was a lead planner. KSM's partner in that planning, Ramzi Yousef, stayed at a bin Laden guest house in Pakistan in the early '90s;[2] Wali Khan Amin Shah, one of the core Bojinka operatives, and Muhammad Jamal Khalifa, a financier of the plot, also linked bin Laden to Bojinka.

Two years before 9/11, author Simon Reeve wrote,

> There is however hard evidence to suggest strong, direct connections between Yousef and bin Laden, maintained by bin Laden's close supporters and acquaintances of the two men—most notably their mutual friends Wali Khan Amin Shah and Muhammad Jamal Khalifa. Shah, who was staying near Peshawar in the summer of 1991, had fought alongside bin Laden during the war, and trained and worked with Yousef on several of his bombing campaigns. "Wali Khan is a Muslim youth," said bin Laden. "In Afghanistan, he was nicknamed 'The Lion.' He is one of the best. We were good friends. We fought in the same trenches against the Russians."[3]

Reeve went on to outline links between Khalifa, bin Laden's brother in law, and various bin Laden operations, links that fellow author Peter Lance has added to.

After this we have two versions of history. This is the Congressional Inquiry's take:

> [This assessment changed in 1996 when a foreign government shared information that bin Laden and KSM had traveled together to a foreign country [Brazil] the previous year. In August 1998, after the bombing of the U.S. Embassy in Nairobi, another foreign government sent CIA a list of the names of individuals who flew into Nairobi before the attack. Based on information delivered by another liaison service, CIA recognized that one of the passengers' names was an alias for KSM. The liaison report also described KSM as close to bin Laden. In an interview, the FBI agent responsible for the KSM case [apparently Frank Pellegrino]

2. Central Intelligence Agency, "Usama bin Laden: Islamist Extremist Financier," 1996, http://www.gwu.edu/~nsarchiv/NSAEBB/NSAEBB55/ciaubl.pdf.
3. Simon Reeve, *The New Jackals: Ramzi Yousef, Osama bin Laden and the Future of Terrorism* (London: André Deutsch, 1999), pp. 156-57.

could not remember this information, even though it had been disseminated by CIA. This information and subsequent reporting led the CIA to see KSM as part of bin Laden's organization. Several CIA cables indicated that following up on information relevant to KSM was essential, given his past activities and his links to al-Qaeda.][4]

The 9/11 Commission went over the same ground and found the opposite:

> Although we readily equate KSM with al-Qaeda today, this was not the case before 9/11. KSM, who had been indicted in January 1996 for his role in the Manila [Bojinka] air plot, was seen primarily as another freelance terrorist, associated with Ramzi Yousef. Because the links between KSM and bin Laden or al-Qaeda were not recognized at the time, responsibility for KSM remained in the small Islamic Extremist Branch of the Counterterrorist Center, not in the bin Laden unit.[5]

This passage is in chapter eight of the Commission's report and was presumably drafted by Barbara Grewe.

If what the Congressional Inquiry says is true—that KSM was recognized on a flight manifest before the embassy bombings and that several CIA cables mentioned his links to al-Qaeda—then it is hard to understand how the Commission could have written what it did. If it is not true, then one would have expected the Commission to debunk it, saying that KSM did not go to Nairobi and that there were no such cables.

Before outlining the evidence the CIA received before 9/11 linking KSM to the plot, the Commission advances its excuse for why the Agency allegedly did not fully appreciate the information it had on KSM:

> Moreover, because KSM had already been indicted, he became targeted for arrest. In 1997, the Counterterrorist Center added a Renditions Branch to help find wanted fugitives. Responsibility for KSM was transferred to this branch, which gave the CIA a "man-to-man" focus but was not an analytical unit. When subsequent information came, more critical for analysis than for tracking, no unit had the job of following up on what the information might mean.[6]

4. 9/11 Congressional Inquiry report, p. 313.
5. *9/11 CR*, p. 276.
6. Ibid.

This passage of the Commission's report is sourced to an interview of CIA officers. The officers are referred to by aliases, but one of them is evidently Michael Scheuer, who ran both Alec Station and the renditions program until mid-1999, when he was replaced by Richard Blee. Another is "John," the alias the Commission used for Tom Wilshire.

After the embassy bombings in 1998, yet more information came in to the CIA linking KSM to al-Qaeda. First, there is the evidence outlined above indicating that KSM attended the Malaysia summit, which was clearly linked to al-Qaeda through the attendance of multiple al-Qaeda operatives and the use of the Yemen hub to arrange it. The summit was monitored by the Malaysians, and the intelligence they gathered was passed on to the CIA.

On September 25, 2000, the CIA received a cable the Commission refers to as "Key UBL personalities." The cable reported that a source had said an individual named Khalid al-Shaykh al-Ballushi was a key lieutenant in al-Qaeda. Al-Ballushi means "from Baluchistan," a region comprising areas of southern Afghanistan, southeastern Iran and southwestern Pakistan; KSM hails from the Pakistani portion. According to the Commission, Alec Station recognized the possible significance of the information, but could not find anything further, and then dropped the matter.[7]

In April 2001 the Agency received information about a man known as "Mukhtar." This was KSM's nickname in al-Qaeda, although the CIA claims it did not know this at this time. Despite this, the information made it clear that Mukhtar was associated with Abu Zubaida and that he was involved in planning possible terrorist activities.

On June 11-12, the CIA generated more reporting on KSM. From the Congressional Inquiry report (emphasis added):

[CIA disseminated a report that KSM had traveled to the United States as recently as May 2001 and was sending recruits to the United States to meet colleagues already in the country[; this][8] did not cause the Intelligence Community to mobilize, even though it contained apparently significant [redacted] information. The report explained that KSM was a relative of convicted World Trade center bomber Ramzi Yousef, *appeared to be one of bin Laden's most trusted lieutenants and was active in recruiting people to*

7. Ibid., pp. 276-77.
8. My brackets.

travel outside Afghanistan, including to the United States, to carry out unspecified activities on behalf of bin Laden. According to the report, he continued to travel frequently to the United States, including as recently as May 2001, and routinely told others that he could arrange their entry into the United States as well. Reportedly, these individuals were expected to establish contact with colleagues already there. The clear implication of his comments, according to the report, was that they would be engaged in planning terrorist-related activities.]

The CIA did not find the report credible, but noted that it was worth pursuing in case it was accurate: "if it is KSM, we have both a significant threat and an opportunity to pick him up." The Joint Inquiry requested that CIA review this particular source report and provide information concerning how CTC, CIA field personnel, and other agencies reacted to this information. That information has not been received.[9]

Throughout this time, the US was intercepting KSM's calls. According to Jonathan Landay, then of Knight Ridder, "[The NSA] monitored telephone conversations before Sept. 11 between the suspected commander of the World Trade Center and Pentagon attacks and the alleged chief hijacker [Mohamed Atta], but did not share the information with other intelligence agencies."[10] Lawrence Wright claims that the FBI was also intercepting KSM's calls and that, out of frustration with the NSA's reluctance to share information, it had built a separate antenna in Madagascar to intercept them.[11]

A key intercept was made on July 20, when KSM and Ramzi bin al-Shibh, who had associated with three of the al-Qaeda suicide pilots in Germany, discussed the 9/11 plot in a call. KSM first instructed bin al-Shibh to send the "skirts," a code word for money forwarded to bin al-Shibh by an associate of KSM, to "Sally."[12] A memo drafted by the 9/11 Commission continues:

Sally is probably [Zacarias] Moussaoui, as there is discussion about sending money to Sally. There is a discussion about Teresa

9. 9/11 Congressional Inquiry report, pp. 314-15. For the precise date of this reporting, see *9/11 CR*, pp. 277, 541.
10. Jonathan S. Landay, "NSA didn't share key pre-Sept. 11 information, sources say," Knight Ridder, June 6, 2002, http://prisonplanet.com/nsa_didnt_share_key_pre_sept_11_information.htm
11. Wright 2006, p. 344. The Alec Station-built antenna for intercepting calls to and from the Yemen hub was also reportedly on Madagascar. Possibly Wright is confusing his information here.
12. *9/11 CR*, p. 246.

being late, which probably refers to [Flight 93 pilot Ziad] Jarrah and possible conflicts with [lead hijacker Mohamed] Atta about Jarrah's isolation from the plot and perhaps uncertainty about whether he would carry out the attacks. It seems that Moussaoui may have been thought [of] as a replacement, since there's an exchange where KSM speaks of Teresa being late so send the money to Sally. KSM is concerned about Jarrah dropping out, stating that if there is a divorce, it will cost a lot of money. Bin al-Shibh tries to reassure him, saying it will be ok. KSM may have been concerned also because he had never met Jarrah and so did not know him personally. There is also a reference to "Danish leather" which is believed to be ["20th hijacker" Mohamed] al Qahtani. At this time, KSM was under great pressure from UBL to carry out the operation as soon as possible.[13]

Another report on KSM came to the CIA in August 2001, when it was reported that KSM's nickname was Mukhtar. The Commission calls this "the final piece of the puzzle" linking KSM to al-Qaeda and the 9/11 plot, but goes on to say that its importance was not appreciated.

In the light of the prevention of key information about Khalid Almihdhar and Nawaf Alhazmi reaching the right components of the FBI before 9/11, it is hard to credit the CIA's protestations that it did not appreciate the link between KSM on the one hand and al-Qaeda and the plot on the other, or that it did not deliberately withhold this from the Bureau. It is even harder to understand how the US government could have failed to appreciate after the attacks that KSM was "Mukhtar" and had been involved in 9/11.

Following 9/11, massive resources were surged into counterterrorism, and investigating and responding to the attacks became the government's number-one priority. Yet, we are told, nobody could figure out that KSM had been involved until the following April. The attacks themselves should have prompted a review of holdings that would have turned up the information that KSM was sending terrorists to the US, was known as "Mukhtar," and was in communication with bin al-Shibh, who had become associated with the plot very early on in the investigation.

---

13. 9/11 Commission, Hyon Kim, "Memorandum for the Record: Moussaoui Team Briefing," March 18, 2004, http://www.scribd.com/doc/20786371/Memo-about-Briefing-of-9-11-Commission-by-Moussaoui-Investigators.

Further, a bin Laden recording that surfaced in late 2001 contained multiple references to a person named Mukhtar, which aroused the interest of Ali Soufan and others. According to a *Newsweek* article, for several months before April 2002, "The FBI had been trying to determine the identity of a mysterious 'Mukhtar,' whom bin Laden kept referring to on a tape he made after 9/11."[14] This recording may be the famous "confession" video, although it is not certain that the multiple references to "Mukhtar" on this tape are to KSM. Nonetheless, these references should have prompted a further search to find out just who this person was, information that was readily recoverable in the CIA's databases.

Even though the CIA was still allegedly suffering from its misapprehension that KSM was not necessarily linked to 9/11 or al-Qaeda, it was trying to assassinate him and al-Qaeda's three other top leaders in Afghanistan. Some time around November 7, 2001, Gary Berntsen, the CIA's leader in Afghanistan, held a meeting with his staff to set out their roles. In a book on his experiences, Berntsen quotes himself as saying to a subordinate (emphasis added),

> You're in charge of high-value targets. I want to find and kill bin Laden, his number two al-Zawahiri, al-Qaeda's military commander Mohammed Atef *and Khalid Shaikh Mohammed*.[15]

If a list of the world's twenty-five most wanted terrorists had been made at this time, KSM would probably have made it due to his participation in Bojinka. Nevertheless, his inclusion among the top four targets in Afghanistan is startling if we accept the narrative that the CIA did not know of his role in the 9/11 operation, thinking of him primarily as "another freelance terrorist." It suggests that the CIA then understood the information it had on Khalid Shaikh Mohammed better than the 9/11 Commission later claimed, and that when the FBI told it that KSM was responsible for 9/11, the CIA was not surprised.

The FBI's discovery that KSM was "Mukhtar" and had been involved in 9/11 has parallels to the situation in December 2001 when Ibn Shaikh al-Libi started talking to Russell Fincher, one of the FBI

---

14. Michael Isikoff, "We could have done this the right way," *Newsweek*, April 25, 2009, http://www.newsweek.com/2009/04/24/we-could-have-done-this-the-right-way.html.

15. Gary Berntsen and Ralph Pezzullo, *Jawbreaker: The Attack on Bin Laden and Al-Qaeda: A Personal Account by the CIA's Key Field Commander* (New York: Three Rivers Press, 2005), p. 114.

agents who had attended the "shouting match" meeting on June 11, 2001. Richard Blee apparently had al-Libi taken away from Fincher, and later Abu Zubaida was to be taken away from Ali Soufan and Steve Gaudin, the FBI agent who had questioned Mohamed al-Owhali after the embassy bombings in 1998.

Abu Zubaida had been shot during his capture on March 28, 2002, but was transferred to a CIA black site in Thailand. Soufan and Gaudin reached it before their CIA counterparts and started questioning him. The first piece of information Abu Zubaida gave them concerned a plot against an ally, presumably Saudi Arabia. According to an article in *Vanity Fair*:

> The team cabled the morsel of intelligence to C.I.A. headquarters, where it was received with delight by Director George Tenet. "I want to congratulate our officers on the ground," he told a gathering of agents at Langley. When someone explained that the F.B.I. had obtained the information, Tenet blew up and demanded that the C.I.A. get there immediately, say those who were later told of the meeting.[16]

However, before their CIA counterparts could get there, Soufan showed Abu Zubaida a photo of KSM. "That's Mukhtar," said Abu Zubaida.[17] And, "How did you know he was the mastermind of 9/11?"[18] The CIA team, led by contract psychologist James Mitchell, arrived a few days later, and Soufan and Gaudin were pushed out of the interrogation process by the use of harsh techniques. The effect of all this was to both cut the Bureau off from information from detainees and to re-erect a barrier between the CIA and FBI.

In contrast to the situation with Alhazmi and Almihdhar, we do not know how the KSM information circulated at the Counterterrorist Center. In the case of the two hijackers, in several instances we know who read exactly what cables and when, what they knew when they read them, and what they did afterwards. This enables an accusation of bad faith to be leveled at some officers, as they repeatedly failed to take reasonable actions, or took unreasonable ones. In the case of the KSM information, we do not know exactly

---

16. Katherine Eban, "Rorschach and Awe," *Vanity Fair*, July 17, 2007, http://www.vanityfair.com/politics/features/2007/07/torture200707.
17. Michael Isikoff, see note 12.
18. Dina Temple-Raston, "FBI: Key Sept. 11 leads obtained without torture," National Public Radio, April 24, 2009, http://www.npr.org/templates/story/story.php?storyId=103475220.

who read and wrote what cables. Concerning the period before 9/11, the only links between the officers who concealed information about Alhazmi and Almihdhar and the KSM issue are that Dina Corsi seemed aware of threat information concerning KSM in late August 2001 and that Tom Wilshire later attended a meeting at which the topic of KSM was discussed with Congressional Inquiry investigators. Nevertheless, the knowledge that the dots were disconnected for Alhazmi and Almihdhar may lead one to suspect that all was not well with the CIA's handling of KSM.

Given the impact of 9/11, the CIA and other agencies should have reviewed their holdings and readily discovered that "Mukhtar" was KSM, and that he was involved in 9/11. The failure to do this after the attacks is much worse than the failure to do it before them. And it is made even worse by the message in which bin Laden repeatedly refers to a Mukhtar, which, again, should have sparked a search to see who the mysterious Mukhtar was. The fact that KSM was number four on the CIA's hit list indicates that the Agency did in fact know KSM had been involved in 9/11, and was merely withholding this information from its partners. The fact that Ali Soufan was forced out of the questioning of Abu Zubaida and, later, other detainees, due to the re-building of the "wall" raises questions about the real motivation of some supporters of the CIA's harsh techniques.

50

We didn't know they were here until it was too late

This story has a significance that goes well beyond 9/11. In late 2005, the *New York Times* broke the news that the US government was engaged in warrantless domestic wiretapping, an operation dubbed the "terrorist surveillance program" by the administration. A major outcry followed, and President Bush led the administration's response, initiated by the radio address where he admitted that hijackers in the US had been openly communicating with al-Qaeda operatives "overseas."

Rather than admitting any wrongdoing, this was seen as an opportunity for spin. Here is a longer excerpt from the president's initial defense of the new program:

> As the 9/11 Commission pointed out, it was clear that terrorists inside the United States were communicating with terrorists abroad before the September the 11th attacks, and the commission criticized our Nation's inability to uncover links between terrorists here at home and terrorists abroad. Two of the terrorist hijackers who flew a jet into the Pentagon, Nawaf Alhazmi and Khalid Almihdhar, communicated while they were in the United States to other members of al-Qaeda who were overseas. But we didn't know they were here until it was too late.[1]

These phone calls were the first justification the administration provided when the warrantless wiretapping was exposed. In addition, this justification was not only advanced on this one occasion, but also on other occasions from 2006 on by other administration officials such as Dick Cheney and Michael Hayden. Nonetheless, we still know relatively little about the calls.

Vice President Cheney chimed in early in 2006, telling the Heritage Foundation:

---

1. George W. Bush, The President's Radio Address, December 17, 2005, http://frwebgate.access. gpo.gov/cgi-bin/getdoc.cgi?dbname=2005_presidential_documents&docid=pd26de05_txt-9. pdf.

Another vital step the President took in the days following 9/11 was to authorize the National Security Agency to intercept a certain category of terrorist-linked international communications. There are no communications more important to the safety of the United States than those related to al-Qaeda that have one end in the United States. If we'd been able to do this before 9/11, we might have been able to pick up on two hijackers who subsequently flew a jet into the Pentagon. They were in the United States, communicating with al-Qaeda associates overseas. But we did not know they were here plotting until it was too late.[2]

Principal Deputy Director of National Intelligence Michael Hayden made the same argument at the National Press Club later that month:

You know, the 9/11 commission criticized our ability to link things happening in the United States with things that were happening elsewhere. In that light, there are no communications more important to the safety of this country than those affiliated with al-Qaeda with one end in the United States. The president's authorization allows us to track this kind of call more comprehensively and more efficiently.... Had this program been in effect prior to 9/11, it is my professional judgment that we would have detected some of the 9/11 al-Qaeda operatives in the United States, and we would have identified them as such.[3]

Hayden neglected to mention that "some of the al-Qaeda operatives in the United States" had *nonetheless* been both detected and identified as such. Two days later, President Bush reiterated the administration line in a speech at the NSA:

We know that two of the hijackers who struck the Pentagon were inside the United States communicating with al-Qaeda operatives overseas. But we didn't realize they were here plotting the attack until it was too late. Here's what General Mike Hayden said – he was the former director here at NSA. He's now the Deputy Director of the National Intelligence – Deputy Director of National Intelligence – and here's what he said earlier this week: "Had this program been in effect prior to 9/11, it is my professional judgment

2. Richard Cheney, Speech at the Heritage Foundation, January 4, 2006, http://www.yourbbsucks. com/forum/printthread.php?t=7489.
3. Michael Hayden, "What American Intelligence & Especially the NSA Have Been Doing to Defend the Nation," National Press Club, January 23, 2006, http://www.fas.org/irp/news/2006/01/hayden012306.html.

that we would have detected some of the 9/11 al-Qaeda operatives in the United States, and we would have identified them as such." The 9/11 Commission made clear, in this era of new dangers we must be able to connect the dots before the terrorists strike so we can stop new attacks. And this NSA program is doing just that.[4]

It must have been comforting to Hayden that Bush would place such stock in his "professional judgment." Later in the year, Cheney again took up the theme:

> If you'll recall, the 9/11 Commission focused criticism on the nation's inability to uncover links between terrorists at home and terrorists overseas. The term that was used is "connecting the dots" – and the fact is that one small piece of data might very well make it possible to save thousands of lives. If this program had been in place before 9/11, we might have been able to prevent it because we had two terrorists living in San Diego, contacting terrorist-related numbers overseas. The very important question today is whether, on five years' reflection, we have yet learned all the lessons of 9/11.[5]

If by *we* these fellows mean to refer only to themselves and other members of their administration, there is every reason to believe that they have not "learned all the lessons of 9/11." In fact, this dis-information onslaught demonstrates that they were determined that the rest of us should draw precisely the *wrong* lessons from that tragic day.

Whatever Bush et al. knew and when they knew it about the hijackers' communications (and perhaps the long-term effort to prevent domestic agencies from foiling their plot) has no bearing whatever on the fact that *these communications were known*, and known by people with enough clout to prevent other authorities from carrying out what should have been routine tasks, especial-ly in the high-alert environment following the African embassy bombings and the *Cole* attack.

And by December 2005 Bush et al. certainly knew that the op-erators' communications had been monitored, and that the plot

4. George W. Bush, "President Visits National Security Agency," White House, January 25, 2006, http://www.gwu.edu/~nsarchiv/NSAEBB/NSAEBB178/surv42.pdf.
5. Richard Cheney, "Vice President's Remarks to the USA Cincinnati Regional Chamber," White House, October 25, 2006, http://georgewbush-whitehouse.archives.gov/news/releas-es/2006/10/20061025-1.html.

should have been easily rolled up. Imagine how our world would look today had the morning of 9/11 brought us breaking news of the simultaneous arrests of four groups of hijackers as they were preparing to board those planes and carry out their missions. The system would have worked, and there would have been no need for the Orwellian "War on Terror," with its dismantling of Constitutional liberties under the veil of necessity. No Patriot Act. No war in Iraq. No war in Afghanistan.

Unfortunately, *you and I* didn't know they were here until it was *far* too late. But the Bush administration after 9/11, for over seven years, did everything it could to ensure that *no one* would be held accountable for the "failures" of that event.

Why?

On October 26, 2001, surrounded by influential members of a Congress that had overwhelmingly approved its passage, President George W. Bush signed into law the so-called USA PATRIOT Act, shorthand for the Uniting and Strengthening America by Providing Appropriate Tools Required to Intercept and Obstruct Terrorism Act of 2001. Its 342 pages created nine new US Code sections and substantially amended over one hundred. Most of it was reauthorized in March 2006. There seems to be widespread agreement that none of the legislators actually read the document.

Epilogue

They were lucky over and over again

Here I would like to summarize the arguments for the two main claims this book contains. Essentially, I have argued that 9/11 was not a failure to connect the dots, but that the Alec Station group deliberately withheld information from the FBI and that, by the summer of 2001, the purpose of withholding the information had become to allow the attacks to go forward. The claim regarding purpose is caveated, being only the most likely explanation based on currently available information.

The first thing to do when discussing why the attacks were not prevented is to dispense with the idea that the hijackers "got lucky." As one of the victim's relatives, Mindy Kleinberg, put it at the first 9/11 Commission hearing:

> The theory of luck. With regard to the 9/11 attacks, it has been said that the intelligence agencies have to be right 100 percent of the time and the terrorists only have to get lucky once. This explanation for the devastating attacks of September 11th, simple on its face, is wrong in its value, because the 9/11 terrorists were not just lucky once, they were lucky over and over again.[1]

Any theory attempting to explain why the attacks were not prevented must explain why the hijackers were not just lucky once, but dozens of times. It must explain, for example, how in January 2000 the CIA failed to watchlist Khalid Almihdhar and Nawaf Alhazmi, how "Michelle" and Tom Wilshire managed to block Doug Miller's cable to the FBI about Almihdhar's US visa, and how "James" told two FBI officials about Almihdhar, but also failed to mention that he had a US visa. It must also explain how the NSA failed to exploit

---

1. Transcript of 9/11 Commission hearing on March 31, 2003, http://govinfo.library.unt.edu/911/archive/hearing1/9-11Commission_Hearing_2003-03-31.htm.

the intercepts of Almihdhar's calls, which handily transformed into a justification for extended domestic spying after the attacks. Other explanations required include those for Dina Corsi's conduct at the June 11 "shouting match" meeting, her withholding of the NSA information from Steve Bongardt even after the NSA cleared it for him, and her misrepresentation of the consultation with Sherry Sabol. Finally, an explanation is needed of why Wilshire, who knew Almihdhar was "very high interest" in connection with a forthcoming al-Qaeda attack against the US, told no one at the FBI of this.

Had there been an isolated failing, it could be viewed as a product of overwork and incompetence. However, as the number of failures mounts—and the bulleted list of them in Appendix A contains dozens of items—it becomes harder and harder to credit such an explanation. There is only a certain amount of incompetence that a group of human beings can commit before the observer begins to wonder whether another explanation might prove more convincing.

Another problem is the magnitude of the failings. The importance of al-Qaeda's Malaysia summit was allegedly not fully recognized at the time, although National Security Advisor Sandy Berger was briefed about it, and the arrival of Alhazmi and his companion in the US, reported in the March 5, 2000 cable, was certainly a significant development. The *Cole* bombing was a major event for the US government and required repeated briefings and discussions among the cabinet principals, including the president, over a period of months. Likewise, the summer of threat in 2001 was the topic of multiple meetings for senior officials, and President Bush was involved, as evidenced by the famous August 6 presidential daily brief item entitled "Bin Laden Determined to Strike in US." The failures did not concern merely low-level radicals, but operatives known to be high-interest al-Qaeda figures. For example, when Khallad bin Attash was identified in a Malaysia photograph by Omar, he was known to be a leader of the *Cole* attack, but the CIA still failed to pass on the identification to the FBI on multiple occasions. While an observer may be willing to attribute the failure to pass on information about a minor figure on one occasion to the usual bureaucratic interagency problems, multiple failures linked to important events must be viewed differently.

A third issue is the ubiquity of Tom Wilshire and his associates. Wilshire was personally involved in the initial blocking of Miller's draft cable, the failure to do anything with the first May 2001 review of the Malaysia cables, the preparations for the June 11 "shouting match" meeting—which appears to have been a fishing expedition to find out what the FBI knew—the second review of the cables by Margaret Gillespie, which Wilshire told her to do in her free time, the Moussaoui case, and the failed hunt for Almihdhar and Alhazmi. People working closely with Wilshire were also involved in the failures, to a greater or lesser degree, including Richard Blee, "Michelle," Dina Corsi, Margaret Gillespie, Clark Shannon, Dave Frasca, Michael Maltbie and Rita Flack.

Wilshire was aware of the NSA's surveillance of the Yemen hub. In addition, several other officers whose poor performance seems inexplicable, officers at CIA stations in Pakistan ("Chris"), Yemen and Thailand, must have been in contact with Alec Station, of which Wilshire was deputy chief. Had the multiple, serious failures been committed by a varied group of officials from a range of agencies, it would be harder to believe that these officials colluded. However, as most of the failures involve the same person or his close associates, one can much more readily accept that the information was withheld not by chance, but by design.

Point number four is that the failures also concerned a small group of al-Qaeda operatives, the key members of which appear to be Almihdhar and Alhazmi, along with bin Attash. While the Alec Station group was withholding information about these men, the CIA was sharing information about other aspects of al-Qaeda and its operatives. In this context, recall the December 2000 cable that contained some information that was about bin Attash and some information that was not about bin Attash—the cable instructed CIA personnel to share the information not about bin Attash, but contained no such instruction regarding the information about him. Recall also the threat briefings in summer of 2001. Richard Blee must have known of Almihdhar, but, although he provided a wealth of other information, there is no record of him mentioning Almihdhar or Alhazmi to his superiors in this context.

Another problem is that some of the surviving documentation contradicts the story later spun by the Alec Station group. Recall the February 2000 message from the CIA stating it was in the middle of an investigation to determine what Almihdhar was up to; this cable came at a time when the CIA later claimed it had ceased all actions regarding Almihdhar. There is also the August 30, 2001 notification informing the FBI of Omar's identification of bin Attash in one of the Malaysia photographs, which disproves the Agency's later claim it thought the Bureau had known of this for months. A further example is in the notes of Stephen Cambone, which state that three of the Flight 77 hijackers had been followed since the Millennium plot and the USS *Cole* bombing. Yet another is in Dina Corsi's notes of the June 11 meeting, which show Clark Shannon was asked about Almihdhar and did provide one piece of information about him—that he was traveling on a Saudi passport.

As the withholding of the information dragged on and became more complex, even Wilshire began to have such problems. In May 2001 he indicated that he knew the photo of Alhazmi that Omar had identified as bin Attash did not show bin Attash, although it is hard to comprehend how he could have known this if the story he later offered investigators is true. Worse, in July 2001 he sent one e-mail linking the Malaysia summit with the current threat reporting and another stating that Almihdhar was "very high interest" in connection with the next al-Qaeda attack. Unfortunately for him, he later became involved in the search for Almihdhar at the FBI and failed to tell anyone else at the Bureau of Almihdhar's significance.

A related matter is that some of the low-level members of the group evidently understood what they were doing so little that they produced documentation that later proved embarrassing. For example: Miller's "Is this a no go?" e-mail from January 2000 provided a documentary link between Wilshire and the withholding of Almihdhar's visa information; Corsi's August 22, 2001 e-mail revealed that she was aware of bin Attash's presence at the Malaysia summit, which she had not communicated to the other agents working on the *Cole* case; and her August 23 e-mail to Wilshire revealed she appreciated Almihdhar's link to the *Cole* bombing, although she later fought to keep the *Cole* agents off the search for him.

We must also question the explanations offered by the members of the Alec Station group and their associates after the attacks. One reason is that they and, for example, Counterterrorist Center chief

Cofer Black and CIA Director George Tenet made a string of false and misleading statements to investigators, often under oath. It is hard to believe they did not know these statements were incorrect at the time they made them. In addition, in some cases the explanations proffered for the failures are not credible, nor are the repeated claims that participants simply could not recall the events that occurred. One of the least believable assertions was made by Wilshire concerning his failure to inform the FBI of Alhazmi's entry to the US after re-reading the Malaysia cables in May 2001. He told the Justice Department inspector general he did not notify anybody at the Bureau of the entry because he was "focused on Malaysia" and the possibility of a terrorist attack there. Of course, at this time he was about to go on detail to the FBI, which focuses on domestic matters.

Finally, there is the matter of Miller and Mark Rossini apparently admitting that they were part of a conspiracy to withhold information from the FBI in January 2000 and identifying two other members of the conspiracy, "Michelle" and Wilshire. If the problem was merely overwork and incompetence, why would two of the allegedly overworked and incompetent officials claim that they could manage their work load and were perfectly competent, but were pressured to deliberately withhold the information, did so, and then lied about it to investigators?

* * *

It is clear that the Alec Station group shielded Almihdhar and Alhazmi from the FBI, and from its *Cole* investigators in particular. The question is, why? Speculation has run the gamut of probability, including the theory that the hijackers were Saudi double-agents in al-Qaeda, who then triple-crossed their Saudi and US handlers. This doesn't stand up, for reasons discussed in Appendix B. Thus, among the many options, two main explanations have emerged.

The first maintains that the Alec Station group deliberately failed to pass the information on, and that they did so to conceal from the FBI a secret CIA operation. Most frequently it is suggested that the operation was trying to recruit Almihdhar and Alhazmi to use against Osama bin Laden. In this scenario, the group did not want the operatives to hijack anything or commit any attacks, they wanted to penetrate al-Qaeda. They were simply loyal intelligence officials keeping the FBI in the dark and indulging in a little illegal activity inside the US.

The second asserts that, at some point before the summer of 2001, one or more people in the group came to desire an attack upon the US and hid Almihdhar and Alhazmi from the FBI—and possibly their own superiors—in an effort to provide them with the time to carry it out. In this case, it is even possible that the hijackers received additional assistance from their supporter(s) within the group, although I am not aware of any direct evidence of this.

A cursory examination of the facts may suggest that the first scenario is the more tenable, although this impression could be influenced by one's natural instinct to assume that, even if the Alec Station group did deliberately conceal the information about Almihdhar and Alhazmi, this must have been for a purpose other than to enable the attacks. However, the more the details are examined, the more the balance shifts in the opposite direction.

First, Almihdhar and Alhazmi must have been under surveillance in the US, either officially by Alec Station or by some parallel group. It makes no sense to assume that the Alec Station group hid the two men from the FBI so that they could ignore them in the US. The point of keeping the Bureau away from the case can only have been for the group to monitor them without having FBI agents get in their way. This applies no matter what the ultimate aim of the operation was; whether the point was to recruit them, to discover their contacts by monitoring them, or to let them attack the US, surveillance must have been involved.

Such surveillance could not have failed to find most or all of the other hijackers. People monitoring the hijackers must also have noticed the various casing flights the hijackers went on and their pilot training. The hijackers' ticket purchases for their 9/11 flights cannot have evaded this group, which would have known it was monitoring operatives of a terrorist organization planning to attack US interests at this time. The purchases should have set alarm bells ringing, had the group been truly interested in preventing a terrorist attack its targets might be involved in. However, the same caveat applies to the presumed surveillance team as applies to Wilshire and his associates at the CIA and FBI: *they might not have desired the outcome that occurred*; they might have been told by a superior that everything was under control.

The second reason to prefer the darker explanation involves three things that Wilshire—and almost certainly Richard Blee—knew in the summer of 2001: that al-Qaeda was planning an attack, that Almihdhar was "very high interest" in connection with the attack, and that Almihdhar was in the US.

At this time the US national security community was well aware of the impending al-Qaeda attack; the 9/11 Commission's chapter on this period is even entitled "The System Was Blinking Red." Nobody in the whole of the US government was more aware of this than Blee, who was the administration's main internal briefer on the flood of warnings of an impending al-Qaeda attack. Wilshire also knew what was coming.

The three e-mails Wilshire wrote in July, culminating in the "very high interest" e-mail of July 23, clearly linked Almihdhar to the current threat reporting. Wilshire could have been in no doubt that one of the men he had been protecting for over a year and a half would probably be involved in the next attack, and he communicated this to Blee.

It is hard to imagine that both Wilshire and Blee were unaware that Almihdhar was in the US in the first half of 2000 and also that he returned on July 4, 2001. One would assume that both of these men would have received reports of the hidden surveillance of Almihdhar and his associates detailing their movements. Whatever the case, Wilshire certainly did learn Almihdhar was in the US on August 22, when Margaret Gillespie, one of Blee's subordinates at the CIA's Counterterrorist Center, told him so.

At this time Wilshire must have appreciated the reason Almihdhar was in the country—to assist an attack against the US inside its borders. Recall that Steve Bongardt reached a similar conclusion six days later—"If this guy is in the country, it's not because he's going to fucking Disneyland!"—based on much less information than Wilshire had. Yet, Wilshire and Dina Corsi continued to protect Almihdhar. In fact, as a consequence of Bongardt learning of Almihdhar's presence, in the three weeks preceding the attacks the Alec Station group had to work harder than ever before to keep the Bureau from finding him and Alhazmi.

Despite knowing what he knew, Wilshire failed to tell anybody at the FBI that Almihdhar may well be linked to a forthcoming major al-Qaeda operation, a crucial fact that would have caused massive resources to be devoted to the hunt for him. Instead, Wilshire supported a procedure—the use of an intelligence investigation instead of a criminal one to look for Almihdhar—that meant that few resources were allocated to the search.

Further, Corsi effectively sabotaged the search. The clearest way this can be seen is in her non-provision to Bongardt of the NSA information linking Almihdhar to the Yemen hub and Malaysia. She should have had this cleared for passage to him immediately after the June 11 meeting, but then waited ten weeks and, even after the NSA had cleared it, continued to withhold it, despite repeated interactions with Bongardt on precisely this topic. In addition, she is accused of fabricating the portion of the legal opinion that prevented Bongardt from being present at an interview of Almihdhar, and committed several other inexplicable errors, such as withholding information about the identification of bin Attash by Omar and preventing Robert Fuller from getting a credit card number from Saudi Airlines.

The logical action of a national security official who wanted to prevent a terrorist attack on the US and knew the identity of one of the probable participants would be to exploit this knowledge to prevent the attack. Yet Wilshire and Blee sat on the information, allowing the plot to go forward. The set of hijackings was a natural and probable result of this inaction, and we should not shy away from attributing a desire to achieve this probable result from at least one member of the Alec Station group.

Counterarguments can be attempted, for example by suggesting that there was an operation in progress to recruit Almihdhar and Alhazmi, that Blee may not have believed Wilshire's warnings, that the surveillance may have ended, or that the hijackers realized they were under surveillance and somehow gave the impression there would be a different attack at a later date. However, I regard such arguments as increasingly bizarre and improbable.

Therefore, in my opinion, the darker explanation is the more likely, although the other, less sinister, scenario cannot be entirely excluded. It is my hope that this book has provided its readers with enough evidence to be able to make informed judgments of their own.

* * *

Tom Wilshire has been the focus of this work's attention because he is the common link among the various failures at the CIA and FBI. However, he was not the most senior officer known to be involved. That would be Richard Blee, his boss at Alec Station. Above Blee is a grey area; it is unclear whether he could have been acting on orders, or if he might have gone "rogue," either acting entirely on his own or with the blessing of influential agency alumni.

If in fact the attacks were deliberately allowed, it does not necessarily follow that all the members of the Alec Station group knew of the intended outcome. In fact, both Doug Miller and Mark Rossini said they did not know the ultimate aim of what they were instructed to do; they were simply given a hint that the CIA did not want the FBI messing with a secret agency operation. Had Miller and Rossini been told of the true aim, they would presumably have refused to go along with it, no matter what they were threatened with.

It is likely that Wilshire's other lower-level associates received similar hints and went along with the operation because they misunderstood its intentions. This may even apply to Wilshire himself—the day after Almihdhar returned to the US in the summer of 2001, he began to send a series of e-mails warning that Almihdhar might be linked to an upcoming major terrorist attack. He nonetheless continued to shield Almihdhar.

What Richard Blee's superiors, in particular Cofer Black and George Tenet, knew of the plot is also a grey area. There is nothing directly implicating them in the wrongdoing before 9/11, no e-mail in which they admit to knowing something they did not officially find out until two weeks later. There is one occasion on which Blee demonstrably misled them: perhaps they were bamboozled by a Machiavellian subordinate, or perhaps Blee withheld the relevant information from them because they had indicated to him that he should do so. What is indisputable is that, soon after 9/11, Blee was rewarded with a promotion to the newly created position of CIA station chief in Kabul. In addition, Black and Tenet made a series of false statements under oath to the various investigations, and their statements had the effect of protecting Wilshire, Blee and their associates.

* * *

It is likely then that one or more of the group of people who protected Almihdhar and Alhazmi did so with the precise intention of allowing them to perform an attack inside the US. In part, this conclusion is based on the rejection of other explanations. "Luck" is a non-starter. "Overwork/incompetence" cannot survive the multiple failings or the admissions of Miller and Rossini. "Recruitment" cannot explain why the surveillance failed when "the system was blinking red." The Saudi theory has multiple problems, as detailed in Appendix B. After the improbable is excluded, we are left with the unpalatable.

This leaves us with one enormous question: why?

Although we can never see into a person's mind—and in this case we do not know exactly whose mind we are attempting to see into—it is possible to sketch some potential motivations.

The first possible motivator is personal benefit. The highest-ranking person clearly involved before 9/11 was Richard Blee, and he certainly did derive a personal benefit from the attacks, winning a major new assignment as station chief in Kabul. "Michelle" was also promoted,[2] although it is far from certain she was fully aware of what was happening in the run-up to 9/11.

The possibility that Blee was acting in concert with loyal CIA alumni has been mentioned. Such alumni often go straight through the revolving door from the Agency to Wall Street or the military-industrial complex. Cofer Black is a good example of this, joining the private military contractor Blackwater USA (renamed Xe after a series of disgraces in Iraq) a few months after leaving the government. Without doubt, companies forming the military-industrial complex did not merely benefit from 9/11, they experienced an unrivalled boom.

---

2. Jane Mayer, *The Dark Side* (New York: Doubleday, 2008), p. 16.

However, people are not motivated merely by money and professional position. Ideas and geopolitical aims are also important. Richard Blee clearly supported at least one policy, stepping up the war effort in Afghanistan through aid to Ahmed Shah Massoud and his Northern Alliance, that he was unable to fully implement due to opposition inside and outside the Agency. 9/11 broke the logjam in spectacular fashion, and the CIA began throwing money at the Northern Alliance.

Given that Blee also ran the rendition program for some time before becoming chief of Kabul station, it is reasonable to assume that he also supported that program. As we know, it was significantly expanded after 9/11, and, in the case of Ibn Shaikh al-Libi, Blee instigated this.

Yet these are only two of the changes that occurred after the attacks. Cofer Black famously told the Congressional Inquiry, "After 9/11 the gloves come off."[3] This was a reference not only to increased rendition and support for the Northern Alliance, but also to a number of other changes, such as black sites where detainees were tortured and the use of unmanned aerial vehicles to carry out targeted killings. All this was accompanied by the CIA's return to its old position of influence, a bigger budget and a hiring boom.

These changes were both the product of, and one of the drivers behind, a larger geostrategic realignment. For some years before 9/11, the US had been attempting to achieve progress in the world by engaging in negotiation: building coalitions, and generally being slightly nicer to other countries than had been the norm during the Cold War. After the attacks, raw American power was displayed visibly, most notably in the "shock and awe" campaign that started the invasion of Iraq. This change was clearly popular with a section of the public, both American and global.

Here, then, is one explanation that can be offered: whoever decided to let the hijackers operate, whether it was ultimately Wilshire, Blee or someone else with de facto authority, did so in order to enable and cause this realignment. Perhaps it was believed that America was losing its will to take difficult, unpopular actions and, with it, its position in the world. Therefore, it would be better

---

3. Testimony of Cofer Black to Joint Congressional Inquiry, September 26, 2002, http://www.fas.org/irp/congress/2002_hr/092602black.html.

to allow an attack, generating the political will to restore America's position. Preventing 9/11 might have led to an even more deadly attack in the future, but by that time the US might have declined so far that its position could not be regained.

Whatever the precise motivation, it seems clear that Blee and some of the group he headed did knowingly withhold information, that he did derive a benefit from withholding this information after the attacks, and that he would have known in advance that this benefit would probably accrue. Given that the attacks were a logical result of withholding the information and allowing the hijackers to operate, we can reach the working premise that either he or someone above him was aware of what was happening and desired the outcome we saw on our television screens.

Yet there remain a number of questions that are unanswered. Primarily, was there any relationship between these failures and the other alleged failures surrounding the attacks, such as the failure to intercept any of the hijacked airliners during the attacks, which, after all, lasted nearly two hours? The only real answer to this is, "We don't know."

The world has been turned upside down since 9/11 and because of 9/11, but we still do not know why it happened. As set out in this book, there are major flaws in *The 9/11 Commission Report*, the 9/11 Congressional Inquiry report, the Justice Department inspector general's report and the CIA inspector general's report. The only way that this issue will ever be satisfactorily resolved is by a new, credible investigation.

Appendix A

... And over again

Any theory about 9/11 emphasizing luck must explain why the hijackers were not just lucky once, but enjoyed remarkable luck over and over again. Let's refresh our memories about a few of the occasions on which the hijackers got "lucky":

- Doug Miller's cable to the FBI about Khalid Almihdhar's US visa was intentionally blocked by "Michelle" and Tom Wilshire.

- "James" failed to inform the FBI of Almihdhar's US visa in two briefings.

- Richard Blee briefed his superiors that the Kuala Lumpur surveillance was ongoing, when it was not.

- The CIA allegedly lost the hijackers in Thailand, despite having information—the phone number of the hotel where they stayed in Bangkok—that could have been used to locate them.

- The CIA failed to watchlist Almihdhar and Nawaf Alhazmi during the Malaysia summit.

- When the CIA's Kuala Lumpur station asked for an update about Almihdhar, its counterpart in Bangkok claimed not to have information it apparently had, then sent a cable which only said Alhazmi and a companion had entered the US.

- The CIA again failed to watchlist Almihdhar and Alhazmi at this opportunity.

- Nor did it inform the FBI about them.

- While they were in the US, Almihdhar and Alhazmi repeatedly called al-Qaeda's operations center, at which Almihdhar lived with his family when not away from home. The NSA intercepted these calls, which contained enough information to roll up the plot, but failed to exploit them.

- The Able Danger data mining project uncovered information about Mohamed Atta, Marwan Alshehhi, Almihdhar and Alhazmi, but was blocked from passing it on.

- Despite several credible reports that the Yemen communications hub was involved in the USS *Cole* bombing, no action was taken against it in the aftermath.

- The FBI's *Cole* investigators asked the CIA for information about the Malaysia summit three times, but the CIA falsely claimed it knew nothing about any such summit each time.

- Some CIA officers discussed Almihdhar and Alhazmi in the aftermath of the *Cole* bombing, but failed to inform the FBI about them.

- The CIA again failed to take this opportunity to watchlist them.

- Photos of Almihdhar and Alhazmi were passed to Omar, the joint FBI-CIA source handled out of Islamabad, under the pretext that some people at the CIA thought Almihdhar and Khallad bin Attash might be the same person.

- When Omar identified Alhazmi as bin Attash, the CIA officer present failed to inform his FBI handler at the time and failed to mention the identification in a cable to the US intelligence community.

- The CIA again failed to watchlist Almihdhar, Alhazmi and, apparently, bin Attash.

- CIA officers met the FBI's *Cole* investigators in late January 2001 to discuss bin Attash, but failed to mention that Omar had seen him in one of the Kuala Lumpur photographs.

- The CIA officer present at the identification then met with the source and the FBI *Cole* investigators to discuss a previous identification of bin Attash by the source, but failed to mention the source's identification of bin Attash in the Kuala Lumpur photographs.

- Shortly before moving to the FBI, Tom Wilshire reread the Malaysia summit cables but did not alert the FBI to the fact that Alhazmi had entered the US with a companion and that Almihdhar had a US visa, ostensibly because he was "focused on Malaysia."

- Again, neither of the two was watchlisted at this time.

- Wilshire initiated a review of the Malaysia cables, but told the reviewer, Margaret Gillespie, to do the work in her free time, and failed to give her the relevant cables, which it took her three months to find.

- Wilshire's associates, Gillespie, Clark Shannon and Dina Corsi, showed photos of Alhazmi and Almihdhar taken in Malaysia to the FBI's *Cole* investigators, but much relevant information was withheld from the FBI agents.

- The *Cole* investigators then requested more information about the photos, but Corsi failed to obtain it for months.

- Learning that bin Attash had been identified by the joint source in Islamabad, Corsi told no one else on the *Cole* investigation for some time.

- The CIA had information indicating that Khalid Shaikh Mohammed, a key al-Qaeda leader, was sending people to the US, but failed to follow this up.

- An intelligence agency, apparently the NSA, intercepted KSM talking to Ramzi bin al-Shibh and possibly others in the summer of 2001, but failed to exploit this.

- Wilshire was involved in the failed Zacarias Moussaoui investigation, sharing FBI headquarters' obstructionist attitude toward the arresting agents and failing to pass on notification about the case to his counterpart at the FBI.

- When information came back to him from the review he had initiated, Wilshire officially learned Almihdhar was in the country, but again failed to take any appropriate action.

- Wilshire then supported a procedure that deprived the FBI's hunt for Almihdhar of resources, agreeing that it should be an intelligence investigation rather than a criminal investigation, despite Almihdhar's having been linked to the *Cole* bombing.

- After New York agents protested that the search for Almihdhar should be conducted as a criminal investigation, an erroneous and probably fabricated legal opinion was used to keep the criminal agents away from Almihdhar.

- After the NSA's general counsel approved the passage of information about Almihdhar to the *Cole* criminal agents, Dina Corsi did not pass it quickly.

- Robert Fuller, a rookie intelligence agent, was assigned the crucial task of searching databases for information on Almihdhar and Alhazmi.

- Fuller's search was intermittent and haphazard, failing to include some obvious checks.

- Corsi told Fuller not to contact Saudi Arabian Airlines to get a credit card number for Almihdhar, although the number could have greatly assisted the search.

This litany of "lucky breaks" for the hijackers demands that we look elsewhere: for a rational explanation.

Appendix B

Alhazmi and Almihdhar were Saudi agents

A n alternative theory is that the CIA's actions regarding Almihdhar and Alhazmi were explained by the two hijackers' relationship to Saudi intelligence, some of which was discussed in Chapter Four. This idea was advanced by investigative journalists Joe and Susan Trento, first in an article, then in a book. Essentially, the theory is that Almihdhar and Alhazmi worked for Saudi intelligence, but had triple-crossed the Saudi authorities.

The initial article said,

> Two of the hijackers—part of the team that flew a plane into the Pentagon—had very visible connections to Saudi intelligence and the CIA. Nawaf Alhazmi and Khalid Almihdhar were well known to the CIA and FBI. The claim that an FBI informant in San Diego who knew the men and assisted them but never mentioned any of this to his FBI handlers has another, darker explanation. A former CIA officer who worked in Saudi Arabia described what he says happened: "We had been unable to penetrate al-Qaeda. The Saudi's claimed that they had done it successfully. Both Alhazmi and Almihdhar were Saudi agents. We thought they had been screened. It turned out the man responsible for recruiting them had been loyal to Osama bin Laden. The truth is bin Laden himself was a Saudi agent at one time. He successfully penetrated Saudi intelligence and created his own operation inside. The CIA relied on the Saudis vetting their own agents. It was a huge mistake. The reason the FBI was not given any information about either man is because they were Saudi assets operating with CIA knowledge in the United States."[1]

In a book three years later the Trentos added more:

---

1. Joe Trento, "The Real Intelligence Cover-Up: America's Unholy Alliance," *Stories that Matter,* August 6, 2003, http://www.storiesthatmatter.org/2003080649/Trento-s-Take/the-real-intelligence-cover-up-americas-unholy-alliance.html. This is more baggage for the enigmatic "professor," Abdussattar Shaikh, referred to here as "an FBI informant in San Diego," although it is unclear how Trento sees Shaikh's role in the "darker explanation."

There were two Saudi intelligence agents the CIA believed had been successfully placed inside al-Qaeda as double agents. The problem was that neither the CIA nor the GID had properly vetted the men. In fact, they were triple agents—loyal to Osama bin Laden. Saudi intelligence had sent agents Khalid Almihdhar and Nawaf Alhazmi to spy on a meeting of top associates of al-Qaeda in Kuala Lumpur, Malaysia, January 5-8, 2000. "The CIA/Saudi hope was that the Saudis would learn details of bin Laden's future plans. Instead plans were finalized and the Saudis learned nothing," says a terrorism expert who asks that his identity be withheld.

... Under normal circumstances, the names of Almihdhar and Alhazmi should have been placed on the State Department, Immigration and Naturalization Service (INS), and US Customs watch lists. The two men would have been automatically denied entry into the US. Because they were perceived as working for a friendly intelligence service, however, the CIA did not pass along the names.[2]

Later in the book we read:

Prior to 9/11 senior CIA officials had convinced themselves that GID, the Saudi intelligence service, had placed agents inside al-Qaeda. Because these two men—Khalid Almihdhar and Nawaf Alhazmi—were thought to be Saudi agents, the CIA did not tell the FBI about them when they came into the United States from a terrorist training summit meeting in Malaysia. Had the CIA shared what it knew, the FBI might have had a chance at preventing the 9/11 attacks....

Why did the CIA stop protecting the two GID agents but not fully inform the FBI as to their whereabouts? Because a month before 9/11 there was a dramatic change in Saudi intelligence. The longtime head of GID, the moderate Prince Turki, trusted by the United States, left GID and became the Saudi ambassador to the court of Saint James in London. Had Turki been forced out by more radical elements in the Saudi royal family? Had he quietly warned the CIA that he suspected that GID's assurances about the penetration of al-Qaeda were not as reliable as thought previously? Had al-Qaeda penetrated GID?[3]

2. Susan Trento and Joseph Trento, *Unsafe at Any Altitude: Failed Terrorism Investigations, Scapegoating 9/11, and the Shocking Truth about Aviation Security Today* (Hanover, New Hampshire: Steerforth, 2006), p. 8.
3. Ibid., pp. 192-93

The Trentos are fine investigative reporters, two of the best in the US. Nevertheless, there are numerous problems with this account.

Primarily, institutional mistrust ran so deep that in 1997 Alec Station, in a memo for Director Tenet, identified Saudi intelligence as a "hostile service" on the issue of al-Qaeda, the product of failed cooperation projects.[4] Author James Risen gave an example of one problem:

> CIA sources say that the agency has had strong evidence that some of the intelligence it has shared with Saudi security officials has ended up in the hands of al-Qaeda operatives. For example, the CIA has in the past given the Saudis copies of NSA communications intercepts, which included conversations among suspected al-Qaeda operatives in Saudi Arabia. But after the CIA gave the intercepts to the Saudis, the suspects quickly stopped using the communications that the Americans had been monitoring, making it far more difficult to track the terrorists.

Risen also recounted another anecdote that reinforced the point:

> Because the Jordanian intelligence service, which is closely tied to the CIA, is renowned in the Middle East for its effectiveness, top Saudi officials asked it to review the Saudi intelligence apparatus and provide them with an assessment. When they began touring Saudi military and security facilities to conduct their review, however, the Jordanians saw something that helped explain why the Saudis had not done a better job in counterterrorism—a number of Saudi officials had Osama bin Laden screen savers on their office computers, according to an American source who heard the story from a top Jordanian official.

Alec Station simply did not trust the Saudis, and it had good reason not to trust them. Therefore, any explanation based on the claim that the CIA trusted the Saudis should be treated with extreme skepticism.

Even if Alec Station had trusted the Saudis enough to allow them to send Alhazmi and Almihdhar to the US and had decided to keep the FBI away from them for this reason, then it would have mount-

---

4. For this detail and the two extended quotations, see James Risen, *State of War: The Secret History of the CIA and the Bush Administration* (New York: Free Press, 2006), pp. 181-82.

ed its own surveillance of the two men inside the US. Intelligence services do not simply let their assets and foreign operatives do as they please; they are kept under surveillance. As discussed above, this surveillance would have uncovered the other hijackers and the ticket purchases for 9/11.

Alhazmi and Almihdhar attended the Malaysia summit and, according to the Trentos, reported back to the Saudis, keeping the real details secret and feeding their handlers bad information. Given the number of al-Qaeda leaders present, the CIA would have been desperate to obtain this report and would have been highly suspicious of any shortcomings in it. This would certainly have increased their wariness of the two men and reinforced the need to keep them under surveillance in the US.

Second, the Trentos made some factual errors with their chronology. For example, they claim,

> The 9/11 Commission reported that two and a half weeks before 9/11 and twenty months after GID agents attended the Malaysia summit, the CIA, as the law requires, finally notified another federal agency – not the FBI, but the Immigration and Naturalization Service.[5]

This is misleading. Margaret Gillespie at the CIA *did* involve the FBI in late August 2001, and the 9/11 Commission's final report spends two pages discussing this. This is also mentioned by the Justice Department inspector general's report, the Congressional Inquiry report and numerous media accounts.

Third, the Trentos claim that Alec Station "stop[ped] protecting" Almihdhar and Alhazmi. This is a reference to the query Gillespie sent to INS to determine whether they were still in the country on August 21 (and her subsequent notification to Dina Corsi at FBI headquarters). However, Tom Wilshire continued to protect the two men by withholding from the FBI the knowledge that Almihdhar was "very high interest" in connection with a forthcoming terrorist attack, which would have led to a lot of resources being devoted to the search. In addition, there was the argument between Corsi and Bongardt and the discrepancies in Fuller's search. It really does not look like the Alec Station group had stopped protect-

---

5. Susan Trento and Joseph Trento, see note 2, p. 193.

ing them, more like protection was continued and they wanted to add embarrassing the Bureau into the bargain.

Further, Gillespie's first call to Corsi came on August 21 and the notification about bin Attash's attendance at the Malaysia summit came on August 30. The Trentos attribute this to Prince Turki's resignation from the GID, which they place "a month before 9/11." However, according to press accounts, Turki was replaced on August 31,[6] ten days *after* Gillespie's initial notification, although it is certainly possible that Turki had informed the US of his forthcoming departure in advance.

Lastly, the Trentos also claim:

> The great secret of why the president and his team were complacent about warnings of an impending 9/11 attack in the summer of 2001 is that the CIA had assured the national command authority that the CIA's cooperative arrangement with Saudi intelligence had resulted in the penetration of al-Qaeda at the highest levels, according to intelligence sources who worked in this area for both the Saudi and US services.[7]

"Intelligence sources" may have made such a claim, but it should be treated with extreme skepticism. There are numerous accounts of CIA Director Tenet running round with his hair on fire in the summer of 2001. Think of the dramatic meeting with Rice in early July, think of the "Bin Laden Determined to Strike in US" presidential daily brief item in August. The White House's counterterrorism and security group was also on full alert, ships were put to sea, embassies were closed. The multiple accounts of what happened all have Tenet extremely agitated, not assuring the White House that al-Qaeda had been penetrated and there was no need to worry. It is possible that somebody at the White House received some sort of back-channel notification, and it might be theoretically possible that all the participants in the meetings have omitted to mention this alleged penetration, but this seems a real stretch.

How, then, are we to explain the Trentos account? One explanation is that they were purposely fed disinformation by the officials they interviewed. Another explanation is that their interviewees

---

6. Simon Henderson, "The Saudis: Friend or Foe?" *Wall Street Journal*, October 22, 2001; "King Fahd Appoints New Head of Intelligence Services," Agence France-Presse, August 31, 2001.
7. Susan Trento and Joseph Trento, see note 2, pp. 193-94.

were lied to, failed to realize this, possibly put the lies together with some other things they knew, and then passed this on to the Trentos.

Documents

Disconnecting the Dots

(Rev. 05-28-2000)

FEDERAL BUREAU OF INVESTIGATION

To: New York From: Counterterrorism
Re: ▓ 199N-NY-NEW, 08/28/2001

Precedence: ROUTINE   Date: 08/28/2001

From: Counterterrorism
    ITOS/Usama Bin Laden Unit/SIOC CAT A
    Contact: IOS Dina M. Corsi (202)323-2808

Approved By: Middleton Rodney D

Drafted By: Corsi Dina M:dmc

Case ID #: ▓ 199N-NY-NEW (Pending)

Title: ▓   Khalid M. Al-Mihdhar
              Khalid Al-Mihdha,
              Khalid Al-Midher

Synopsis: ▓ Request to open a full field intelligence investigation.

Administrative: ▓ The following contains information from ▓
This information is not cleared for review by agents working Usama Bin Laden criminal
matters. Prior approval from FBIHQ must be obtained before forwarding this
information to any agent working Usama Bin Laden criminal cases.

Details: ▓ FBIHQ has recently received information from INS
that Khalid M. Al-Mihdhar arrived in New York City on July 4,
2001, via Saudi Arabian Airlines Flt. 00053. Al-Mihdhar's I-94
indicates that he arrived on a B1 visa issued in Jeddah, KSA on
6/13/01 and provided his address in the United States as the
Marriott Hotel(NFI), New York City.

        According to INS Al-Mihdhar had previously
traveled to the United States on January 15, 2000 with an
associate identified as Nawaf Al-Hazmi. Al-Mihdhar and Al-Hazmi

NA-88-1653

SECRET

NA-1653

Declassified Upon Use at Trial
by: UC, CTLU1, OGC, FBI
on: 03/17/2006

Draft request on August 28, 2001 from the bin Laden unit at FBI headquarters, drafted
by Dina Corsi, to open full field intelligence investigation of Khalid Almihdhar. Note the
injunction not to share information with criminal investigators.

(Rev. 01-25-2000)

SECRET/
SECRET/
FEDERAL BUREAU OF INVESTIGATION

To: New York From: Counterterrorism
Re: ███ 199N-NY-NEW, 08/28/2001

arrived in the United States via United Airlines Flt. 00002 from
Bangkok, Thailand. Both carried B2 visas. Al-Mihdhar and
Al-Hazmi stayed at the Sheraton Hotel (NFI), in Los Angeles, CA.
On that occasion, Al-Mihdhar remained in the United States until
June 10, 2000, when he departed via Lufthansa Flt. 457. The date
of Al-Hazmi's departure is unknown at this time.

> In late-1999 the CIA was monitoring potential operational planning
> by an Islamic extremist identified only as Khalid LNU. As part of their
> analysis, CIA obtained information from NSA that in late 1999, a suspected
> Islamic extremist known as Khalid was planning to travel to Malaysia with an
> associate, identified only as Nawaf. Khalid was associated with a suspected
> terrorist facility in the Middle East used by individuals in the attacks against
> the East Africa embassies and USS Cole. The facility is well known to the
> intelligence community as providing support to Al-Qaeda world-wide.
>
> Al-Midhar eventually finalized plans to depart for Kuala Lumpur,
> Malaysia in early 2000. Al-Midhar planned to meet Nawaf in Kuala
> Lumpur.
>
> The United States Government obtained information that on January
> 8, 2000, Al-Midher, traveling under the name Khalid al-Midhar, and an
> individual identified as Nawaf al-Hazmi, departed Kuala Lumpur and traveled
> to Bangkok, Thailand.

███ The similarity in the names and travel destinations
indicate that Khalid Al-Midher and Nawaf Al-Hazmi are
identifiable with the individuals who traveled to the United
States on January 15, 2000. The correlation of Al-Midher's
original travel to Malaysia with operational activity by Al-Qaeda
and his association with a known Al-Qaeda ████ make his possible presence in the United States ████ Facility ████
threat to United States' interests.

SECRET ████

NA-88-1654

That injunction was included despite Almihdhar's stated connection to the African
Embassy and *Cole* bombings, see inset above. The inset appears to have been created
in the declassification of the document where sensitive elements could not be blacked
out without preventing comprehension, analogous to the bracketed textual redactions
in the reports.

(Rev. 08-28-2000)

To: New York From: Counterterrorism
Re: 199N-NY-NEW 08/28/2001

FEDERAL BUREAU OF INVESTIGATION

Furthering that suspicion is a potential
association between Al-Midher and USS Cole suspects, Fahd Al-Quso
and Ibrahim Nibras. During his interview by FBI agents in Yemen,
Al-Quso originally told interviewers that on approximately
January 6, 2000, he and Nibras traveled on a Gulf Air flight from
Yemen to Kuala Lumpur via Dubai, UAE.
Al-Quso and Nibras ultimate destination was
to be Bangkok, where he and Nibras would pass Khallad Bin Attash,
the suspected financier of the Cole operation, $36,000 (US) which
had been sent to Khallad from his parents. Al -Quso later
retracted that statement and claimed he and Nibras traveled from
Yemen to Bangkok where Thai authorities refused to allow the two
to travel onward to Singapore because they did not possess the
proper travel documents. Thus the money was passed to Khallad in
Bangkok. Investigation of the USS Cole attack to date has not
developed evidence to support either version of Al-Quso's story.

Of further interest is the fact that

According to Al-Quso,
Nibras contacted his home where he left a message for Khallad as
to where they could be reached when the two were not able to make
their final travel destination.

Based on the above, FBIHQ suggests FBINY review
this matter and consider opening a full field intelligence
investigation to determine if Al-Mihdhar is still in the United
States. Al-Mihdhar's confirmed association with a
facility which provides support for terrorist operations and
potential association with two individuals who were involved in
the attack on the USS Cole make him a risk to the national
security of the United States. The goal of the investigation is
to locate Al-Mihdhar, determine his contacts and reasons for
being in the United States, and potentially conduct an interview
of him. FBIHQ has already requested Department of State to
provide the visa applications filed by both Al -Mihdhar and
Al-Hazmi.

NA-88-1655

SECRET

NA-1655

>From   Tue Aug 28 15:48:12 2001
Subject: RESPONSE TO FBI Sanitization Request
To:
Cc:

Your request on behalf of Dina Corsi to share sanitized information on Khalid M al-Midhar with FBI investigators in the New York office has been approved as proposed.

The tracking number for this request is NSA ORCON

Cheers,

... a suspected Islamic extremist known as Khalid al-Midhar   was planning to travel to Malaysia with an associate, identified only as Nawaf. Al-Midhar made the arrangements

Al-Midhar eventtually finalized plans to depart for Kuala Lumpur, Malaysia
Al-Midhar planned to meet Nawaf in Kuala Lumpur."

After arriving in Malaysia, al-Midhar was associated with   Nawaf, who had also arrive in Malaysia, was associated with

The   are critical in making the connection between the suspects and al-Midhar. FBI would appreciate priority handling on this request, since al-Midhar is already in the U.S.

Page 1

NA-1528

NA-88-1528

Prompt NSA approval of a request information about Almihdhar and Nawaf Alhazmi could be shared with FBI criminal investigators, noting that the FBI "would appreciate "priority handling" as Almihdhar was "already in the U.S." This contradicts the actual "routine" designation on Corsi's draft request that an investigation be opened. Perhaps the NSA detailee who sent Corsi's request had something to do with the change, but this is conjecture. In the event, the "routine" designation prevailed, with tragic consequences.

397

DINA CORSI - Fwd: Re: FFI request

Page 1

From: DINA CORSI
To: LIGUORI, JOHN
Date: Wed, Aug 29, 2001 7:39 AM
Subject: Fwd: Re: FFI request

John,
  I think I may have caused some unnecessary confusion with this issue. I sent the EC on Al-Midhar to Craig via email marking it as a DRAFT so that he could read it before he went on vacation. There is material in the EC from ▆▆ which had not yet been approved and which is not cleared for criminal investigators. I should have been more specific in the email. My fault.
  Steve called and Rod and I spoke with him and tried to explain why this case had to stay on the Intel. side of the house. I had a very brief follow-up conversation with Jack about the case as well. In order to be confident that we were providing the proper recommendation for this case to be a 199, and to answer some questions that Steve had, Rod and I spoke with the National Security Law Unit (NSLU) yesterday afternoon. I will pass the information on to Steve and Jack as well. The opinion is as follows:

  Al-Midhar can be opened directly as a FFI. I have finalized the EC with the ▆▆ info. properly marked and I will forward it to Rob Fuller as soon as it is signed out. The EC is still not cleared for criminal investigators.
  Per NSLU, if Al-Midhar is located the interview must be conducted by an intel agent. A criminal agent CAN NOT be present at the interview. This case, in its entirety, is based on intel. If at such time as information is developed indicating the existence of a substantial federal crime, that information will be passed over the wall according to the proper procedures and turned over for follow-up criminal investigation.
  I have the I-94 forms and have requested the visa applications which I will forward to Rob when I get them. Once the case is opened, Rob is free to initiate all possible and appropriate efforts to locate the individual and make any arrangements necessary to receive notification should he attempt to leave the country.
  Rob can call me with any questions about the origins of the case or for additional information. Again, I apologize for any confusion.

                    Dina 3/2808

CC: Middleton, Rodney

M-HQI-88000458

Declassified by: UC, CTLU1, OGC, FBI
on: 02/17/2006

NA-1664

Dina Corsi's August 29, 2001 description of what the FBI's National Security Law Unit had told her regarding passage of the Almihdhar information to intelligence agents only, along with her apologies for any "confusion" she may have caused.

UNITED STATES v. ZACARIAS MOUSSAOUI (NO. 01-455)
SUBSTITUTION FOR THE TESTIMONY OF
"JOHN"

If called to testify, this witness would say the following:

"John" is a former Deputy Chief of the Usama Bin Laden Unit at the CIA. In May 2001, John was "detailed" to FBI Headquarters in the International Terrorism Operations Section (ITOS). (A detailee is an employee from one organization who is loaned to another.) In that capacity, John acted as the CIA's chief intelligence representative to ITOS Section Chief Michael Rolince. John's primary role at the FBI was to assist the FBI in exploiting information for intelligence purposes.

Khalid al-Mihdhar and Nawaf al-Hazmi

Shortly before assuming his duties at the FBI, John asked management in the CIA's Counterterrorism Center (CTC) to assign a CTC desk officer with "getting up to speed" on the early 2000 meetings in Kuala Lumpur, Malaysia and determining any potential connections between those meetings and the October 2000 terrorist attack on the U.S.S. Cole. This assignment was given to "Mary," who was an FBI detailee in the CIA's CTC.

After joining ITOS in May 2001, John had continuing concerns about the early 2000 meetings in Kuala Lumpur, especially whether they had any nexus to the attack on the Cole. On May 15, 2001, John reminded several of his CTC colleagues that after the Malaysia meetings, Khalid al-Mihdhar had traveled with Nawaf al-Hazmi and another person who he (John) believed were couriers that had traveled between Malaysia, Bangkok, Los Angeles, and Hong Kong.

Around this same time in May, John began inquiring about the Malaysia meetings with a CIA analyst in the CTC named "Peter." John knew that Peter had been "down in the weeds" and knew the "nuts and bolts" of the Cole investigation because Peter has been assigned to prepare a CTC report on who was responsible for the Cole attack.

Page 1 of 4

DEFENDANT'S EXHIBIT
U.S. v. Moussaoui
Cr. No. 01-455-A

Tom Wilshire's "Substitution for Testimony" at the Zacarias Moussaoui trial, with attached e-mails.

John and Peter discussed the Malaysia meetings, and Peter provided John with a copy of the timeline of events related to the Cole investigation that Peter had compiled as part of his work on the Cole attack. In an e-mail to Peter in mid-May 2001, which was copied to "Mary," John noted that he (John) was interested because Mihdhar was traveling with two "companions" who had left Malaysia and gone to Bangkok, Los Angeles, and Hong Kong and "also were couriers of a sort." John noted in the e-mail that "something bad was definitely up." Peter replied in an e-mail dated May 18, 2001, "My head is spinning over this East Asia travel. Do you know if anyone in [the CIA's Bin Laden Unit] or FBI mapped this?"

At some point before the end of May 2001, John discussed with Dina Corsi, who was an Intelligence Operations Specialist in the FBI's Usama Bin Laden Unit, the East Asian travel of some UBL operatives in January 2000. John also began looking in CIA records for the surveillance photographs taken of the meetings in Kuala Lumpur, Malaysia in January 2000. John obtained three of the photographs, which included Mihdhar. At that time, John thought he recalled hearing that an identification of Khallad in the photographs had been made.

At some point before the end of May 2001, John gave to Corsi the three Malaysia meeting photographs. He does not recall ever discussing with Corsi, or anyone else at the FBI, his recollection that Khallad had been identified in the photographs. John believed that since the photographs had been given to Corsi, they could be further distributed within the FBI.

On July 13, 2001, John wrote another e-mail to CTC managers stating that he had discovered a CIA cable stating that a joint CIA-FBI source had, in early January 2001, identified Khallad in the Kuala Lumpur surveillance photographs with a high degree of certainty. John began the e-mail by announcing "OK. This is important." He then described Khallad as a "major league killer who orchestrated the Cole attack and possibly the Africa bombings." The e-mail recommended revisiting the Malaysia meetings, especially in relation to any potential information on Khallad. John ended the e-mail asking, "can this [information] be sent via [Central Intelligence Report] to [the FBI]?"

Page 2 of 4

John received a responsive e-mail dated July 13, 2001 from a CTC Bin Laden Unit supervisor. That e-mail stated that "Mary" had been assigned to handle the request for additional information on the Malaysia meetings.

On July 23, 2001, having seen no action, John e-mailed a CTC manager inquiring as to the status of his request to pass information to the FBI. In the e-mail, John noted that, "When the next big op is carried out by UBL hardcore cadre, Khalad will be at or near the top of the command food chain--and probably nowhere near either the attack site or Afghanistan. That makes people who are available and who have direct access to him of very high interest. Khalid Midhar [sic] should be [of] very high interest anyway, given his connection to the [redacted]."

On August 22, 2001, John met with Corsi and Mary in his office at FBI Headquarters. They discussed Corsi and Mary's discovery that Mihdhar recently had entered the United States and that there was no record of his departure. All of them agreed that it was important to initiate an investigation to determine whether Mihdhar was still in the United States and locate him if he was.

Zacarias Moussaoui

On August 24, 2001, John e-mailed Michael Maltbie about the Moussaoui case. Maltbie was a Supervisory Special Agent in the Radical Fundamentalist Unit (RFU) in ITOS. Maltbie was working on the request from the Minneapolis Field Office of the FBI for a Foreign Intelligence Surveillance Act (FISA) warrant to search Moussaoui's property. Copied on this e-mail were two others in the RFU who also were working on the Moussaoui case, David Frasca, the Chief of the RFU, and Rita Flack, an Intelligence Operations Specialist in the RFU. In the e-mail, John asked Maltbie for an update on the Moussaoui case. Maltbie responded in an e-mail the same day, stating, among other things, that "Photos of [Moussaoui and Hussein al-Attas] were . . . forwarded to [Charles] Frahm this afternoon." (Frahm was the FBI's detailee at the CIA.) Maltbie concluded by stating, "Please bear in mind that there is no indication that either of these two [Moussaoui and Hussein al-Attas] had plans for nefarious activity, as was apparently indicated in an earlier communication." A copy

Page 3 of 4

of these two e-mails is attached as Defendant's Exhibit 639.

Agreed: _____ _____
              Counsel for Mr. Moussaoui   Counsel for the United States

Date: March 11, 2006

Documents

RITA FLACK - Re: request for update

DEFENDANT'S
EXHIBIT
639
U.S. v. Moussaoui
Cr. No. 01-455-A

From: Michael Maltble
To:
Date: Fri, Aug 24, 2001 5:29 PM
Subject: Re: request for update

███ Legats London and Paris were furnished photos and bio info on Moussaoui earlier this week. These were shared w ██████████████ and both were asked to attempt to i.d. and determine background on the guy.

██████████ pocket litter of Moussaoui and al-Attas were sent to C Frahm today w/ req to pass to ███████████ Photos of these two were also forwarded to Frahm this afternoon. We'll pass along add'l info when/if we obtain it.

Please bear in mind that there is <u>no</u> indication that either of these two had plans for nefarious activity, as was apparently indicated in an earlier communication.

Mike Maltble, 3-2106

>>> ████████ 08/24 7:19 AM >>>
Dave, Please advise when you get a chance this AM where we are re the Minneapolis Airplane IV crowd. Has the tasking gone out to try and obtain more bio info on the guys, ████████████████ Do we have photos yet? Can the agency get the photos so they can get them on the wire to assets?

Thanks

CC: David Frasca, RITA FLACK

M-MP1-88800414

M-MP1-90000414

M-MP1-88880414

Declassified by:
UC, CTLU1, OC, FBI
On: 03/03/2006

403

Bibliography

9/11 Commission. *The 9/11 Commission Report: Final Report of the National Commission on Terrorist Attacks upon the United States.* New York: W.W. Norton, 2004. [*9/11 CR*]

Atwan, Abdel Bari. *The Secret History of al-Qaeda.* London: Saqi Books, 2006.

Baer, Robert. *See No Evil.* London: Arrow Books, 2002.

Bamford, James. *Body of Secrets: How America's NSA and Britain's GCHQ Eavesdrop on the World.* London: Arrow Books, 2002.

Bamford, James. *A Pretext for War: 9/11, Iraq, and the Abuse of America's Intelligence Agencies.* New York: Anchor Books, 2005. [Bamford 2005]

Bamford, James. *The Shadow Factory: The Ultra-Secret NSA from 9/11 to the Eavesdropping on America.* New York: Doubleday, 2008. [Bamford 2008]

Bergen, Peter. *Holy War Inc.: Inside the Secret World of Osama bin Laden.* London: Phoenix, 2002.

Berntsen, Gary and Ralph Pezzullo. *Jawbreaker: The Attack on Bin Laden and Al-Qaeda: A Personal Account by the CIA's Key Field Commander.* New York: Three Rivers, 2005.

Burke, Jason. *Al-Qaeda: The True Story of Radical Islam.* London: Penguin, 2004.

Clarke, Richard A. *Against all Enemies: Inside America's War on Terror.* London: Free Press, 2004.

Coll, Steve. *Ghost Wars: The Secret History of the CIA, Afghanistan, and bin Laden, from the Soviet Invasion to September 10, 2001.* London: Penguin, 2004.

Coll, Steve. *The Bin Ladens: The Story of a Family and its Fortune.* London: Allen Lane, 2008.

Corbin, Jane. *The Base: Al-Qaeda and the Changing Face of Global Terror.* London: Pocket Books, 2003.

Crile, George. *Charlie Wilson's War: The Extraordinary Story of How the Wildest Man in Congress and a Rogue CIA Agent Changed the History of Our Times.* New York: Grove, 2003.

Farmer, John. *The Ground Truth: The Untold Story of America under Attack on 9/11.* New York: Riverhead Books, 2009.

Fouda, Yosri and Nick Fielding. *Masterminds of Terror: The Truth Behind the Most Devastating Terrorist Attack the World Has Ever Seen.* Edinburgh: Mainstream, 2003.

Fury, Dalton. *Kill Bin Laden: A Delta Force Commander's Account of the Hunt for the World's Most Wanted Man.* New York: St. Martin's Griffin, 2008.

Gaffney, Mark H. *The 9/11 Mystery Plane and the Vanishing of America*. Walterville, Oregon: TrineDay, 2008.

Graham, Bob with Jeff Nussbaum. *Intelligence Matters: The CIA, the FBI, Saudi Arabia, and the Failure of America's War on Terror*. New York: Random House, 2004.

Joint Inquiry Into Intelligence Community Activities Before And After The Terrorist Attacks Of September 11, 2001. *Report Of The Joint Inquiry Into The Terrorist Attacks Of September 11, 2001 – By The House Permanent Select Committee On Intelligence And The Senate Select Committee On Intelligence*. December 2002. [9/11 Congressional Inquiry report]

Kean, Thomas H. and Lee H. Hamilton, *Without Precedent: The Inside Story of the 9/11 Commission*. New York: Alfred A. Knopf, 2006.

Lance, Peter. *1,000 Years for Revenge: International Terrorism and the FBI*. New York: Regan, 2003.

Lance, Peter. *Cover-up: What the Government Is Still Hiding about the War on Terror*. New York: Regan, 2004.

Lance, Peter. *Triple Cross: How bin Laden's Master Spy Penetrated the CIA, the Green Berets, and the FBI—and Why Patrick Fitzgerald Failed to Stop Him*. New York: Regan, 2006.

Levy, Adrian and Catherine Scott-Clark. *Deception: Pakistan, the United States and the Global Nuclear Weapons Conspiracy*. London: Atlantic Books, 2006.

Mayer, Jane. *The Dark Side: The Inside Story of How the War on Terror Turned into a War on American Ideals*. New York: Doubleday, 2008.

McDermott, Terry. *Perfect Soldiers: The 9/11 Hijackers, Who They Were, Why They Did It*. London: Pontico's, 2005.

Miles, Hugh. *Al Jazeera: How Arab TV News Challenged the World*. London: Abacus, 2005.

Miller, John and Michael Stone with Chris Mitchell. *The Cell: Inside the 9/11 Plot and Why the FBI and CIA Failed to Stop It*. New York: Hyperion, 2003

O'Neill, Sean and Daniel McGrory. *The Suicide Factory: Abu Hamza and the Finsbury Park Mosque*. London: Harper Perennial, 2006.

Reeve, Simon. *The New Jackals: Ramzi Yousef, Osama bin Laden and the Future of Terrorism*. London: André Deutsch, 1999.

Risen, James. *State of War: The Secret History of the CIA and the Bush Administration*. New York: Free Press, 2006

Schroen, Gary. *First In: An Insider's Account of How the CIA Spearheaded the War on Terror in Afghanistan*. New York: Ballantine, 2005.

Scott, Peter Dale. *The Road to 9/11: Wealth, Empire, and the Future of America*. Berkeley: University of California Press, 2007.

Shenon, Philip. *The Commission: The Uncensored History of the 9/11 Investigation*. New York: Twelve, 2008.

Suskind, Ron. *The Price of Loyalty*. London: Free Press, 2004.

Suskind, Ron. *The One Percent Doctrine: Deep Inside America's Pursuit of its Enemies Since 9/11*. London: Simon & Schuster, 2006.

Suskind, Ron. *The Way of the World: A Story of Truth and Hope in an Age of Extremism*. London: Simon & Schuster, 2008.

Tenet, George. *At the Center of the Storm: My Years at the CIA*. New York: HarperCollins, 2007. [Tenet 2007]

Thompson, Paul. *The Terror Timeline: Year by Year, Day by Day, Minute by Minute*. New York: Regan, 2004.

Trento, Joseph J. *Prelude to Terror: Edwin P. Wilson and the Legacy of America's Private Intelligence Network*. New York: Carroll & Graf, 2005.

Trento, Susan B. and Joseph J. Trento. *Unsafe at Any Altitude: Failed Terrorism Investigations, Scapegoating 9/11, and the Shocking Truth about Aviation Security Today*. Hanover, New Hampshire: Steerforth, 2006.

US Department of Justice, Office of the Inspector General. *A Review of the FBI's Handling of Intelligence Information Related to the September 11 Attacks*. November 2004.

Waugh, Billy and Tim Keown. *Hunting the Jackal: A Special Forces and CIA Soldier's Fifty Years on the Frontlines of the War Against Terrorism*. New York: Avon Books, 2004.

Weiner, Tim. *Legacy of Ashes: The History of the CIA*. London: Penguin, 2007.

Woodward, Bob. *Plan of Attack: The Definitive Account of the Decision to Invade Iraq*. New York: Simon & Schuster, 2004.

Woodward, Bob. *State of Denial*. London: Pocket Books, 2006.

Wright, Lawrence. *The Looming Tower: Al-Qaeda's Road to 9/11*. London: Allen Lane, 2006. [Wright 2006]

Zegart, Amy B. *Spying Blind: The CIA, the FBI, and the Origins of 9/11*. Princeton, New Jersey: Princeton University Press, 2007.

Index

Symbols

9/11 Commission x, 2, 4, 11-12, 25, 30-33, 40-45, 49, 59, 62, 65, 71-81, 84-86, 90-91, 94-95, 98-99, 108, 116, 118, 122-26, 129, 132-34, 139, 141, 143, 146-47, 154, 156-58-167, 170, 173, 177, 180, 187, 189-90, 194-95, 197-200, 202, 209, 211, 226-227, 230, 232-33, 238, 249-53, 262, 269, 272, 277-79, 285, 300-02, 305-06, 310, 315-16, 318, 321-323, 327-31, 334, 339, 343-49, 358-67, 371, 377, 390

9/11 Commission Report, The (9/11 CR) x, 2, 4, 17, 25, 30, 31, 37, 41, 44-49, 62-63, 71-72, 79-81, 84-85, 90-91, 95, 97-98, 108, 122, 125-126, 132-33, 140, 142, 156, 158, 160, 163, 165-67, 170, 177-79, 187-88, 190-91, 197-99, 209-11, 225-227, 230, 232, 234, 238, 244, 249, 251-253, 261-62, 268-69, 272, 275, 277-79, 285, 298, 300-02, 308-10, 312, 314-15, 318, 320-324, 326, 328-29, 335, 340, 345-47, 350, 359, 361-62, 382, 390

9/11 Congressional Inquiry (Joint Inquiry) ix-x, 2, 4, 22-23, 25, 29, 37-38, 46, 53, 59, 61, 82-84, 86, 90-91, 95, 115, 119-20, 122-23, 129, 132, 139, 141-43, 147, 149-50, 154, 156-57, 161-63, 171-72, 177, 179, 187, 197, 205-09, 230-31, 236-37, 248, 277-79, 301-02, 309, 324-25, 334, 339, 342-43, 357-58, 364, 381-82, 390

9/11 Congressional Inquiry report x, 2, 22-25, 29, 37, 46, 59, 83, 90-91, 95, 115, 123, 129, 139, 141-43, 147, 150, 154, 156-57, 171-72, 177, 179, 187, 197, 277, 302, 309, 334, 337, 359-62, 382, 390

9/11 Mystery Plane and the Vanishing of America, The 167

1993 World Trade Center bombing 86, 17, 30, 33, 86.171, 217-18, 356

A

Abdul-Rahman, Sheikh Omar ("Blind Sheikh") 33-34, 139, 169-73, 217-18

Able Danger 102, 168-73, 384

Abouhalima, Mahmud 218

African embassy bombings 9-10, 13-16, 18-21, 25, 28-29, 43, 48, 61, 87, 93, 124, 146-47, 155, 159, 166, 180, 182-83, 185-86, 191-92, 211, 214, 218-19, 261, 263, 268, 274, 359-60, 364, 368, 395

Airplane 297

Airplane II 297

"Airplane IV" 297-98

Ajaj, Ahmad 30

Alanssi, Mohamed 353-55

al-Bayoumi, Omar 102, 171

Albion, Alexis 78, 80, 125

Alec Station (CIA bin Laden Unit) 1, 2-3, 7-12, 19, 37-39, 40, 43-44, 51, 52, 63, 67-69, 74, 80-81, 83, 96-99, 106-07, 110, 119-20, 127, 135-36, 143, 145-48, 168, 197-98, 203-04, 208, 211, 225, 228, 230, 238-39, 241, 251, 265, 269, 271, 273, 283, 287, 311-12, 327, 334-36, 360-61, 371, 373-76, 378-79, 389-90

al-Gama'a al-Islamiyya 33

Alghamdi, Ahmed 6, 32, 128-29, 131-34, 315

Alghamdi, Hamza 6, 133, 292

Alghamdi, Saeed 6, 32, 133

al-Hada, Ahmed 7-10, 13-15, 17-22, 26-27, 139, 142, 148, 159, 177, 180-82, 188, 192, 214-17, 219-20, 222, 261-64, 274 al-Hada, Hoda 20, 140-142, 158-160, 177

al-Hada, Samir 20-21, 181, 263

al-Hawsawi, Mustafa 292

Alhazmi, Nawaf 1, 3, 6, 19, 22-25, 28-30, 32, 37-38, 41-42, 45, 47, 54, 60, 67, 69, 71, 73, 80, 82, 84-85, 89-95, 99, 102, 104, 107, 112, 115-21, 123, 127-29, 131-35, 139-40, 142-44, 150, 156-57, 159, 165, 168, 170, 172, 177, 180, 187-88, 193-94, 196-97, 201-05, 207-08, 210-12, 226-28, 230, 232, 234-35, 237-41, 243-44, 246, 247, 249, 252-254, 252-56, 261-62, 265-70, 275-76, 280, 282-83, 287-88, 292, 302, 304, 307-08, 310-14, 325, 330, 335, 341-42, 344-52, 356, 361, 363-65, 371-76, 378, 380, 383-90

Alhazmi, Salem 6, 30-32, 37, 89, 91, 128, 131-34, 156-57, 177, 314

Alhaznawi, Ahmed 6, 31-32, 133, 292

al-Iryani, Abd al-Karim 186

al Kahtani, Mohamed 237-38

al-Libi, Ibn Shaikh 110-12, 114, 362-63, 381

Almihdhar, Khalid 1, 3, 6-7, 9-10, 19-30, 32, 37-38, 41-43, 45-63, 67, 69, 71, 73, 81-82, 98, 83-84, 89-93, 95, 97-99, 102, 104, 107, 112-13, 115-23, 127-29, 131-36, 139-42, 144-45, 148, 150-52, 154, 156-60, 162, 166, 168, 170, 172, 177-80, 182, 186-89, 191-94, 196-97, 201-05, 207-08, 210-12, 220, 226-32, 234-35, 237-43, 245-47, 249, 252-56, 259, 261-63, 265-69, 271, 273-76, 278-83, 286-89, 292, 302, 304, 307-08, 310-19, 322-35, 338-39, 341-53, 356, 361, 363-65, 371-80, 383-90

al-Moayad, Mohammed Ali Hassan 355

Alnami, Ahmed 6, 31-32, 133

al-Nashiri, Abd al-Rahim (Bilal) 13, 20, 84, 87, 89-90, 128, 182, 187-88, 191, 193, 214, 284

al-Noor, Waleed 172

Alomari, Abdulaziz 6, 32, 128, 131-34, 172, 314

al-Owhali, Mohamed 7-8, 13-17, 19, 87, 182, 211, 214-17, 219-20, 364

al-Qaeda 2, 7, 10, 12-13, 16-20, 22, 24, 26-30, 37-40, 42-43, 46-48, 50, 56, 58, 60, 64-65, 71, 73, 82-84, 87, 89-90, 92-95, 100, 106-107, 111, 114, 116-17, 119, 121, 135, 139-40, 142-44, 146-47, 153, 155, 157-58, 163-66, 168-69, 171, 177-78, 180-81, 183, 186-88, 190-93, 195-96, 199, 201-04, 208, 211-15, 217, 218-22, 225-28, 232, 243-44, 249, 256, 259-62, 265-69, 272, 274-76, 282-84, 286-87, 292, 308, 310, 312, 315, 322, 324-26, 330, 332-34, 342 354, 356, 358-62, 365-7, 372-8, 383, 385, 387-92

al-Quso, Fahad 89, 93, 97, 188, 193-96, 201-02, 226, 243-48, 268, 281

"Al S." (see Soufan, Ali)

Al Saud, Bandar bin Sultan bin Abdul-Aziz 28-29

Al Saud, Turki bin Faisal 28-29, 388, 391

Alshehhi, Marwan 6, 89, 102, 117, 131, 168, 171-72, 291-92, 384

Alshehri, Mohand 6, 133

Alshehri, Wail 6, 32, 133

Alshehri, Waleed 6, 32, 292

al-Shibh, Ramzi bin 89, 91-93, 117, 140, 188, 238-39, 292, 360-61, 385

al Suqami, Satam 6, 292, 314

al Taizi, Abu Bara 82

al-Thawar, Ibrahim 97, 187-88, 193, 195, 202, 268

al-Thumairy, Fahad 102

al-Owhali, Mohamed (Azzam) 7, 8, 20, 220

al-Zawahiri, Ayman 284, 356, 362

American Foreign Service Association 32, 196

Anderson, Thad 127

Anticev, John 17

Ashcroft, John 195

Atef, Mohammed 357, 363

Atta, Mohamed 6, 89, 102, 131-32, 134, 168-73, 238-39, 241, 291-92, 315-6, 360-61, 384
At the Center of the Storm 49, 52, 87
Avrakotos, Gust 102-103
Ayyad, Nidal 218

B

Badeeb, Saeed 28-29
Bafana, Faiz abu Baker 40-41
Baker, Stewart 162
Bamford, James 8, 10-11, 14-15, 29-30, 38-39, 42-43, 49, 53-54, 66, 91, 98-99, 107, 140-141, 152-53, 185, 219, 239, 323
Bangkok station (CIA) 98-99, 115-18, 211, 307, 373
Banihammad, Fayez Ahmed 6, 133, 292
Bank of Credit and Commerce International 101
Bashir, Abu Bakar 88
Basnan, Osama 102, 171
Beghal, Djamel 17, 262
Berger, Sandy 38, 83, 124, 372
Berntsen, Gary 16, 49, 108-09, 362
bin Abdul-Aziz, Nayef 87
bin Attash, Khallad 13, 15, 20, 24-25, 27, 37, 41, 46-47, 82, 84-85, 89-90, 93-95, 97, 115, 117-118, 128, 140, 156-57, 160, 178, 181, 187-89, 191, 193, 195, 197-99, 201-12, 226, 235-37, 240, 243-47, 252, 265-66, 268-70, 272, 274, 276-77, 283, 308-09, 311-12, 315, 321, 325, 330, 333, 337-40, 353, 372-74, 378, 384-85, 391
bin Laden, Osama 7-10, 14-15, 19, 43, 48, 50, 90, 108-10, 116, 124-25, 128-29, 134, 142, 144, 160, 164-65, 180-82, 188, 190-91, 196, 210-11, 217-22, 238, 274, 284, 290, 293-94, 316, 333, 357-60, 362, 364, 372, 375, 387-89, 391
Black, Cofer 49, 69, 83, 97, 104-05, 109, 119, 205-06, 283-85, 326, 375, 379-81

black sites 110, 112, 166, 381
Blackwater USA (Xe) 69, 380
Blair, Tony 20-21, 186
Blee, David 49, 104
Blee, Richard (also "Rich," "Richard," and "Rich B.") 44, 49, 69-70, 78, 97-99, 104-12, 119, 126-27, 131, 135-36, 148, 204, 231, 236, 240-41, 267, 269, 273, 277-78, 283-88, 310, 326, 335, 359, 363, 373, 377-83
"Blind Sheikh" (see Abdul-Rahman, Sheikh Omar)
"Bob" 55-57, 235
Bodine, Barbara 196
Bojinka plot 7, 41, 84-86, 88, 90, 357-58, 362
Bongardt, Steve ("Steve B") 60, 78, 112, 197, 199, 206-207, 248-51, 254, 256-58, 307, 311, 314-17, 319-23, 326-28, 330, 334, 336, 339, 341, 351, 353, 372, 377, 378, 390
Bowman, Marion "Spike" 78
Bureau of Diplomatic Security (State Department) 342-43
Burke, Jason 220-221
Burr, Richard ix, 61, 206, 208, 230
Bush, George W. x, 1, 80, 111, 124-25, 139-40, 143, 150, 305-06, 365-67, 370, 372
Bush-Gore election 190

C

Cambone, Stephen 127, 130, 135, 176, 374
Caine Mutiny, The 107
Canada 24
Carey, David 68
Casey, William 100-01
Central Intelligence Agency (CIA) 1-2, 4, 9-12, 16-19, 23-24, 26-29, 31, 33-34, 37-39, 41-47, 49-60, 62-65, 67-73, 76-126, 129-30, 135, 139, 143, 146-48, 151, 155, 157, 160, 163-64, 166, 168, 171, 173, 178, 188, 190, 192, 194-99, 201-

12, 221-22, 225-27, 230-37, 239-47, 251-55, 265-66, 269-73, 275-79, 281-85, 290, 292, 296, 298, 300-12, 318, 333-40, 347, 357-65, 371-75, 377, 379, 380-85, 387-91

CENTCOM 109

"C" formation battle 8, 177, 214, 215

Chechen mujaheddin 294, 296

Chechnya 40, 290

Cheney, Dick 113, 365-67

ChoicePoint database 345-50, 352

"Chris" 78, 201, 203-06, 208, 373

Church Committee 99, 100

CIA inspector general 2, 4, 51, 55, 59, 62, 67-70, 116, 121-22, 146-47, 382

Clarke, Richard 49, 260, 262, 283, 285-287, 312

Clinton, Bill 9, 80, 110-11, 124-25, 142, 190

Cloonan, Jack 42-43, 83, 110-11, 119, 302, 316

Cole (see USS Cole)

Coleman, Dan 143-144, 151

Coll, Steve 49, 106, 108

Commission: The Uncensored History of the 9/11 Investigation, The 80, 86, 123, 163, 300

Congressional Quarterly 44, 64-66, 79

Copeland, Miles 100

Corsi, Dina (also "Donna" and "Jane") 78-79, 198-99, 237, 242, 244-45, 248-54, 256-58, 270, 276, 278-80, 307-27, 329-43, 350-51, 353, 364, 372-74, 377-78, 385-86 390-91, 394, 398

Counterterrorism Division (FBI) 122, 195

Counterterrorist Center (CTC)[CIA] 9, 12, 38, 45-46, 51-52, 56, 59-60, 64-65, 67-69, 83, 97, 104, 107-09, 122-23, 146-47, 204-06, 232-34, 236, 239-40, 266, 269-70, 281, 283-84, 287, 302, 337-338, 358, 360, 363, 377

Counterterrorism Security Group 262, 313

Crowley, Robert 100

D

"Dadang" 42

Dailey, Dell 109

Dar al Hijra mosque (Virginia) 172

Dark Side, The 38, 43, 83, 90, 114, 380

Day of Terror plot 33, 169, 172, 217

Dime Savings Bank 133

Directorate of Operations (CIA) 45, 147

Director of Central Intelligence (DCI) 68, 108, 125, 224, 301

domestic no-fly list 313

"Donna" (see Corsi, Dina)

Downing, Jack 68

Dubai 17, 42, 262, 319

"Dwight" (see Miller, Doug)

E

E-4B 166-67

EATSCO 101

Echelon 91

el-Atriss, Mohammed 172

El-Hage, Wadih 48

El-Shukrijumah, Adnan 171-173

El-Shukrijumah, Gulshair 171-73

Engelberg, Stephen 260-61

"enhanced" techniques 110, 117

F

Farmer, John 166, 167

Federal Aviation Administration 313

Federal Bureau of Investigation (FBI) 1, 8-9, 13, 15-17, 21, 24, 30, 37-39, 41-46, 48-65,-74, 76-78, 83-85, 87-88, 90, 92, 95-96, 98, 104-05, 107, 110-12, 114-15, 118-23, 125-36, 140, 143-45, 148-53, 155, 157, 159-63, 166, 168, 171-73, 179-82, 187, 190, 192-99, 201-06, 208-14, 220-21, 224-37, 239, 24-48, 250-54, 257-58, 263, 265-7, 269, 270-79, 28-84, 287, 289, 292-304, 307-57, 360-63, 371-79, 383-85, 387-91, 394-97

Fenner, Lorry 11-12, 76, 163-65

Financial Crimes Enforcement Network 312

Financial Review Group 312

Fincher, Russell 78, 110-112, 248-49, 363

First Union National Bank 133

FISA (Foreign Intelligence Surveillance Act) 144, 149-50, 161-62, 292-96, 298, 303, 318-21, 325-26, 329-30, 333-34

"Five Eyes" 24

Flack, Rita 293-300, 302, 373

Flight 11 (American Airlines) 128, 132, 133, 314

Flight 77 (American Airlines) 7, 128, 131, 133-34, 176, 181, 314, 352, 374

Flight 93 (American Airlines) 132-33, 361

Flight 175 (United Airlines) 131, 133, 314

Fouda, Yosri 117, 238

Frasca, Dave 293-304, 373

Freedom of Information Act (FOIA) 127, 159, 176, 349

Freeh, Louis 180, 195, 197

Frontline (PBS) 196

Fuller, Robert (also "Richard") 78, 341-55, 378, 386, 390

G

Gaffney, Mark 167

Gaudin, Stephen 214-16, 364

General Intelligence Directorate (GID) [Saudi Arabia] 28-29, 81, 386-90

Gillespie, Margaret (also "Mary") 54, 62-63, 78, 230-38, 240-41, 243, 245, 248-49, 254, 257, 269, 271, 273, 276, 279-80, 307-08, 310-13, 323-24, 326, 373, 377, 385, 390-91

Global Objectives 134

Gordon, John 12

Gore, Al 87, 190

Goss, Porter ix-x, 68, 69, 70

Government Communications Headquarters (GCHQ) [UK] 18, 24

Graham, Bob ix, 45, 84

Graham, Mary Margaret 240

Grewe, Barbara 65, 71-79, 157-58, 198-99, 209, 227, 230, 249, 252-53, 268, 279, 315, 328-29, 349, 358

Ground Truth, The 166-67

Guantanamo 1, 354-55

Gunaratna, Rohan 84-85, 92

H

Hadley, Stephen 170, 285

Hambali (see Isamuddin, Riduan)

Hamdan, Salim 354-56

Hamilton, Lee x, 25, 74, 80, 86, 405

Hanjour, Hani 6, 32, 115, 127-28, 131-34, 172, 292, 314

Harper's 49, 107

Hasbi, Fauzi 41, 88

Hassaine, Reda 289

Hayden, Michael 149-53, 161-65, 183-85, 366-68

Hercules (CIA database) 234

Hezbollah 16, 164

Hill, Eleanor 53

Holy Capital (reference to Mecca in Saudi passports) 29, 30

House Intelligence Committee ix-x, 25, 156

Hudson United Bank 133

Hussain, Shahed 355

I

INS (Immigration and Naturalization Service) 98, 128, 227, 232, 235, 307, 318, 342-43, 353, 388, 390

Intelink database 234

International Terrorism Operations Section (ITOS) [FBI] 56, 225, 301, 304

Iran-Contra affair 100-01

Isamuddin, Riduan (Hambali) 41, 84-85, 87-89, 90, 92-93, 119

ISI security agency (Pakistan) 101-02

Islamiyya, Jemaah 33, 40-42, 84, 88

Israeli-Palestinian peace process 190

J

Jacobson, Mike 25, 77
"James" 55-58, 235-36, 311, 371, 383
Jandal, Abu 187, 188
"Jane" (see Corsi, Dina)
Jarrah, Ziad 6, 17, 89, 117, 131-32, 134, 290, 292, 361
"John" (see Wilshire, Tom)
Jones, Greg 295
July 13 email 236, 266-67, 270-73, 277, 279, 281
July 23 email 266-68, 271, 273-283, 288, 301, 304, 310, 313, 351, 374, 377
June 11 meeting 112, 236, 248-254, 256-58, 307, 309, 311, 315, 320, 330, 339, 353, 363, 372-74, 378

K

Kabul station (CIA) 108-11, 380-81
Kahane, Meir 356
Kaplan, David E. 17, 154, 162, 182, 262
"Kathy" 244-45, 308
Kean, Tom 25, 74-75, 86, 124
Kelley, David 248
Khadr, Omar 353-55
Khan, A.Q. 86, 101, 357
Khattab, Ibn 290
King Fahd mosque (Los Angeles) 172
Kleinberg, Mindy 371
Kolb, Larry 100
Konsonjaya 41
Krongard, A.B. "Buzzy" 68
KSM (see Mohammed, Khalid Shaikh)
Kuala Lumpur station (CIA) 94, 116

L

Landay, Jonathan 361
Land Information Warfare Unit 169
Lederman, Gordon 11, 12, 76
Lehman, John 349
Levin, Carl ix, 60, 120-21, 252-53
Linden, Sarah 72
Looming Tower, The 15, 42, 63, 196
Los Angeles Times 10, 42, 84, 92-93, 141, 219, 289

M

MacEachin, Doug 78, 164
Maitner, Jennifer 78
Malaysia summit 37-99, 118, 123, 177, 188, 194-97, 199, 201-08, 226-27, 230, 234-36, 243-45, 249, 256, 263, 266, 268-69, 271-72, 274-76, 279, 283, 290, 292, 307-09, 311, 315, 330, 337, 339, 356, 359, 372, 374, 383-84, 390-91
Maltbie, Michael 293-98, 300, 302, 373
Manson, Charles 106
map of al-Qaeda's global network [FBI] 17, 19, 155, 180
"Mary" (see Gillespie, Margaret)
"Max" (see "Michael D")
Maxwell, Kenneth 144
Mayer, Jane 38, 43, 83, 90, 114, 380
May, Ernest x, 166
McCarthy, Mary 283
McDermott, Terry 10, 15, 17, 42, 140, 189, 219
McLaughlin, John 190, 283, 300
McNamara, Barbara 11, 12
Mecca, Saudi Arabia 30, 110
MI5 289, 290
"Michael D" ("Max") 78, 198, 201, 204-05, 208-09
"Michelle" 37-39, 43-44, 46-55, 57-58, 62, 67, 71-72, 78-79, 81-90, 114, 120, 123, 197, 203, 228, 230-31, 235-36, 253, 269, 312, 331, 371, 373, 375, 380, 383
Middleton, Rodney ("Rob") 78, 280, 313, 316-17, 326-27, 330-31, 334, 337-40, 351
Millennium Plot 37, 46, 89, 127, 176, 324
Miller, Doug ("Dwight") 43, 44, 47, 48, 49, 50, 51, 52, 53, 55, 57, 58, 59, 60, 61, 62, 63, 64, 65, 66, 67, 71, 72, 76, 79, 81, 95, 129, 172, 182, 202, 228, 230, 231, 235, 236, 253, 259, 260, 261, 262, 273, 276, 277, 286, 301, 304, 311, 312, 371, 373, 374, 375, 379, 380, 383
Miller, Judy 259, 286

minders 74-76, 304
Minneapolis field office (FBI) 289, 291, 292, 295, 299
Mitchell, James 363
MITRE Corporation 79
Mohammed, Ali 48
Mohammed, Khalid Shaikh (KSM, aka al-Ballushi, Khalid al-Shaykh) 20, 41, 46, 68-69, 82-86, 88-91, 113, 117-19, 166, 178, 187-89, 211, 238-39, 290, 308, 357-65, 385
Moqed, Majed 6, 128-29, 131-34, 314, 347
Mossad 102
Moussaoui, Zacarias ("Sally") 1, 40, 62, 72, 76, 78-79, 95, 110, 224, 226, 282, 289-304, 306, 324-25, 361, 373, 385, 399
Mueller, Robert 111, 132, 179
Mukasey, Michael 217
"Mukhtar" (see Mohammed, Khalid Shaikh)
Myers, Lisa 218, 221

N

Nacchio, Joe 152
National Archives 49, 72, 78-79, 164-65, 199
National Security Council 114, 283
National Review 31, 218
National Security Agency (NSA) 2, 7-12, 14-15, 17-19, 22-29, 37-38, 42, 68-69, 71, 73, 76, 79, 91-92, 99, 122, 129, 139-40, 142-47, 149-58, 160-66, 168, 170, 177, 178-79, 182-85, 187-88, 190, 192, 194, 210, 221, 234, 239, 249-50, 252, 256-58, 260-62, 265, 284, 315, 318-22, 328, 330, 333-34, 351, 353, 360, 366-69, 372-73, 378, 383, 385, 389, 397-98
National Security Law Unit (FBI) 327, 333, 398
NCIC (National Crime Information Center) [FBI] 345-352
Newburgh Four 354, 356

Newsweek 9, 41, 85, 92, 93, 95, 107, 108, 114, 140, 173, 182, 222, 290, 313, 362
New York Daily News 20, 356
New Yorker, The 18, 64, 112-13, 141, 193, 195, 199, 226, 263, 316
New York Field Office (FBI) 205-06, 208, 248-258, 278, 310-322, 323-335, 341, 343-355
New York Observer 94, 95, 346-47
New York Times 17, 20-21, 30, 49, 53, 68, 74, 86, 104, 113, 121, 129, 169-70, 172, 186, 199, 221-22, 231, 259-261, 285, 366
Northern Alliance 7, 108, 381
Nosair, El Sayyid 356
NOVA (PBS) 10, 14, 37, 44, 45, 144, 185

O

Obaid, Nawaf 28, 29
Observer (UK) 16, 93-94, 220-21, 290
O'Connell, Jeff 68
Odeh, Mohammed Saddiq 16
Office of Intelligence Policy and Review (OIPR) [DOJ] 249-50, 296
Office of Strategic Services 104
"Omar" 201, 203-08, 235-36, 246, 265-66, 269-70, 276, 304, 308, 311, 337, 339, 372, 374, 378, 384
O'Neill, Joe 33
O'Neill, John 44, 95-96, 193, 196-97, 239-241, 313
Orion Scientific Systems 169

P

Parkinson, Larry 330
PATRIOT Act 349, 370
Pavitt, James 68
Payne, James F.X. 152
Pellegrino, Frank 113, 119, 357
Phoenix field office (FBI) 128, 302
Phoenix memo (FBI) 128, 294, 302, 316
Pickard, Thomas 195, 301, 303-04, 348
Powell, Colin 114
Presidential Daily Brief (PDB) 305-06

Q

Qwest 152, 153

R

Rabat mosque (San Diego) 172
Radical Fundamentalist Unit (RFU) [FBI] 56, 293-94, 296-98, 302
Rashid, Ahmed 101, 214
Red Book (CIA publication) 31
Reeve, Simon 16, 41, 357
Reid, Richard 110, 290
Renditions Branch [CIA] 69, 84, 359
Reno, Janet 317-18
Ressam, Ahmed 324
Rice, Condoleezza x, 80, 283, 285-88, 305, 326, 391
"Rich" (see Blee, Richard)
"Richard" (see Blee, Richard)
"Richard" (see Robert Fuller, 345)
"Rich B." (see Blee, Richard)
Rigler, Erik 279-80, 313, 350-51
Risen, James 49, 104, 111, 199, 389
"Rob" (see Middleton, Rodney)
Robustelli, Peter 344
Roemer, Tim ix-x, 25, 85, 156, 300, 305-06
Rolince, Michael 60, 225, 293, 298, 300-01, 303, 325
Rossini, Mark 37, 43-44, 46-52, 58, 63-66, 76, 79, 90, 144, 202, 228, 230-31, 235, 304, 311, 374, 378-79
Rumsfeld, Donald 109, 127

S

Sabol, Sherry ("Sherry S" and "Susan") 78, 143, 222, 327-33, 353, 372, 387
Salameh, Mohammed 218
Salvetti, Lloyd 164-65
Samit, Harry 293
Sánchez, Ilich Ramírez (Carlos the Jackal) 26
Saudi embassy (Washington, DC) 173
Scheid, Kevin 75-76, 78, 164-65
Scheuer, Michael 9-12, 18-19, 44, 81, 110, 147-48, 184, 359
Shackley, Ted 101
Shah, Wali Khan Amin 86, 357

Shaikh, Abdussattar 45, 115, 197, 385
Shakir, Ahmad Hikmat 82, 92, 94-95, 312
Shannon, Clark 78, 235, 236, 243-46, 248-49, 252-54, 257, 270, 280-81, 308, 373-74, 385
Shenon, Philip 65, 74, 76, 80, 86, 123-25, 163-5, 170, 285, 300, 306
Silverstein, Ken 49, 107
Smith, Derek 346-47
Smith, James D. 169
Soufan, Ali ("Al S.") 78, 112-13, 193-99, 201, 206, 208-209, 226, 239, 240, 248, 263, 266, 312, 339-40, 356, 362-64
Soviet-Afghan War 33-34, 101-102
Special Projects (9/11 Commission team) 76, 157
Sphinx Trading 172
State of Denial 285, 348
Steinger, Shayna 32, 196
Strategic Information Operations Center (SIOC) [FBI] 55-56
Sufaat, Yazid 82, 88, 93, 292
Sungkar, Abdullah 88
Sunni Extremist Group (CIA) 107, 108, 283
Survival, Evasion, Resistance and Escape (SERE) [DOD] 113-14
Suskind, Ron 91, 114, 143-44, 151-52,

T

Taliban 7, 101
Team 6 (9/11 Commission) 73-74, 76-77, 157-58
"Ted" 56-57, 235
Tenet, George 44, 49, 52-53, 68, 83, 87, 90, 104-05, 108, 119-26, 163, 190, 224, 231-232, 252-253, 283-86, 288, 300, 303-07, 326, 347, 363, 374, 378-79, 389, 391
Terrorist Travel report (9/11 Commission document) 30-33, 129, 132, 171, 173, 314, 343
The Sullivans (see USS The Sullivans)
Time magazine 42, 88, 132, 285
Trento, Joseph and Susan 33, 100-01, 143, 386-87, 390-91

U

UBL (see bin Laden, Osama)
USA ID card 132
US Consulate Jeddah, Saudi Arabia 32, 33, 170
US News and World Report 17, 154, 161, 162, 182, 262
US Department of Justice, inspector general 2, 4, 37, 44, 45, 50-51, 55-57, 59, 62-66, 72-73, 78-79, 90, 95, 178-179, 197-98, 200, 202-03, 209, 211, 225-26, 228, 233-36, 243-46, 249-54, 256, 258, 267-68, 270-71, 277, 279-82, 287, 293, 295, 303-04, 309-10, 314, 321-24, 326-27, 329-32, 335, 338-40, 342-43, 345-47, 349-52, 354, 375, 382, 390
US Department of State 18, 45, 69, 109, 219, 249, 312, 318, 342-43, 388
USS *Cole* 3, 14, 19-21, 26-27, 39, 78-79, 83-84, 89-90, 93, 95, 97, 112, 119, 127-28, 141-42, 148, 151, 153, 155, 159, 176, 178, 180-203, 205-10, 212, 222, 226, 228-29, 233, 237, 243-49, 251, 254-61, 263, 265-70, 272, 274-76, 280-281, 284, 286, 287, 308-09, 313-17, 319-21, 323, 325, 332, 338-40, 342, 345, 352, 367, 371, 374-75, 384-86, 395
USS *The Sullivans* 84, 89, 90, 142, 187-89, 267-68, 287, 308, 352

V

Valerie Plame Affair 259
Vanity Fair 364

W

"wall" 78, 112-113, 293, 313, 317-19, 326-27, 329, 331-33, 340, 364
Washington Hotel 97, 195, 199, 226
Washington Post 16, 26, 87, 89, 109, 129, 285, 306, 312, 354
Watson, Dale 195, 301
Waugh, Billy 26, 100
Weldon, Curt 169, 170

Whitelaw, Kevin 17, 154, 162, 182, 262
Wiener, Tim 33
Wigmore, Barry 18, 24-25
Wilhelm, Kirsten 78-79, 164-65, 199
Wilshire, Tom 2-3, 38-39, 43-44, 46-49, 51, 52, 54, 55, 57-63, 65, 67, 69-72-74, 78-81, 97, 105, 112, 114, 119-20, 122, 127, 130-31, 135-36, 144, 197-99, 204, 206, 208, 225-32, 234-36, 240-48, 251-54, 257-58, 266-84, 287-89, 293, 297-02, 304, 308, 310-11, 313, 318, 323-26, 330, 334-35, 337-38, 347, 351, 353, 358-59, 364, 371-75, 377-81, 383-85, 390, 399-403
Wilson, Edwin 100-01
Woodward, Bob 285-86, 348
Wright, Lawrence 15-18, 28-29, 37, 42-44, 50, 63-64, 92-93, 97, 112, 141, 144, 188, 193-97, 199, 226, 234, 239-40, 246, 249, 253, 263-64, 266-68, 316, 319, 333-34, 339-40, 360

Y

Yatim, Rais 95
Yemen hub 8-10, 12-14, 16-21, 24-27, 37-39, 76, 138-44, 146, 150-58, 165-66, 177-84, 186, 188-89, 191-92, 210, 214-22, 259-63, 265, 274, 286, 318, 359-60, 372, 378, 384
Yemen station (CIA) 26, 194-95, 201-204, 209, 340
Yemen Times 21
Yousef, Ramzi 16, 30, 41, 88, 217, 357-58, 360

Z

Zelikow, Philip x, 25, 76-78, 80-81, 124-25, 163-65, 285
Zubaida, Abu 112, 114, 283, 356, 359, 363-64

ACKNOWLEDGEMENTS

I would like to thank Paul, Matt, Mike, Erik, Allan and Mike.